OFFICIAL SECRETS
The Use and Abuse of the Act

In OFFICIAL SECRETS, David Hooper examines the leading cases brought to trial decade by decade against such people as Compton Mackenzie, Jonathan Aitken, Sarah Tisdall (not the first Foreign Office clerk to be prosecuted) and Clive Ponting. He also describes a host of less well-known cases, the majority of which should not have been brought or were brought for the wrong reasons against the wrong person.

But above all he shows convincingly, with style and humour, that the law at present on the Statute Book is so vaguely drafted and all-embracing that few citizens can be absolutely sure that they will not suddenly find themselves at risk.

Praise for OFFICIAL SECRETS

'A splendidly farcical postscript to the Peter Wright case'

Graham Lord in the Sunday Express

'Balanced and instructive narrative history of British official secrecy'

Geoffrey Marshall in the Listener

'He has done a great service in producing the handbook – the official guide to the Official Secrets Act'

Ludovic Kennedy in Cover to Cover BBC

'A quite outstanding authoritative work of the history of the Official Secrets Act . . . It cannot be too highly commended'

Solicitors Journal

**Also by the same author,
and available from Coronet:**

PUBLIC SCANDAL, ODIUM AND CONTEMPT

About the author

David Hooper was born in Lisbon in 1949 and educated at Eton and Balliol. He practised at the Bar for a few years before becoming a solicitor. He has two sons and is a partner in a firm of solicitors – Biddle & Co. – in the City of London.

OFFICIAL SECRETS
The Use and Abuse of the Act

David Hooper

CORONET BOOKS
Hodder and Stoughton

First published in Great Britain in 1987 by Martin Secker & Warburg Limited

Coronet edition 1988

British Library C.I.P.

Hooper, David, *1949–*
    Official secrets: the use and abuse of the Act.
    1. Great Britain. Official secrets. Disclosure, 1911–1986.
    Legal aspects
    I. Title
    344.105'23

ISBN 0-340-42650-0

Printed and bound in Great Britain for Hodder and Stoughton Paperbacks, a division of Hodder and Stoughton Ltd., Mill Road, Dunton Green, Sevenoaks, Kent TN13 2YA. (Editorial Office: 47 Bedford Square, London, WC1B 3DP) by Cox & Wyman Ltd., Reading, Berks.

For Edward and James

" So far the legal fees come to approximately £10,000,000—wouldn't it have been cheaper to have increased the old codger's pension in the first place? "

Contents

Acknowledgements

I hope that I have thanked the very many people in this country, Australia, Canada, New Zealand and the United States who have assisted me in relation to this book. It would be a very long list and would include a number of people who would not agree with a number of the conclusions I have reached, and others who would wish their assistance to remain anonymous. I hope, therefore, that my failure to list those who have assisted is not taken as any lack of gratitude.

Thanks are also due to Chatto & Windus Ltd for permission to quote from *My Life and Times: Octave 7, 1931–1938*, by Compton Mackenzie, and to Weidenfeld & Nicolson Ltd for permission to quote from *The Castle Diaries 1964–1970*, by Barbara Castle.

London, November 1986

Introduction

My first encounter with the Official Secrets Act was when I was asked by Peter Grose of Secker & Warburg to advise whether publication of the book *The Sinking of the 'Belgrano'* by Desmond Rice and Arthur Gavshon would infringe the Official Secrets Act. This book set in motion the events that led to the prosecution of civil servant Clive Ponting in 1985. It caused questions to be put to the government by Tam Dalyell MP, and by Denzil Davies MP, the Labour Party spokesman for defence. The government's failure to give proper answers to these questions led Ponting to the conclusion that there was a concerted attempt to cover up the true circumstances of the sinking of the *Belgrano* during the Falklands war and to leak two Ministry of Defence documents to Dalyell (see Chapter 12).

The theory advanced by Gavshon and Rice, that the *Belgrano* was sunk to scupper the Peruvian peace plan, was questionable, but their research was impressive. Their information came, it seemed, from a very well-placed source in the British nuclear submarine *Conqueror*. I was asked by the publishers to advise whether a problem could arise under Section 2 of the Official Secrets Act. It appeared that the authors had access to the diary of an officer on *Conqueror*. I said that, if this were the case, it would be unwise to reveal the source of any such information. Otherwise the publishers could confidently expect a visit from the Treasury Solicitor and his flying pickets.

No prosecution was brought against the authors under the Official Secrets Act, nor was any other attempt made to stop the book. As it turned out, my advice was vindicated by subsequent events; in his book, *The Right to Know*, Ponting described the impact of *The Sinking of the 'Belgrano'*:

> It was the first detailed account of events to be publicly available and it directly contradicted the government's version in virtually every respect. It contained details of the Peruvian peace proposals and the orders to the Argentinian fleet. It also contained long extracts from the diary kept by Lieutenant Sethia (the supplies officer on the *Conqueror*), but without attribution, and it was not immediately apparent where they [the authors] had obtained the information.

Only later did I learn of the dramatic effect my advice had had on the publishers. One of them, whom for legal reasons I can refer to only as P.G., went out with his spade and buried a copy of Lieutenant Sethia's diary at the end of a friend's garden.

My small part in these events led me to review the cases brought under Section 2 of the Official Secrets Act 1911 and to examine the curious history of the Act. The circumstances in which the Act passed through all its stages in Parliament are described in Chapter 1, and the way in which Parliament was misled by Attorney-General Sir Gordon Hewart KC as to the scope of the amendments being made to the Act is considered in Chapter 2. Chapter 4 discusses some of the cases in the 1930s, when Hewart, by then Lord Chief Justice, made a number of rulings on the Official Secrets Act which were diametrically opposed to what he had said in Parliament. An examination of the cases brought under Section 2 of the Act reveals that a large number of the people prosecuted were either inadequates or a little unlucky to be prosecuted when their briefcases had been stolen. These cases can be contrasted with the failure of succeeding governments to prosecute ministers of the Crown or influential television companies.

Whatever one's views on freedom of information and on the need to maintain discipline in the Civil Service it is difficult to escape the conclusion that there is far too much secrecy in Britain and that Section 2 of the Official Secrets

Act is a fairly ineffective way of protecting state secrets. There is no reason to suppose either that secret government necessarily means good government or that Section 2 deters the determined leaker. Section 2 is so widely drafted, and so discredited, that it has now become difficult for the government to have much prospect of prosecuting successfully under it – even where there has been serious betrayal of trust and the documents concerned can be shown to be of a genuinely secret nature. The balance between the need for secrecy and a greater degree of open government is not an easy one to draw. However, this book contends that there is too much secrecy in Britain and that much may be learnt from countries such as the United States, Australia and Canada, which have freedom-of-information legislation. In any event, in its present form, Section 2 no longer merits a place on the statute book.

The failure to reform Section 2, described in Chapter 21, makes unhappy reading, and there is no good reason for it. Until now all governments have found Section 2 a useful weapon and until the acquittal of Ponting in February 1985 the use being made of Section 2 was increasing. No previous Attorney-General has used Section 2 more than the former incumbent, Sir Michael Havers QC. However, government would be better served by a statute that protected the secrets that really matter. Trust and confidentiality are not the exclusive ingredients of government service – they are equally important in many other occupations. There is no significant qualitative difference between a clerk in a government department and a comparable employee in a major company or solicitors' office who leaks sensitive material. Yet the government clerk can be sent to prison for up to two years plus an unlimited fine, whereas the employee in the private sector or practice faces nothing worse than the sack. He can be sued in a civil court, but by then the damage has probably been done and he may have insufficient means to meet any judgment against him.

Section 2 is a formidable piece of legislation. Various additional offences were tacked on to the 1911 Act by the Official Secrets Act 1920. Section 2 has been calculated to be

capable of producing 2,314 different offences, and contains a
sentence of more than three hundred words. Its text is to be
found in Appendix 2. The section is, as the Franks
Committee reported in 1972, a mess and it blurs the
important distinction between espionage and leakage. The
obscurity of its drafting meant that for a time there was
genuine doubt as to whether a person had to know or believe
that he was communicating information in breach of the
Official Secrets Act before he could be convicted, or whether
the prosecution had to prove merely that the information had
in fact been communicated without authority. In the 1970
Sunday Telegraph case (Chapter 9) Mr Justice Caulfield
inclined to the view that the person could be convicted only if
he knew he was communicating information in breach of the
Act, whereas Mr Justice McCowan in the Ponting trial
(Chapter 12) took the view that breach of Section 2 is an
absolute offence and it matters not that the accused thought
he was entitled to communicate the information if in fact he
did so without authority.

Section 2 is to be distinguished from Section 1, which deals
with spying and sabotage and carries a penalty of fourteen
years' imprisonment. The principal offences under Section 2,
punishable by two years' imprisonment and an unlimited fine
– but by only three months' imprisonment and a maximum
fine of £50 if the Attorney-General agrees to the prosecution
taking place in a magistrates' court – are communicating
official information without authority and receiving such
information knowing or believing it has been communicated
in breach of the Act. Section 2 applies to everyone and is not
confined to people who work for the government. Many
people have at some time signed the Official Secrets Act.
They may range from people who work for the Security
Service to students weeding the palace gardens at Hampton
Court or doing a Christmas delivery round for the Post
Office. In Appendix 3 a typical Official Secrets Act
declaration is reproduced: this would normally be signed by a
government employee, or by someone having access to
government information, on joining the government service
or transferring from one government job to another. Signing

the Official Secrets Act is of no particular legal significance. Crown servants could equally well be prosecuted without having signed a declaration that they have had the terms of Section 2 drawn to their attention and have read these terms. The signing procedure serves two main purposes: first it is useful evidence in any prosecution under Section 2 that the employee knew he was bound by the Official Secrets Act (not that the employee has to be shown to know that he was breaking the Act to be guilty of an offence); secondly, it helps initiate the employee into the freemasonry of secrecy. Much is to be said for limiting the number of those who sign the Official Secrets Act declaration and for redrafting Section 2 in terms that people would find easier to understand.

Section 2 applies to unauthorised communications by people working for the Crown, government contractors, people who have received information relating to a 'prohibited place' (which includes not only naval dockyards and RAF establishments but even mines and telephone establishments), and people who have received information entrusted to them in confidence by a Crown employee or government contractor, and to others who have received such information in contravention of the Act. Such people commit an offence under Section 2 if they communicate this information to a person to whom they are not authorised to pass it, or if they use it for the benefit of a foreign power or in any other manner deemed to be prejudicial to the safety or interests of the state, or if they retain the information when they had no right to do so, or if they disregard a lawful order to return it, or if they fail to take reasonable care of the information. The permutations of these offences are enormous. The principal offence is the unauthorised communication of information by any person who holds or has held office under Her Majesty. However, it is also an offence under Section 2 to use information for the benefit of any foreign power, to communicate information about munitions of war directly or indirectly to a foreign power, to retain official papers which should be returned, to fail to take reasonable care of official papers, and to receive information knowing or having reasonable grounds to believe that it is communicated in contravention of the Official Secrets Act 1911. People are generally charged under Section 2 with leaking documents (communicating them without authority), hoarding them (retaining then, normally at home, without authority) or losing them (failing to take reasonable care of them).

Under Section 2 (ii) there is the further offence that if a person receives official information knowing or having reasonable grounds to believe that the information was communicated to him in contravention of the Act, he is guilty of an offence. The Franks Committee recommended in 1972 that the mere receipt of official information should no longer be an offence, but people are still charged with this offence.

Other provisions in the Official Secrets Act 1911 and 1920 confer wide powers on the government. Section 7 of the 1911 Act makes it an offence for any person knowingly to harbour a person who has committed or is about to commit an offence under the Act. Although the section is headed 'penalty for harbouring spies' it is not restricted to offences under Section 1; a wife who is told by her husband how many cups of tea his minister drank that day theoretically permits him to stay under her roof at her peril! Under Section 10 of the 1911 Act a British subject can be punished for a breach of the Act in any part of the world. Under Section 6 of the 1920 Act it is an offence not to supply information about a suspected breach of the Act to a senior police officer who demands your co-operation. There is not the normal right of silence. Initially this applied not only to cases of spying but to any breach of Section 2. It caused a sufficient outcry for an amending Act to be passed in 1939 confining the powers under Section 6 to cases of spying. Section 7 of the 1920 Act makes it an offence to perform an act preparatory to the commission of an offence under the Official Secrets Act. This enabled the government to prosecute Crispin Aubrey in 1977 for making a telephone call to arrange a meeting at which information was communicated in breach of the Official Secrets Act (Chapter 10).

In addition to the powers under the Official Secrets Act

there is the D-notice system. D-notices are formal letters of request which should cover 'naval, military and air matters, the publication of which would be prejudicial to the national interest'. D-notices are circulated confidentially to newspaper editors, news editors in sound and television broadcasting and the editors of a number of periodicals concerned with defence. Their purpose is to advise editors and publishers of categories of information whose protection is considered by the government to be essential for national security. D-notices have no legal force as such but serve to warn of items which may be protected under the Official Secrets Act. Some 960 people are on the D-notice circulation list. The system is also supported by private and confidential letters sent out from time to time to editors about such matters as the protection of oil rigs or the dangers of revealing the identities of senior intelligence officers. The shortcomings of the D-notice system are considered in Chapter 20.

There is a further weapon to prevent the publication of material that the government considers to be contrary to the national interest: the civil law of confidence. This branch of the law can be used where information is communicated in breach of an obligation of confidence either by someone who was under an obligation not to disclose confidential information he had acquired or by someone who received the information knowing that it had been passed to him in breach of an obligation of confidence. This has been used with varying success and consistency by the government to restrain the publication of memoirs of Crown servants of which it disapproves or to try to stop authors such as Nigel West publishing what they have been told by various MI5 and MI6 officers (Chapter 18). The civil law of confidence has the advantage of speed and privacy compared to invoking the criminal law and Section 2. Rather than the Crown having to prove its case beyond reasonable doubt to the satisfaction of a jury – which it was unable to do in the Ponting prosecution – the government can, under the law of confidence, obtain an injunction at a private hearing before a High Court judge, initially without any need to notify the person against whom it is being sought. If an injunction is obtained – and it normally will be when the judge has the opportunity of hearing only one side – the other party then has to produce evidence to persuade the judge not to renew the injunction.

The present position, following the Ponting case, is that the government has dropped a number of prosecutions, such as the very trifling toy-typewriter case brought against Alan Lowther (Chapter 13). There are those who feel that the Ponting affair tolled the death-knell of prosecutions under Section 2, but I would question whether they are right to be so confident. After the acquittals in the *Sunday Telegraph* case in 1971, people expected Section 2 to be substantially reformed or abolished. A distinguished committee under Lord Franks recommended the abolition of Section 2 and its replacement by an Act to protect secrets that really matter. Nothing has happened. Within six years of the Franks Report the government (at the time a Labour administration) felt it appropriate to prosecute two journalists, Crispin Aubrey and Duncan Campbell, in the 'ABC' case (Chapter 10) – not only under Section 2 but also under Section 1. The story of such attempts as there have been to reform Section 2 (Chapter 21) is an unhappy one. The present government's attitude that nothing can be done, because it tried and failed to reform the law with its inept performance over the Protection of Information Bill in 1979, seems unnecessarily defeatist.

No one has been prosecuted as yet for revealing how many lumps of sugar the Secretary of State has in his cup of tea, but an examination of the cases in this book shows that people have been prosecuted in a number of bewilderingly petty cases, because someone at some stage has stamped 'confidential' or 'secret' on a document. Dusty old documents have frequently been fished out of attics, where they were left years before by overworked or inefficient employees, to form the basis of prosecutions under the Official Secrets Act. Just as it is not safe to rely on the wisdom of the Attorney-General's department to ensure that prosecutions are brought only in serious or important cases, so it is unwise to rely on courts taking a suitably lenient view of prosecutions which need hardly have been brought. The cases of Robert Oakes, Barbara Fell and Ronald Cox are an indication of the severe penalties which the courts can and do impose for relatively innocuous breaches of Section 2.

This book is not concerned with the prosecution of spies under Section 1 of the Act. It deals instead with the history of the creation and use of Section 2, which aims principally to prevent the unauthorised communication, receipt and retention of official information.

There is no definition in the Act as to what constitutes an official secret. The best working definition is that given to the Franks Committee by the then Director-General of the Security Service, Sir Martin Furnival Jones: 'It is an official secret if it is in an official file.' The question of whether a document is classified as 'top secret' or 'restricted' depends on the view that a particular government department takes of its secrecy. The working rules are that the classification 'top secret' means that the disclosure of the document could result in exceptionally grave damage to the nation; 'secret' envisages serious injury to the national interest; 'confidential' that disclosure could be prejudicial to the interests of the nation; and 'restricted' that disclosure would be undesirable in the national interest. There are additional classifications, as can be seen from the Jackson case (Chapter 13), of 'commercial in confidence', aimed at protecting confidential information of a commercial nature, and 'staff in confidence', which designates confidential information regarding staff and appointments in a particular government department. As the journalist David Leigh has pointed out, these words have no objective meaning. They could equally well be 'earth-shatteringly secret', 'very, very secret', 'very secret' and 'secret'. Leigh feels that a sensible paraphrase would be 'secret', 'rather secret', 'mildly secret' and 'hardly secret at all'. It is difficult to improve on the words of the Security Commission's report produced after the publication of Chapman Pincher's book *Their Trade Is Treachery* (Appendix 7): 'In the Commission's view over-classification is the error that is most commonly committed in carrying out current security procedures.'

The English courts seem happy to swallow these classifications, which after all are only departmental decisions. It is worth contrasting the attitude taken in Canada in the *Toronto Sun* case (Appendix 6) and in Australia in the *Anzus Papers* case (Appendix 4), where the question of classification was treated purely as a matter of administrative convenience which was not binding on the court.

Successive governments appear to have lost sight of what Winston Churchill said about the Official Secrets Act in 1939: 'The Official Secrets Act was devised to protect the national defences and ought not to be used to shield ministers who have strong personal interests in concealing the truth about matters from the country.' For a general criticism it is difficult to improve on the comment made by Mr Justice Caulfield, the judge who presided over the *Sunday Telegraph* case, to the Franks Committee: 'I could add many other worries I have about this section, but perhaps it is sufficient to say that I think the section in its present form could be viciously or capriciously used by an embarrassed executive.'

It will be seen in Chapter 21 that the Labour, Social Democratic and Liberal parties have committed themselves to reforming the law. The Labour Party has a chequered career in its operation of the Act, and its attempt to reform the law during the period 1974–9 was half-hearted. The leading figures in the Social Democrats were part of that government, although apparently they have now seen the light. It was a Liberal MP, Clement Freud, who introduced the Official Information Bill in January 1979, which would have repealed Section 2 and introduced access to official information: this might have been enacted but for the fall of the Labour government. However, we have a Liberal government under Asquith to thank for the passage of the original Act. Despite heading the administration which steered the Official Secrets Act through Parliament, Asquith used to write about Cabinet secrets to his lady friend, Miss Venetia Stanley. Even Churchill, Home Secretary at the time of the passage of the Act, was not above revealing Cabinet secrets. In October 1912, Wilfred Blunt (a forebear of Sir Anthony) described how Churchill stayed the weekend at his house in Sussex: 'The secrets of the Cabinet were gloriously divulged – Winston told us admirable stories of his experiences as Home Secretary.' Churchill was in fact especially prone to retain government documents for use in his books – something not permitted to those below Cabinet rank. He used secret material from the War Cabinet Records in his book about the First World War, *The World Crisis 1911 to 1918*, which was published over the period 1923–9, and for *The Second World War*, published between 1949 and 1952. He even acknowledged Crown copyright when he had done so.

In the 1930s the government attempted to use the Act to bully journalists into revealing their sources (see the cases of Frederick Truelove and Ernest Lewis in Chapters 2 and 4). On one occasion the same powers were unsuccessfully used against an MP, Duncan Sandys, in respect of a parliamentary question he had put down in the House of Commons (Chapter 5). The 1930s also produced one of the clearest examples of the failure to prosecute a minister for breach of the Official Secrets Act, where J. H. Thomas, the Colonial Secretary, had revealed Budget secrets not just once but twice to his cronies, who then made a killing at Lloyd's and on the stock market (Chapter 4). No minister has ever been prosecuted for a breach of the Official Secrets Act: the nearest thing to this was in 1934 when Edgar Lansbury, the son of the leader of the Labour Opposition, was prosecuted for publishing information which had been given to him by his father. His father was not prosecuted and nor has any Speaker of the House of Commons – despite Michael Foot's whimsical suggestion that Viscount Tonypandy could have committed an offence under the Act by publishing in his memoirs his exchanges with Foot behind the Speaker's chair. There are also examples of officials who have been prosecuted for the failure to take care of government documents – such as Robin Gordon-Walker, who had his briefcase stolen on the tube, and Lt-Commander Emary, whose papers fell off the back of his bicycle.

For an informative contrast, consider what happened in May 1965, when Richard Crossman left some Cabinet papers in Prunier's Restaurant, where he had been dining. The documents were scooped up by a fellow diner, Major Geoffrey Blundell-Brown, who dropped them off at the nearby flat of Chapman Pincher, the *Daily Express*'s defence correspondent, for onward transmission to Crossman. Among these papers were details of an embarrassing disagreement between Crossman and the Home Secretary, Sir Frank Soskice, on the question of positive discrimination in housing for New Commonwealth immigrants. When the Labour government learnt that the papers had come into the possession of Pincher, it unleashed its security watchdog, George Wigg, who appealed forlornly to Pincher's sense of charity, before threatening a prosecution under the Official Secrets Act. This appeal fell on barren ground. Pincher very reasonably reminded Wigg of his own lack of charity over the Profumo affair, and of the false accusations he had made against Julian Amery in the House of Commons of not just leaking about the Ferranti affair but being positively incontinent – an accusation that was particularly unfair, as Pincher's source was Ferranti rather than Amery. Wigg's attempts to threaten the *Daily Express* proved counter-productive, and the story was published the following day. The incident is memorable for being the occasion of a joke by Edward Heath, who suggested that Crossman should not be allowed to have such working dinners unless he had Wigg with him to ensure that he collected up his papers at the end. Like many Official Secrets sagas, there was a little more to this than met the eye: what had caused concern to the Labour government was the revelation that Crossman was in the habit of engaging in the unsocialist activity of having working dinners alone at Prunier's. It was curious that such an incident should have involved Crossman, who had a reputation for leaking documents to the press himself and was generally considered to be the source of information contained in Cabinet papers on government housing policy. It will be seen in Chapter 19 that after Crossman's death a case was brought seeking to prevent his diaries from being published.

The Official Secrets Act hovers like a vulture over those

connected with government service and the media and
produces an atmosphere of needless and sometimes absurd
secrecy. While there is certainly an argument for enabling
ministers to receive confidential advice without it being
leaked to the newspapers, and for the maintenance of
discipline in the Civil Service, the existence of Section 2 will
probably not deter a Tisdall or a Ponting, but it does cause
anxiety to many people in the service. The case of William
Miller and Paul Thompson in 1958 (Chapter 7) is an example
of how a prosecution could somewhat cynically be used to
deter others. If criminal sanctions really are required to keep
errant civil servants in line, they should be strictly defined.

An indication of the degree of secrecy in Britain can be
found in a parliamentary reply in 1967 by Niall MacDermott,
the Financial Secretary to the Treasury. He announced that
no less than 1,700 tons of classified waste paper had been
burnt in the five years up to 1 March 1967.

When the Australian Royal Commission under Mr Justice
McCelland, enquiring into British nuclear tests in Australia
and the South Pacific in the 1950s and early 1960s, wished to
examine British government documents, it transpired that
there were no less than 38 tons of documents of various
security classifications, access to which was prohibited under
the thirty-year rule. In the face of Australian protests the
Ministry of Defence relented in allowing positively vetted
groups of Australians to inspect the documents, provided
these did not relate to weapons designs or to information
about individuals' personal health.

There are eighty-nine statutes making the disclosure of
information relating to particular statutory bodies an
offence. They range from the Covent Garden Market Act
1961 to the Sewerage Scotland Act 1968.

In many instances the Official Secrets Act can be used
oppressively and contrary to the national interest, or merely
stupidly. In 1950 information was passed to Chapman
Pincher that the walls of one of two giant uranium reactors
being built at Windscale (Sellafield) were porous, and that
this could lead to an escape of radioactivity. This was based
on a leaked memorandum drafted by the inappropriately

named Sir Charles Mole, Director-General of Works at the
Ministry of Works. He had expressed the view that the
furnace might have to be scrapped. When the government
learnt that the *Daily Express* had this information and
intended to publish it, Sir Archibald Rowlands, the
Permanent Secretary to the Ministry of Supply, telephoned
the chief editor and warned that he would be prosecuted
under the Official Secrets Act if he published the information. The result was that the story was held up for a year,
long enough for repairs to be carried out. Sir Archibald later
admitted to Pincher that the threat of prosecution was a
bluff.

In 1957 the *Daily Sketch* was threatened with prosecution
if it published a photograph taken of the vertical-take-off
aircraft, which had by then acquired the irreverent name of
'The Flying Bedpan'. The editor subsequently decided not to
print the photograph, but was dismayed when a fortnight
later Duncan Sandys, the Minister of Aviation, made a
speech about the plane at the Farnborough Air Show and
released photographs of it to every newspaper. In other
words, the Official Secrets Act was used as a form of press
embargo. In 1960 the editor of the *South-East London
Mercury* was warned that a story he was planning to run
about trees being blown down in a gale in Greenwich Park
contravened not only a D-notice but also the Official Secrets
Act. This produced the sarcastic comment by John Gordon
of the *Sunday Express* that not only did the government
harass the press with D-notices but it had now invented
something called Tree-notices. In 1964 a *Daily Mail* reporter,
making enquiries as to where the corned beef cans thought to
be the source of a typhoid epidemic in Aberdeen were stored,
was told that the information was covered by the Official
Secrets Act. In February 1973 postman Alan Grimwood
unwisely wrote to the *Chingford Guardian and Independent,*
replying to complaints in its correspondence column about
the slow service at Chingford post office. He said that he did
not consider the counter staff of six to be sufficient. He may
or may not have been right but he certainly was surprised to
receive a letter from the Eastern District of the Post Office

accusing him of contravening the declaration he had made to observe the Official Secrets Act. He was not prosecuted, but this was a good example of how stupidly the Act can be used. In 1973 the London bureau chief of *Newsweek* was informed that photographing the Shoreditch employment office to accompany a story on unemployment constituted a breach of the Official Secrets Act.

The *Railway Gazette* published on 8 October 1972 a report on a confidential railway study being prepared as a discussion document by economists at the Department of the Environment. This study concerned a plan to cut the railway network by some 40 per cent over the next ten years, from 11,600 miles to 8,000 miles. Police raided the editorial offices of the *Gazette* on 29 November 1972, armed with a warrant under the Theft Act. They found nothing. On 7 December the police interviewed Harold Evans, editor of the *Sunday Times*, and cautioned him that he might have committed an offence under the Official Secrets Act by publishing the story.

An incredulous Evans was asked, 'Did you realise that the document was a classified government paper?'

He replied, 'If you ask me did it have a red tag on top saying "top secret – do not give to the Russians" – no.' The *Sunday Times* was not prosecuted.

In 1979 Yorkshire Television was making a programme on Rampton Mental Hospital. The government considered it prudent to make the staff sign the Official Secrets Act, to discourage them from participating in the documentary.

Examples of this official obsession with secrecy are endless. Ludovic Kennedy, no doubt at some peril to himself, revealed recently in the correspondence column of *The Times* that his daughter Ailsa had to sign the Official Secrets Act while working on a holiday job pricking out marigolds at Hampton Court. The official explanation given to her was not that she might reveal the way out of the maze, but that documents from a nearby defence establishment might be blown her way! More alarming examples are to be found in Chapter 17.

This preoccupation with secrecy, which is in any case absurd, is made more ridiculous by inefficiency. It is difficult to see how well the national interest was served when, upon the appointment of the new heads of M15 and M16 in 1978, a letter was sent out to newspaper editors indicating that their names should not be disclosed, particularly as they were not given police protection. A copy of this worthy missive was sent to the editor of the Communist *Morning Star*, Anthony Chater, even though he was, not surprisingly, not on the D-notice mailing list.

Moles themselves are not always completely efficient. In May 1983 a concerned citizen felt that a report from HM Inspectorate of Schools, concluding that spending cuts in education were depriving some pupils of the basic education they needed, was being suppressed, not on the grounds of illness as was claimed, but because of the forthcoming general election. However, as the mole omitted to put a stamp on the envelope which he sent to the *Guardian*, the Post Office opened the letter and returned it to the Department of Education, from which the leaked document had originally emanated.

Sometimes the leakers of official information understandably feel that their tracks will be better covered if they retype the contents of the document they are trying to disclose, so that it cannot be traced by various inter-departmental markings on the documents, or through marks left by a particular office photocopier. However, when a mole leaked a confidential memorandum quoting a remark by Sir George Young, Under-Secretary at the Department of the Environment, that he considered that the effect on certain boroughs such as Lewisham of the non-payment of rate support grant was 'political dynamite', the mole rather lessened the impact of the revelation of this document to a bemused Dr John Cunningham, shadow environment spokesman, by retyping the document showing it as referring to Leicester and not Lewisham.

Another worrying feature of Section 2 is that political considerations can influence this question of whether or not to prosecute. There is no evidence to suggest that any law officer has been influenced by improper political pressure in recent times, but the Attorney-General is in an equivocal position, being a member of the government as well as a law officer. Various holders of the office have had differing views as to the extent to which they can properly consult their colleagues. There seems little objection to them sounding out their colleagues' views on a prosecution, although it is ultimately their decision.

Sir Hartley Shawcross KC, who was Attorney-General in the first post-war Labour government, laid out the criteria that he felt should be applied to a prosecution. The Attorney-General should acquaint himself with all the relevant facts, including the effect that the prosecution – successful or unsuccessful as the case may be – would have on public morale and order; but he must exclude from consideration the repercussions of the decision upon his personal or his government's political future. He can properly consult his colleagues for the purpose of informing himself of the relevant implications of any decision to prosecute, but he must not defer to his political colleagues when making his decision.

The test applied by Sir Michael Havers QC in recent times is rather different. He operates under the normal criteria for prosecution, which he published in March 1983, and which applied to the prosecution of all offences, taking into account such matters as whether a conviction is more likely than an acquittal before an impartial jury. He has told Parliament that he does not consult his ministerial colleagues on the question of prosecutions. Since prosecutions under the Official Secrets Act have a political element, he is unwise not to do so. His predecessor, Sam Silkin QC, pointed out that, while law officers must take instructions from nobody, they are free to consult colleagues, particularly those with a departmental concern, observing that Sir John Simon – an Attorney-General and later Lord Chancellor – rightly said there are times when they would be fools not to do so. Sir Michael Havers QC did, however, when in opposition on 15 June 1978, state the principles that he thought should apply: 'But the public interest requires that there is no misuse of secrecy to cover up errors or bungling or to avoid criticism.' It is open to question whether under his stewardship Section 2 has been used to prosecute the right people. Havers told the House of Commons that Section 2 would be used only sparingly and when absolutely necessary.

The prosecution of John Campbell under the Incitement to Mutiny Act 1797 shows how political pressure can be brought upon the Attorney-General, in that case Sir Patrick Hasting KC. On 25 July 1924 an article was published in *Workers' Weekly*, at that time the official organ of the Communist Party, calling in an open letter to the fighting services 'to let it be known that neither in the class war nor in the military war will you turn your guns on your fellow workers'. They were also encouraged to smash capitalism for ever and institute the reign of the whole working class. This was hardly the stuff likely to appeal to the average squaddie. However, Sir Patrick took a very serious view of the matter and instructed the Director of Public Prosecutions to bring such proceedings under the Incitement to Mutiny Act 1797 (passed to deal with the aftermath of the Nore and Spithead mutinies) as he thought fit.

A warrant was accordingly issued for the arrest of John Campbell, the acting editor of *Workers' Weekly*. This immediately led to questions being raised in the House of Commons and to uproar in the Labour Party. Hastings was told by the left-wing Labour MP James Maxton that Campbell had an excellent war record, that he had been only the acting editor while the editor was on holiday and had not written the article himself. In the face of this political pressure Sir Patrick now considered his initial decision 'an unfortunate mistake'.

Ramsay MacDonald was furious when he heard about the intended prosecution. He called for the Attorney-General and the Assistant Director of Public Prosecutions and gave them a piece of his mind. According to MacDonald their reply was that the whole matter could in fact be dropped, but he retorted that now a charge had been brought they had better go through with it. 'I would rather go through what's started than show a white feather.' After a certain amount of soul-searching and head-scratching, Sir Patrick reaffirmed his decision that, having learnt of Campbell's gallantry during the First World War and of the fact that he was prepared to write a letter amounting to an apology, the matter was best forgotten.

After considerable discussion, the Cabinet resolved on 7 August that no prosecutions of a political character should be undertaken without the prior sanction of the Cabinet. It did agree to accept the Attorney-General's recommendation. It was a classic case of political pressure being brought to bear on the prosecution.

This carve-up of legal proceedings did the government little good. In a debate in the House of Commons at the end of September, Ramsay MacDonald said: 'I was not consulted regarding either the institution or the subsequent withdrawal of these proceedings. The first notice of the prosecution that came to my knowledge was in the press. I never advised withdrawal but left the entire matter to the discretion of the law officers.' The normally restrained Cabinet Secretary, Sir Maurice Hankey, was moved to observe that this was a 'bloody lie'. Following publication of the forged Zinoviev letter, Labour lost a vote of confidence by 364 votes to 198.

The carve-up did not do John Campbell much good either. He was prosecuted for the same offence a year later with eleven other communist leaders and on this occasion was sent to prison for six months.

There is no doubt that there are secrets which must in a democratic country be properly safeguarded. The contention of this book is that the Official Secrets Act does not properly achieve this object. Recollect, for example, the words of two traitors who gratefully embraced the Official Secrets Act as a means of ducking questions at press conferences which raised questions about their duplicity. The first occasion was in 1956, seven years before his defection, when Kim Philby declined to comment on his possible role as the 'third man' who had tipped off Burgess and Maclean. Philby was asked:

'The disappearance of Burgess and Maclean is almost as much a mystery today as it was when they went away about four years ago or more. Can you shed any light on it at all?'

To which he replied:

'No, I can't... In the first place I am debarred by the

Official Secrets Act from saying anything which might disclose to unauthorised persons information derived from my position as a former government official.'

The second incident was at a press conference given in 1979 by Anthony Blunt:

'At that time your main activity in the cause of anti-fascism was to be a talent spotter?'

Blunt: 'Yes.'

'Were there any other duties you performed at that time?'

Blunt: 'No.'

'How many of them did you spot?'

Blunt: 'This is, I'm afraid, something where I must take refuge behind the Official Secrets Act.'

Many people, including Mrs Thatcher, argue that a system of freedom of information would be inconsistent with the type of parliamentary democracy that we have in Britain, with ministers accountable in Parliament. It is also said that changes have already been introduced resulting in more information being released to the public. However, as Appendices 4 and 6 confirm, Australia and Canada have successfully introduced freedom-of-information legislation without damaging their Westminster-style elements. It is, moreover, questionable whether government departments will of their own accord release the information to which the citizen could properly be said to be entitled without damaging the decision-making process or national security. When the question of access to public records was reviewed in 1903 it was discovered that the Admiralty and the War Office were refusing access to documents dated later than 1830; the Foreign Office drew the line at 1780, and the Treasury was even more cautious, maintaining the secrecy of all documents since 1759. In 1958 documents in the Public Records Office were opened to inspection after fifty years, and were in general to be opened to public inspection fifty years after the date they had come into existence, although there were a number of important exceptions – notably that the Suez papers of two years previously should not be opened for one hundred years. In 1967 the fifty-year period was reduced to thirty years but with wide-ranging exemptions for particularly sensitive papers, the disclosure of which would be contrary to the public interest, whether on security or on other grounds.

One of the more significant inroads made into the apparatus of secrecy is to be found in an Act of Parliament, the Public Bodies (Admission to Meetings) Act 1960, which was introduced as a Private Member's Bill by, of all people, the newly elected Margaret Thatcher MP. Mrs Thatcher appears now to have had second thoughts on the reduction of government secrecy (Chapter 21). In some areas, however, there have been faltering steps towards a lessening of secrecy and greater freedom of information. These can be found in the Local Government (Access to Information) Act 1985, which permits members of the public to attend council meetings and examine official council papers, and in the Data Protection Act 1984, which sets up a machinery for people to examine computer records that are kept about them and to correct errors in those records. These measures are piecemeal but they are a step in the right direction. However, it is the argument of this book that the steps so far taken are too little and too late.

1

The Growth of Official Secrecy

In the nineteenth century people began to realise the commercial value of government papers. The Foreign Office obtained an injunction in 1833 to prevent the sale of Lord Hanley's documents concerning Britain's foreign relations with Bavaria, Denmark, Austria and Prussia in the period 1777–89. Four years later, the Foreign Office was unsuccessful in its attempt to prevent the publication of the dispatches from Spain that Lord Wellesley had written in 1809. The Foreign Office had taken this action to try to stamp out the practice of selling government papers.

In 1847 the government tried and failed to stop *The Times* publishing correspondence between Lord Castlereagh and representatives of Imperial Russia on the Polish Question at the Congress of Vienna in 1815. *The Times* argued that this was of public interest and that its readers were entitled to the information, but in conceded that the government had a residual right to prevent publication of such papers 'as often as their suppression may be presumed to be most expedient to the interests of the country'.

The Foreign Office was more successful in 1862, when it obtained an injunction against Lady Jackson, the widow of a British diplomat. She was attempting to sell to the Foreign Office for £3,000 some dispatches that had passed between London and Berlin in the period 1771–1800, which had been in her late husband's possession. Despite warnings from the British Ambassador in Paris, where she then lived, that her approach to the Foreign Office was most unwelcome, and

despite some conspicuous spying on her hotel by British
agents, Lady Jackson was determined to press on with the
sale. The hints from the ambassador were to no avail, and she
was in consequence served with an injunction when she
arrived in London. The Foreign Office agreed to pay Lady
Jackson £800 for the papers, although it drew the line at her
request for a widow's pension.

These were all cases brought in the civil courts. In 1858 the
government decided to bring the first prosecution for
unauthorised leaking of government information. There was
at that time no Official Secrets Act for it to use, so a charge
was brought under the nineteenth-century Larceny Act. The
leak was a serious one, and the reaction of the government
would become increasingly familiar in the twentieth century.

On 8 November 1858 a mission headed by William
Gladstone had left England to investigate the situation in the
Ionian Islands, where the inhabitants demanded union with
Greece. Gladstone had been asked by the Colonial Secretary,
Sir Edward Bulwer Lytton, to prepare a report which he
could then lay before Parliament. On 12 November, 1858 the
Daily News – 'to the unspeakable surprise and astonishment'
of the Colonial Office – published two dispatches, dated June
1857 and June 1858, that had been sent to the Colonial Office
by the Lord High Commissioner of the Ionian Islands, a man
with the suitably Gilbertian name of Mikado. These
dispatches appeared to prejudge the report that the mission
was due to make. The leaked documents were published at a
particularly embarrassing time for the government, since
Gladstone had by then gone overseas but had not yet started
his work; the mission was compromised before it arrived.

Mikado's dispatches had reached the *Daily News* from
William Guernsey, who had on 23 October succeeded in
removing a printed copy from the Colonial Office library,
where he was friendly with the sub-librarian. Guernsey did
not seek any payment from the *Daily News*. His motive was a
grudge against the Colonial Office for not offering him a job.

The leak was traced to Guernsey, and he was arrested on 26
November. He was tried before Mr Baron Martin and a jury
at the Central Criminal Court on 5 December 1858. Almost

by way of precedent for the future, the Attorney-General was wheeled in to conduct the prosecution, opening the case in suitably blood-curdling terms. It was, he told them, impossible to overrate the serious consequences that might result from the publication of such important documents. It might have the effect of plunging the country into war and causing enormous sacrifices of blood and treasure.

Guernsey was skilfully defended. Mr Baron Martin was persuaded to direct the jury that the *Daily News* had acted quite properly in publishing the dispatches, although they were marked 'confidential'. He also raised a doubt in the jury's mind as to whether there was, as was required to prove the offence of larceny, an intention permanently to deprive the Colonial Office of these dispatches. It took the jury no longer than fifteen minutes to restore Guernsey, like W. S. Gilbert's burglars, triumphantly to his friends and relations.

The next case arising out of the improper disclosure of government information was brought in 1878. Charles Marvin was a twenty-six-year-old temporary clerk in the treaty department of the Foreign Office. He was charged under the Larceny Act 1861 with removing a document from a government office and stealing the paper on which he had passed the information to a newspaper. In fact, Marvin had used his own paper and had copied the contents of the government document on to it. This dealt a severe blow to the government's chance of securing a conviction, as he could not be said to have stolen its paper but only the information written on it.

Marvin's motives in the matter were a mixture of resentment, injured pride and greed. He was employed by the Foreign Office to copy out Cabinet documents and, in his own view, was grossly underpaid – despite his leisurely hours of 12.30 to 5.30 with an hour for lunch. He was paid tenpence per hour, with a supplement of fourpence ha'penny per page of any document copied in a foreign language. Contrasting his remuneration with that of the permanent staff, Marvin said: 'I was so disgusted with the Foreign Office for sucking the best years of my life for the miserable sum of £90 per year that I resolved to place upon the market every piece of information that chance threw in my way.'

He decided to augment his income by occasional contributions to the *Globe* newspaper, receiving forty guineas for revealing details of the Berlin treaty. On 30 May 1878, he was asked by Foreign Secretary Lord Salisbury's private secretary to copy out the memorandum of the secret agreement reached between Lord Salisbury and Count Schouvaloff, the Russian Ambassador in London. He was told that Lord Salisbury required it for a statement in Parliament that evening and that it would appear in *The Times* the following day.

Marvin decided that if the press were to have the memorandum on the morrow, he would let the *Globe* have it that evening. By a considerable feat of concentration he committed it to memory, so that he was able to write it out in the newspaper's offices. The *Globe* rushed out a special edition at 9 p.m. on 30 May, headlined 'The Berlin Congress decided upon! Terms of agreement between England and Russia'. Marvin hoped that when he arrived at work next morning the talk in the office would be about the article in the *Globe*. Unfortunately, no one at the Foreign Office appeared to read the *Globe*, and it was not until 4 p.m. that word of the leak reached Whitehall. When it did, blame immediately fell on the hapless Count Schouvaloff.

The matter might have ended there, had not the Marquess of Salisbury reacted to the leak with a lack of candour that was itself to set a precedent for the twentieth century. Earl Grey asked Salisbury in the House of Lords whether the newspaper report was true. Salisbury replied, 'The statement to which the noble Earl refers and other statements I have seen are wholly unauthentic and not deserving of the confidence of your Lordship's House.' A relieved but misled Earl Grey then said: 'I should not have supposed that what was said with regard to the retrocession of Bessarabia was correct. It appeared too monstrous to be believed that Her Majesty's government could have made such a stipulation as was alleged.'

In fact Marvin's account was correct. He was outraged that

doubt had been cast on his credentials as a leaker of information. He wrote a number of letters marked 'Private and Confidential' to several newspaper editors, saying that, as a Foreign Office clerk, he knew the *Globe*'s disclosure of the Anglo-Russian agreement to be accurate. He did not reveal that he was the source of the leak. Marvin also decided that, since the paper had hitherto received only a summary of the agreement, it should now have the whole text, in order 'to retrieve my reputation as a contributor of reliable news'. He therefore copied out the text onto his own paper and sent it to the *Globe*, which published the first eleven clauses of the proposed Anglo-Russian treaty on the front page on 14 June.

The Berlin Congress, which had convened to settle the Eastern Question, had started the previous day, 13 June. The diplomats of Germany, France and Austria-Hungary were dismayed to learn that Britain and Russia had come to the congress with a secret agreement already concluded.

There followed an intensive operation to catch the leaker. Marvin's letters were intercepted; even the contents of his blotter were examined. He was kept under observation by a police officer with a telescope on the roof of the adjoining India Office. In fact the police had little difficulty in finding the source of the leak. The editor of the *Morning Advertiser*, Captain Hamber, as a measure of his dissatisfaction at not having been able to publish the scoop himself, had informed the police about the private and confidential letter he had received from Marvin confirming the accuracy of the *Globe*'s story. Marvin was arrested on 26 June 1878 and locked up at King Street Police Station, where he complained volubly about the bugs and fleas with which he had to share his cell. He appeared before Mr Vaughan, the chief magistrate at Bow Street. After the head of the Treaty Department at the Foreign Office had admitted under cross-examination that there was no rule which forbade Foreign Office clerks writing to the newspapers, the magistrate was able to take a surprisingly charitable view of Marvin's conduct:

Originally I thought it a great breach of trust, but it now appears that Marvin had good reason to believe that the information would be circulated among the press the next morning; it was not unnatural that he should endeavour to secure priority for a journal with which he himself was connected.

The magistrate considered that Marvin had obtained the document by surreptitious means, but concluded that there was insufficient evidence of larceny, and dismissed the summons. He nevertheless criticised the *Globe* for accepting such an item from a young man whom it knew to be employed at the Foreign Office. Marvin was summarily dismissed from his job, but he became something of a celebrity. His next book, *The Russians at the Gates of Herat*, sold 60,000 copies. He wrote about his arrest and trial at some length in his rather verbose memoirs, which carried the pointed dedication: 'To my benefactor Captain Hamber, the Editor of the *Morning Advertiser* and the Discloser of the Discloser, I dedicate these pages with sentiments of gratitude and esteem.'

In the meantime, there had been attempts to tighten the rules to prevent such leaks. In 1873 Sir Ralph Lingen, Permanent Secretary to the Treasury, had circulated a minute entitled 'Premature Disclosure of Official Documents'. This appealed to the better instincts of civil servants, pointing out that breaches of official confidence were 'offences of the gravest character to which most civil servants would not stoop. The unauthorised use of official information is the worst fault a civil servant can commit. It is on the same footing as cowardice by a soldier. It is unprofessional.'

A Treasury minute of 1875 attacked the links some civil servants had with the press, pointing out that 'any gentleman with such connection would be held liable for breach of confidence by such journals and would be liable to instant dismissal'. It was not until after the Marvin case that such links with newspapers were expressly prohibited.

In 1884, following leaks to the press of the proclamation by General Gordon before it was read in Parliament, and the disclosure of information about the re-organisation of the

Exchequer and Audit office and about a possible pay rise for suburban letter carriers, a further Treasury minute was circulated. This reminded civil servants that the publication of official information without authority was grounds for dismissal, and that the need for secrecy was 'not confined to matters still under discussion, but included also the unauthorised disclosure of matters finally decided upon'.

Despite these exhortations, the problem was becoming worse rather than better. There were two serious cases in 1887. The text of the instructions to the intelligence department of the Royal Navy was published in the press. In Parliament the First Lord of the Admiralty called this 'a grave breach of trust'. The scale of the problem and the deficiency of the law were highlighted by the treatment of a dockyard draughtsman named Young Terry. He had sold, probably to the French, confidential tracings and designs of a warship. He had been dismissed for betraying trust, but it was felt that there was insufficient evidence to prosecute him. In Parliament the First Lord of the Admiralty reported that a criminal law which allowed someone like Young Terry to escape could not be regarded as satisfactory; consideration was being given to strengthening the law.

The Admiralty began work in 1887 to make it an offence improperly to disclose official information. The drafting of the legislation was taken over by the Treasury with assistance from the War Office and the Foreign Office. The Official Secrets Act 1889 started life in 1888 as the Breach of Official Trust Bill. It was introduced shortly after Lord Salisbury, who had suffered in the Marvin case, had become Prime Minister. It was designed to provide sterner measures against civil servants who disobeyed instructions and betrayed the trust placed in them by the government.

The Lord Chancellor, Lord Halsbury, explained to the House of Lords: 'In recent years we have had very conspicuous examples of the necessity of guarding official secrets, and protecting official documents.' The Bill was intended to remedy existing defects in the law. Much of the debate was directed to espionage, but the Lord Chancellor told the House of Lords that 'another class of offences is the

disclosure of official secrets'. His concern was with
'Government servants who communicate with those who
may become the Queen's enemies', and his remarks were
evidently directed at disclosures which harmed the security of
the state rather than making the business of the government
more difficult or inconvenient.

In the event, there was remarkably little debate about the
Act. In the House of Commons the Attorney-General, Sir
Richard Webster QC (later the Lord Chief Justice, Lord
Alverstone), felt it necessary to expend only sixty-nine words
in introducing this important new piece of legislation:

> Sir, I wish to say just a word or two with regard to this Bill.
> It has been prepared under the direction of the Secretary of
> State for War and the First Lord of the Admiralty in order
> to punish the offence of obtaining information and
> communicating it against the interests of the state. The Bill
> is an exceedingly simple one and I beg to move its second
> reading.

An Irish MP, Dr C. K. Tanner, strongly objected to this
attempt to shepherd the Official Secrets Bill through the
House of Commons without proper debate. He referred to
the 'miserable explanation' of the Bill by the Attorney-
General and suggested that he was 'trifling with the House'.
He did not, however, succeed in obtaining a fuller debate of
the Bill; the main emphasis in the debate was on treason and
espionage. Such debate as there was on Section 2 showed that
at least one MP, Robert Hanbury, appreciated the dangers of
such legislation. He objected to the fact that the Bill penalised
the disclosure of information contrary to the interests not
only of the state but also of any part of the government. With
some prescience of the use to which Section 2 was to be put,
he complained that, if the words 'contrary to the interests of
any part of the Government' remained, criticism of a
government department – which might in many instances be
for the benefit of the state – would become a crime. This being
the only substantive point raised in opposition to the Bill, the
Attorney-General conceded it, but not before rapping

Hanbury's knuckles by observing that it was a little unfortunate that the Honourable Member should have 'imported so much feeling into this matter'.

The Bill was passed. But the Act was limited in scope and turned out in practice to be difficult to operate. Unlike the later Act of 1911, it did not apply to everyone but only to Crown servants and certain government contractors. Furthermore, an offence was committed only if it could be established that information had been communicated to a person to whom it ought not have been, and, that his communication was not in the interests of the public.

The Act was very seldom used. Its shortcomings were revealed by the case brought against Edward Holden, a former quartermaster in the Royal Engineers. Because of the difficulty of proving treachery under Section 2, which carried two years' imprisonment or (until its abolition) penal servitude for life, he had to be tried under Section 1, permitting maximum imprisonment of twelve months.

While in the Royal Engineers, Holden, who was a chief draughtsman, had worked on the construction of forts in Malta. After leaving the Army, he had become a surveyor and had supplemented his income by selling secrets to the French. On 20 January 1892 he had written to a Lance-Corporal M'Cartney, who had served under him. He asked to be supplied with plans of forts and gun batteries in Gibraltar and Malta and with details of the guns. He wrote in the language of a petty criminal, but there was no doubt that his conduct was a threat to British security – it would under present law merit prosecution under Section 1 of the Official Secrets Act 1911. Holden's letter ran:

Dear M'Cartney, You will be, no doubt, a little surprised to hear from me. However, I am in the land of the living, and I am glad to hear you are on the staff and doing A1. Now, I want you to do me a little favour, only it must be strictly confidential. I want certain information according to enclosed form, and I feel sure you can get it for me by writing to one of the draughtsmen at Malta that you know and can trust ... I shall pay both you and the individual who gives the information for your trouble . . . I want the information without delay, so kindly send off by post and let me know what you have done and how you are getting on.

With best wishes, yours faithfully, E. Holden, late Qr. M. Sergt. R.E.

PS. Destroy this as soon as you have noted what I want. E.H.

Unfortunately for Holden, M'Cartney showed the letter to an officer, and Holden was arrested at the address he had given for his reply. Holden had not followed his own advice about destroying letters; he was found in possession of two mysterious letters signed only with a hieroglyph. These letters indicated that Holden was being regularly paid by the French.

The jury at Liverpool Assizes soon found him guilty. The Lord Chief Justice, Lord Coleridge, expressed regret that he could not have sentenced him to a long period of penal servitude. As he had been charged with the lesser offence, he could pass a sentence only of twelve months' imprisonment. *The Times* called Holden's crime 'the basest treachery'.

An attempt was made in June 1896 to amend the law by another Official Secrets Bill. This would have placed the burden of proof on the accused in such cases, to show that he had obtained the information for innocent purposes and not illegally for the use of a foreign government. It would also have raised the penalty for the offence of which Holden had been convicted from one year to two years' imprisonment. The legislation was again outlined very briefly by the Attorney-General, Sir Richard Webster QC. Objection was taken by opposition MP E. H. Pickersgill to the way the Attorney-General had made light of shifting the burden of proof from the prosecution to the accused. The debate was adjourned, and the Bill was subsequently withdrawn.

The only prosecution brought under the 1889 Act which did not deal with military or naval secrets was the case of John Doe, a clerk in the supply reserve depot at Woolwich

Dockyard. He had access to documents which gave details of government supply contracts, and wrote to one of the contractors offering to let them have details of prices charged by their competitors. This was the first case involving a government contractor. It was pointed out on behalf of Doe that he had not been told that these documents were confidential; nor was there a copy of the Official Secrets Act in his office. He was found guilty, but the jury said that they did not think Doe knew he was committing a criminal offence. Testimonials were produced as to Doe's excellent character, and the judge was told that he had a wife and six children. Mr Justice Darling was sufficiently impressed to impose no penalty upon Doe other than to bind him over to come up for judgment if called upon to do so.

Concern was growing about German espionage. This was an era when every dachshund was viewed as a potential spy. A Bill to remedy the defects in the Official Secrets Act was introduced in March 1908. It would not only have strengthened the law against spying but would also have prohibited the unauthorised publication by any person of official information, if publication was not in the interests of the state. The Bill extended the law against the disclosure of official information beyond Crown servants and government contractors to any member of the general public.

The Lord Chancellor, Lord Loreburn, assured the House of Lords that 'anyone in the press conducting his duties honourably would be quite safe'. The press were understandably unconvinced. A law that depended on whether the government thought the press were acting honourably would give that government far too wide a discretion. The Bill therefore met spirited opposition in Parliament; its main purpose, it was suggested, was to support officialdom, bureaucracy and 'weak ministers who cackle in society'. The legislation was abandoned, but it was to serve as a prototype for Section 2. On 21 May 1908 the Lord Chancellor told the House of Lords that the government was postponing the second reading of the Official Secrets Bill because of representations made by the metropolitan press that it would interfere with the legitimate enterprise and freedom of the press. His Majesty's government had no such designs, he reassuringly added.

As fears about German spying grew, the government became increasingly determined both to protect national security and to safeguard the administration against the disclosure of official information. R. B. Haldane, the Secretary of State for War, set up a subcommittee of the Committee of Imperial Defence to consider 'the nature and extent of foreign espionage that is at present taking place within this country and the danger to which it may expose us'. The subcommittee collected and faithfully recorded evidence which bordered on the trivial and the anecdotal. Mr Schweiger, a German barber in Southsea, had been 'discovered by accident to wear a wig over his own thick head of hair' and showed 'much interest in naval gossip'. A lieutenant in Chatham felt it necessary to report that the proprietor of the Sun Hotel was a Mr H. A. Klockenbosch.

Books on invasion scares were avidly read. Erskine Childers's *The Riddle of the Sands* had been published in 1903; it described how Carruthers of the Foreign Office and his companion Davies had learnt while on a yachting holiday of plans to use the Frisian Islands as a springboard for a German assault on the unprotected east and south-east coast of England. The Earl of Selborne, the First Lord of the Admiralty, was sufficiently concerned by the reaction to the book to call for a report to see if the invasion plan was feasible. He was assured by the Naval Intelligence Department that it was not.

One writer of such invasion-scare books, William Le Queux, was also responsible for a particularly bizarre piece of evidence to the subcommittee, which no doubt was all good for business. He told them of a sinister incident when on a lane between Portsmouth and Chichester he had nearly run over a cyclist who was looking at a map and making notes. The man swore in German but had explained this to Le Queux by saying that he was studying at Oxford for the Church and swore in German to ease his conscience! Le Queux had returned to the neighbourhood on several subsequent days and found the cyclist and his companions still engaged in exploring tracks and lanes.

In the House of Commons, Colonel Lockwood, the Member for Epping, frequently raised the question of espionage by a foreign power (meaning Germany) by recounting lurid incidents of doubtful origin. Military men from a foreign nation had since 1906 been up to no good in his constituency, and a foreign power had the effrontery to organise a staff ride through England. He alleged that enemy agents were taking naval soundings off Holyhead. Little credence was given to what Lockwood said, but it heightened the impression that there was a serious problem of espionage and helped produce a suitable climate of opinion for introducing the Official Secrets Bill in 1911.

In 1909 a counter-espionage department was set up under Captain Vernon Kell. It was originally called MO5 but subsequently became MI5. Kell pressed for tougher legislation against spies. His campaign received some assistance in 1910 from the lenient treatment of Lieutenant Siegfried Helm of the 21st battalion of the Nassau Regiment of the German Army. The affair became known as the Portsmouth Spy Case. However, as in many such cases, on closer examination it turned out not to be serious and had, for good measure, an element of absurdity. When the case opened before magistrates at Fareham Police Court there was so much interest that the magistrates ordered that admission should be by ticket only. Helm was accused under the Official Secrets Act 1889 of feloniously making sketches and plans of fortresses in the Portsmouth area, intending to communicate them to the Empire of Germany.

He had been apprehended on 5 September by Captain Horace Martelli, who was out riding with a Lieutenant Salmond and an eleven-year-old boy, Leslie Hamilton. The two officers were in dress uniform. Helm himself was unusually dressed for a spy in that he was wearing a white suit with a panama hat. He appeared to be taking notes not far from the perimeter fence of Fort Wildey. He was allowed to walk back in the direction of Portsmouth for one mile. The British officers then decided to question Helm further and asked him whether he had any other papers on him. Helm then produced a *Portsmouth Times* map of Portsmouth but he aroused their suspicions by initially proffering them the cover of this publicly available document without the map inside. He was asked to mount the spare horse and to accompany them to Fort Widley, where, unaccountably, he was blindfolded.

Helm had behaved in a way likely to draw suspicion on himself but he was scarcely a serious threat to national security. His principal motive for coming to Portsmouth had been to pay court to a Miss Wodehouse, about whose charms he had heard from his brother officer, Lieutenant Wohlfart. Helm had planned on seeing Miss Wodehouse in Brixton, at an address he had been given by Wohlfart. (The opportunities for espionage in Brixton in 1910 were distinctly limited.) He had written to the lady in his stilted English: 'I am very sorry to hear from you that you are not in Brixton. I did hope to have a jolly time here in London. I would like a lady friend to sometimes accompany me and show me the city.' On learning that she was at Fratton, he wrote: 'I will come to Fratton in the forenoon and hope to see you. Will Fratton be far from Portsmouth? I will willingly see the harbour and the big harbour steamers.'

Miss Wodehouse took a dislike to the twenty-three-year-old lieutenant. She found his insatiable desire for the sights of Portsmouth suspicious and reported him to the military garrison. No doubt he felt that he would be assisting his country by finding out details of the disposition of fortifications at Portsmouth, but his interest appeared to be largely the product of an excess of zeal and an overdeveloped sense of curiosity. Even travelling down on the train to Portsmouth, Helm had found it necessary to jot in his notebook about a clergyman wearing a frock-coat; and for reasons never entirely clear at the trial he had made detailed notes of the furniture at his lodgings in Portsmouth, including the distance between the chest of drawers and the bed.

When challenged by Captain Martelli, Helm had responded by producing his calling card. The sketches in his notebook had been traced from a hanging map that was available for anyone to look at on the South Parade. He had made his drawings of the forts after looking through a powerful telescope on the Clarence Pier, which was available for use by the public on payment of a penny.

There was some evidence that Helm had tried to make notes of the military fortifications in Portsmouth and Southsea and had marked the location of gun positions on the map. However, his counsel, Travers Humphreys, was able by skilful cross-examination to indicate how amateur Helm's efforts had been. He persuaded the magistrates to rule that there was insufficient evidence of Helm having made these sketches for the purpose of wrongly obtaining information, intending to communicate it to a foreign state. That was a felony punishable by penal servitude for life. Helm was instead committed for trail on the lesser charge, the misdemeanour of making sketches and plans of those fortresses without authority, carrying a maximum sentence of twelve months. At his trial at the Winchester Assizes before Mr Justice Bankes in November 1910, Helm pleaded guilty to this lesser charge.

The prosecution case was presented with considerable moderation by the Attorney-General, Sir Rufus Isaacs KC. He pointed out that this was the first time there had been a prosecution of any officer of a foreign state for this offence under the Official Secrets Act. While Sir Rufus agreed that the question of punishment was entirely a matter for the court, he felt it right to say that Helm had been held in prison for four weeks before being released on bail and had admitted the offence, expressing his unfeigned regret. Accordingly the Attorney-General would ask his Lordship in his discretion to treat the prisoner with the utmost leniency he might see fit to exercise. This made the task of Travers Humphreys very much easier. He said that Helm wished to state that he had been treated with the utmost courtesy and the most absolute fairness. He would not be exceeding his instructions if he added an acknowledgement of the very generous way the case for the prosecution had been presented by the Attorney-General.

The real reason for this lenient treatment was that there

had been pressure from Captain Cumming of the Secret
Service Bureau, and this had been passed on to the Attorney-
General. The Security Service did not want the Germans to
think that it was taking the spy problem seriously.

Germany sent its gunboat the *Panther* to Agadir in Morocco
in June 1911, increasing international tension and the fear of
war. This event provided an excellent occasion to pass the
Official Secrets Act, which had been prepared for just such an
eventuality. The subcommittee on foreign espionage of the
Committee of Imperial Defence had been researching the
subject since 1909 and had prepared a draft Bill in 1910,
drawing on the draft Bills of 1896 and 1908.

The Bill was read on 17 July 1911 and was guided through
its second reading in the House of Lords by Viscount
Haldane, the Secretary of State for War, on 25 July. A total
of four peers spoke in the debates, and they were concerned
not with Section 2 but with the danger of espionage. Viscount
Middleton was worried about protecting the secrets of the
Brennan torpedo. Lord Alverstone, who as Sir Richard
Webster had introduced the 1889 and 1896 Official Secrets
Bills, made a characteristically short speech recollecting the
extreme difficulties he had had in instituting prosecutions
under the 1889 Act. Lord Ellenborough welcomed the Bill,
which he felt was all the more necessary after the Schultz trial.
All the peers were concerned about spies and felt that this Bill
merely strengthened the procedures of law. Viscount
Haldane told their Lordships that the Act had been prepared
after a good deal of deliberation. Its purpose was to
strengthen the law for dealing with the violation of
obligations with regard to official secrets and with espionage
generally, not to enact new restrictions but to make the
existing law more effective. There was nothing new about the
Act, it was merely a change in procedure. Viscount Haldane
took up the theme of the intelligence reports and waxed
anecdotal:

Not many months ago we found in the middle of the
fortifications at Dover an intelligent stranger, who

explained his presence by saying that he was there to hear the singing of the birds. He gave the explanation rather hastily, because it was mid-winter. Then there was another case, in which somebody was found looking at the emplacement of guns in a battery at Lough Foyle, and he declared that he was there for the purpose of paying a call on somebody.

The Bill passed through its committee stage without amendment and went through all its stages by 8 August. It reached the House of Commons on 18 August. It passed through all its stages there on a Friday in less than one hour's debate. Owing to the exigencies of the grouse season, only 117 MPs were present.

The Official Secrets Bill was steered through the House of Commons by Colonel J. E. B. Seely, the Under-Secretary of State for War. He told the House that it would be a great convenience if the Bill passed through all its stages that day and that it was highly necessary that it should. Even Colonel Seely seems to have been surprised by the readiness of the House of Commons to allow this Act to go through so quietly and wish so little debate:

I got up and proposed that the Bill be read a second time, explaining, in two sentences only, that it was considered desirable in the public interest that the measure should be passed. Hardly a word was said and the Bill was read a second time; the Speaker left the Chair. I then moved the Bill in Committee. This was the first critical moment; two men got up to speak, but both were forcibly pulled down by their neighbours after they had uttered a few sentences, and the committee stage was passed. The Speaker walked back to his chair and said: 'The question is, that I report this Bill without amendment to the House.' Again two or three people stood up; again they were pulled down by their neighbours, and the report stage was through. The Speaker turned to me and said: 'The third reading, what day?' 'Now, Sir,' I replied. My heart beat fast as the Speaker said: 'The question is that this Bill be read a third time.' It was open to any one of all the members of the House of Commons to get up and say that no Bill had ever yet passed through all its stages in one day without a word of explanation from the Minister in charge.... But to the eternal honour of those members, to whom I now offer, on behalf of that and all succeeding governments, my most grateful thanks, not one man seriously opposed, and in a little more time than it has taken to write these words that formidable piece of legislation was passed.

There was some resistance to the Bill. Mr Alpheus Cleophas Morton complained admist laughter that it was a very unusual and very extraordinary thing to pass such a Bill without an opportunity of discussing it and that it upset Magna Carta altogether. However, he said he would not press the point and, when the division came, he voted for the Bill.

There was, then, no serious debate in the House of Commons. Assurances were given by the Attorney-General, Sir Rufus Isaacs KC, that the principle of the Bill was not new. It was merely a remodelling of the 1889 Act to deal with certain points which had not been foreseen at the time that Act was passed. The first, second and third readings were passed before lunch, and a motion that the Bill be reported without amendment was passed by 107 votes to 10. The ten opponents included Keir Hardie, Arthur Henderson, George Lansbury (whose son fell victim to the Act), Ramsay MacDonald and Philip Snowden, but they made no contribution to the debate. The House was soothed by the assurance of Colonel Seely that none of His Majesty's loyal subjects ran the least risk whatever of having their liberties infringed in any degree or particular whatever.

In truth the 1911 Act introduced a number of changes. It extended beyond Crown servants and government con- tractors to anyone who received or communicated official information without authority. The Act was presented as a measure against foreign espionage, but official papers show that it was also intended to operate as a restraint on Civil Service leaks, of which the Welsh Church Commission leak in

1910 was the latest example. In contrast to the controversy in 1908, the press allowed the Act to pass without comment, as attention was focussed on the fears of war with Germany.

The Act altered the burden of proof in spying cases under Section 1 in that the prosecution no longer had to prove that the accused's purpose was prejudicial to the safety or interests of the state. It was sufficient if from the circumstances of the case, or the defendant's conduct, or his known character, it appeared that his purpose was prejudicial to the safety or interests of the state. In those circumstances the purpose would be deemed to be prejudicial unless the accused could prove otherwise. Although the harsh penalties under Section 1 of fourteen years' imprisonment were headed 'Penalties for spying', they were interpreted in 1964 by the House of Lords as applying to 'saboteurs', so that the CND protesters at Wethersfield air base were gaoled for eighteen months.

The 1911 Act produced a battery of new offences under Section 2 for the wrongful communication or retention of official documents, sketches, notes and the like, and for failing to take reasonable care of them. The Act extended to any citizen who came into possession of such documents in contravention of the Act, or to whom such documents had been entrusted by anyone working for the government. The Act made it an offence to receive such documents if they were communicated in contravention of it. People in possession of such documents were presumed to be guilty unless they proved that the document was communicated to them contrary to their desire. The Act introduced penalties for harbouring people who were reasonably suspected of committing offences under the Act. It also conferred worldwide jurisdiction on the English courts to try offences under the Act, wherever they were committed.

There had been no serious discussion in Parliament of these greatly enlarged powers. The alterations in the law were presented as purely procedural.

2

Clamping the Powers of War on to the Liberties of the Citizen in Peace

During the First World War, the Official Secrets Act was used principally against spies. There were, however, some prosecutions brought under Section 2 which, not surprisingly, had a strong wartime flavour. Details of those cases are given in Appendix 1. The most significant prosecution during this period was that of Albert Crisp, a clerk in the War Office who dealt with Army clothing contracts, and Arthur Homewood, a director and company secretary of a firm of tailors. The case, which occurred in 1919, had only a marginal connection with the war. Crisp was charged with communicating details of contracts, relating to the supply of khaki tunics costing £3.5s., which he had obtained during his employment in the statistical department. This involved him tabulating the contracts that various clothing firms had made with the government for the supply of officers' uniform. This information was of interest to Homewood, as his company from time to time tendered for government clothing contracts.

Crisp had been a friend of Homewood for three and a half years. There was no evidence that any illicit profit was made by Homewood or that Crisp had obtained any corrupt advantage. On three occasions in 1911 Crisp had borrowed a total of £40 from Homewood, but he had repaid most of this by the time he was charged. It was accepted by the court that these were merely loans from one friend to another and that the information was not communicated from any corrupt motive but out of friendship. As often happens, this matter came to light when Homewood left his office unattended and took his first holiday for four years. His desk was found to contain particulars of the clothing contracts supplied by Crisp. Crisp was charged with communicating official information to an unauthorised person, and Homewood with receiving it.

The magistrate at the Westminster Police Court took a robust view of the meaning of Section 2. The Act was, he commented, called the Official Secrets Act and was intended to apply to matters that were or should be secret. There was nothing secret about clothing contracts; while the details of tenders should be kept secret, there was no public interest in keeping details of executed contracts secret. Indeed, it was arguable that it was in the public interest that such details be known.

In order to get around this set-back, the Attorney-General preferred an indictment against Crisp and Homewood, and the ruling by the Westminster magistrate was considered afresh by Mr Justice Avory. He held that Section 2 applied to any official document or information obtained by a person as a result of his employment by the Crown. After this ruling Crisp and Homewood pleaded guilty. They were fined 40s. each and were ordered to pay the costs of their prosecution.

The case was significant in that it revealed for the first time the breadth of the Official Secrets Act. It made all the more inexplicable the subsequent claim by the Attorney-General, Sir Gordon Hewart KC, that the Official Secrets Act related to spying and attempts at spying.

After the First World War, the Defence of the Realm Regulations lapsed, and the government wished to retain some of the wide powers that those regulations gave it. The War Office Emergency Legislation Committee had proposed a National Security Bill, but in the event what was pushed through Parliament was a series of wide-ranging amendments to the Official Secrets Act 1911, in the form of the Official Secrets Act 1920. Again, debate was very limited, and concentrated more on espionage than on the increased powers which were taken to deal with offences under Section 2.

The parliamentary debates were remarkable for what was said about the Act by the Attorney-General. He produced a series of misleading and wrong answers to those who questioned the need for such wide-ranging powers. Hewart was a brilliant advocate but a man of illiberal views, despite starting his career as parliamentary reporter for the *Manchester Guardian*. He had become Attorney-General in 1919. In 1922 he became Lord Chief Justice, a post he held until his retirement in 1940. He presided over a number of courts which interpreted the powers given under the Official Secrets Act in diametrically the opposite way to that by which he had sought to reassure the House of Commons while shepherding the 1920 Act through Parliament.

The office of Lord Chief Justice at that time was considered to be the prerogative of the Attorney-General whenever he wanted the post. Not until the appointment of Lord Goddard in 1946 did it become the practice to appoint the most suitably qualified High Court judge to the position of Lord Chief Justice, rather than the Attorney-General. When Sir Rufus Isaacs KC accepted the Vice-Royalty of India in April 1921, Hewart decided that the time for him to become Lord Chief Justice was not yet appropriate; so the senior judge, Mr Justice Lawrence, was appointed at the age of seventy-seven. In March 1922 Lord Trevethin, as Lawrence had become, learnt of his resignation in *The Times*. It is true that he was aged seventy-nine, but he was in as good health as he had been when appointed the previous year, and he remained so until he died while fishing for salmon in the Wye in August 1936, above Builth Wells, aged ninety-two.

In any event, the post was open for Hewart. Lord Devlin, himself a Law Lord, has this to say about Hewart's term of office:

Hewart, who had towards the end of his term the misfortune of ill-health to contend with as well as those of his temperament, clung to office until 1940. He has been called the worst Chief Justice since Scroggs and Jeffreys in the seventeenth century. I do not think that is quite fair. When one considers the enormous improvement in judicial standards between the seventeenth and twentieth centuries, I should say that, comparatively speaking, he was the worst Chief Justice ever.

The Official Secrets Bill was introduced in 1920 against the background of increasing worries about Bolshevik agitation and the threat of full-scale civil war in Ireland. It added a new list of misdemeanours. It was now possible to be sentenced to two years' imprisonment, with or without hard labour, for a wide range of activities, such as unlawfully wearing military or police uniform, or making a false statement, or forging a military pass, or using a secret official code-word, or possessing an official stamp, if this was done for the purpose of gaining admission to a prohibited place within the meaning of the Official Secrets Act 1911, or – to use the very wide words of the 1920 Act – 'for any purpose prejudicial to the safety or interest of the State'. It also became an offence under the 1920 Act to retain, for any purpose prejudicial to the state, any official document without authority and, if one happened to find such an official document or secret official code-word, to fail to restore it to the relevant authority or even a police constable. If a person was charged with an offence where a purpose prejudicial to the state had to be shown, the burden effectively rested on the accused to show that his purpose had not in fact been prejudicial to the state.

The Bill was debated only briefly in the House of Lords. The principal opposition came from Viscount Burnham. With some irony he commented:

I am loath to interrupt the silent course of proceedings on this Bill, and I shall not detain your lordships for more than a minute... I think the words in the subsection are dangerously wide... I do not believe any editor would be safe if the Bill were passed in its present form... I do not know a single editor of a national paper who from time to time has not been in possession of official documents which have been brought into his office, very often not at his own request, and which it may be inconvenient to the

Minister of the responsible Department should they have gone out.

Lord Parmoor, a Lord of Appeal, regretted that such a Bill was necessary, 'because it will seriously interfere with our ordinary freedom in various directions'.

These objections were met with some surprise from the government front benches. Viscount Peel pointed out that, as no noble lords had taken any part whatsoever in the second reading, it had been assumed that no one was going to raise any points on the third reading. Consequently he had no notice which would have given him the opportunity of consulting with the authorities. He suggested that the question of amendments should be dealt with in the House of Commons. The Bill was accordingly passed through the House of Lords. It came for its second reading in the House of Commons on 2 December 1920. This was shortly after the killing of twelve British intelligence officers in Dublin on 21 November 1920, 'Bloody Sunday', which produced a suitably sombre atmosphere that aided the passing of the legislation.

The Act also created a new offence of interfering with a police officer or member of His Majesty's forces in a prohibited place, under Section 3. This undebated provision was, with considerable effect, used in the 1960s against CND demonstrators at British and American military air bases. Powers were given to the government to require the production of telegrams sent to and from any place out of the United Kingdom by any private cable service. Powers were also given under Section 5 to require the regulation of all accommodation addresses, including records of persons using them. It will be seen later that in 1935 a bookmaker called Fulton was prosecuted, despite the fact that no official information was involved. The case inevitably came before Lord Hewart, who found no difficulty in upholding Fulton's conviction.

The powers sought by the government became more astonishing as the Act went on. Section 6 made it an offence to fail to give information as to the commission of any offence under the 1911 or 1920 Act. This removed the traditional right of silence, and was used against a Stockport journalist in the Lewis case, another case to come before the Lord Chief Justice Lord Hewart. It was used on several occasions to try to compel journalists to reveal their sources.

Section 7 of the 1920 Act made it a crime to do any act preparatory to the commission of an offence under the Official Secrets Act. It was this section which enabled Crispin Aubrey to be charged in the 'ABC' case for doing nothing more sinister than making a telephone call fixing an appointment for Duncan Campbell and him to meet John Berry.

The second reading of the Official Secrets Bill was introduced by Hewart, on the basis that it was strengthening and updating the law against spies. Sir Gordon told the House of Commons that 'unfortunately one of the things which increase and develop in an imperfect world is the ingenuity of spies'. He told them that as the Defence of the Realm Regulations were being repealed it was necessary to have laws against gaining admission to a prohibited place by means of wearing naval or military uniforms, and against tampering with official documents, because 'experience during the war has made it quite plain that a provision of that kind is necessary if the work of foreign agents is to be checked'. The law relating to communications with enemy agents, he told the House of Commons, was necessary because 'modern spying, assisted by contrivances like invisible ink, is extremely difficult to detect'.

The main purpose of the rules contained in Clause 4 of the Bill, relating to postal and cable censorship, was 'to enable the authorities to detect and deal with attempts at spying by foreign agents'. He then went on to say:

There are in this country some businesses which consist in the receipt of letters for persons whose real addresses are elsewhere, and this bill provides for the registration and regulation of persons who carry on the business of receiving postal packets. It is required that they shall register the names and addresses of their clients, and also register the particulars of business done. No honest or innocent person can have any objection to that provision.

Sir Gordon was asked in the course of the debate by Lieutenant Commander Kenworthy whether the powers in the Bill were intended to deal with people who forged passports, passes, official permits and things of that sort, rather than being merely confined to cases where such acts were done for the purpose of obtaining access to official secrets. The Attorney-General replied by shaking his head vigorously and answering: 'It is not only not in our minds but it is not in the Bill.'

Although at the outset of the debate Sir Gordon said that he could not possibly say that the Bill only dealt with spying, when he was asked specifically about the powers under Section 6 of the Official Secrets Act 1920, which made it an offence not to answer questions put by a police officer relating to a possible offence under the Official Secrets Acts, he had replied rather sharply: 'We are dealing only with offences or suspected offences under the principal Act, or this Act, in other words, to put it shortly, we are dealing with spying or attempts at spying.' This was demonstrably wrong. He appears to have forgotten that in the previous year, 1919, Crisp and Homewood had been convicted under Section 2, for the disclosure of details of military tailoring contracts.

It was also suggested to Sir Gordon that the Act severely restricted the powers of the press. To this he replied with some vigour:

It is said that this bill deals with the press. That seems to me to be an astonishing statement, and it is very strange that persons connected with the press should say that this Bill deals with them ... So far from asserting that this is something aimed at journalists, I should have thought that the first comment of a journalist reading this provision would be this: 'Whosoever may be the persons referred to, they are certainly not journalists.'

Section 6 was later used to try to compel journalists to disclose their sources of information. For example, in 1930 the government used these powers in an attempt to find out how news of Gandhi's impending arrest had been leaked forty-eight hours before it took place; and in 1938 Lord Hewart, sitting as the Lord Chief Justice, upheld the conviction of a journalist for failing to disclose to a police superintendent how he had obtained a copy of a police message which he had used as the basis of a story in the *Southport Daily Dispatch* (Chapter 4).

The Attorney-General referred in the House of Commons to the powers in the 1920 Bill as being 'certain ancillary provisions, the better to secure the end already sought to be secured'. There was fierce opposition from Sir Donald Maclean MP (whose son Donald was to be the subject of a warrant under the Official Secrets Act after he defected to Moscow). He complained that the Act would hit at the legitimate exercise of the functions of the press, and would impinge most harmfully on the liberty of the individual. Dealing with the section that effectively reversed the burden of proof when it came to proving that a person's purpose was 'prejudicial to the safety and interests of the State', Sir Donald complained that a private individual or the editor of a newspaper who was prosecuted would be dealt with in the same way as an enemy spy in time of war. It was 'the complete abrogation of any semblance of justice'. When Sir Donald came to the powers to compel information to be given to senior police officers under Clause 6, and to hear cases in secret under Clause 8, his indignation knew no bounds: 'I find it difficult to confine my language in regard to this Bill within the range of parliamentary propriety. It is another attempt to clamp the powers of war on to the liberties of the citizen in peace.'

Despite this opposition, and despite criticism in the press, the Act was passed by 143 votes to 34, without any significant changes, and with little scrutiny or debate of the detailed provisions of the Bill.

In the absence of any specific legislation against IRA terrorists, charges were brought under Section 2 of the Act in the early 1920s. It was not felt appropriate to bring charges under Section 1, because of doubts as to whether as British citizens they could be 'an enemy' within the terms of the section. Brief details of those cases appear in Appendix 1.

Twice during the 1920s the Official Secrets Act was used to bring prosecutions for unlawful communication of information which did not relate to national security. The first was in November 1926, when the former Governor of Pentonville Prison, Major Frederick Blake, was prosecuted for communicating information to the editor of the *Evening News*. The editor was not prosecuted for receiving it, although he had paid Blake's literary agent, Raymond Savage, 300 guineas for the story. During his twelve-year tenure as prison governor, Blake had presided over eleven executions, before in November 1925 being placed on the sick list and retired. He agreed to share with the British public the last hours of the life of twenty-year-old Frederick Bywaters before his execution three and a half years before for the murder of an Ilford shipping clerk, Percy Thompson. Bywaters had been having an affair with Thompson's wife, Edith, who was also executed, so the case had aroused considerable public interest.

What appeared in the *Evening News* was, as Sir Travers Humphreys KC observed for the prosecution at the trial, in execrably bad taste, although he pointed out that the court was not concerned with sentimental considerations. The article was headlined 'What Bywaters Told Me' and was said to be an account of a long talk he had with Governor Blake, when he had told the story of his life. Bywaters had also requested a last talk with the governor on the morning of his execution:

'It's her I want to speak to you about, Sir. I swear she was not guilty. I can't bear to think of their mauling her about.'

'My boy [Blake recorded himself as saying], that is no good now. She was tried and found guilty. She appealed, and there is nothing left. In any event it would not have been a happy life for her after all that has happened. They will be very gentle. Don't think of it. There is only a minute or two left. I should like to hear you say that you are sorry for what you did.'

'I am, Sir, damned sorry.'

The door opened and we shook hands.

'Yes, Sir, I really am sorry. Goodbye.'

Then, as related in the *Evening News*, they marched Bywaters off to the shed and shot him off on his last voyage.

This lurid narrative contrasted with the more prosaic recollections of the two prison warders, Albert Bickman and Alfred Alders, who were on execution duty. They considered the governor's account somewhat embroidered, as all they had heard was Bywaters saying, 'I am sorry I murdered Thompson, Sir.'

Bywaters at least showed himself to be a man of some quality for, when he had been convinced, he had said, 'I say the jury is wrong. Edith Thompson is not guilty.'

This was a sentiment with which she agreed, for she said, 'I am not guilty. Oh, God, I am not guilty.'

Both were hanged on 9 January 1922. Bywaters apparently met his end like a gentleman, protesting Edith Thompson's innocence to the last. His fears about her were well founded, as she had to be carried to the scaffold in a state of collapse by two wardresses.

Confessions of the sort reportedly made by Bywaters were regarded as highly confidential. They were, under prison regulations, to be communicated only to the Under-Secretary of State at the Home Office. This rule was so strictly enforced that the confessions were not even to be divulged to the coroner; it was felt most undesirable for such statements to be made, for 'there were always persons who believed that what a man said just before his death must be true'.

Blake pleaded not guilty at his trial before Mr Justice Roche at the Central Criminal Court, and he was vigorously defended by Roland Oliver KC. He contended that to come within the ambit of the Official Secrets Act, there must be something which it was contrary to the public interest to reveal. The existence of the prison regulations had nothing to do with the question of whether there had been a breach of the Act. Blake was guilty of nothing worse than an error of taste, and annoying some people at the Home Office. He commented that this matter could have been dealt with at the police court. It was the Attorney-General who had required the matter to go for trial at the Central Criminal Court and had sent the Solicitor-General, Sir Thomas Inskip KC, to prosecute.

The judge enquired whether this was the first case of prosecution of an official for using information for journalist purposes. Roland Oliver KC replied that it was, although other officials had published their reminiscences without being prosecuted. (In fact there had been two cases, in 1916 and 1918, when officials had communicated information to the press.)

'I would rather not be informed of that,' Mr Justice Roche replied. 'If other people deserve prosecution I hope they will be.' So saying, he fined Blake £250, and ordered him to pay the costs of the prosecution.

In 1928 an Air Ministry clerk, Archibald Taylor, was prosecuted and sent to prison for two months after being convicted of communicating information about Air Ministry tenders for the supply of 35,000 practice bombs, without authority, contrary to the Prevention of Corruption Act 1906.

When the tender of one of the companies had been accepted in July 1928, Taylor wrote to one of the unsuccessful bidders:

> I write to inform you no part of the order will go to your firm. If you wish to send in another tender I am prepared to give you a complete list of prices quoted by your competitors in consideration of the payment of £100. I suggest that the excuse for revising your tender should be that a mistake was made by your costing department. If you wish to avail yourself of this offer, place an advertisement in the personal column of the *Daily Express* in the name of Williams.
>
> I have two objects in making this offer. One is that I am in great financial difficulties and the second is that I do not agree with orders going to large companies.

The letter was signed 'Wellwisher'.

This company reported the matter to the ministry, and, acting under its instructions, made contact with Taylor, having put an advertisement in the *Daily Express* agreeing to meet him at London Bridge Station. The firm's representative met Taylor at a tea-shop at London Bridge and handed him no more than £10, receiving the list of tenders in return. Taylor was arrested as he left the shop and immediately admitted what he had done. The case was one of corruption, and the charge under the Official Secrets Act added nothing, but was perhaps included as a precaution in case the main charge failed.

The Official Secrets Act became an increasingly useful tool for suppressing leaks of official information. It was soon used for purposes far removed from those outlined by Hewart. Lord Parmoor, who as a Law Lord had expressed liberal sentiments (as befitted the father of Stafford Cripps) during the Bill's passage through Parliament, voiced a rather different view when he became the Labour Leader of the House:

> After an Act has been passed, on the question as to what it means, how it should be interpreted and how it should be used, we are guided by the words of the Act itself and not by a statement made by either one side or the other at the time the Bill was before your Lordships' House or another place.

Section 6 was found to be particularly handy. In 1925 the Home Office threatened a prosecution against the author of a book about Sir Roger Casement. Casement had been executed for his activities in Ireland in 1916, leaving behind him his notorious 'black' diaries which listed his homosexual encounters. The government had refused to allow the diaries to be published (their existence had helped hang Casement). The Home Secretary, Sir William Joynson Hicks, justified his decision on the basis of the security situation in Ireland.

In 1927 Joynson Hicks used the powers of search given

under Section 9 of the Official Secrets Act 1911 to enable the police to raid the premises of the Russian Trade Delegation. It was ironical therefore that he found himself the butt of a later allegation that he had breached the Official Secrets Act when he allowed a series of articles to be published in *Tit-Bits* about his experiences as Home Secretary. It was stated on his behalf that no breach of the Act had taken place. This inevitably led to the supplementary question, 'Is the Right Honourable Gentleman not afraid of the threat to the Constitution if the articles in *Tit-Bits* get into the hands of the Russians?'

During the 1920s there was considerable concern about the disclosure of information. A Cabinet minute of 11 March 1925 records Prime Minister Stanley Baldwin as dealing with the following matter:

Leakage of information – the attention of the Cabinet was drawn to several recent instances of premature disclosure in the Press of decisions taken by the Cabinet. The Prime Minister made an appeal for the utmost reticence in revealing outside discussions which have taken place in Cabinet.

Similar platitudinous requests have been made by successive Prime Ministers without success.

A detailed report of a Cabinet discussion on retirement pensions appeared on 3 November 1929 in the *Manchester Guardian* and the *Yorkshire Post*. In the same year George Lansbury, the Commissioner of Works, who was known to have close links with the *Daily Herald,* was strongly suspected of having leaked the report of the Snowden Committee on Unemployment to that newspaper. His refusal to comply with Cabinet rules of secrecy was one of the reasons why the opportunity to prosecute his son was taken in 1934.

The worry about the need for government secrecy led to a particularly ill-advised attempt in 1930 to use the powers under Section 6 – which was the section requiring a person, under the pain of two years' imprisonment, to answer questions from a senior police officer who had reasonable grounds to believe that an offence under the Official Secrets Act had been committed. Despite what the previous Attorney-General, Sir Gordon Hewart KC, had said in the House of Commons, Section 6's use was threatened against journalists when news of Gandhi's impending arrest in India was disclosed to the press forty-eight hours before the event. The background to the investigation shows that there was no question of any spying or threat to national security, merely embarrassment to the government.

On 30 April Frederick Truelove, the lobby correspondent of the *Daily Sketch*, learnt from a parliamentary private secretary that earlier in the day the Cabinet had approved Gandhi's arrest. In order to confirm this story Truelove went to see the Home Secretary, J. R. Clynes, who was an old friend. During his conversation he obtained confirmation and he passed the story to two lobby colleagues, Jack Kirk of the *News Chronicle* and William Forse of the *Daily Telegraph*.

Kirk's article read:

The Government of India is preparing, I understand, to take decisive action against Gandhi.

His arrest is to be expected at any time.

The matter is entirely within the province of the Government of India.

Nevertheless, the latter has taken the precaution of ascertaining the views of home government before moving.

The British Government has decided to support the Viceroy and his advisers.

The matter was reviewed at some length at yesterday's meeting of the cabinet. The conclusion was reached with natural regret.

Within hours the police had visited the offices of the three newspapers. They were sent away empty handed by the more resolute editors of the *Daily Telegraph* and *Daily Sketch* but they were a little more successful at the *News Chronicle*, where they found a deputy editor. The deputy editor was sufficiently alarmed at the arrival of Special Branch officers at his paper to express his regret at the fact that the report had been published. He supinely gave the police the name and address of Kirk. Three officers went to Mr Kirk's house, where they interrogated him for five hours, during the course of which Mrs Kirk had a fainting fit. When the police threatened to arrest him under the Official Secrets Act, Kirk felt that the time had come to telephone Truelove, who had originally passed him the story. At that stage the enquiry turned to farce. Truelove told the chief inspector who had been questioning Kirk that it might be as well if he let the Commissioner of Police know that the source of the information was none other than the Home Secretary! It was suggested to him that he might like to call off his sleuths.

The Home Secretary had been unaware of these enquiries being made under Section 6, because the initiative for the enquiry had come from the Attorney-General, Sir William Jowitt KC. What had happened was that King George V had been outraged to learn of this Cabinet decision through what he read in the newspapers. He was after all Emperor of All India and expected to be kept fully informed of government policy. He had telephoned the Prime Minister, Ramsay MacDonald, at 10 Downing Street and had used colourful language from his naval days to communicate his displeasure. MacDonald, concerned at the apparent lack of security at No. 10, called in the Attorney-General – without consulting Home Secretary Clynes. The moment the Commissioner of Police was told that the source of information was none other than the Home Secretary the enquiry was terminated.

The Prime Minister, however, spoke sternly to his Cabinet on 7 May about the question of leaks of information. The minutes record:

> The attention of the Cabinet was drawn to several cases that had occurred recently of leaking to the press of Cabinet discussions or of the contents of secret documents communicated to the Cabinet, some of which had been circulated under the same precautions as are taken in the case of Cabinet minutes.

In one case, namely the decision of the Cabinet to approve the Government of India's proposal to arrest Mr Gandhi, the possible consequences of leakage had been so serious that steps had been taken, under the threat of prosecution, to ascertain the source from which certain newspapers had derived the information. This investigation indicated the desirability that all persons in possession of Cabinet secrets should avoid answering any questions whatsoever, whether apparently innocent or not, by pressmen and others, in regard to Cabinet business.

The Prime Minister appealed to his colleagues to observe these rules.

The Attorney-General was closely questioned about the matter in the House of Commons. Jowitt explained that the drastic power given by Section 6 should, in his view, be used sparingly and only where serious issues were involved. He gave the House some indication of where the blame for the fiasco lay; he said the Prime Minister had informed him of his view that, in the existing situation, this was a gravely serious publication from which tragic consequences might have ensued. Sir William nevertheless went out of his way to deny categorically that the police enquiries had revealed the fact that a Cabinet minister had disclosed information relating to the intention of the Indian government to arrest Gandhi, or about the fact that there had been consultations between the governments. This statement was utterly untrue. This was possibly the extent of Sir William's knowledge, but, if so, the truth had been concealed from him. He was able to reassure the House that the police had conducted their enquiries with tact and consideration and that he did not contemplate any further proceedings.

The Attorney-General declared to the House:

I should certainly desire to uphold the freedom of the press in every possible way. I would point out that there is no question of this journalist either being guilty or innocent. He was merely asked to comply with the duty which the statute imposes on him, namely, to give the source of his information.

3

Not a Prosecution but a Malicious Persecution: Sir Compton Mackenzie

Few prosecutions under Section 2 of the Official Secrets Act are likely to parallel, for its air of unremitting farce, the case brought in 1932 against Edward Montagu Compton Mackenzie – who, despite his conviction, became Sir Compton Mackenzie. During the First World War, Mackenzie had served as a captain in the Royal Marines. Before retiring on sick-leave to Capri, he had a number of intelligence postings from 1915 to 1917. He was seconded to the Intelligence Department in Athens, being Military Control Officer in the British Legation in Athens and Director of the Aegean Intelligence Service. He was decorated by the British, French, Greek and Serbian governments.

Mackenzie wrote more than a hundred books, and the First World War accounted for three volumes of his memoirs. The first, *Gallipoli Memories*, was published in 1929. As the war had been over for eleven years, he considered that what he wrote about would no longer be secret. No complaints had been made about this first volume, despite his recounting his experiences as an intelligence officer, including various plots he had hatched to eliminate enemy agents in Asia Minor. The second volume, *First Athenian Memories*, followed in March 1931. This also quoted various Foreign Office telegrams relating to his intelligence activities, but it did not give rise to any action by the government.

A third volume, *Greek Memories*, was planned for 1932. Before it was completed, Sir Basil Thomson's *The Allied Secret Service in Greece* was published in March 1931. Sir Basil's credentials to write such an account seemed impeccable. He had been head of the Special Branch and the CID from 1921 and had been previously Director of Intelligence.

Mackenzie considered that Thomson's book was scurrilous and mendacious. It had, he stated, been subsidised by funds provided for propaganda by the Greek Royal Family. Accordingly, he doubled his efforts to produce his book to counter what he termed the 'untrustworthiness' of the author. In the preface to *Greek Memories* he did not mince his words about Thomson:

His description as Director of Intelligence from 1919 to 1921 (a civil post connected with the police) suggested a more intimate knowledge of Greek affairs than he possessed. His official position gave him very little more opportunity to know what was happening in Greece in 1915 to 1917 than the man in the street. Experienced intelligence officers should take steps to check the accuracy of information that reaches them in this way.

As Thomson's book quoted various secret and unpublished material, Mackenzie decided to draw more deeply on his intelligence sources, such as the texts of telegrams, and dispatches from the then Foreign Secretary, Sir Edward Carey, and the Permanent Under-Secretary of State at the Foreign Office, Sir Arthur Nicolson, to the British Minister in Athens, Sir Francis Elliot. The pre-publication publicity for *Greek Memories* referred pointedly to 'ill-informed propagandist and apologetic writing'. The book's hopes of success were short-lived, however, for intervention by the Foreign Office led to its being withdrawn on the day of publication. This followed the issue of a summons, not on literary grounds or due to delayed shock at the use of the words 'tart' and 'bitch' in his novel about lesbians in Capri, *Extraordinary Women* (the words had been deleted from the

United States edition), but rather because he had allegedly
infringed Section 2 of the Official Secrets Act 1911.
Mackenzie's alleged offence was that he had in July 1932
communicated without authority to his publishers, Cassell,
information he had obtained as an officer in the Royal
Marines.

For all its absurdity, this was a serious charge, which in the
normal course of events would carry a sentence of
imprisonment. But the flavour of what was to follow became
apparent when the summons to appear at the Guildhall
Magistrates' Court on 16 November 1932 was delivered by a
City of London Police inspector at the offices of his solicitor,
Sir Reginald Poole. The summons had previously been sent,
rather unnecessarily, to the Chief Constable in Inverness, to
serve upon Mackenzie in Scotland.

As the inspector handed Mackenzie the summons, he
confided: 'Well, sir, this is one of those times when one wishes
one had stuck to one's original job, instead of going in for the
law. Still I've had many interesting gentlemen through my
hands.'

He then went on to reveal that his earlier career had been in
publishing. He had, he explained, been a packer at
Macmillan. By now the inspector was warming to his task.
He spoke of a convicted fraudsman – 'Mr Clarence Hatry,
one of the nicest gentlemen I've ever met. He was always
helpful and saved us no end of time in going through the mass
of papers. Yes, sir, we were very grateful to Mr Hatry at the
Old Jewry' (where the inspector was stationed in the City),
'and when Mr Justice Avory gave him fourteen years, we
thought the sentence very harsh.'

With these comforting words, the police inspector turned
and left.

The committal proceedings to decide whether Mackenzie
should stand trial at the Central Criminal Court were heard
before Alderman Sir George Truscott at the Guildhall. The
case was confidently opened by Eustace Fulton for the
prosecution. A library clerk from the Foreign Office told the
court that Mackenzie had paraphrased secret and confidential telegrams passing between London and Athens in

1916, and that he had no authority to do so. This was scarcely startling evidence, as the Foreign Office had not declassified any documents since 1885!

Mackenzie was represented by a contemporary of his at Magdalen College, Cambridge, St John Hutchinson, and the first blow was not long in falling.

'So far as you can see, is there anything in the document which at present is in any degree secret?'

Before the alarmed clerk could reply, Eustace Fulton intervened for the prosecution:

'I don't think it is in the public interest for the witness to answer that question.'

Sir George Truscott agreed and said that he did not think the witness should answer the question. The case was adjourned to enable the prosecution to produce someone from the War Office of greater authority who could deal with such matters.

After the adjournment, Mackenzie found himself invited for a series of pink gins by the police inspector who had served the summons on him. With unusual camaraderie, one of the police officers concerned with the case launched into a short speech.

'I know I'm speaking both for the Metropolitan Police and for Old Jewry when I say we do not consider this a prosecution but a malicious persecution. Here's to you, Sir.' And he raised a pink gin to his lips.

The cause of this good fellowship was the fact that Mackenzie had, by publishing *Greek Memories*, attacked the veracity of Sir Basil Thomson. Sir Basil had been Assistant Commissioner of the Metropolitan Police. Shortly after leaving the police force he was convicted of an act of public indecency with a Miss Thelma de Lava on a park bench in Hyde Park and fined £5 – despite calling a former Home Secretary, Reginald MacKenna, as a character witness. He protested that he had been framed and accused the police of perjury. The police were infuriated by Thomson's accusations and were delighted to see him being attacked.

At the resumed hearing the prosecution produced a more senior member of the Foreign Office library staff. Only the secretary of state, he explained, could have given permission for those documents to be published, and his consent had not been requested. He too was pressed by Hutchinson to say what damage might be done by the book. He replied, no doubt quoting from his Foreign Office brief:

'I do not think that in this case the public interest has been prejudiced. No detriment has been suffered.'

Fulton then requested that the court go into camera – always a good way of reminding a court of the threat to national security, with the added advantage of no publicity. What followed can scarcely have pleased the prosecution.

They called a witness named, in the best traditions of Official Secrets cases, 'Major X'. He was able to tell the court that Mackenzie had disclosed the names of fourteen intelligence officers who had served in the First World War. He had also revealed the fact that the passport control departments of embassies and consulates were used as cover for intelligence work and had disclosed the existence of a department of the Secret Intelligence Service called M1(c). If this was signally to impress the gravity of his offence on Mackenzie, it failed to do so. As he recounts in his memoirs, *My Life and Times*:

> The Crown Prosecutor went on to enumerate a list of more than a dozen names I had mentioned in my book of people connected with the Secret Service sixteen years ago, because it might be necessary to use them again in the event of another war. I was staggered when I heard the list of names. Even I, with all my first-hand experience, should have hesitated to impute such stupidity to the Intelligence pundits who drew up the list.

Poor Major X was subjected to merciless cross-examination by Hutchinson:

'Major X, you have told my learned friend that, by publishing in his book the names of these gentlemen who worked on intelligence duties in the war, Mr Mackenzie had jeopardised their future.'

'Because when war comes –'

'When war comes? Are we indebted to our intelligence service for knowing when war will come?'

'I meant, if another war comes.'

'Ah! Please go on, Major X.'

'If another war comes, we may want to call upon their services again.'

'I see. So that you must know where all these gentlemen are and what they are doing now.'

After some hesitation Major X replied, 'I have no doubt we know, yes.'

'Then shall we go through the list? The first name is Mr C. E. Heathcote-Smith. Do you know where he is now?'

'I don't myself know, but I have no doubt that it is known.'

'Perhaps you don't know that he is now His Britannic Majesty's Consul-General in Alexandria?'

'I hear you say so.'

'You can trust your ears, Major X. Have you read Mr Mackenzie's two previous volumes of war memories?'

'I have, and if I may say so with very much pleasure.'

'I'm sure Mr Mackenzie and his publishers will appreciate that unsolicited testimonial. . . . Then don't you remember, Major X, that in *Gallipoli Memories* he wrote at some length of Mr Heathcote-Smith's intelligence work when he was Vice-Consul at Mytilene? And perhaps you are not aware, Major X, that in the entry in *Who's Who* under his name, Mr Heathcote-Smith says that he was working in intelligence from 1915 to 1916.'

Major X was not enjoying himself. 'I hear you say so.'

'You can take it from me, Major X, that I am not indulging in fantasy. Well, so much for the Consul-General of Alexandria. Let us take the next name on the list. Mr A.J.B. Wace. Do you know where Mr Wace is now?'

'I do not know myself.'

'Then perhaps you do not know that he is the Deputy Keeper of the Victoria and Albert Museum?'

'I hear you say so.'

'Perhaps you do not know that Mr Wace was never in the Secret Service?'

Major X did not answer, but gulped his third tumbler of water.

'And now, Major X, the last name on your list? Captain Christmas. Surely, Major X, the page in Mr Mackenzie's book about Captain Christmas shows that Captain Christmas was nothing more than a figure of fun?'

'Well, as a matter of fact, Mr Hutchinson, we do not wish to press that name.'

'No? Why not?'

'Because we have found out that Captain Christmas is dead.'

'Indeed? When did he die?'

'I believe it was about ten years ago.'

'Indeed! So that not even the Secret Service will be able to call upon Captain Christmas when war comes – I should say *if* another war comes.'

Major X was then asked about another agent whose name Mackenzie had mentioned in his book. This was Pirie Gordon, who it turned out had reviewed *Greek Memories* in *The Times* without realising the enormity of what he was doing.

Despite the virtual demolition of the prosecution's case, Sir George Truscott felt compelled to commit Mackenzie for trial at the Central Criminal Court, after he was reminded by the court clerk that no less a person than the Attorney-General had given his consent for the prosecution to take place. However, some indication of the gravity that the court took of the charge could be gauged from the reduction of his bail to his own recognisance of £100 and the removal of any need to have sureties. Before the proceedings concluded Mackenzie made a statement that his object in writing *Greek Memories* was not financial gain but to tell the truth about Mr Eleftherios Venizelos and the patriots who followed his lead sixteen years before: 'I thought it my duty to answer the propaganda which for many years has been carried on against the Allies and Venizelist Greeks. I plead not guilty and reserve my defence.' (Venizelos was republican and pro-Ally, whereas the King of Greece was pro-German and married to the Kaiser's sister.)

Mackenzie's hopes of a triumphant acquittal after these encounters in the magistrate's court were soon dashed. He was taken by his solicitor, Sir Reginald Poole, to the Temple to see the King's Counsel engaged on his behalf, Sir Henry Curtis-Bennett. He was advised that the case would be heard in camera and the jury would be directed that he had no authority to use the information he had revealed in his book. He might well go to prison for nine months and have to pay the costs of a three-week trial.

There was, on the other hand, some good news in that Sir Henry had spoken about the case to the Attorney-General, Sir Thomas Inskip KC. The Attorney-General had indicated that, should Mackenzie see his way to pleading guilty, the prosecution might be able to take a different view of the letter Lt. Colonel Sir Eric Holt-Wilson, an MI5 officer, had written to Mackenzie when he was planning to write the book. Now the prosecution would concede that Mackenzie might have interpreted the letter as an encouragement to write the book. Even more providentially, the Attorney-General had been able to have a word with the trial judge, Mr Justice Hawke, who had indicated that he would not impose a greater penalty on Mackenzie than a £500 fine and the payment of £500 costs.

It was a classic plea bargain. No embarrassing trial for the government and no prison sentence for the author. Despite his utter astonishment at such a judicial carve-up behind the scenes, Mackenzie agreed. Even so, the penalty would be severe, as he had received only £1,500 for the three volumes of memoirs, and the case had already cost him £2,533 in legal fees. However, the *Daily Mail* offered him £1,000 for his account of the trial.

There was a convention that Attorney-Generals prosecuted in official secrets cases, and Sir Thomas Inskip followed the practice in this case. As it turned out, it was most fortunate that he did, for his inept performance meant that Mackenzie escaped with a fine of no more than £100, and similar costs.

Sir Thomas later progressed to the posts of Lord Chief Justice and Lord Chancellor, and he took the title Viscount Caldecote. He was not, however, a particularly good advocate. *The Dictionary of National Biography* put it very tactfully: 'There was in his advocacy neither drama nor rhetoric. His approach was straightforward rather than subtle.' When Inskip was appointed Minister for the Co-ordination of Defence in 1938, Desmond Morton wrote to Winston Churchill: 'I hear from legal friends of his that he is bad at conducting cases in the courts and that he revokes at bridge more frequently than any professed player of the game.'

Even though the outcome of the case had been decided, Sir Thomas's was not a distinguished performance. He told the increasingly irritated judge about the case in some detail. He laid stress on the fact that Mackenzie had revealed the mysterious consonant 'C', by which the chief of the Secret Service was known.

'But Mr Attorney, if "C" is such a dangerous consonant, why is it still used nearly fifteen years after the war?'

'That I can't say, M'Lud.'

'No, I shouldn't think you could. That consonant should surely have been changed by now.'

The Attorney-General moved to what he hoped was safer ground. Mackenzie had revealed that 'C' stood for Sir Mansfield Cumming, the chief of the Secret Service.

'But surely this officer's name was perfectly well known during the war?' the judge interjected.

'I think not, M'Lud.'

'Come, come, Mr Attorney, in clubs both you and I belong to?'

'No, M'Lud, with great respect, I think not.'

'Oh well, have it your own way, Mr Attorney, but please be quicker. I'm growing excessively tired of this case. What did this officer do?'

Neither the Attorney-General nor Fulton knew. Nor did the head of MI5, Sir Vernon Kell, who with a distressing lack of secrecy was known as 'K'. They certainly should have known. Sir Mansfield Cumming had been head of the Secret Service and had instituted the practice of the heads of Secret Service signing official documents in green ink. He had been a flamboyant character who enjoyed testing the ingenuity of his spies with his disguises, and had carried a sword-stick.

At this point, Mackenzie intervened to help the prosecution

out of its temporary embarrassment, as he later recalled:

> I prodded the silver-haired old gentleman who was guarding me in the dock and asked for paper, intending to write down the answer to the judge's question.
>
> 'Do you wish to tell me something?'
>
> 'Yes, My Lord, with great respect, the officer died in June or July 1922.'
>
> 'Thank you, I accept that,' the judge pointedly commented as he glared at the prosecution.

When it came to the plea in mitigation on behalf of Mackenzie, there was the unusual spectacle of the Lord Rector of Edinburgh University, General Sir Ian Hamilton, testifying as to the excellent character of the Lord Rector of Glasgow University, who was presently sitting in the dock. Mackenzie had joined Sir Ian's staff in 1915. His conduct at Gallipoli had shown him to be an honourable and efficient officer, Sir Ian told the court.

Mr Justice Hawke, maintaining the charade that there had been no discussions as to sentence, told Mackenzie:

> I have thought very deeply over the matter and hesitated very much whether I ought to send you to prison. But I say at once, because I do not want you to have any anxiety about it, that I have come to the conclusion that I can do justice without sending you to prison. But you must be punished. You have already suffered a great pecuniary loss, which to some extent I will consider, although these losses were inflicted on yourself by yourself.

No harm had come, the judge observed, as a result of the defendant publishing these documents, except possibly in one case, but he should have obtained official permission. 'No testimony to your character could have been stronger than that given today, but I cannot pass this over. In the circumstances you must pay a fine of £100 and a further £100 towards the costs of the prosecution.'

Fearing a greater penalty, Mackenzie had brought more

than enough money for it to be paid at once and his release secured.

It is difficult to see what was achieved by this costly and well-publicised prosecution, except as an unjustified and mischievous attempt to deter other authors. The absurdity of the trial was masked by the fact that nearly all of it was held in camera. It seemed unjust that Mackenzie should find himself being prosecuted for writing about not particularly secret matters so long after the event.

Mackenzie did have one piece of revenge against what he considered a needless and spiteful prosecution, when he wrote a satire on the Secret Service in his book *Water on the Brain*. Sinclair, the then head of the Secret Service ('C'), and Vernon Kell ('K') were mercilessly satirised as 'N' and 'P'. So too was Valentine Vivian, the SIS head of counter-espionage, needless to say known in the service as 'VV', who became Hunter-Hunt, 'H-H'. As this was fiction, and as it followed the débâcle over *Greek Memories*, the government took no action.

Mackenzie went to some lengths to avoid a further prosecution in relation to *Water on the Brain*. The book contained what he insisted was a fireproof disclaimer; it was a 'grotesque fairytale', based on improbability rather than probability, 'since the latter would have involved me in the odium of striking at men incapable of defending themselves, except in camera'.

Greek Memories reappeared in a suitably edited second edition. Although no further action was taken, it remained accident-prone, as it formed part of Mackenzie's first twenty copyrights, which he sold for £10,000 in 1943, believing that this would be a capital transaction. The Inland Revenue took him to court and won a ruling that he would have to pay income tax in the year of the sale. An echo of the prosecution can still be found in the Bodleian Library, where anyone wishing to read the first edition of *Greek Memories* has first to apply to the Foreign Office.

The motives of the government in this matter were characteristically inglorious. Word had reached Mackenzie's solicitor, Sir Reginald Poole, before the trial, that the government took a serious view of his conduct and wanted to make an example of him if it could, in order to warn Lloyd George and Churchill that they could go too far in using information that they could have acquired only in office. To that limited extent the prosecution was successful, since Churchill admitted to Mackenzie four years later that he had taken the precaution of burning a few of his papers, something he always regretted.

In a vain attempt to see what could be done to reform Section 2, Compton Mackenzie wrote to two members of the Labour shadow cabinet about his case. They replied that they could not help, because they might want to use the Act when they were next in power!

4

Victim to the Two Weaknesses of his Class

When the Official Secrets Act 1911 passed through the House
of Commons in August of that year with such unseemly
haste, one of the Act's opponents was George Lansbury MP.
There was a certain irony in the fact that his son fell victim to
these provisions in a particularly cynical prosecution that
discriminated without any real justification between a
famous father, who was not prosecuted, and an unknown
son, who was. In 1934 Edgar Lansbury had published a book
unimaginatively called *Lansbury, My Father*. George
Lansbury was at the time leader of the Labour Party. In order
to convey the flavour of his father's political views, Edgar
quoted from a number of his writings. There was a passage in
the book of some four pages which presented his father's
opinions on such matters as unemployment, raising the
school-leaving age and a special tax for those with higher
incomes. George Lansbury's views on these matters were
public knowledge, but the difficulty was that Edgar quoted
from two memoranda prepared in 1930 and 1931 by his
father for circulation to the Labour Cabinet, of which he had
been a member. Both memoranda were marked as the
property of His Britannic Majesty's Government, and it was
no doubt felt that this was a good opportunity to deliver a
warning to Cabinet ministers who misused official papers.

Since 1919 a practice had grown up whereby senior
ministers were able to retain such Cabinet documents with
which they had been concerned as they wished, and this
privilege had been exploited to the full by Churchill and

Lloyd George. An opportunity to cut back on the use of Cabinet papers for private purposes presented itself when the deputy Cabinet Secretary, Sir Rupert Howorth, spotted an article in the *Manchester Guardian* entitled 'Last Labour Cabinet: Papers Disclosed'. The article stated that 'Mr Edgar Lansbury gives long extracts from memoranda submitted to the Cabinet by the First Commissioner of Works (his father), which casts a little light on its internal struggles.' Howorth reported back to the Cabinet that 'the subjects discussed in these two memoranda deal with extremely controversial issues of very recent date, and very much alive'. He said that immediate action was imperative, 'either under the Official Secrets Act, or in some other way', if a further compromise of Cabinet secrecy was to be prevented.

George Lansbury had been strongly suspected of being responsible for the publication in the *Daily Herald* in 1931 of a detailed account of the last Labour Cabinet meeting, which even included names of ministers who had voted against the reduction in unemployment benefit. Howorth had commented: 'I think the Prime Minister knows the name of the person who, there is the strongest reason to believe, must bear responsibility for this act.'

It was now felt that there must be a prosecution, and Sir Thomas Inskip KC, the Attorney-General, was called in. It was not considered expedient to prosecute the leader of His Majesty's Opposition, but there was no suggestion that Edgar Lansbury had procured these memoranda from any source other than his father. Sir Thomas had no doubts about the propriety of the case: 'It is obvious in a matter of this sort, concerning documents circulated to the Cabinet, that the Official Secrets Act must either be, so far as possible, enforced or it must be treated as a dead letter.' He did not suggest that Edgar Lansbury had sought to do anything 'contrary to the interests of the country'. It was, it seems, a case of visiting the sins of the father upon the son and prosecuting under the Official Secrets Act *pour encourager les auteurs*. Edgar Lansbury was fined £10 on each of the two summonses he faced, which alleged that he had unlawfully received certain information contained in two Cabinet memoranda, having reasonable grounds to believe that they had been communicated to him in contravention of the Act; he had to pay twenty-five guinea costs. The charges rather coyly did not say who the prosecution alleged had communicated the information. The magistrates imposed the penalty to mark 'the seriousness of the offence', and observed that 'the main object of the prosecution is to establish the principle that Cabinet documents are confidential documents and must not be disclosed to any persons other than members of the Cabinet'. The publishers had meanwhile recalled all copies of the book.

Whether this had the desired deterrent effect upon George Lansbury is doubtful. It seems that he retained a dislike of excessive official secrecy. During a parliamentary debate in 1932 he had commented on how, when in office, he had been exhorted in Cabinet not to breathe a word about the matter being debated but, as he later wrote, 'as I walked down Downing Street and bought an *Evening Standard* at the corner, it had the whole story'. Now, after the Lansbury case, the rule permitting ministers to keep Cabinet documents they had retained while in office was changed; but the attempts made by Howorth to put an end to the practice fell on stony ground as far as George Lansbury was concerned:

> This Cabinet has no moral or legal right to tell the members of previous Cabinets what they shall do with their papers, or to interfere with the discretion of previous governments with regard to public documents. I have not the slightest intention of complying with the request. Parliament is the only authority which has the right to decide on such an issue.

The two principal offenders, Lloyd George and Churchill, also declined to return their papers. However, when George Lansbury came to publish his memoirs, *My England*, in 1943, he exercised some caution in what he wrote, even though he did not submit his manuscript in advance. The Cabinet Office did not feel compelled to take action against him, as 'no documents are quoted and little, if any, information is given which is not already public property'.

Despite being unsuccessful during Lansbury's lifetime, after his death the Cabinet Office was able to apply to him the change in the rules. In accordance with the instructions he had given, several boxes of official papers about the Labour government were delivered to his biographer and son-in-law, Raymond Postgate. In 1943 Norman Brook, the deputy Cabinet Secretary, interrupted his wartime duties to write from the War Cabinet Office requesting Postgate to return all Lansbury's secret Cabinet papers that were in his possession. Brook did not specify which documents he required, however. Postgate replied that he did not propose to spend time sorting the papers out and trying to work out which were the secret papers he had to return, as he was busy with his Home Guard duties.

In 1944 Ian Lansbury, George's other son (Edgar having died in 1935), received a letter from the War Cabinet Office, this time from the Cabinet Secretary, Sir Edward Bridges. Bridges requested the return of the secret Cabinet papers from Ian Lansbury as executor of his father's will. Ian complained that he could not identify which of the papers were secret. The Treasury Solicitor indicated that his office would sort out the 'dozen or at most a score' of very secret papers which might be among George Lansbury's effects; he indicated that they could be recognised by the fact that they were written on blue paper with a caption in red saying that they were secret. By this time Postgate was on active service in North Africa and he had little choice but to accept the Treasury Solicitor's offer of assistance.

Accordingly, the Treasury Solicitor and a member of his staff collected no less than thirty boxes of papers from Ian Lansbury. The government proved reluctant to return the remaining documents; the Lansburys received back only an application signed by George Lansbury to subscribe to the *Labour Gazette* in 1893. Postgate was never certain whether this was 'an official's jest or not'. Even when the Labour government came to power under Attlee, the papers were not returned, and Postgate's request for permission to quote from the correspondence relating to the confiscation of the documents was refused. The incident was described with some feeling by Postgate, whose job as Lansbury's biographer was as a consequence much more difficult; and his *Life of George Lansbury*, published in 1951, was not the book it might have been.

J. H. (Jimmy) Thomas, the Secretary of State for the Colonies, leaked financially sensitive details of the Budget to two friends – Sir Alfred Butt and Alfred Bates – on two separate occasions. The failure to prosecute him was proof of the double standards applied to the rich or famous under Section 2. The attempts in the House of Commons to justify this lack of punitive zeal were wholly unconvincing. Thomas had had a distinguished career. He had left school at the age of twelve and rose from being an engine cleaner on the Great Western Railway Company to General Secretary of the National Union of Railwaymen in 1918. He was Colonial Secretary in Ramsay MacDonald's Labour government in 1924. He joined the National government in 1931 and became Secretary of State for the Colonies. His loyal support of MacDonald cost him his office as General Secretary of the NUR and even his membership of the union and accrued pension rights.

On 9 April 1936 Thomas was at the Cabinet meeting at which the Chancellor of the Exchequer revealed his proposals to raise income tax by 3d. to 4s.9d. in the £ and the tax on tea by 2d. from 4d. to 6d. per pound weight. Not only would some share prices react to that announcement, but contingent life insurances could be written against such tax changes. Speculation against such changes was conducted through Lloyd's rather than Ladbrokes, although the transaction seemed to be more in the nature of a gamble than a genuine insurance on one's life. (Such insurances could also be effected on the date and result of the general election, and indeed Thomas had made a profit of £600 from insuring himself against an election being held in 1935. This insurance had been written by Sir Alfred Butt on his behalf, but not in Sir Alfred's name.) Unfortunately for the loquacious Mr Thomas, the Budget speech was not due to be delivered until 21 April.

The first person to receive the Budget details from Thomas was his friend and publisher Alfred Bates. Even in those days it seems that there were publishers prepared to advance substantial sums for political memoirs of limited appeal. Bates had on 26 November 1935 agreed to pay Thomas the considerable sum of £20,000 for his autobiography. He had at the beginning of April 1936 advanced Thomas £15,100 to enable him to purchase a house. On 8 April, Thomas had given Bates a receipt for this advance.

Of this transaction the subsequent Tribunal of Inquiry – consisting of a High Court judge, Mr Justice Porter, and two King's Counsel, Gavin Simonds and Roland Oliver – said, somewhat charitably:

> The payment of £20,000 and an advance of £15,100 and the failure to take any security may seem an unbusinesslike transaction. But Mr Thomas and Mr Bates are old friends and Mr Bates is a rich man. We see no connection on Mr Bates' part between the payment of £15,100 and the suggested Budget leakage save that it accentuates the close connection and friendship of the two men and put Mr Thomas under obligation to Mr Bates.

As far as Bates's evidence was concerned, the tribunal said that he was guilty of misstating and suppressing the truth.

In the euphoria of purchasing his house and receiving the advance on his autobiography (despite not having written a single word nor having done anything except put his press cuttings and books together), Thomas let slip the details of the Budget during a weekend that he and Bates had spent together on 10 April. Bates was not slow to take advantage of this information. He sold out a large block of securities likely to be affected by the raising of the tax on tea. Bates also effected insurance against a change in the income tax rates.

Sir Alfred Butt, Conservative MP for Balham and Tooting, also had the good fortune to receive premature details of the Budget from Mr Thomas. He was a Lloyd's underwriter and had been happy enough to effect a £3,000 insurance against a rise in income tax for a Mr Matheson on 20 April, the day before the Budget, at the very reasonable

rate of ten guineas per cent. However, on his way to obtain a
seat in the House of Commons for the Budget debate on 21
April, Sir Alfred dropped in at the Colonial Office before
lunch to see Thomas. During a convivial conversation when
they discussed racing, a subject close to Thomas's heart, Sir
Alfred gave him a winning tip to back a horse called Quashed.
Thomas provided Sir Alfred with an even safer tip by letting
slip the details of the Budget. Sir Alfred learnt that he would
be paying out on Matheson's insurance. He delayed his trip to
the House of Commons to sell Budget-sensitive securities, to
cancel the wretched Matheson's insurance and to effect his
own insurances on the Budget – not in his own name, as was
his normal practice, but, rather less sportingly, in those of his
broker and his son.

The advantage taken of these windfall drops of information was so great and the insurances taken out relating to the
tax changes were so heavy that a Budget leak was suspected
almost immediately. The suspicion increased when it was
discovered that the two heaviest insurances were taken out by
two close friends of Thomas. The Secretary of State denied
having disclosed the details of the Budget, but his account
was not accepted by the Tribunal of Inquiry. There were
those in the Labour Party who were not sorry to see him
discomfited, although the abiding feeling on the part of his
colleagues in the National government was one of sympathy.
The tribunal had no doubt that there had been an
unauthorised disclosure by Thomas to Bates and Sir Alfred,
who had both used it for their own private gain. The tribunal
was kinder to Thomas, referring to his 'incautious error and
inadvertence'. It did not make any reference to the fact that
Thomas may very well have been under the influence of drink
when he disclosed details of the Cabinet discussion – he was a
notorious soak.

The Prime Minister, Stanley Baldwin, when talking over
the matter with Tom Jones, the deputy Cabinet Secretary,
had a simple if somewhat patronising explanation.

He has fallen victim to the two weaknesses of his class...
He has been a terrific gambler. They say the turf agents'

clerks had to work overtime to make an inventory of his debts. I don't think Jim deliberately gave anything away. What he most likely did was to let his tongue wag when he was in his cups. He just wanted to show that he carried great secrets.

It seems likely that a less distinguished malefactor would have been charged, but neither Thomas nor Bates nor Sir Alfred was prosecuted. Sir Donald Somervell KC, the Attorney-General, explained this decision by saying that there was a gap in the Official Secrets Act in that those who used information disclosed in breach of the Act were not guilty unless the informant could first be proved guilty. He considered that the Act did not extend to the improper use of information obtained through mere inadvertence. He told the House of Commons that he would see whether this gap in the Act could be filled. Needless to say, it was not, once this problem had been resolved. No such change in the law was made when the Official Secrets Act was amended in 1939. It is instructive to compare Sir Donald's protection of a colleague in government with his later attempt to bully Duncan Sandys into revealing the source of his information by threatening to use the powers under Section 6 – see Chapter 5.

In the House of Commons, Sir Stafford Cripps argued (impressively in the view of *The Times*) that there was no such gap in the Act. He made the point that the Act did not require that disclosure must be deliberate. People have subsequently been prosecuted for acts of negligence.

Thomas resigned from his post as minister, and both he and Sir Alfred resigned from the House of Commons. Thomas left a son in the House of Commons, who sat for the constituency of Leek. He made a moving farewell speech in the House, whereas Sir Alfred complained bitterly about the findings of the tribunal and of the injustice of the fact that the Attorney-General refused to bring him to trial. Then Thomas had an audience with Edward VIII to relinquish the Seals of Office. In a moving interview, which recalled the very good relations he had enjoyed with George V, he said to the King, 'Thank God your old dad is not alive to see this.'

After his resignation the former Secretary of State found he had the time to write his memoirs. However, his attempts to obtain access to the Cabinet papers were frustrated by Sir Maurice Hankey, the Cabinet Secretary, who was much later to complain bitterly himself of being unfairly prevented from writing his memoirs. Thomas's request to be allowed to examine at home Cabinet papers relating to five major incidents that he wished to write about was denied. There was, Hankey argued with some justice, a danger of the papers falling into the wrong hands. All that he would allow Thomas to do was to refresh his memory from Cabinet documents. He could not refer to proceedings in Cabinet nor quote from Cabinet meetings or documents. Thomas agreed to submit his manuscript to the Cabinet Secretary, who required a number of cuts. Thomas, he said, ought not to be allowed to describe what happened and what was said in Cabinet, even if his account was not correct.

The result was a book, published in 1937, of breathtaking dullness and certainly not worth the £15,100 paid. It had chapters such as: 'Some Cherished Memories of the Royal House', 'A Gallery of Portraits' and 'I Recall Some Stories'. The memoirs came to life only briefly when Thomas set out his views on horse-racing and the turf.

Under Section 6 of the 1920 Official Secrets Act, a person who fails to give any information relating to an offence or a suspected offence under the Official Secrets Act 1911 when asked by a senior police officer is guilty of an offence. It was perhaps only a matter of time before this power, which removed the traditional right of remaining silent when questioned by a police officer, was used against the press as a means of discovering the source of a particular story.

On 11 June 1937 the Southport police issued a warrant for the arrest of a confidence trickster called Tansley Munnings. His description and his *modus operandi* were circulated by the Chief Constable of Southport on 14 June to other local police forces. Although clearly intended to be an internal document, there was nothing on the police report to indicate that it was secret or confidential. It was the sort of information which might have been displayed on a police-station notice-board. A Southport newspaper, the *Daily Dispatch*, published an article on 17 June 1937 headed 'Frauds on Workless alleged: Warrant for Man with Scar'. The story was based on information in the police circular and was written by a journalist named Ernest Lewis. Superintendent Arnold Cattle extracted this information as to the article's origins from Nathaniel Booth, managing editor of the *Daily Dispatch*, using his powers under Section 6.

The police were interested to know which of their number had passed the story to Lewis. Accordingly, Lewis opened his front door on 29 July to find Superintendent Cattle on his doorstep telling him that the Attorney-General had consented to police enquiries being made under Section 6 and that Lewis was now required to give him the name of the person from whom he had received his information. Superintendent Cattle was less successful with Lewis than he had been with Booth. The journalist refused to reveal his police source: 'My mind is made up. I refuse to give you the information you require.' He was told he would be summonsed.

The Stockport magistrates later fined Lewis £5, despite eloquent pleas by the defendant's counsel, J. C. Jolly, that

> This Act of Parliament gives a right of interrogation which seems to me to be reminiscent of the old procedure of Star Chamber. Lewis was being asked to do something inconsistent with the code of professional conduct of the National Union of Journalists regarding the protection of his sources of information.

Lewis was understandably aggrieved at his conviction. He received some support from his union, the National Union of Journalists, when he appealed to the High Court on the rather tenuous grounds that a police officer 'is not a person holding office under His Majesty' within the meaning of Section 2. That argument was skilfully demolished by Valentine Holmes, appearing for Cattle, who finished his argument by quoting the sergeant in the *Pirates of Penzance*

'On your allegiance we've a stronger claim . . . We charge you
yield in Queen Victoria's name.'

Any feeling of relief that Lewis may have felt on finding
that the judge presiding in the court was none other than
Lord Hewart – who had reassured Parliament that Section 6
would not be used against the press – soon evaporated. He
swiftly dismissed the appeal: 'In my opinion this case is really
too plain for argument, and I think that the appeal must be
dismissed.'

The mess had to be cleared up by the Home Secretary, Sir
Samuel Hoare, who told the House of Commons on 12 May
1938 that the Official Secrets Act would be confined to cases
of 'serious public importance'. On 7 December 1938 he went
further by saying that Section 6 would be used only 'in cases
of the gravest importance to the safety and the welfare of the
state' – by which he was understood to mean something
rather more serious than the convenience of Superintendent
Cattle.

Section 6 has not been used since the Lewis prosecution,
owing to the furore of this and the Sandys case. But as long as
it remains on the statute book, it is more probable than not
that, on past form, its very convenient powers will at some
stage be used.

Following the Lewis case, on 24 May 1938 Dingle Foot,
subsequently a Solicitor-General, introduced the Official
Secrets Act (Amendment) Bill to amend Section 6. He did
not want the powers to be exercised without the express
permission of one of the law officers or the Home Secretary,
and he wanted it to be confined to cases where there
were reasonable grounds for believing that the information related to matters affecting the safety of the state.
Foot reminded the House that Hewart had in 1920 said of
Section 6: 'In other words, to put it shortly, we are dealing
with spying and attempts at spying.' Interestingly, in the
debate there were cries of 'no' from Honourable Members
when he said that it was theoretically possible for an MP to be
approached by a superintendent of police clutching Hansard
requiring him to disclose information that may have been
entrusted to him in breach of the Official Secrets Act. It was

characteristic of the entire history of the Official Secrets Act that, despite these protests, just such an action would be taken, only a few weeks later, in the case of Duncan Sandys MP, not by a superintendent, but by the Attorney-General himself.

Foot's Bill did not become law, although it did form the basis of the Official Secrets Act 1939, which was introduced after the Duncan Sandys affair.

5

A Gross Violation of the Relationship between MPs and Ministers: Duncan Sandys

With the wide powers that existed under the Official Secrets Act there were few cases in which the government did not succeed. One notable exception was the attempt in 1938 to use the powers under Section 6 to compel Duncan Sandys, MP for Norwood and a second lieutenant in the 51st (London) Anti-Aircraft Brigade RA (TA), to disclose the source of his information about the state of anti-aircraft defences around London. The government underestimated Sandys as an opponent and it twice ended up on the wrong end of a report of the Committee of Privileges of the House of Commons. On the first occasion the Attorney-General appears to have lied about his questioning of Sandys to compel him to disclose his source of information. On the second the Army was criticised for convening a military tribunal to order Sandys, under military discipline, to disclose his source.

Out of a mixture of incompetence, complacency and wishful thinking the government had produced a stream of inaccurate information about the state of its defences. Duncan Sandys was not the only MP obtaining leaked information from members of the armed services and civil servants. Winston Churchill (Sandys's father-in-law) received such disclosures from a variety of sources. Foremost amongst these was Major Desmond Morton, director of the

Committee of Imperial Defence Intelligence Centre. After Stanley Baldwin had stated in the House of Commons that German air strength was not 50 per cent of that of Britain, Morton let Churchill know that the true position was that the Germans had 950 fighter aircraft against our 1,247. Asked by the government to refute a statement made by Churchill based on information that he had supplied, Morton replied: 'I am sorry, but Mr Churchill's information is correct.' Churchill also regularly received information from Ralph Wigram, head of the Central Department at the Foreign Office, and on occasions from Sir Robert Vansittart, the Permanent Under-Secretary of State at the Foreign Office, and from RAF officers.

Sandys himself found that he was receiving inaccurate answers from the government but that there were officials and RAF officers who were prepared to leak documents to him, so that he could establish the truth. When in May 1938 Earl Winterton announced that the government planned to have 3,500 first-line aeroplanes, Sandys was able to point out that the Germans already had 3,500, with a capacity for an additional 500 per month.

On 17 May, Leslie Hore-Belisha, Secretary of State for War, gave Sandys the reassuring but inaccurate information that the Territorial Anti-Aircraft Division was equipped with up-to-date instruments and could be supplied in wartime without drawing on the regular Army. In fact the shortage was so chronic even in peacetime that only half the required training could be carried out. Sandys expressed these anxieties to his adjutant, Captain H. T. Hogan, and told him that he intended to raise the shortage of guns with the Secretary of State. Hogan responded sympathetically to this and gave Sandys some precise figures about anti-aircraft defences from the secret emergency plan of defence of the capital drawn up by the Air Officer Commanding-in-Chief in 1938. He gave this information to Sandys so that he could use it as the basis of his comments to Hore-Belisha. There were fifty copies of this plan, but there was no question but that paragraph 844 of the Territorial Army Regulations 1936 made it clear that the publication of official documents without official sanction would constitute a breach of the Official Secrets Act.

On 24 May 1938 Sandys took the opportunity of raising the matter privately with Hore-Belisha. The latter denied that there were gaps in the anti-aircraft defences and assured Sandys that the 3.7-inch guns were complete with the required scale of instruments and were equipped with up-to-date electronically controlled instruments for aiming. He said that the figures Sandys was quoting were inaccurate. Sandys responded by drafting a parliamentary question about the shortage of 3.7 anti-aircraft guns and the need to improve aiming techniques as a result of changes in the method of firing. He sent this to the Secretary of State on 17 June, accompanied by a letter:

> Dear Hore-Belisha, When we had a talk the other day about the anti-aircraft defence position, I told you that before taking any further action in the matter, I would consult with you again.
>
> I am accordingly sending you a copy of a question which I am thinking of putting down for answer on Tuesday June 28th. As, however, I do not wish unnecessarily to create alarm, I am anxious before doing so to give you an opportunity to contradict the statement contained in this question.

Hore-Belisha was sufficiently taken aback by this question to report his concern to the Prime Minister at 'the disclosure of such highly secret and important information'. On 23 June, Sandys received a letter from the Attorney-General, Sir Donald Somervell KC, asking him to go and see him that evening. In his letter to the Speaker of 27 June, Sandys explained what then happened:

> At this interview the Attorney-General informed me that the question which I had sent to the Secretary of State for War showed, in the opinion of the War Office, a knowledge of matters covered by the Official Secrets Act, and he asked me to reveal the sources of my information.

He added that I was under a legal obligation to do so. When I enquired what would be the consequences, were I to refuse to comply with his request, he read me the text of Section 6 of the Official Secrets Act and pointed out that I might render myself liable to a term of imprisonment not exceeding two years.

Somervell's account of this interview would not be worthy of serious examination had it not been given by an Attorney-General. (Sandys was not a lawyer and was not conversant with Section 6; his account of the interview was fully set out in the letter he wrote to the Speaker on 27 June.) If the Attorney-General's account of the matter is correct, it is surprising that Sandys felt it necessary to burn two papers that might have revealed the source of his information, consisting of some handwritten notes given to him by Captain Hogan for his parliamentary question, and the original draft parliamentary question, which had been amended in Hogan's handwriting.

What the Attorney-General said had taken place at the interview, at 7.30 p.m. on 23 June, was this:

I told him that a rather serious position had arisen. I told him that I was not operating under the powers of the Official Secrets Act. I was not threatening him with them or pressing him in any way.

Just on 8 o'clock Sandys had got up and said that he wanted to get back to the House, whereupon I said to him, 'Well, if you like I will read you the section.' I got it down out of the shelf where it was behind me and I read it through. When we came to the word 'misdemeanour' he asked me, 'What is the maximum penalty for that?' I said, 'I think it is two years.' I remember thinking, 'Well, perhaps that sounds a little alarming', so I added, 'I think in the last case we were talking about just now, the man was fined a fiver.'

Of this conflict of evidence the Privileges Committee said that it acquitted (an odd word to use of a law officer) the

Attorney-General of any intention to threaten Sandys with compulsory powers of interrogation. The committee stated nevertheless that it was undesirable that a senior law officer should discuss with an MP the desirability of giving information when he might be responsible for launching a prosecution. Any error of judgement on the Attorney-General's part was attributed to his lack of opportunity of considering the matter fully. The committee accepted the Attorney-General's evidence that he had written to Hore-Belisha saying that he had told Sandys that he was not operating under his special powers, but was asking him whether he was prepared to assist. What Hore-Belisha really said to Sandys was less clear.

The committee thought it was unfortunate that Somervell had decided he was the proper person to talk to Sandys and that Hore-Belisha had taken the Attorney-General's advice instead of seeing Sandys himself. The committee further criticised Somervell for not giving an undertaking on 23 June (which he did on the next day) that he would not use his powers under Section 6 against Sandys.

On 24 June, Sandys had reported to the Speaker that he was being threatened, in connection with his parliamentary work, with the use of the powers under Section 6. This produced a remarkable transformation in the Attorney-General's attitude; Somervell asked Sandys to see him again and told the MP that he had been under a misapprehension if he thought he had been threatened with the use of the powers of interrogation under the Official Secrets Act. Somervell said he would give Sandys an assurance that 'there was at present no intention' of using these powers against him.

Sandys indicated that the words 'at present' were unsatisfactory, whereupon Somervell offered to drop the words and to give an assurance that 'there was no intention' of taking any action against him. Following this meeting, Sandys said that even this was not satisfactory, because an intention could change at any time. Once more the Attorney-General backed down. On 24 June he wrote to the MP: 'I am writing to confirm the assurance that I gave you this afternoon, namely that there is no question of seeking to exercise against you now or hereafter the police powers of interrogation under the Official Secrets Act.'

If Somervell thought that was the end of the matter, he had once more underestimated Sandys, who wrote on 27 June:

I am naturally relieved to know that no further pressure will be exerted upon me to reveal the source from which I obtained the information which I communicated to the Secretary of State for War in my letter to him of June 17th. However, as I pointed out to you at our interview yesterday, this does not, of course, entirely dispose of the matter.

The marked reluctance and hesitancy with which you gave me this assurance at our second interview and the fact that you informed me that in giving this assurance you were exceeding the instructions given to you by the Secretary of State for War confirm the fact that the possibility of exercising against me the police powers of interrogation was being seriously contemplated.

The use of these powers in circumstances such as these raises an important question of Parliamentary privilege vitally affecting the freedom of the Members of the House of Commons in the discharge of their public duties. You will therefore appreciate that in spite of your assurance in regard to my personal position, I should not, in the interests of the House as a whole, be justified in abandoning my intention to seek Mr Speaker's guidance. I shall accordingly raise the matter after questions on Monday next.

On 25 June, Sandys wrote to the Speaker:

After seeing you yesterday, I have had a further interview with the Attorney-General. The result of this interview has been more than ever to confirm the fact that I was being threatened with the police powers of interrogation under the Official Secrets Act.

The fact that, in the hope of preventing this matter being raised in the House, the Attorney-General has now given me an assurance that in my case these powers will not be exercised does not, in my opinion, dispose of the matter.

Therefore with your permission, I propose to raise the question in the appropriate manner in the House on Monday next.

Sandys had thus been successful in referring the conduct of the Attorney-General and the Secretary of State for War to the Committee of Privileges – no mean feat for a thirty-year-old back-bencher. However, having failed under Section 6 the government felt that it might be more successful by invoking military discipline against Sandys, under which, as a serving officer, he could be ordered to answer the question of who leaked him the information. Accordingly on the very day that he was raising the matter in the House of Commons, 27 June, a telegram was sent to Sandys's home at 79 Chester Square, which read: 'You are detailed to attend a Court of Enquiry at Horse Guards. Dress uniform and sword.'

Again the government had underestimated the young MP. He replied curtly: 'Your telegram received.'

At 4.20 p.m. he raised the matter in the House of Commons. He felt emboldened not to attend the court of enquiry, but he sent a message that 'one of your witnesses, Second Lieutenant Sandys, cannot come'. With something approaching resignation, the Inspector-General Overseas Forces, General Sir Edmund Ironside, replied: 'If he cannot come, I cannot hold the court.' It had been Ironside's intention to ask Sandys who had supplied him with the information and it would have been difficult for Second Lieutenant Sandys to refuse to answer a General.

By this stage the Cabinet had become concerned at the way events were progressing. The Home Secretary expressed the view that the Attorney-General's interview with Sandys was 'difficult to defend'. The Attorney-General commented that 'it was notorious that information had been leaking to Members of Parliament for some time'. Henry Pownall, Director of Military Operations and Information at the War Office, wrote: 'The fact is that Sandys, having seduced an officer from his allegiance, then shelters under the umbrella

of privilege – not in order to withhold the name of the officer
– he must know perfectly well that we have got that – but to
save himself.' He went on to refer to him as 'a slippery young
gentleman who is certainly backed up by Winston'. A curious
feature of the Attorney-General's and the Army's behaviour
in the Sandys affair was that they appeared to be unaware of
the fact that the War Office already *knew* Hogan was the
source of the leak!

This attack on parliamentary privilege was thought even
more serious than the first. The Committee of Privileges,
which included the Prime Minister, the Leader of the
Opposition and Winston Churchill, was convened immediately. They concluded on 30 June that the order to Sandys to
appear before a military court enquiring into the circumstances of the leakage of information that formed part of his
original statement to the House of Commons was a serious
breach of privilege but they decided that no action was
required.

The original Committee of Privileges reported in June
1939, and its criticism of the government was no less severe.
The Prime Minister admitted (in words reminiscent of the
Westland affair in 1986) to the committee that the Sandys
case was poorly handled and that there had been 'a most
extraordinary catalogue of misunderstandings'. The committee's report concluded that the conduct of the Attorney-
General was to be condemned as a gross violation of the
proper and traditional relationship between Members of
Parliament and ministers and that it was a breach of privilege
to use Section 6 against an MP on account of his questions or
speeches in Parliament. It considered that the Secretary of
State for War had committed an error of judgement in
allowing the interview with Mr Sandys to pass out of his own
hands. This, it said, was due partly to touchiness over the
covering letters that Mr Sandys had sent with his question.
The committee felt that the whole fiasco could have been
avoided had there been proper liaison in the War Office,
which ought to have led them to learn that Captain Hogan
had in fact admitted that he was the source of Sandys's
information. The conclusion was that Sandys was justified in

bringing the conduct of the Attorney-General to the attention of the House. The committee observed that the affair had brought home to MPs the need for discretion in framing questions or seeking information regarding matters affecting the safety of the realm, but there was no doubt where responsibility was felt to lie.

Following as it did the Lewis case, the Sandys affair produced a change in the law, in the form of the Official Secrets Act passed in November 1939. What this Act did, in the words of Sir John Simon, was 'to substitute for Section 6 of the 1920 Act an entirely new section which limits those special powers of interrogation to cases of offences or suspected offences under Section 1 of the 1911 Act – that is to say in practice cases of espionage'. A parliamentary answer given by Somervell in February 1939 revealed that Section 6 had been used on six occasions. Three of these did relate to espionage, one to the suspected Cabinet leak and two to the disclosure of police information.

If it is no longer possible for the government to use the powers of interrogation in respect of Section 6, it would still be possible to achieve that result by treating what is really a Section 6 matter as a Section 1 offence. The 'ABC' case (Chapter 10) showed that the government's view of a threat to national security can be very different to that of the general public.

6

We Have Been a Naughty Boy

During the Second World War the Official Secrets Act was scarcely used. Wide powers to safeguard national security were taken under the Defence of the Realm Regulations, which extended to careless talk and the disclosure of any information relating to the country's defences. Examples of prosecutions brought under the Defence of the Realm Regulations are given in Appendix 1. Many of the cases were conducted in secret.

There was no attempt after the Second World War had ended to keep these emergency powers in peacetime, as had happened with the Official Secrets Act 1920 at the end of the First World War. Prosecutions under Section 2 started again in 1945, and a number retained a wartime flavour, but the first significant case did not.

On 26 May 1948 a journalist named James Atkinson was prosecuted and fined a total of £10 in respect of two charges under Section 2. The case provided another example of how Section 2 could be used against journalists obtaining information by unauthorised means when their conduct should have been dealt with, if at all, under a specific statute (as was done in the very similar case of James Goodrich in 1938 – see Appendix 1). Atkinson was a journalist of high reputation in Yorkshire and a member of his urban district council. A local telephone operator in Driffield, Mark Appleyard, was friendly with Atkinson and used to pass him the occasional titbits he overheard at the telephone exchange. When Appleyard heard a police inspector telling a constable that an identity parade might be necessary to determine the assailant of a WAAF at a local aerodrome, he called Atkinson. Forty minutes later Atkinson telephoned the desk sergeant at the local police station, who immediately realized that the information must have been leaked.

The police decided to try to trap Atkinson. A police offer was deputed to telephone a colleague and to say slowly and distinctly over the telephone that the partly dressed body of a woman had been found by a lorry driver on the Bridlington Road. While Appleyard was eavesdropping on this hot news, a police sergeant was stationed outside Atkinson's home so that he could hear the telephone ringing when Appleyard called to tip him off, and could also listen to the journalist calling Driffield Police Station to ask about the body on Bridlington Road. At that stage the sergeant was authorised to burst in on Atkinson and arrest him.

The villain of the piece was Appleyard, whom the magistrate fined £20. Telephone operators have no business to eavesdrop or to use information that they overhear to their own advantage. However, this was something that should have been dealt with under the Telegraphy Act. It is highly questionable whether Section 2 should have been used for such petty offences, which had nothing whatever to do with national security, and whether a journalist should be bound to check that his informant did not obtain the information in breach of his duty to his employers.

The case was raised in the House of Commons on 24 June 1948 on the adjournment motion by Tom Driberg. He reminded the House of what Sir Gordon Hewart KC had said in 1920 and complained of the triviality of the charge. He quoted from an editorial in the *Manchester Guardian* which had said: 'The Attorney-General should not let it happen again. It is not necessary to kill a fieldmouse with a fieldgun.'

The Attorney-General, now Sir Hartley Shawcross KC, whose views on press matters were markedly more liberal than those of his predecessors, stoutly defended the prosectuion. He had perhaps little choice, as the prosecution was brought by the Director of Public Prosecutions with his authority. He said that he had no reason to doubt that justice was properly done. He made it clear that the Official Secrets Act was not limited to spying; nor did journalists have any special immunity from the operation of the Act:

> I hope this will be the last case in which a journalist will be able to say, as the defendant did here, 'I have a complete answer being a journalist.' If journalists so far betray the honour of their profession as to secure the disclosure of official information which it is contrary to the public interest to disclose, I have no power to undertake in advance that the ordinary law may not be put into operation against them.

However, this justification of the decision to prosecute rang hollow when measured against the triviality of the case:

> We do not prosecute unless we come to the conclusion that the information disclosed, and improperly disclosed, is something which is quite contrary to the public interest to disclose; something which for instance might interfere with the detection of criminals and the ordinary course of justice. We do not initiate proceedings in these cases too lightly.

The aftermath of the Second World War produced one rather curious prosecution for retaining official documents without authority. The person prosecuted was Donald Cameron Watt, then a sergeant in the Field Security Section of the British Army Occupation Forces in Austria. His duties consisted of checking the Hungarian refugees who were pouring into the British zone, escaping from the Communist regime that was taking power in Hungary. The Hungarians gathered at Graz, and Watt had to find out what he could about these refugees before they applied for Displaced Persons status. Many of the Hungarians there were professional people, who passed their time writing about their experiences in Hungary. Watt – subsequently to become

Professor of International History at the London School of Economics – felt that these accounts would be worth publishing when he was demobilized in 1948. They were not directly connected with his work and were collected by him privately. While he would not have had access to them had he not been serving with Her Majesty's forces in Austria, the documents contained nothing secret, nor were they official in the sense of being collected or examined for any official purpose.

As Watt could take only one suitcase with him when he returned to England, he decided to send these transcripts by post in thirteen parcels. Not realizing that he was committing a heinous offence under the Official Secrets Act, and marking the documents as of no interest save to the recipient, he posted them addressed to himself in England. The packages were intercepted by an alert member of the Customs, who noticed that they had come from someone serving with Field Security.

When Watt returned to England to his demobilisation centre, he was called for interrogation at the Intelligence Corps depot. His demobilisation was postponed for three months while he was questioned by the special investigation branch of the Corps of Military Police. He succeeded in obtaining leave of absence from the Army to go up to Oxford University, where he had obtained a history scholarship at Oriel College. This university career had lasted no more than ten days, however, before Watt was ordered to report to Chelsea Barracks, where he had to rejoin the Army, on attachment to the 1st Battalion, Middlesex Regiment.

The presence in the Middlesex Regiment's barracks of a sergeant in Field Security was at first resented. The regiment had unhappy memories of how Field Security had been responsible for two of its members being gaoled in Marseilles for selling arms to the Jews in Palestine. But when it was discovered that the only reason for Sergeant Watt of Field Security's presence at the Middlesex Barracks was that consideration was being given to prosecuting him under the Official Secrets Act, the regiment saw the humour of the situation and invited him to play rugby and to help administer literacy tests on recruits. Watt was asked by the colonel of the regiment, with commendable courtesy, whether he would like to be court-martialled before or after Christmas. As he had by this time taken the opportunity to read the Official Secrets Act, he realised not only that he had no real defence even though he had not divulged any secrets, but that he faced two years' imprisonment. He therefore opted for a court martial after Christmas. This took place on 28 December 1948. Watt received excellent testimonials from the Middlesex Regiment at his court martial. He was skilfully defended by Edward Clarke, who demonstrated that there had been no damage to national security and obtained specific findings that certain of the documents did not fall within the Act.

Clarke complained at a large part of the hearing being in camera. It meant that the case obtained greater publicity because it appeared to be shrouded in mystery. All that Watt had done was to retain certain documents that came into his possession in the course of his duties. For the prosecution, Major J. J. G. Cumberledge asserted that there was no suggestion of Watt being concerned in espionage or anything of that nature, although he added darkly that some of these documents contained information about individuals in foreign countries, and that if they fell into some hands there was no knowing what might happen.

After hearing testimonials as to Watt's conduct in the Army, the court martial imposed an extremely light sentence: he was to be reprimanded and reduced to the rank of corporal. As it was a rule in the Army that on demobilisation you reverted to your original rank, the penalty was meaningless; he received his demobilisation pay at the sergeant's rate. It was probably just as well that he received this lenient sentence, as a plan spearheaded by Niall MacDermott MP, who had served in intelligence in 21 Army Group, existed in the event of a prison sentence: to subpoena for the appeal the senior officers of 21 Army Group who had retained secret documents for their own purposes – from Field Marshal Montgomery downwards.

When Watt left Oxford, he applied for a job at the Foreign

Office to edit captured German documents. He was given a form to fill in, asking him whether he had ever been convicted. No doubt much to the surprise of the Foreign Office – which was probably more used to hearing about speeding convictions in Hyde Park – he filled in the details of his conviction under the Official Secrets Act. This was very far from being fatal to his application, for he was summoned to the Foreign Office library, where his interview with the librarian, Jim Passant, started with the immortal words, 'Well, Mr Watt, we have been a naughty boy!'

So began the first and only occasion when the Foreign Office engaged a person with a conviction under the Official Secrets Act. There followed a distinguished career, which led to Donald Cameron Watt becoming not only Stevenson Professor of International History at the London School of Economics, but also in 1973 official historian to the Cabinet Office historial section. Most appropriately he became an adviser to the government on the disclosure of public documents, giving evidence to the Radcliffe Committee of Privy Councillors on the publication of ministerial memoirs. He was also a member of the working party of historians that produced recommendations reducing the period for which government records were closed from fifty years to thirty years, as well as of a Social Science Research Council working party on government information.

7

Blown up out of All Proportion

It is difficult to find any case brought under Section 2 that justified the Official Secrets Act's wide powers. For the most part Section 2 was used to punish personal inadequacy and carelessness; numerous examples are to be found in Appendix 1. Despite the width of the provisions of Section 2, a surprising number of prosecutions failed, and it is difficult to discern a consistent reason for starting such proceedings. One feature of the cases was the potential embarrassment to the authorities when lost documents fell into the hands of third parties. Occasionally, as in the Miller and Thompson case (see below), there was a desire to deter others. However, in many cases the reason for the decision to prosecute itself remains an official secret: the papers relating to the Attorney-General's decision will remain under wraps in the Public Records Office for seventy-five years.

In February 1951 Section 2 was used as a sledge-hammer to crack three very small nuts. The chief security officer at the Royal Aircraft Establishment in Farnborough had found a letter in the desk of a twenty-year-old apprentice student there, Richard MacDemitria, from another twenty-year-old, John Webb, who was employed by the Society of British Aircraft Instructors. Webb's letter asked MacDemitria to send him any information he obtained – not, he said, for the purpose of sending it to the USSR, but to enable him to 'criticise or applaud the government'. MacDemitria responded to this naïve approach by sending Webb details about the types and numbers of aircraft at Blackbushe

Airport. A twenty-two-year-old associate of Webb, Alan Gardiner, also found himself in the dock for an offence, which foreshadowed the case later brought against Crispin Aubrey (chapter 10), of performing an act preparatory to the committing of an offence under the Official Secrets Act. This was nothing more sinister than posting Webb's letter to MacDemitria!

The prosecution was good enough to indicate that there had in its view been nothing subversive about the young men's conduct; it was purely a result of over-enthusiasm. Each of the defendants was nevertheless fined £50. Their appeal against sentence was heard by Ewen Montagu KC, the Chairman of Hampshire Quarter Sessions – himself to raise some Security Service eyebrows two years later when he wrote a highly successful book arising out of his experiences as a wartime intelligence officer, *The Man Who Never Was*. Montagu ruled that the imposition of the maximum fines was excessive. Although any breach of the Official Secrets Act was an extremely serious offence, the three young defendants had all lost their jobs, and he felt that the fines could safely be reduced to £20; this suggests his view of the gravity of the case. It was the only occasion when a sentence under Section 2 has been reduced on appeal.

The prosecution of Geoffrey Palmer in 1956 is an example of the sort of inadequacy that tends to be punished under Section 2. Palmer was a twenty-three-year-old print-room operator at the Bristol Aircraft Company. His ambition was to become a press photographer. When an aircraft drawing came into his possession in the course of his work, he thought that it might perhaps provide him with the opportunity of getting his foot on the first rung of the Fleet Street ladder. He took the sketch of the aircraft to Rafael Steinberg, the London editor of *Time* magazine, and tried to sell it to him for twenty-five guineas. As the judge at his trial patronisingly put it, 'You were not to know Mr Steinberg was an honest man.' In any event, Steinberg called the police. As Palmer left the office of *Time*, he walked into the arms of Detective Inspector C. Rhodes. He was convicted of two charges under Section 2: one of having a sketch used in a prohibited place, namely the Bristol Aircraft Company factory at Filton, which he unlawfully communicated without authority to Rafael Steinberg; and secondly of having in his possession a sketch used in a prohibited place and unlawfully retaining it. He was sent to prison for six months.

Palmer's case was followed by the even more trivial prosecution of Frederick Harrington in May 1956. Harrington was a fifty-year-old higher executive officer at the Department of the Director of Ordnance Factories at Nottingham. He wished to write an article for a national newspaper exposing waste in government departments and to this end wrote to Douglas Stoneman, who had been his assistant. His action hardly threatened the fabric of society:

> You will not be surprised to hear I have resigned from the Civil Service. The Ministry of Supply was hard enough. The War Office was beyond description. I have a proposition to put to you which if you agree will give you a very nice Christmas present but I would like to discuss the matter with you, before going any further. All this may sound very mysterious to you, but believe me, you will be very pleased to hear what I have to tell you. In the meantime you had better keep this to yourself.

Stoneman wished to have nothing to do with the proposal and refused to give any information, saying that he was disappointed that Harrington even thought he might consider breaching his duty. He reported the approach, and Harrington was fined £50 at Woolwich Magistrates' Court for trying to persuade Stoneman to commit an offence against the Official Secrets Act.

Harrington had not wished to obtain any secret information. His offence arose out of nothing more sinister than attempting to obtain information about government departments without authority. The offence was a very minor one and would seem to have fallen well short of the sort of corruption against which it is necessary to protect the public service.

*   *   *

The leading case in the 1950s was that brought against two undergraduates at Oxford University, William Miller and Paul Thompson. The article in the Oxford University magazine *Isis* on 26 February 1958, entitled 'Frontier Incidents – Exposure' and accompanied by a photograph captioned 'Mercedes-Benz spy boat', would now be considered fairly tame. The photograph had been obtained from a fellow undergraduate, who had taken it, without objection from the Royal Navy, during his national service. However, it resulted in the two undergraduates being sent to prison for three months and marked the start of a concerted campaign to prevent any revelation of the activities of the Government Communications Headquarters (GCHQ). The prosecution of Miller and Thompson ensured widespread national and international publicity for an Oxford undergraduate publication. A large part of the article was read out on the BBC and was published in the national press, as well as being read aloud in court. The government seems to have thought this was worthwhile, and the imprisonment of the two undergraduates was meant as a warning to journalists of the limits of free speech.

That particular issue of *Isis* was devoted to nuclear disarmament and was edited by four undergraduates, including Miller and Thompson. The *Guardian* had taken an interest in the anti-nuclear campaign, and there had been a meeting at Oxford town hall with Victor Gollancz and other speakers. The *Guardian* published extracts from the *Isis* article the day after its appearance in Oxford. Miller and Thompson had done their national service in the Royal Navy Special Reserve and had been taught Russian before being sent to Germany to listen to Soviet signals traffic. Like many national servicemen, their overwhelming feeling was one of boredom. Posted to Cuxhaven and Kiel, with occasional outings on fishery-protection vessels, Miller and Thompson had heard little of any significance. But they were troubled by what they learnt of incidents that had taken place on the Russian frontier. The argument which was then put forward for having a nuclear deterrent was that the Soviets would not dare to enter one inch into Allied territory, nor would they

attack Western aircraft. The reality was a little different;
every so often there would be a deliberate penetration of
Soviet air space or territorial waters by the Western Allies to
gauge the USSR's response and to listen to its signals traffic
as it reacted to the invader. This is what Miller and
Thompson sought to describe in their article in *Isis*:

Frontier Incidents – Exposure
The doctrine of Western sincerity and the good fight
against Russian wickedness is fostered in many little ways;
and not the least of these is the misreporting of news. We
wish to expose one variety of this. Frontier incidents are
almost invariably reported as ferocious and unjustifiable
attacks by Russian fighters on innocent Western aircraft
peacefully cruising well within their own frontiers.
Sometimes it is conceded that the victim had lost its way.
This is British understatement at its best. All along the
frontier between East and West, from Iraq to the Baltic,
perhaps further, are monitoring stations manned largely
by national servicemen trained in morse or Russian, avidly
recording the last squeak from Russian transmitters –
ships, tanks, aeroplanes, troops and control stations. It is
believed, perhaps rightly, that this flagrant breach of the
Geneva Convention can provide accurate estimates of the
size and type of Russian armaments and troops, and the
nature of their tactical methods.

In order to get this information the West has been willing
to go to extraordinary lengths of deception. British
Embassies usually contain monitoring spies. When the
Fleet paid a 'goodwill' visit to Danzig in 1955 they were on
board. And since the Russians do not always provide the
required messages they are sometimes provoked. A plane
'loses' its way; while behind the frontier tape-recorders
excitedly read the irritated exchanges of Russian pilots:
and when the latter sometimes force the plane to land an
international incident is created, and reported in the usual
fashion. The famous Lancaster bomber incident near
Berlin was deliberately provoked in this way.

In a moment of crisis irresponsibility of this kind could

well frighten the Russians into war. Certainly if Russian planes were to fly over American bases the American reply would be prompt. But there is no controlling the appetite of the statistical analysers at Cheltenham. Perhaps the best example of their activities is in the Baltic. After the war a fleet of half-a-dozen exceedingly fast Mercedes-Benz torpedo-type boats were built, and, manned by sailors from Hitler's navy, were sent out under English Captains to provoke and listen to the Russians. They would head straight for the Russian Fleet at exercise and circle round a battleship taking photographs. When they had succeeded in concentrating all the guns of the fleet and recorded enough messages they fled. When in Swedish waters, contrary to all international conventions, they flew the Swedish flag. One British captain, who was suitably equipped with a wooden leg which lent a certain glamour to the Quixotic behaviour, so far exceeded the normal practice, which was merely to enter Russian territorial waters, as to go into Leningrad Harbour and on another occasion to land a small party in Russia. It was incredible that this should have been allowed, but the irresponsibility bred and sheltered by the Official Secrets Act is uncontrollable. In 1956 the new German navy took over the full control of these boats and are doubtless happily continuing our own policy.

The reference to the statistical analysers at Cheltenham, with their inexhaustible appetite for monitoring the responses of the Soviets, and to the monitoring stations from Iraq to the Baltic, related to GCHQ. Not only the role but even the existence of GCHQ were secret, although it was listed in the telephone directory and various reference books and presumably was therefore known to the Soviets.

Miller and Thompson were aware of the Official Secrets Act and had signed declarations that they would abide by it while in the Navy; the article itself had referred to the Act. They felt that what they were writing was not secret, was well known to the Soviets, and did nothing to damage national security. Nevertheless the publication of the article caused considerable agitation in naval intelligence circles. On 13 March, Detective Inspector Swan and Detective Sergeant James Bateman were sent to interview the undergraduates to find out who had written the article. As the article was in Thompson's handwriting and the title in Miller's they freely admitted their part, and the police task was a simple one. While police investigation proceeded at a leisurely pace, Miller happened to go the *News Chronicle* for an interview for a job on leaving university. He mentioned that he had written an article which had resulted in his being interviewed by the Oxford police. Miller did not get the job but he made the headlines in the next edition. The *Isis* article was reproduced in a number of newspapers before a hastily prepared D-notice was issued, resulting in its being excluded from later editions.

Following this further publicity Miller and Thompson were seen by Detective Superintendent George Smith of the Special Branch. In Parliament, Frank Allaun MP asked questions about the provocation of the Soviet Union. On 2 May, Miller and Thompson were charged with three offences under Section 2; the first was that they had on 26 February 1958 communicated official information to an unauthorised person, a Mr Bennett at 71 Pall Mall. Neither Miller nor Thompson had any idea who Bennett was. It turned out that he was the secretary of the Oxford and Cambridge Club, who subscribed to *Isis* and had been sufficiently taken aback by the 26 February issue to report it to the club's committee. When the police told Miller who Bennett was, he commented with some justification, 'Oh, the bloody thing has blown up out of all proportion.' They were further charged with using official information in a manner prejudicial to the safety and interest of the state, and with receiving information, having reasonable grounds to believe that it was communicated to them in breach of the Official Secrets Act. The day after they had been charged they were called up as reservists for duty at a secret establishment in Germany. This inappropriate order, it emerged, was something which had been planned some months before, and in the circumstances Miller and Thompson were not required to go back into the Navy. To underline the gravity with which the offence was viewed the police took the precaution of posting a plain-clothes officer at the corner of Walton Street near Miller and Thompson's student digs, until they were due to take their final examinations.

Both defendants came from respectable backgrounds. Thompson was twenty-two and had won an open scholarship in history at Corpus Christi College. His father was managing director of a grocery company, and his mother was a Justice of the Peace. Thompson had joined the Labour Party but he did not belong to any form of radical group. He was then a practising member of the Church of England but came from a pacifist nonconformist background and supported the recently formed Campaign for Nuclear Disarmament. Miller had won a scholarship to Lincoln College. He supported CND, had been on the first Aldermaston march and was a member of the Labour Party. The police had little time for the activities of CND. Superintendent Smith of the Special Branch was asked by defence counsel:

'From your enquiries it is right to say that among a certain group of people at Oxford there was considerable emotional feeling as to whether the hydrogen bomb should be banned?'

He replied frostily: 'I cannot say I know anything about the emotional feelings among certain people at Oxford.'

At the magistrates' court the case was outlined by Mervyn Griffith-Jones (the man later to bring *Lady Chatterley's Lover* to the notice of the popular press as a book unsuitable to show your butler), who said that there had been a deliberate contravention of the Official Secrets Act, an utter and dishonourable breach of the solemn undertakings each had entered into. The prosecution had been brought because some of the matter contained in the article was true and, he said, because Miller and Thompson well knew it was of a highly secret nature.

When their trial started at the Central Criminal Court on 17 July, the case was opened by Sir Harry Hylton-Foster QC, the Solicitor-General, who said that Miller and Thompson had published their article with a total disregard of the law, if not in defiance of it, and in dishonourable breach of the undertakings they had given during their national service.

Their attention had been drawn to the Official Secrets Act at what he called 'a solemn little procedure known as indoctrination'. It would seem, he commented, as if they both regarded their undertakings as being pieces of paper. The reason for this slightly more conciliatory approach may have been that, although Miller and Thompson had pleaded not guilty, they had, through their counsel, privately indicated that they would change their plea of guilty to the first count of the indictment, after they had had an opportunity to explain their conduct. A succession of naval officers was called to prove that Miller and Thompson had signed the Official Secrets Act and that they knew that their work was secret. The court then went into camera so that the jury could hear about the work of GCHQ.

Miller's evidence was that there were at least a hundred people in Oxford who knew the facts about which he had written. He had not received any secret information from any third party, and he had no wish to damage the security of the state. Miller said that he did not expect to be prosecuted; he thought that the Official Secrets Act would be invoked only if national security was endangered, and that this article certainly did not endanger it. Virtually all the information in this article had been published elsewhere – for the most part in the United States. He explained that he still felt strongly about nuclear disarmament.

Thompson's evidence was to similar effect. He supported nuclear disarmament:

> I had several friends at Oxford who felt very strongly about the matter and I was in sympathy with them. The article was not written on a political basis at all. A special issue of *Isis* dealing with nuclear disarmament had been discussed and I felt it was my moral duty to support it. I felt that the article was part of a rational argument and that it could be written without breach of national security.

He explained that he objected to these provocative incidents on the Russian frontier; the idea of the nuclear deterrent was not in his opinion consistent with any continuous activity along the frontier. He told the jury that he had no intention of provoking a prosecution.

Miller, on the other hand, had unguardedly said to the police that they were aware of the possibility of a prosecution but felt that it might do their cause good. Both students agreed that they had signed a declaration drawing their attention to the Official Secrets Act and had been subjected to indoctrination and de-indoctrination on the need for the secrecy.

Evidence was called as to their exemplary character from such witnesses as the chaplain and Modern History tutor at Lincoln College, who spoke very highly of them. These tributes had only a limited effect on the Lord Chief Justice, Lord Goddard. When he was told by Thompson's tutor that he had an extremely good academic record and could be described as an industrious and unusually intelligent young man, Lord Goddard commented, 'And capable of appreciating the gravity of what he had done.' He later remarked: 'The more it is emphasised to me that these are unusually intelligent young men, the harder it is for me to take the view that what they did was not done deliberately.'

The moment came when they faced Lord Goddard for sentence. He treated them more leniently than most people expected:

It is not for young men employed in these matters, either at university or elsewhere, to decide for themselves what is vital to the security of this country, and what secrets must be maintained and what secrets are of less value than others. You had all the provisions of the Official Secrets Act made clear to you, and it is to your credit that you did not deny that the work you were engaged upon was secret and, I have no doubt, in some instances highly secret.

I cannot treat this matter as merely trivial, otherwise I would be making a farce of the Official Secrets Act. I take into account particularly the fact that this was an act of more or less youthful folly and that you were led astray by the enthusiasm you were showing for other causes. I will communicate with the Home Secretary to ensure that your sentence will be served in the most favourable circumstances, which will, I hope, keep you away from criminals.

He then sentenced them each to three months' imprisonment, most unusually backdating the sentence to the first day of the Old Bailey sessions, 16 June. As sentence was passed on 18 July this meant that they were treated as already having served one month in prison, although they had been out on bail. There is no recorded example of Lord Goddard, not a man known for leniency, passing such a sentence on any member of the criminal classes who was not an Oxford undergraduate. Miller and Thompson were sent to an open prison at Eastchurch.

After starting his sentence, Thompson learned that he had been awarded a first-class degree in his final Oxford examination. Miller had been permitted to discontinue his studies after he had been charged, but was allowed to return to the university the following year.

The treatment accorded to Miller and Thompson was curious, as if there was some embarrassment about imprisoning these well-educated undergraduates. They were not, for example, fingerprinted by the police or prison authorities. Upon his release Thompson was even permitted by the Law Society to begin employment as a solicitor's articled clerk, despite the known fact that he had just come out of prison. He decided after six months to become an academic, subsequently becoming a Reader in Social History at Essex University, where there was no suggestion that a prison sentence was any form of disqualification. Miller became a publisher and literary agent.

Having decided to prosecute the editors of *Isis*, the authorities had turned their attention to the other Oxford University newspaper, *Cherwell*. In order to discourage the publication of an article in support of Miller and Thompson, a bowler-hatted member of the Special Branch had visited its editor, Michael Sissons. He failed in his mission. *Cherwell* carried an editorial in terms that the Special Branch had indicated would be most unwelcome. No attempt was made to enforce the earlier threats, and Sissons himself also became a literary agent, without having to serve any apprenticeship in Eastchurch Prison.

8

A Position of High Trust

In February 1962 there was a further extension of the use of
the Official Secrets Act, this time under Section 1; it was not
used in relation to spies or saboteurs, but against members of
the anti-nuclear Committee of One Hundred. Five members
were gaoled for eighteen months and one for twelve months
following a demonstration at Wethersfield air base in Essex.
The protesters were convicted of a conspiracy to incite people
to commit a breach of the Official Secrets Act for a purpose
prejudicial to the safety and interests of the state, by entering
the RAF station. The jury, in convicting them, recommended
mercy, but as they refused to undertake not to commit further
criminal acts Mr Justice Havers passed severe sentences. The
allegation against them was that they were trying to enter the
base to surround aircraft and to prevent the base – which
occasionally served squadrons of the United States Air Force
– being used.

The imprisonment of Barbara Fell in 1962 showed the
viciousness of prosecutions under Section 2. Aged fifty-four,
she held the OBE and was the daughter of Sir Godfrey Fell, a
distinguished member of the Indian Civil Service, who had
become Under-Secretary to the Government of Burma. She
had worked in the Central Office of Information for twenty-
three years and was the acting controller of Overseas
Services. Her job was to distribute government information
among foreign embassies, but it was the manner in which she
chose embassies to distribute government information
among that led to her proseuction.

In June 1958 Miss Fell had met the Yugoslav Embassy's

press officer, Smilian Pecjack, a married man and fourteen
years her junior, when he made an official visit to the Central
Office of Information. He sought to persuade her that his
sympathies were with the West and that he was anti-Soviet.
Miss Fell swallowed the story, and in the spring of 1959 she
and Pecjack became lovers. In a scene reminiscent of General
Alexander's dinner party (Chapter 9), during the course of an
argument she showed Pecjack a government report she had
received at the Central Office, in order to persuade him that
what she was saying was true. She allowed him to take it away
to read overnight. Pecjack returned it the next day; she lent
him a number of other confidential documents over the next
two and a half years.

There was no question of Miss Fell being entitled to show
Pecjack these papers. Each was marked 'confidential' and
stated that it was the property of Her Britannic Majesty's
Government. The documents consisted of reports and
dispatches to the Foreign Secretary on various matters
relating to Yugoslavia. No doubt they were of considerable
interest to the Yugoslavs, including as they did reports by the
British Ambassador in Belgrade upon the effect of Yugo-
slavian foreign policy on the West, and a valedictory dispatch
on the political situation in Yugoslavia by a British
Ambassador relinquishing his post. Miss Fell would have
known that she was not entitled to pass these confidential
documents on to Pecjack. In July 1961, at the very time she
was committing the offence under the Official Secrets Act,
she wrote a memorandum on the question of security relating
to such reports, suggesting they be distributed in black boxes,
which she felt were more secure.

The reason the Central Office of Information received
copies of these reports was for the very purpose of
distributing government information among foreign embassies that were considered to be deserving recipients. As
Communists, the Yugoslavs were not considered sufficiently
deserving. However, none of the papers was classified secret,
and at no stage at Miss Fell's trial did it become necessary to
sit in camera – proof of the lack of secrecy surrounding the
documents.

Barbara Fell was subjected to rigorous questioning on the day of her arrest, 30 October 1962, and was interviewed on three occasions between 2.30 p.m. and 12 midnight without having any access to a solicitor. She readily admitted what she had done; she had in her own words been 'a lunatic'. Yet it was not until 17 November that she was told she would be prosecuted.

The case arose after William Vassall had been sentenced, earlier in October 1962, to eighteen years' imprisonment for spying. His trial – with its homosexual overtones – had raised considerable alarm about the general state of British security. Although there were those who expressed relief that in Miss Fell's case the Official Secrets Act had on this occasion been breached by a heterosexual, that was a minority view. Despite the concessions made at her trial by Sir Peter Rawlinson QC, the Solicitor-General, that Miss Fell had not acted to prejudice the interests of the state and that she was probably emotionally influenced and had had her judgement overborne by Pecjack, Mr Justice Gorman took a severe view of the case at her trial in December 1962. She had great responsibilities, he told Miss Fell, and a substantial salary for those days (£3,865). It was unrealistic to approach this case as other than one of gravity and seriousness: 'You have completely broken the trust that was imposed upon you.' He passed the maximum sentence permitted under Section 2, which was two years' imprisonment.

Regardless of having vociferous support in Parliament, Miss Fell's appeal was rejected by the Lord Chief Justice, Lord Parker. He observed that Section 2 was an absolute offence, and he rejected Gerald Gardiner QC's pleas that the maximum sentence was wholly inappropriate, remarking that the judge could have imposed a consecutive sentence. As Miss Fell had faced eight charges she could therefore have been sentenced to sixteen years' imprisonment. The sentence, Lord Parker ruled, should 'mark the seriousness of the offence committed by a person in a position of high trust'. To add insult to injury, she lost the benefit of the four weeks she had already served in prison by the time of her appeal, as her sentence was treated as starting to run from the day of the rejection of the appeal. She had been spotted by a plausible and personable foreign agent as a vulnerable, ageing spinster. She had undoubtedly breached her obligations of trust and had behaved foolishly and irresponsibly, but was it necessary to send her to prison for two years to stop civil servants like her going to bed with Communists?

Barbara Fell was badly treated in prison. The inmates of Holloway treated her like a spy, and her conditions did not improve until she was transferred to Askham Grange open prison. Her career was, of course, ruined by her conviction, but she did marry a blind former COI colleague when she was released, whom she looked after devotedly until his death. It was a sentence of needless harshness, which was not repeated in the very similar case of Miss Rhona Ritchie (Chapter 13). Speaking in the November 1979 debate in the House of Lords on the government's Protection of Information Bill, Lord Gardiner, by then a retired Lord Chancellor, called the Fell case an absurd example of a prosecution under the Official Secrets Act and an absurd sentence.

9

Storm in a Port Glass: Jonathan Aitken

Although there are still prosecutions under Section 2, the case brought in 1970 against Jonathen Aitken, Colonel Douglas Cairns, Brian Roberts and the *Sunday Telegraph* marked the beginning of the end for the Act. Following the case the Franks Committee was set up, which recommended the repeal of Section 2 and its replacement by a section confined to the protection of government secrets.

It was perhaps fitting that the wide net of Section 2 succeeded in trapping a Conservative parliamentary candidate (Aitken), a distinguished soldier who had been seconded from his retirement job with Barclays Bank to the British observation team in the Nigerian civil war (Cairns), the respected sixty-four-year-old editor of the *Sunday Telegraph* (Roberts) and the newspaper itself. They were prosecuted for their parts in the publication in the *Sunday Telegraph* on 11 January 1970 of an official report entitled 'An Appreciation of the Nigerian Conflict'. It was scarcely the stuff of which martyrs were made. Aitken's literary agent, Graham Watson, described the report as 'of breathtaking dullness', observing that although it was obviously from an official source and confidential, it had no secrecy classification nor any distribution list of those to whom it could be safely entrusted. Nevertheless, it was published with great enthusiasm by the *Sunday Telegraph* under a front-page headline: 'Secret Biafra War Plan Revealed'. The article was highly critical of the British government's policy and sought to rally support for Biafra, but as a scoop it was torpedoed by the surrender of the Biafran forces just as the story was being prepared for publication.

There were allegations that the trial was a political one, brought by a government infuriated by revelations that it had been less than truthful about its support for the federal Nigerian forces and by the publication of a British government report which accused the Nigerian regime of being corrupt and inefficient. The decision to prosecute was taken by the Labour government, whose policies over Biafra had been severely criticised in the report, but it was left to the incoming Conservative administration to conduct the prosecution – for which it can have had little appetite. It was noticeable that neither the Conservative Attorney-General, Sir Peter Rawlinson QC, nor the Solicitor-General, Sir Geoffrey Howe QC, exercised the traditional right of the law officers to conduct such prosecutions.

While there was some measure of agreement that Aitken was a suitable candidate for prosecution, if proceedings under Section 2 were taken, there was considerable criticism of the decision to prosecute Colonel Cairns rather than Major-General Henry Templer Alexander CB, CBE, DSO. Cairns's 'crime' was to send the confidential report not to the *Guardian* but to a Major-General who had been his superior in the British observation team in Nigeria and who gave lectures supporting the British government's line on Nigeria. Alexander was not prosecuted for his role in the affair – passing the report on to Aitken, whom he knew to be a journalist. The wrong selection of defendants was to present considerable difficulties to the prosecution, which became clear when the trial judge, Mr Justice Caulfield, summed the case up to the jury.

The background to the case was to be found in the instruction given in December 1969 to Colonel R. E. Scott, the defence adviser to the British High Commission in Lagos, to update an earlier report, 'An Appreciation of the Nigerian Conflict'. The civil war, between the Hausa and Yoruba tribes of federal Nigeria, and the Ibos of Biafra, had lasted thirty months. Scott's brief was to assess the military position. He correctly forecast that the federal Nigerian forces would win by the end of the dry season, that is to say by April 1970.

Scott's report showed that the statement by Michael Stewart, then Foreign Secretary, to the House of Commons in July 1969 – that 'the arms which we have supplied to the Nigerian government have been broadly both in quality and quantity what we were supplying before the war began' – did not lie easily with Scott's own assessment that the British supply of arms had increased tenfold. On 15 November 1969 this had been amended to a statement that the British government was supplying approximately 15 per cent in value of the federal forces' arms. Scott, however, thought the correct figure was nearer 70 per cent. The federal Nigerian government, moreover, did not greatly care for Scott's reference to the 'inefficiency, corruption, muddle and waste' of its army's high command. This was picked up by the *Sunday Telegraph* in its subheadline, 'Muddle, Corruption, Waste by Federals'.

None of this was especially secret. Scott had distributed fifty-one copies of his report and had read out the less critical passages at a press conference in Nigeria. The Israeli and even the Irish embassies were known to have copies, and extracts had appeared in the French press. The report was marked 'confidential', which Scott agreed at the trial was not a particularly high security grade. Scott supplied a copy of the report to Cairns, the senior British member of an international team of observers set up to monitor the civil war. Cairns – who had a distinguished military career behind him, including quelling a mutiny amongst the Ghanaian forces in the Congo, and who was described by his character witness, Brigadier Sir Bernard Fergusson, former Governor-General of New Zealand, as a man of unimpeachable loyalty – sent a copy of the report to Major-General Alexander.

Cairns had been deputy to Alexander and had succeeded him when he retired. The General was, according to Cairns, a man who never really retired and who liked to be kept informed on developments. Cairns considered him to be a man of unquestionable loyalty, bound by the Official Secrets Act as he was. He later told the jury that it had never crossed his mind that he might be breaking the Official Secrets Act by sending a copy of the report in confidence to a major-general, whom he described as a trusted colleague. Unwisely as it turned out, however, Cairns had written in a covering letter to Alexander that he should not tell Bob Scott that he had been sent a copy of the report. The reason for this was that he himself wanted to tell Scott that he had sent Alexander a copy rather than having it come from Alexander.

The scene shifts from Lagos to General Alexander's dining room in Brandsby, Yorkshire. There, on 21 December 1969, Alexander was entertaining a number of guests, including Aitken. Aitken was prospective parliamentary candidate for Alexander's constituency, Thirsk and Malton. This led Alexander, in his own words, to treat Aitken 'not as a second-class journalist but as the prospective Tory candidate in my own constituency and as a close and trustworthy friend, who had accompanied my daughter to a dance'. Alexander had maintained contact with Aitken since December 1967. From time to time he had sent him maps and documents on the Nigerian civil war as background information which he could use in his articles without attributing his source.

Alexander had already had one unfortunate encounter with the press. In October 1961 he had spoken rather too freely about the Ghanaian situation with *Topic* magazine's feature writer at his club, White's. This occurred after his dismissal by President Nkrumah from his post as Chief of Defence Staff, on the grounds that there was no place in his army for an 'imperialist general' who wanted to send Ghanaian cadets to Sandhurst rather than Peking. Although Alexander repudiated the *Topic* interview as inaccurate and as in breach of an agreement not to publish, he was a serving British officer and ought not to have given an interview. He was passed over for the post of GOC Scottish Command, and after a term as Chief of Staff, Northern Command, he retired.

Nevertheless, Alexander had lost none of his appetite for discussing African politics with journalists. Over the port, following 'a convivial dinner at which we were all on good form', he found himself opposing Aitken's view that the federal Nigerians could not win and that the British government should impose an arms embargo. He told Aitken he was wrong; he had received a report from Lagos which he would show to him to prove that the federal government was going to win the war.

Precisely what he said as he handed the report over to Aitken became the subject of considerable dispute, and neither party emerged with complete credit. The nearest to independent evidence came from one of the dinner guests, Anthony Cliff, who said at the trial that Alexander gave Aitken the report like a race-card. Mr Justice Caulfield suggested that Alexander might perhaps have taken greater care of his race-card, and the witness was inclined to agree. Alexander said that he told Aitken that he should not have been in possession of the report anyway, and it was secret and confidential and that Aitken should read it as background information. It seems unlikely that Alexander would have felt it necessary to make this little speech as he passed the report around with the decanter. When he gave this explanation he was in some danger of being prosecuted. He may perhaps have remembered the case of Barbara Fell (Chapter 8). However, Alexander was neither a Communist nor a Yugoslav, nor was he Aitken's lover. He was not prosecuted.

No doubt the General intended that Aitken should read it overnight and return it to him. He did not expect Aitken to photocopy the document six times, nor to sell it to a newspaper (albeit for a fee donated to charity). Aitken felt he was free to communicate the report to whomever he pleased provided that he did not disclose his source. Alexander, it seems, approached the matter on the basis that Aitken was a friend and his prospective MP, whereas Aitken approached it as a working journalist and as someone firmly committed to the Biafran cause.

Some measure of the depth of misunderstanding between the two men can be found in the fact that, during the twenty-four hours Aitken had the report, he ran off half a dozen photocopies. Yorkshire Television received two; Hugh Fraser MP, a leading figure in the pro-Biafran lobby in the House of Commons, had two; Aitken kept two himself, one for a newspaper article he was planning to write, and one for a television programme. Although Alexander may well have embroidered his account of how he handed over the report, he certainly did not expect the journalist to exploit the overnight loan of the report for background information in this way.

Aitken discussed the use he would make of the document with Hugh Fraser, with whom he was staying over the New Year. It was agreed that it should first be submitted to the *Sunday Telegraph*, whose editor, Brian Roberts, was sympathetic to the Biafran cause and which had supported an arms embargo against Nigeria. It had also published a number of articles by Aitken. He arranged for this to be done on 8 January 1970 through his literary agent, Graham Watson of Curtis Brown. The enterprise was initially cloaked in secrecy, Watson's instructions being that he should not mention Aitken's name until he had the *Sunday Telegraph*'s acceptance. Thereafter the *Sunday Telegraph* could check the document's source and authenticity with Aitken. The paper was not at that stage told that the document came from an occasional contributor to its columns. Watson telephoned Fraser about the report and was told that he intended to ask seven parliamentary questions about it, and to display a copy in the House of Commons library. Watson was satisfied that the document could be sold to the newspaper and he agreed a fee of £500 with Ralph Thackeray, the features editor.

Apart from the fact that this fee was sent to the Biafran Save the Children Fund, this appeared to be an unexceptional transaction to Graham Watson. He realised that it was out of the ordinary only when, on 27 January, as he was about to leave his office, he found Detective Chief Superintendent Kenneth Pendred and Detective Sergeant Digby of the Special Branch at the door. They told him that they had just seen Brian Roberts, the *Sunday Telegraph*'s editor, who had told them he had received the report from 'a literary agent of the highest repute, one with which we deal in this field' – which he later revealed to be Curtis Brown. Watson declined to name the source but it was evident that the police had a very good idea, as they asked him to confirm that Aitken was a client of Curtis Brown. Since Aitken's name appeared in the firm's brochure, there seemed little point in denying it.

The police officers left, and Watson telephoned his solicitor. He received the scarcely reassuring advice that he might have committed two offences under Section 2 by receiving and communicating official information, having reasonable grounds to believe that it had been obtained in contravention of the Official Secrets Act. Watson was not prosecuted, but he was called as a prosecution witness. He next saw Pendred and Digby on 3 March, when they were rather more friendly to him; they confided that if there was a prosecution it would be for political reasons, and as he was unpolitical it was unfortunate that he had been involved. This was a messy affair, they said, and if he had known what was behind it, no doubt he would not have touched it with a barge-pole.

When the *Sunday Telegraph* had been offered the report on 8 January 1970, its concern had been to check whether it was genuine and whether publication would harm national security. The assistant editor, Gordon Brook-Shepherd, was asked by his editor to make the necessary enquiries. He showed the document to a Foreign Office friend, Johann Welser, who expressed some surprise that the newspaper should be in possession of it and said he would enquire to see if it was genuine. At 4 p.m. on 9 January, Vice-Admiral Sir Norman Denning, the secretary of the Defence, Press and Broadcasting Committee – the D-notice committee – telephoned Brook-Shepherd expressing some doubts as to whether the document was genuine. He said, however, that as the report did not refer to British forces it would not appear to affect national defence security. Denning later told the court that he added that if it was an official confidential document it would be covered by the Official Secrets Act. Brook-Shepherd telephoned Welser at 4.30 p.m. to obtain his opinion, telling him that he was under pressure for a decision as to whether the *Sunday Telegraph* could publish. Welser told him not to touch the document. This, needless to say, convinced Brook-Shepherd of its authenticity, and at 5 p.m.

he agreed to buy it from Watson. At 6 p.m. Denning called Brook-Shepherd and told him that the document appeared to be Scott's official report. As a matter of courtesy, Brook-Shepherd telephoned Welser and said that the *Sunday Telegraph* intended to publish it.

At the trial Welser told the jury that he had given Brook-Shepherd a friendly warning that if the document was published there might be trouble under the Official Secrets Act. Brook-Shepherd described the meeting as part of the old-boy network. Welser was a member of his club. 'At no time did Mr Welser put on his bowler hat and brandish his umbrella and say I am telling you officially.' It was perhaps only appropriate that Welser, who had the task of dissuading the paper from publishing, should have worked for the information and research department of the Foreign Office.

One of the weaknesses of the newspaper's case was the suggestion that it had published the Scott report after being warned of the risk of prosecution under the Official Secrets Act. However, there was some question as to precisely what Denning had said. Brook-Shepherd's recollection was that Denning said only that the report did not affect British national security, and did not mention the Official Secrets Act. Welser's advice not to publish was informal – that it was better not to publish. When he was told by Brook-Shepherd that the paper's lawyers had advised that the report could be published, he had said, 'Be it on your own head; it cannot be helped.'

If the prosecution had been a little more alert, it might have discovered that Ronnie Burroughs, an assistant under-secretary at the Foreign Office and a friend of Brook-Shepherd, had gone steaming around at 5.15 p.m. to the *Sunday Telegraph* offices when he learned of the plans to publish the Scott report. He was sufficiently alarmed about the proposed publication to go there in person. He warned Brook-Shepherd that the paper was heading for serious trouble if it printed the document. This view was passed on to the editor, but he decided to take the risk and publish.

No mention was made at the trial of this unusual visit by an assistant under-secretary. Had the jury known of this very clear warning, the *Sunday Telegraph* and its editor might very well have been convicted. Burroughs also brought the unwelcome news that a telegram had been received at 4.45 p.m. at the Foreign Office from Lagos that the war was over. Thus Scott's report was no longer the main news from Nigeria. Biafra did not formally capitulate until 13 January, but the war was over by the time the report was published, and as a journalistic coup it was a flop.

The insistence on describing the report as secret, coupled with Nigerian fury at its contents, caused urgent enquiries to be set in progress in Whitehall and a certain amount of fluttering in the dovecotes in Brandsby. General Alexander wrote to Colonel Cairns a curious letter: 'I am shattered about Bob Scott. What happened? How did the report leak?' He recollected lending the report to Aitken and wrote to him asking him not to divulge the fact that he had been shown the Scott report, 'otherwise there will be trouble for both of us'. Aitken replied that he would 'maintain a grave-like silence about this. Frankly I am rather surprised by all the fuss other people are making.' He denied being responsible for the document's appearance in the *Sunday Telegraph*.

After a visit from the ubiquitous Pendred and Rigby of the Special Branch, Alexander became more concerned. He noticed that the staple in his copy of the Scott report had been interfered with, presumably when a photocopy had been made. Alexander wrote courteously enough to Aitken saying that he would have to admit he had shown him the report, but he wished to have his permission to do so. He mentioned that he had noticed that the report's staple had been interfered with. On 24 January, Aitken replied that he had not made a photocopy.

Alexander was at some risk of being prosecuted himself. He wrote a number of letters setting out the position as he now saw it. He told Cairns: 'I'm afraid we've been shopped. He [Aitken] has told a good many lies. He has behaved in a dishonourable way.' He said that it had never occurred to him that the communication of the report to him by Scott was in breach of the Official Secrets Act. He then went on to tell Cairns his version of events, that 'at the end of the port

session I offered to lend it to Aitken and asked him to treat it
in the strictest confidence'. He regretted that he had landed
Cairns in the cart, yet he wrote, without apparent irony,
'however bitter you may feel, you must remember that I got
you to Nigeria in the first place'.

On 11 March, Alexander invited Aitken to tea at his home.
Somewhat unusually for a British major-general, he had
bugged his library, where tea was served. This conversation
assited the prosecution by producing evidence of how the
report was copied and circulated. It may well be that
Alexander hoped that by this cooperation with the police he
would avoid being prosecuted. Nevertheless, when Alexander
gave evidence for the prosecution at the Old Bailey, the judge
told him that he could refuse to answer questions on the
grounds that the answers might incriminate him. It is not that
unusual to hear witnesses being told of the rule relating to
self-incrimination, but it is rare to hear it being explained to a
major-general. The playing back of the tape was a matter of
some embarrassment to Aitken. He placed the blame on
Hugh Fraser MP, who he said had copied the report and sent
it to the *Sunday Telegraph*. Later he explained that he had
been given. *carte blanche* by Fraser to say this. Aitken's
friendship with Fraser survived the case; he was executor of
Fraser's will and dedicated his book on the case, *Officially
Secret*, to Hugh and his then wife, Lady Antonia Fraser.

Less dignified perhaps was the verbal sparring which took
place in the library. 'I gather you said to one or two people
that you feel anyone who betrays a confidence and that sort
of thing is not a person who ought to be a candidate,' Aitken
observed acidly to Alexander. 'If you sort of, as it were,
repeat that charge, the only way I am going to cope with it is
to deny it and say it was a misunderstanding. I would produce
things like that letter which Lord Goodman has a copy of
which said, "I would be very grateful if you would not
mention to anyone that you have seen the report." It might
have repercussions for both of us, so it would be very
unseemly for us both.'

Shortly after this interview, on 17 March 1970, Jonathan
Aitken, Colonel Douglas Cairns, the *Sunday Telegraph* and

Brian Roberts, its editor, were charged under Section 2:
Aitken with receiving the report, knowing or having
reasonable grounds to believe it had been communicated to
him in breach of the Act; Cairns with communicating a
confidential report entitled 'An Appreciation of the Nigerian
Conflict', which he had obtained in his official capacity, to
Major-General Alexander. Roberts and the *Sunday Telegraph* were both charged with receiving a confidential report,
knowing or having reasonable grounds to believe it was
communicated to them in breach of the Act, and with
publishing it in breach of the Act.

   The selection of defendants reveals something about the
operation of the Act. Alexander was not prosecuted; nor was
Fraser, a former Secretary of State for Air, who had let it be
known in a letter to *The Times* dated 18 March, on the BBC,
in the House of Commons and on practically any platform
where he was permitted to speak that he had received the
report and had encouraged its publication in the *Sunday
Telegraph*. In his evidence to the Franks Committee, Aitken
said he had been told by the police that they had not been
permitted to interview Fraser. The Attorney-General, Sir
Elwyn Jones QC, denied this, saying that the Director of
Public Prosecutions had advised that there was no real
evidence against Fraser since they did not know which copy
he had obtained nor how he came by it. It would, they
concluded rather surprisingly, be a complete waste of time
interviewing Fraser. The fact that he was an MP was, it
seems, coincidental. Lord Hartwell, at that time the
proprietor of the *Sunday Telegraph*, wrote to the Attorney-
General saying he took full responsibility for the publication
and that he personally fixed the amount of money the
newspaper was prepared to pay to Aitken for the report. In
effect he invited the authorities to prosecute him; for good
measure he sent a copy of his letter to the Prime Minister,
Harold Wilson, in the latter's capacity as head of the Security
Service. Sir Elwyn replied that he had sent a copy of Lord
Hartwell's letter to the Director of Public Prosecutions.
When, after four weeks, Lord Hartwell had heard no more,
he published the correspondence. It was no great surprise

that the government declined the opportunity to prosecute a newspaper proprietor.

The Attorney-General's justification for not prosecuting Fraser was not altogether convincing. He said that notwithstanding Fraser's 'admissions' there was insufficient evidence to prosecute him. The letter to *The Times* was not, he said, evidence against him, and he had declined to be interviewed by the Special Branch. However, a confession is not essential to launch a prosecution under the Official Secrets Act. Fraser's role in the affair was clear and could with relatively little effort have been proved by admissible evidence.

On 22 April 1970 the committal proceedings commenced before the magistrates at the Guildhall. The case was opened in vigorous terms by John Mathew for the Crown. Aitken had promised to return the report the next day, he told the magistrates, and the understanding between Alexander and him had been disgracefully dishonoured. His categorical assurance that he had not copied the document was a deliberate and dishonourable lie. The defendants' conduct could, it was asserted, have endangered diplomatic relations between Nigeria and the United Kingdom. They had revealed military secrets of a Commonwealth power.

The defence adopted what has become a standard ploy in subsequent cases: by minute cross-examination it showed that what was claimed to be confidential had been published elsewhere. Scott spent two and a half days in the witness box going through his report with Basil Wigoder QC, Aitken's counsel.

Welser dealt with the question of why certain documents were classified as confidential rather more frankly than the prosecution might have wished: 'A government official who thought that the disclosure of a document might cause embarrassment to Her Majesty's government might well classify it as confidential... Embarrassment and security are not really two different things.'

The court had to read thirty pages of transcript of the conversation of 11 March. This started with the domestic detail of Mrs Alexander returning from the library, having seen the approaching Aitken, saying, 'Here he comes now in his blue sports car. Good luck, darling!'

After Alexander had been cross-examined, informal approaches were made to the defence whereby it was made clear that, if the defendants would plead guilty, the committal proceedings (a preliminary to trial at the Central Criminal Court) would be dropped. At the magistrates' court the maximum penalty was three months' imprisonment and a £50 fine. Although three of the defendants were reluctantly prepared to plead guilty and to pay a fine – rather than risk the costs and the possibility of a prison sentence at the Old Bailey (where the maximum was two years) – Cairns refused to admit any guilt. The case had to proceed, and the defendants were committed to stand trial at the Old Bailey.

Aitken took advantage of the rarely exercised right of defendants to make a statement at the committal proceedings; in this it was possible to discern the hand of Lord Goodman:

> I would like to make it clear that throughout this affair I have told no dishonourable lie, that I have broken no promise, that I have violated no confidence, that I have in no way acted dishonourably.
>
> If there was a misunderstanding between General Alexander and myself I regret it. I also regret that my actions have unintentionally caused such embarrassment and inconvenience to Colonel Scott and Colonel Cairns.
>
> I believe that this document was of vital public interest. In revealing it I was upholding the right of a free press to publish non-secret material affecting government policies.

At the trial at the Central Criminal Court, the opening by Mathew was, after the cross-examination at the magistrates' court, more low-key. It was not claimed that diplomatic relations with Nigeria had been threatened or military secrets revealed. The criticism of Aitken was now that he had acted in an underhand manner. The *Sunday Telegraph* was said to have ignored two warnings not to publish (from Denning and Welser) and to have put forward the lame excuse that the Scott report could have been an unofficial document intended only for private distribution.

Brook-Shepherd explained the difficulties that confront a newspaper when presented with a document such as the Scott report: 'Half our time we live with a government persuading us not to publish something we think we ought to, the other half we spend resisting attempts by the government to print things we are not interested in.'

'It is a wonder that you produce a newspaper at all,' Mr Justice Caulfield, the trial judge, observed. He expressed some sympathy for the quandary of editors when they were given documents which did not affect national security.

Brook-Shepherd denied that he was ever told that publishing the report might contravene the Official Secrets Act. His discussions with Denning were about the authenticity of the document, and he was told that British national security was not involved, he said.

Welser was pressed on the question of how documents were classified as confidential. There were, he conceded, written rules about classification, but they were probably classified themselves!

Watson's evidence was particularly helpful to the *Sunday Telegraph* and its editor. He had discussed the report with Fraser at the House of Commons. He was asked if anything said by the MP had led him to believe that he might be committing an offence against the Official Secrets Act. 'No, rather the contrary,' he replied. He did not feel he was doing anything wrong and he assumed that a newspaper like the *Sunday Telegraph* would have its own legal department. After his evidence Mr Justice Caulfield directed the jury to acquit the paper and Roberts of receiving the document knowing it to have been communicated in breach of the Act, because there was no evidence to support the charge.

Alexander's evidence was less dogmatic. He admitted that the dinner party had been a convivial one and that there had possibly been a misunderstanding, although as far as he was concerned there was no misunderstanding.

Major Paul Gray, Colonel Cairn's deputy on the team of observers, told the court that he remembered Colonel Scott saying that he had marked his report confidential to ensure a wide distribution. 'Well, he certainly achieved that,' the judge wryly commented.

Scott himself agreed that there was nothing in the report that was secret or affected national security; it was more in the nature of a confidential document whose publication could embarrass Her Majesty's government, particularly if the Nigerians knew it was written by a British diplomat. That prediction certainly was correct. The report had been published in the *Sunday Telegraph* on 11 January. Scott was declared *persona non grata* on 12 January and was given twenty-four hours to leave Nigeria. He left the country by lunchtime on the 13th with a justifiable sense of grievance at being expelled as the result of an act perpetrated by Colonel Cairns.

Aitken's defence was that he had believed General Alexander to be lawfully in possession of the report and that he was entitled to use the document provided he did not disclose its source. He said there was a gentleman's agreement not to embarrass the General. He denied that Alexander had told him the document was given in the strictest confidence. It never occurred to the twenty-seven-year-old journalist that a general, in handing over this document, could be breaking the Official Secrets Act. His main impression on reading the report was that it completely contradicted the Foreign Minister's statements in the House of Commons.

Aitken admitted that he had laid a false trail by blaming Fraser for leaking the document. He regretted that he had taken that panicky step and that he had told a number of lies; he did however feel that the General was not free from blame in the matter and was himself being less than candid about the circumstances in which he had handed over the report. In a reference to Alexander's run-in with *Topic* magazine, he said he did not want to be the General's second journalistic victim.

He called Fraser to give evidence on his behalf. Fraser said he had not given a statement to the police because he saw no reason why he should furnish them with evidence to enable them to prosecute him. He considered that the case was an abuse of the Official Secrets Act and that the Labour government had brought the prosecution for political purposes. The suggestion (for which there appeared to be no evidence) was that the Labour government wanted a prosecution of a Conservative figure to distract attention from the fact that one of its MPs, Will Owen, was locked up in Brixton Prison accused of spying for Czechoslovakia. Fraser said that he had read the report during the New Year when Aitken was staying with him and found some of the government statements in the House of Commons 'outrageously mendacious'. He had some experience of secret documents as a minister in Macmillan's government and he did not suppose that a general would have handed over officially secret documents to a young journalist. As a leading supporter of the Biafran cause, Fraser did not in any event much care for Alexander, who had supported the bombing of Uli Airport, where Red Cross stores had been landed.

Aitken also called Lord Chalfont, a former Labour Minister of State at the Foreign Office. Chalfont said he was surprised that the report did not have an official stamp or crest. He would have worried more about the document being a fake rather than a breach of the Official Secrets Act. He thought it was at best 'a private document, written as a mind-clearing exercise'. If he had received it from a retired general he 'might have thought it a joke, a hoax or a fake'.

Aitken's star witness was Selwyn Lloyd QC, the Speaker of the House of Commons, whose private secretary Aitken had been in 1965–6. He told the jury that he had complete confidence in Aitken's trustworthiness; he was a man of the highest integrity.

Colonel Cairn's defence, with which Mr Justice Caulfield evidently had much sympathy, was that he considered the General – who still gave lectures setting out the government's case on the Nigerian Civil War – was bound by the Official Secrets Act just as he was. It never occurred to him that he might be breaking the Official Secrets Act when he sent Alexander a copy of the much duplicated report on 12 December 1969. He thought he was acting in accordance with his duty when he sent the report to Alexander, whom he considered to be a man of unquestioned loyalty.

Brian Roberts was a most improbable man to find in the dock of No. 1 Court at the Old Bailey. He had been editor of the *Daily Telegraph* for four years and was well respected in

Fleet Street. He had a strong personal sympathy with the
Biafran cause; his paper had even sent out Frederick Forsyth
to write about the war – an experience which led to his book
The Dogs of War. Roberts had acted correctly and
honourably when he had been offered the Scott report. He
had consulted the D-notice committee and had caused
enquiries to be made at the Foreign Office. His view was that,
if publication of the report was seriously detrimental to the
government, the Foreign Office should have told him so
when it was contacted.

Roberts explained to the jury that there had been three
main considerations in his decision to publish. First, it was
the task of the press to disclose information of public interest,
provided that it could do so within the limits of the law. The
Scott report, which he described, perhaps with a little
exaggeration, as of continuing public interest, had been
cleared on security grounds. It never occurred to him that
publication might be a breach of the Official Secrets Act.
Secondly, the term 'confidential', which had been applied to
the report, was meaningless unless it could be shown to be
confidential to someone. Anyone could write 'confidential'
on a document. There was no indication as to whom the Scott
Report was confidential to. Thirdly, even if the report had
some quality of confidentiality about it, this had been entirely
negated by the fact that it was in the possession of a Member
of Parliament and that questions about the report were being
tabled in Parliament. The literary agent's leaflet had said that
the report was in the hands of Hugh Fraser MP and was
circulating among pro-Biafran circles in London. Colonel
Ojukwu, the Biafran leader, was also said to have a copy.

Mr Justice Caulfield clearly had some sympathy with the
dilemma Roberts had faced on deciding whether or not to
publish. As if to underline Robert's caution in making this
decision, the Judge asked him:

'You do not want to be in the dock for one month?'

'The role of the martyr is not congenial to me.'

The summing up by Mr Justice Caulfield of the issues of
law and fact that had emerged in the sixteen-day trial savaged
the prosecution case and showed an unusual degree of

judicial distaste at the proceedings. The issues of fact were for the jury to decide, but there was little doubt what Mr Justice Caulfield thought of the case. The judge's directions on the law relating to Section 2 were the most favourable ever heard in court, with their emphasis on the defendants having to know or have reasonable grounds to believe that they were acting in contravention of the Act. Far from viewing Section 2 as an absolute offence, the judge seemed to be opening up the door for defendants to argue (as did Clive Ponting in 1985) that they had reasonable grounds for believing that they were entitled to act as they did. This door was belatedly slammed by Mr Justice McCowan. There are those who feel that Mr Justice Caulfield's summing up in this case was a factor in his remaining a High Court judge and not being promoted to the Court of Appeal. His comments on the role of the press were helpful to the defendants:

> We all recognise that an opinion-forming medium like the press must not be muzzled. The warning back is necessary to help maintain a free society. If the press is the watchdog of freedom and its fangs are withdrawn, all that will ensue is a whimper, possibly a whine, but no bite. If the press is muzzled you may think it becomes no more than a political pawn.

He then went on to attack the very existence of the law it was his duty to enforce: 'The 1911 Act achieves its sixtieth birthday on August 22nd this year. This case, if it does nothing else, may alert those who govern us at least to consider, if they have the time, whether or not Section 2 has reached retirement age, and should be pensioned off.'

Alas, the law has now reached its seventy-fifth birthday. More happily, Mr Justice Caulfield remains on the High Court bench, having celebrated his seventy-second.

The judge's summing up of the case against Cairns came very close to a direction to acquit. The Crown, he said, had to prove not only that Cairns had communicated the report to Alexander, but that he knew at the time that he was acting unlawfully and that the General was not authorised to receive

the document from him. The Crown had to disprove Cairn's
defence that it was his duty in the interests of the state to send
it to Alexander. The judge then reminded the jury that the
report had no distribution list, no official stamp from the
High Commission and no covering letter from Scott. Cairns
was a man of loyalty and experience who worked for the
High Commission, and Alexander enjoyed the confidence of
the Foreign Office and might have returned to Nigeria. He
had been encouraged by the government to give lectures on
the country. The jury might, Mr Justice Caulfield suggested,
find it easy to conclude that the Crown had not only failed to
prove its case, but that Cairns had satisfied them (which he
did not have to do) that he was authorised in his action.

The terms in which the judge described the prosecution of
Cairns were remarkable. By the time the prosecution counsel,
John Mathew, had made his closing address to the jury, he
was saying that there was hardly any blame on Cairns and
that the breach of the Act might be technical. However, the
judge pointed out that it was important for the prosecution to
obtain a conviction of Cairns so that it could establish a chain
of guilt. It would not be right, he warned the jury, to convict
Colonel Cairns as a scapegoat in order to make the
conviction of Jonathan Aitken and the *Sunday Telegraph*
possible. The jury were advised to be all the more on their
guard because the prosecution has chosen not to prosecute
General Alexander, but to use him as a witness against
Jonathan Aitken. Prosecuting counsel had, the judge said,
suggested that an enormous conflagration had spread from a
small fire started by Colonel Cairns; but if there had been a
conflagration, it was Colonel Scott who sent the document
outside the Civil Service.

The judge was less polite about Aitken. He had confessed
to telling a number of lies and with some embarrassment had
given the jury his reasons. However, the case was not about
whether Aitken had done the dirty on Alexander, but
whether, however much mud was thrown, the Crown had
proved a crime under the Official Secrets Act against him.
The judge was not altogether impressed by Alexander's
evidence. The jury might, he suggested, think that when the

balloon went up Alexander did not want to implicate himself or anyone else, but they might think that he became perturbed once the police came on the scene.

One of the problems of the way the prosecution was mounted was that, if Colonel Cairns was acquitted, the jury had to be satisfied, before convicting Aitken, that General Alexander had committed an offence in communicating the report to him. The prosecution became very difficult to sustain once one of the defendants (Cairns) was acquitted because the Crown would have to prove Alexander himself guilty of an offence under the Act. It would have to prove that Alexander knew he was acting unlawfully in giving the report to Aitken and that when Aitken received it he knew or had reasonable grounds to believe that Alexander had passed him the report in contravention of the Act.

The judge directed the jury to acquit Roberts and the *Sunday Telegraph* of the charge of receiving the report knowing it had been communicated to them in contravention of the Act. That charge was not sustainable in the light of Welser's evidence. The only charge against Roberts and his newspaper they had to consider was that of publishing the report in contravention of the Act. The issue here, the judge directed, was whether they knew the report had been obtained in breach of the Act. The judge suggested that by approaching the Foreign Office and the D-notice committee, and by telephoning Aitken and Fraser, the *Sunday Telegraph* and its editors had taken great pains not to put the paper in jeopardy of breaching the Act.

There is no censorship in this country; there is no duty in law for an editor or his newspaper to go running to Whitehall to get permission to print articles or news. Indeed, it would be absurd for a government official to have the power to dictate to an editor what he should or should not publish.

The judge suggested that the case was not so much a storm in a teacup or a wineglass, as had been put forward by defence counsel, but a storm in a port glass. It was perhaps not so much a matter of not seeing the wood for the trees, but of deciding whether there were any trees at all. He directed the jury to decide the case on the evidence and to put aside any political opinions of their own, but in doing so he permitted himself a fairly acid comment about the prosecution's disclaimer of any political motive in bringing the prosecution:

> It may be that prosecutions under the Official Secrets Act can serve as a convenient and reasonable substitute for a political trial, with the added advantage of achieving the same end without incurring the implied odium. This court is entirely independent of politics. It is independent of the executive, and the trials that take place must be conducted according to the principles of our law and not in prejudice.

It took the jury no more than two hours and ten minutes to acquit the four defendants of all charges. They were all awarded their costs. Cairns had been defended for a modest £5,511; the *Sunday Telegraph* and its editor for £10,150; Aitken's defence cost £10,562.

None of the defendants suffered severely as a result of the case. Aitken was elected to Parliament for Thanet South in 1974, where Detective Sergeant Digby became one of his constituents. Colonel Cairns received an OBE for his services in Nigeria. Brian Roberts remained editor of the *Sunday Telegraph* for another six years. The principal loser was Colonel Scott. He had been told in 1969 of his appointment as military attaché in Tokyo. This was cancelled after he was expelled from Nigeria, and he received the considerably less exalted post of Deputy Commander of the West Midlands District at Shrewsbury.

There was widespread criticism of this unsuccessful prosecution, which it was generally felt should never have been brought. If it had to be brought, Alexander should have been prosecuted instead of Cairns. The need to establish a chain of guilt underlined the difficulty of operating Section 2. Had there been a conviction, the press would have been in grave danger of being prosecuted each time they published a leaked document. The only positive feature of the case was that it hastened the advent of the Franks Committee.

10

Ferrets Not Skunks: the ABC Trial

Hopes that the government might have learnt something
from the Franks Report and the Aitken trial proved ill-
founded. In 1977 Crispin Aubrey, John Berry and Duncan
Campbell were prosecuted not only under Section 2 but, for
good measure, under Section 1. Section 1 was designed for
use against spies and saboteurs, and carries a maximum
sentence of fourteen years. It is not unusual for consecutive
prison sentences to be passed under Section 1, as in the case of
the spy George Blake, who was sentenced in 1961 to forty-two
years' imprisonment. Aubrey and Campbell, however, were
not spies but journalists; Berry was a community worker who
looked after delinquent children. This was the first and only
time that a chrage under Section 1 has been brought against
journalists, and it led to what became known as the 'ABC'
case (after the initials of the defendants' names). It started
with the prosecution believing that it had uncovered a nest of
spies and ended, despite the defendants' conviction under
Section 2, on a note of absurdity.

The case had its origins in an article published in the
magazine *Time Out* in May 1976 entitled 'The Eavesdroppers'. It was written by Duncan Campbell and Mark
Hosenball, although it was nearly all Campbell's work.
Hosenball was an American journalist who had been a staff
reporter on *Time Out* before moving to the less subversive
waters of the *Evening Standard*. 'The Eavesdroppers'
described the partnership between GCHQ, whose activities,
despite its large budget, were not officially acknowledged,

and the United States National Security Agency (NSA), which did officially exist but only just. 'The Eavesdroppers' was the most detailed description of the work of GCHQ, its monitoring and administrative sites. The article described how GCHQ eavesdropped electronically not only on military traffic but also on diplomatic and commercial communications.

The government was less than overjoyed by this article, and a few months later Winslow Peck, an American who had formerly been an analyst at NSA and who had been named in 'The Eavesdroppers' as an informant, was banned from entering the United Kingdom by the Home Secretary, Merlyn Rees. It subsequently transpired that very active consideration had been given, at the request of GCHQ, to prosecuting Campbell under the Official Secrets Act, but this had been turned down owing to insufficient evidence.

However, government attention had turned to Hosenball and a former CIA officer, Philip Agee, who had assisted in providing information for 'The Eavesdroppers'. To the fury of the United States government, Agee had written a whistle-blowing book on the activities of the CIA called *Inside the Company: CIA Diary*. He had named a number of agents, and the anger of the US government increased when one of those agents was murdered.

On 16 November 1976 Agee and Hosenball were informed by the British government that they were to be deported on the grounds of national security. This was sanctioned by Rees shortly after he had become Home Secretary; his predecessor, Roy Jenkins, had declined to make any such order. They were not then or ever given any detailed reasons for their deportation, but 'The Eavesdroppers' appears to have been the reason. The objection to Agee was, it seems, that he was assisting radical journalists investigating US intelligence activities in Great Britain. In his foreword to the book *British Intelligence and Covert Action* by Jonathan Bloch and Patrick Fitzgerald, Agee produces a suitable epitaph on his stay in this country when he quotes from a US Embassy telegram: 'Agee is leaving on Saturday, thank God.' It was less clear why Hosenball was deported, but this was probably

the result of muddled thinking by the government. He seems
to have been held responsible for much of the research in the
Time Out article. In fact he was by then working at the
Evening Standard and was required by that newspaper to
cover the Jeremy Thorpe case.

An Agee-Hosenball defence committee was set up to
contest the Home Secretary's order. Merlyn Rees appointed
a tribunal of three wise men to decide whether the
deportation orders should be enforced. They were all knights
in their late sixties. Sir Derek Hulton was a solicitor who had
served in British intelligence and had become President of the
Immigration Appeals Tribunal; Sir Clifford Jarrett was a
retired civil servant; and Sir Richard Hayward was a retired
trade union official. The tribunal met in the distinguished
surroundings of the United Services Club in Pall Mall. The
allegations against Agee and Hosenball were never spelt out.
Agee was told darkly that his deportation was 'conducive to
the public good', Hosenball that he was 'involved in
disseminating information' and with 'aiding and abetting
others in obtaining information for publication'. These might
have seemed unexceptionable activities for a journalist, but
the government apparently thought that he and Agee had
maintained regular contact with foreign intelligence officials.

John Berry had read 'The Eavesdroppers' with interest. On
11 February 1977 he wrote to the defence committee with a
brief statement of his views and an offer, as a former member
of the Intelligence Corps, to assist in the committee's work.
By then he had become a social worker in Tottenham. He had
been in the Army for seven years – with his four O-levels a
natural recruit for the Intelligence Corps. He had spent five
years in the 9th Signals Regiment, reaching the rank of
corporal. During his military service he had spent two years
in Eastern Cyprus, analysing Iraqi radio traffic at the RAF
base of Ayios Nikolaos. The base's functions were not
officially acknowledged, although it had been there for thirty
years.

Berry's military career had come to a bizarre end in 1970
when, following a drunken party in Famagusta, he and his
friends sent a hoax bomb warning to the sergeants' mess,

where a dance was taking place with the commanding officer present. In his befuddled state, Berry had not expected the call to be taken seriously. He was court-martialled and reduced to the rank of lance-corporal. He was sent back to the United Kingdom with the option of being discharged from the Army or transferred to another unit. He left the Army and had a succession of jobs. His political views had become increasingly radical and he now felt he should try to assist the defence of Agee and Hosenball.

In the statement he sent the defence committee care of the National Council for Civil Liberties, Berry said: 'It appears to me that secrecy is one of the most important keys to power and the existence of an organisation capable of spending vast sums of money in the total absence of public control should do much to dispel any illusion about the democratic nature of our government.' No one at the NCCL took much notice of the statement until it was shown to Crispin Aubrey, who was *Time Out*'s community affairs correspondent. He thought it convoluted and alarmist, possibly that it came from someone seeking personal publicity.

While Aubrey was nevertheless making arrangements to see Berry, Rees confirmed the deportation orders. An appeal against this decision, based on a breach of natural justice in failing to supply Agee and Hosenball with proper details of the allegations, was unsuccessful. Even Lord Denning seems to have felt that Britain would be a better place without Agee and Hosenball: 'When the state is in danger our cherished freedoms and even the rules of natural justice have to take second place.'

On 18 February, Aubrey and Campbell went to see Berry at his flat in Muswell Hill. Aubrey had written to Berry to fix a meeting and had telephoned from the offices of the Agee-Hosenball committee to confirm that they would arrive at his flat at 6.30 p.m. In the event they arrived half an hour late. Over a bottle of Italian wine Berry spoke into Aubrey's recorder for three hours of his experience in signals intelligence. Aubrey found the interview tedious, and Campbell soon discovered that he himself knew a great deal more about the subject than Berry did, although he was able to fill some gaps in his knowledge.

As the two journalists left Berry's flat at about 10.15 p.m. they were arrested by Detective Chief Superintendent Harry Nicholls, who had assembled a force of thirteen Special Branch officers. Exactly how Nicholls and his men came to be there was something of a mystery. They managed to lose their way on the journey of a mile to Muswell Hill Police Station – it had been considered tactically unwise to involve any local police officers in this mission. At the trial, Nicholls denied any knowledge of Aubrey's mail being opened or his telephone being tapped. He was able to say only that he had been told to go to Berry's address earlier in the evening. The probability is that someone intercepted Aubrey's telephone call to Berry. If they did, their suspicions were no doubt increased by Campbell's referring to Berry as 'Percy' and as having worked for 'British Rail', rather than Signals Intelligence.

The Special Branch officers were there to arrest a social worker (Berry), an Oxford graduate working for *Time Out* (Aubrey) and another Oxford graduate, with a first-class physics degree (Campbell). All came from respectable backgrounds. Campbell was the son of a professor at Dundee University. His mother had worked during the war for the Government Code and Cipher School in the Special Communications Unit at Hanslope Park, near Bletchley – a precursor of GCHQ, which was to feature so prominently at the trial.

In the event they were bundled into police cars. When they eventually reached Muswell Hill Police Station, courtesy of directions from a cab driver, they were held incommunicado and without access to a lawyer for forty hours, while they were interrogated and their addresses were searched. A filing cabinet containing more than one hundred files was removed from Campbell's flat and four hundred books, including one which was carefully logged as '*The Female Unok* by Germaine Greer'. After forty-four hours in police custory, they were charged under Section 2. The first charge under Section 1 was not added until seven weeks later. They were brought before the Tottenham magistrates, who, although offers were made to post substantial sureties, remanded them to Brixton Prison. An entire floor of the gaol's top-security wing was cleared for them, a privilege normally accorded only to terrorists and particularly dangerous criminals. Aubrey and Campbell succeeded in obtaining bail from Mr Justice Bristow a few days later with two sureties in a much lesser sum than had originally been offered, but Berry remained in custody for two weeks before being released on bail.

Aubrey, Berry and Campbell were prosecuted because of the government's extreme sensitivity about GCHQ. One of the ironies of the case was that GCHQ's existence was not officially admitted until Colonel Hugh Johnstone ('Colonel B') came to give his evidence. Even then little more was stated publicly about GCHQ until Margaret Thatcher made a statement in the House of Commons in 1982, following the arrest of the spy Geoffrey Prime. Any attempt to describe GCHQ's work in detail or to expose its activities was likely to lead to a prosecution. Furthermore, the intelligence services had observed the growth of investigative journalism in the United States with distinctly mixed feelings, and wished to discourage a spate of Watergate-type investigations into British intelligence operations.

Having decided that there was insufficient evidence to prosecute Campbell for 'The Eavesdroppers' article, the Attorney-General decided to proceed in respect of the interview with Berry. On the face of it there was a watertight case, as the police had seized the tape-recording of the interview given by Berry in clear breach of the Official Secrets Act. The prosecution failed to come to terms with Campbell's motives in building an encyclopaedic knowledge of defence communications, finding it difficult to accept that Campbell merely wished to know how the system operated in order to be able to criticize it. It was felt that he must have some political link with a foreign power. Even during the trial it was possible to hear one Labour Cabinet minister – presumably with the aid of a briefing from the Security Service – plying his fellow dinner guests with innuendos about Campbell and berating the editor of the *New Statesman*, Bruce Page, for having employed him.

Not only had the government seized all Campbell's papers but it tried to work through his contacts. One of these, Steven

Wright, a student at Lancaster University, had supplied Campbell with a photograph of his local Post Office tower; he found himself questioned and detained on suspicion of having committed an offence under the Official Secrets Act. Wright was researching a thesis on the social and political implications of new police technology. He remained on police bail for a month, until, after protests by the Vice-Chancellor of Lancaster University, he was told by the police that he would not be charged. Even so, not all his papers that had been seized by Special Branch officers from Preston were returned to him.

Seven weeks after their arrest, Aubrey, Berry and Campbell found themselves facing charges under Section 1 for communicating information calculated to be directly or indirectly of use to an enemy for a purpose prejudicial to the safety and interests of the state. By the time of the committal proceedings at Tottenham Magistrates' Court a formidable array of charges had been assembled which would have enabled Aubrey and Campbell to have been locked up for thirty-two years, out of all proportion to what they were alleged to have done. Berry was charged under Section 1 with communicating to Campbell information which might be useful to an enemy. Campbell was likewise charged under Section 1 with receiving information from Berry at that interview, and Aubrey with aiding and abetting Campbell to commit such an offence. In addition Aubrey was charged with performing an act preparatory to the commission of an offence under Section 1, which turned out not to be the preparation of microdot messages or the placing of explosives, but making the telephone call to Berry to fix the time and place for their meeting. Campbell was further charged under Section 1 with collecting sketches, notes and information regarding defence communications for a purpose prejudicial to the safety and interests of the state.

They each faced an additional charge under Section 2: Berry with communicating information to Campbell without authority; Campbell with receiving it, having reasonable grounds to believe it was communicated in contravention of the Act. Aubrey was once more charged with aiding and abetting, and his telephone call was tossed in to found a charge of perpetrating an act preparatory to the commission of an offence under Section 7.

A defence committee was formed, and the committal proceedings, to see if the defendants had a case to answer, were vigorously defended. After a lacklustre performance by the prosecution counsel, Michael Coombe, the defendants were committed for trial at the Central Criminal Court. Counsel for the prosecution pitched his case at a high level. The defendants had, he suggested, put the lives of British troops in Northern Ireland at risk and had provided information that would be of use to a foreign power. As the case progressed, so the prosecution's case moderated from the way it had been opened.

The committal proceedings introduced the shadowy figure of 'Colonel B', who was to become a source of discomfiture for the prosecution. His name was Colonel H. A. Johnstone, and for two years until November 1977 he had been head of Army Signals in the United Kingdom. He had to be referred to as Colonel B as it was felt that national security required that his name should not be given in court, although it was made available to the magistrates and the defence. As he was persuaded to reveal his Army number and service designation (Col Gen. Staff D124) and as his photograph and appointment to the Ministry of Defence had appeared in *Wire*, the magazine of the Royal Signals Association, which had jocularly referred to him as the 'don of the communications underworld', his real identity was readily discoverable. When the court clerk inadvertently asked Campbell's counsel which issue of *Wire* he was referring to, all Fleet Street was let into the secret of Colonel B's identity!

The prosecution had intended to call 'Lieutenant-Colonel A', a serving officer in military intelligence. The defence wanted to know his identity, but the prosecution would not reveal it. The magistrates retired to consider the question of whether the defence was entitled to know the identity of this prosecution witness. They ruled that he need not be named in court, but his name must be supplied to the magistrates and to the defence. This was not acceptable to the prosecution;

Colonel A was withdrawn from the trial, and Colonel B was called to give evidence in his place. However, one month after the committal proceedings Colonel B was publicly named in an article in the *Leveller* headlined 'Who are you trying to kid, Col. H. A. Johnstone?' He was also named in *Peace News* and the *Journalist*.

Colonel B's evidence revealed the nature of the prosecution's case and the chasm which existed between investigative journalism and the almost obsessive secrecy of the world of signals intelligence. He asserted that the identification and location by the defendants of defence communications establishments with a description of their tasks could provide a potential enemy with a possible target, or with a very great stimulus to take counter-measures. As his evidence unfolded, his complaint was that the defendants had revealed the nature and size of the Army signals intelligence effort, its co-operation with other services and agencies, the location of 'Sigint' (signals intelligence) units and their tasks and successes. His firm assertions, such as that 'any revelation which pushes aside the veil must inevitably adversely affect our ability to defend ourselves', were undermined by the production of a wealth of published material. After rigorous cross-examination of Colonel B, the prosecution case did not look so strong. The prosecution planned to replace Colonel B by a civilian, inevitably known as 'Mr C' – a superintending director of GCHQ – his name was so secret it could not even be revealed to the judge. But fortunately for the defence, the prosecution stuck to Colonel B.

While awaiting trial, Campbell planned a sixty-hour trip to France with his girlfriend. She telephoned him one Sunday evening to discuss how many French francs they would need. The following morning a Special Branch officer contacted his solicitor and informed him that there was to be a hearing on Wednesday to 'clarify his bail conditions'; he had presumably obtained this information by means of a tap on Campbell's telephone. At this hearing Mr Justice Thesiger soon put paid to Campbell's trip. He could not, he told him, see why anyone would wish to go abroad in July anyway, unless they were particularly fond of garlic.

The trial opened on 5 September 1979 before Mr Justice
Willis – a rather inappropriate choice as a former officer in
the Royal Signals TA division. It lasted ten days before it was
abandoned amid recriminations about the vetting of the jury.
Without notifying the defence, the names and addresses of
the panel of eighty-two jurors from whom twelve would be
selected to try Aubrey, Berry and Campbell had been given to
the prosecution, so that their backgrounds could be checked
by the Special Branch to ensure that the tape-recording of the
interview in Berry's flat could safely be played to them.
Defence counsel had contrived to learn about the vetting by
making informal enquiries of the court clerk to find out if any
checks had been made on the jury. No one had been rejected
as unsuitable to serve on the jury, but the prosecution had the
benefit of knowing that on this vetted jury there was a former
SAS soldier who had worked in security in Northern Ireland,
the Far East and Cyprus, a former squadron security clerk in
the Army and a civil servant – all of whom had signed the
Official Secrets Act and had been subject to its disciplines.

It turned out that twenty-four juries had been vetted since
1975, twelve of which had sat in terrorist trials and two in
official secrets cases. It was not until 1986 that the
government revealed that juries were vetted twice, not only
by the Special Branch, which was admitted in 1978, but also
by the Security Service. What was objectionable was the
failure of the prosecution to disclose this practice or to share
the results of the vetting with the defence.

The defence sought unsuccessfully to have the jury
discharged on the basis that people who had signed the
Official Secrets Act were likely to have some preconceived
ideas on the subject, particularly if they had been de-
indoctrinated. There was also an unsuccessful application to
discharge the foreman of the jury. Campbell had written an
article in *Time Out* that was highly critical of the SAS, which
it had been proposed to place before the jury when the
defence case opened. The defence feared that this would
harden the foreman's views, which were later reported as
having been that Berry should have faced a military trial.

The judge ordered that this ruling should not be reported,

but it was perhaps inevitable that, in a case about leaks, this should itself leak out. On a chat show presented on London Weekend Television by Russell Harty, the jury-vetting beans were spilt by Christopher Hitchens, a journalist with the *New Statesman*. His comments did not slip out in animated conversation but were read off autocue. The script had a built-in malapropism for Russell Harty to mouth, for he had introduced the item thus:

'Now, for your further vituperation, Mr Hitchens has some further news which you will not even have read or heard.'

Some of the jurors saw the programme on television and reported the fact to the judge. He reluctantly discharged the jury, condemning the programme as 'a quite lamentable piece of gratuitous journalistic gossip'. The disruption of the trial was reported to the Attorney-General, Sam Silkin QC, to consider whether there should be any proceedings against LWT. Large and powerful television companies are not usually prosecuted by governments, and this case was no exception. The company had, the Attorney-General concluded, 'acted in the sincere belief that it would not prejudice the trial'. As the conversation was scripted – and its whole purpose was to reveal news which had not been published elsewhere – Silkin was perhaps a little more charitable to LWT than he had been to Aubrey, Berry and Campbell, who still faced charges potentially carrying fourteen years' imprisonment.

At the first trial the defence had successfully shown that virtually all the sketches, notes and information concerning defence communciations that Campbell was alleged to have collected for a purpose prejudicial to the state had in fact been compiled from published sources. John Leonard QC remarked in a distinctly audible *sotto voce* that the prosecution would continue with that charge over his dead body. It was little surprise that the charge was dropped before the second trial.

Before the retrial could take place, Mr Justice Willis fell ill. With a fine sense of courtesy the defendants sent him red roses in hospital and were graciously thanked by the judge. The defence was fortunate that the trial did not continue in front of Mr Justice Willis. He told one of the defence counsel after the trial that the defendants were lucky to get rid of him and that he would have sent them inside. He was due to be replaced by the conservative judge who had refused Campbell's application to visit France for the weekend, Mr Justice Thesiger, the son of a major-general and, at seventy-five, nine years older than the Official Secrets Act. However, he was unable to hear the case, and Mr Justice Mars-Jones was appointed in his place. It was a stroke of luck for the defendants, as he was to take an independent-minded view of the prosecution case. The second jury was also vetted, but on this occasion the defence was informed of the intention to vet and was permitted to ask if any of the jurors had handled secret materials in the last fifteen years and were subject to the Official Secrets Act. One juror said that he had and was excused from service; none was excluded on security grounds.

Not surprisingly, Mr Justice Mars-Jones was anxious that there should be no further mishap which could lead to the abandonment of the second trial, so he ordered that there should be no publicity about the jury vetting. As part of the continuing chapter of accidents, this information did not reach the office of the Attorney-General. Unaware of the judge's order, Silkin issued a press statement setting out the guidelines for screening juries. No doubt LWT would have welcomed the opportunity of stating that the Attorney-General had acted in the sincere belief that he would not prejudice the trial, but they were prevented by Mr Justice Mars-Jones's order from mentioning it on Russell Harty's chat show. In any event, no mention was made of ignorance of the law being no defence, and the Attorney-General apologized to the judge for this oversight.

The second trial began on 5 October 1978. Like the first trial, it was opened to the jury by John Leonard QC in tones distinctly more moderate than those adopted at Tottenham Magistrates' Court. This reflected the inroads which had been made into the prosecution's case at the first trial. Instead of talking of threats to troops' lives, he paid tribute to the press, the profession to which, he explained to the jury,

Aubrey and Campbell belonged. If it had not been for the press and journalists, liberties in Britain would be in danger, he said, but there was no special law for journalists. They were subject to the ordinary law of the land. Aubrey and Campbell had been seeking information which they knew Berry was not entitled to give.

Campbell was, he said, trying to build up a complete picture of communications in this country, using documents on the ballistic early warning system, the Polaris submarine fleet, radar installations and Post Office microwave communications. The prosecution appeared unsure what to make of Campbell with his obsessive and, in its view, unhealthy interest in communications. Leonard asserted that what Campbell had done went beyond the ordinary inquisitiveness of a journalist. He illustrated this by referring to Campbell's filing system of seven hundred index cards and pictures of radio antennae, including one of a NATO radar installation.

The trial introduced a new line of jargon to the general public: 'Sigint' (signals intelligence), 'Commit' (communications intelligence) and 'Elint' (electronic intelligence). The case was given a greater air of secrecy not only by a number of witnesses appearing by letter, but also by the description of 9th Signals Regiment as 'Unit A', and its base at Ayios Nikolaos as 'Location 1'. At one stage, Mr Justice Mars-Jones was persuaded by defence counsel to permit proper names to be used after being told that the regiment's name, location and function had been mentioned at the first trial. Leonard strongly resisted this ruling and sought an adjournment to challenge it. When the court reconvened, he prevailed upon the judge, after a hearing in camera, to reverse his ruling. This curious incident came about because the prosecution claimed that the disclosure of the use of Ayios Nikolaos as a British electronic intelligence base would embarrass the Greek Cypriot government. The press counsellor at the Cypriot High Commission was prepared (on instructions from his government) to assist the defence by stating that the base's role as a monitoring centre was well known. Before he could give evidence, the counsellor was notified by the Foreign Office that it would be contrary to normal practice for foreign diplomats to give evidence in English court proceedings. The prosecution's contention was therefore unchallenged and it got its order for anonymity.

The result was that six Sigint units had to be referred to by letter, and each base they used had to have a number. The jury needed a crib to enable them to follow the evidence. This also provided the defence with a good opportunity to exploit the absurdity of the situation. One witness was asked to look at a photograph of a sign at the entrance to the base.

'Is that the name of your unit?'
'I cannot answer that question, that is a secret.'
'Is that the board that is up outside the door of your unit?'
'Yes.'
'Read it out to the jury.'
'I cannot do that, that is a secret.'

The damage that this obsession with secrecy can do is well illustrated by the fact that the prosecution let slip the fact that they were 'targetting' the signals traffic of one of their NATO allies, Turkey. Colonel Johnstone justified this on the basis 'Friends don't always stay the same. There's a perfectly legitimate reason for the British to be extremely concerned in what is happening. [We] try to stay one jump ahead of the game.' But, he said, if the Russians found out we were intercepting Turkish national military communications and could understand what was said it would be 'disruptive... The Turks are our allies in NATO and one of the main bastions of the southern flank.'

Berry was alleged to have revealed the fact that intercepting the Turkish naval signals was one of our tasks and that we were able to read traffic on Turkish naval nets. In fact the information Berry disclosed about Turkish naval moves to invade Cyprus came from no more sinister source than the *Daily Telegraph* and this secret had been let out of the bag quite unnecessarily by the Government.

It was established by the defence that information about the activities of the 3rd Squadron Intelligence Unit of the 9th Signals Regiment at Ayios Nikolaos had been published in an article by the *Guardian*'s defence correspondent in November 1974. The newspaper had informed its readers that the 3rd Squadron Intelligence Unit was 'a key listening and surveillance post for the United Kingdom and hence NATO purposes'. It had been mentioned in Parliament by Robin Cook MP. One prosecution witness, Major Frederick Everson, the security officer of the 9th Signals Regiment – the man who, unsuccessfully it would appear, had given Berry his indoctrination and de-indoctrination lectures – conceded that the regiment's name and location, the name of its commanding officer and its changes of personnel were not secret. However, he insisted its role was secret, although it had been published in the *Guardian*. Colonel B told the court that the exact name and location of the regiment were not a secret, but its strength was. He was then shown a cartoon in *Wire* with the caption, 'With a strength of just over 1,000, 9th Signals obviously contains many characters.'

The value of this charade of concealing the identities of the Sigint units was maintained despite the fact that in 1969 RAF Sergeant Douglas Britten, a chief technician at the RAF Sigint centre at Digby, Lincolnshire, was convicted of supplying information over a period of five years to the Russians regarding his activities monitoring Soviet air force units' radio signals at Digby, and his earlier work at the RAF Sigint base at Pergamos, Cyprus. He was sentenced to twenty-one years' imprisonment. Britten had been posted at an RAF base only a few miles from Unit A. Brian Patchett, a corporal in the Intelligence Corps, working in Sigint in the 13th Signals Regiment, had in 1962 deserted through the Berlin Wall from Unit B, the GCHQ post at Teufelsberg in West Berlin. He had no doubt told the Soviets of the identity of Unit B and about his work of the last four years monitoring Soviet and East German radio signals from stations in Berlin and Birgelen.

The atmosphere of needless security was further illustrated by the answers given by various prosecution witnesses. Hugh Webb, for example, refused to answer questions about GCHQ, explaining that it was covered by the Official Secrets Act. When asked whether it was a fact that the *Civil Service*

Yearbook showed Sir Arthur Bonsall as director of GCHQ, he preferred neither to confirm nor deny it. His answer was the same when he was asked whether it was the case that the location of GCHQ was revealed as 2 Priors Road, Cheltenham, in graduate recruitment brochures.

The prosecution found Campbell's fascination with communications so significant that it called a monk, Don Anselm Cramer, a teacher at Ampleforth College. He and a pupil, Philip Quigley, had been on what was described as a 'microwave treasure hunt' to supply Campbell with a photograph of a Post Office microwave tower near the school, after Quigley had got in touch with Campbell following an article he had written in the *New Statesman*. However, Don Anselm Cramer was a disappointing witness for the prosecution; he did not feel that this activity belonged to the realms of sabotage or spying, and said he considered that it could do no more harm than train-spotting.

The prosecution also attached considerable importance to a map of the United Kingdom found in Campbell's possession. This showed fifty-two locations, thirty-two of which were Post Office structures and stations, all but one carrying radio traffic that formed part of UK defence communications. The remaining twenty included thirteen RAF and five Army establishments. To complete the picture the jury were given the not particularly sinister information that Campbell owned a camera with five lenses, and had seventy colour slides and eighteen photos of communications installations.

When evidence came to be given of Aubrey and Campbell's three-hour interview with Berry, the court went into camera. However, the prosecution's case was chipped away by cross-examination by Lord Hutchinson QC, Campbell's counsel, who showed that practically every piece of information in Campbell's files was available from published sources such as *Flight International, Wire* and *Rose and Laurel*, the magazine of the Intelligence Corps. Campbell even received a renewal notice for his £2.10 annual subscription to *Wire* during the trial. The prosecution tried vainly to counter arguments that virtually all Campbell's material had been published elsewhere by the jigsaw argument, namely that he was putting the pieces together for the USSR. It was not fair, the prosecution claimed, to rely on articles in *Wire* and the *Rose and Laurel*; no one, and least of all the Soviets it seems, would have placed much reliance on these publications, which were not official magazines but 'inexpert journalistic publications'.

One prosecution witness, Major Philp of the Royal Signals Corps, told the court that he had a high opinion of Campbell as a technical journalist. He had been prepared to discuss technical signals matters with Campbell, and they had talked, amongst other things, about Ceres, which in this context was not the goddess of plenty but an acronym for computer-enhanced radio emission surveillance.

The crucial prosecution witness was Colonel B – by this time unmasked as Colonel H. A. Johnstone, but in court he remained Colonel B – who had for two years commanded Unit B. He was in the witness box for twenty hours. He exemplified what the defence castigated as an obsession with secrecy, and he was subjected to cross-examination that highlighted some of the more absurd aspects of the case. He was asked by Lord Hutchinson QC how secrets were classified, when so much of the classified material had already been revealed.

'What remains secret is what is designated secret by whoever makes the designation,' he replied, without shedding too much light on the subject.

'You mean the rules that are laid down for what is and is not secret are themselves secret?'

'Yes,' was his unflinching reply.

Colonel B was accused of being obsessed with secrecy; but in denying it, he revealed the importance attached to secrecy by the prosecution:

'Because of my knowledge of the subject I am better aware than most people of the critical need to ensure that some secrets that are more secret than others are kept as secret as possible. Sigint is one. This matter should remain as secret as possible. An individual having information concerning Sigint in his possession may only communicate it to someone else having the same type of indoctrination or if he has been previously authorised in writing by an officer not below the rank of major-general.'

His description of the damage to national security ranged from its being 'prejudicial to the national interest' to its 'potentially causing grave damage'. Its value to the Russians was as 'manna from heaven' or (less biblically) 'hitting the jackpot'.

It was pointed out that the *Guardian* had published a number of articles about the activities of the 9th Signals Regiment and that much of the information which was claimed to be secret in this case was no longer secret. This did not worry Colonel B.

'Quite apart from its accuracy or inaccuracy, I deplore articles of this sort.'

This was not mere shadow-boxing, because under Section 1, if the prosecution could prove that information was collected in a prohibited place for what appeared to be purposes prejudicial to the safety of the state, the burden of proof was reversed. The defendants would have to prove their innocence by showing that it had not in fact been collected for such a purpose.

As the case progressed, it became apparent that Campbell had assembled his material from published sources for the purpose of his research and writings. Much of what the prosecution claimed to be secret had been widely published. Mr Justice Mars-Jones took the view that the charges under Section 1 were oppressive. He told prosecution counsel that he could not say that Section 1 was only for sabotage and spying, but it should be applied only to the clearest and most serious of cases. He signalled his view of the case when he told the prosecution that, just as the Attorney-General has the power to start a prosecution, so he had the power to stop it. The prosecution took the hint, and the next morning, on the sixteenth day of the retrial, after consultations with the Attorney-General and the Director of Public Prosecutions, the prosecution said it would be dropping the four remaining charges under Section 1.

This was a considerable triumph for the defence. It

removed the charges which carried a maximum sentence of fourteen years and a virtually inevitable prison sentence in the event of conviction. Berry had been warned by his lawyers that he might face a seven-year sentence if he was convicted under Section 1. Now the defendants faced nothing worse than a maximum of four years in prison.

In his defence, Aubrey said that he had had no intention of embarrassing the government. 'Never in my wildest dreams did I imagine that the Official Secrets Act would cover a private conversation between two journalists and someone who wanted to talk to them.'

Berry had undoubtedly communicated official information without authority. He had been indoctrinated when he joined the Royal Signals Regiment and de-indoctrinated when he left it. He told the police officer who interviewed him that it had been rammed down his throat that his work was secret and that he could be subject to serious penalties if he disclosed details of it. On no less than six occasions he had been made to sign documents committing him to abide by the Official Secrets Act. He had no defence to the charges under Section 2. It was little surprise therefore that he chose to make a statement from the dock, which meant that he could not be cross-examined on his evidence. He said that the deportation of Agee and Hosenball had focussed his attention on the lack of accountability of the intelligence agencies, which are effectively beyond public control: 'There is a state within a state – a secret state – where you are not encouraged to ask questions.'

He considered signals intelligence illegal in that it was contrary to various international agreements and was in effect espionage. Possibly with some rationalisation after the event, he said he felt he was entitled to act as he did because of the Labour government's commitment in its manifesto to more open government, along Swedish lines. When he had left the Army, he explained, he had had to sign a document which told him he was prohibited for two years from travelling to the USSR. He felt that this meant that the information would be of no value after two years, and that in the circumstances he could speak to journalists four years and eleven months after leaving the Army.

Campbell had signed the Official Secrets Act when he was shown around GCHQ. He told the jury that Sigint was in his opinion illegal because it was contrary to a number of international conventions. He said that he had been misled by a statement on 22 November 1976 by the Home Secretary, Merlyn Rees, that the mere receipt of official information would no longer be an offence. On his behalf, Lord Hutchinson QC contended that the role of the Official Secrets Act is to prevent harm to the nation's safety and not to save the government from embarrassment or to block Watergate-style newspaper investigations.

Before starting his summing up of the case Mr Justice Mars-Jones had taken the unusual step of telling the defendants (in the absence of the jury) that even if they were convicted he had no intention of locking anyone up. If this was an invitation to the defendants to plead guilty it was not accepted. It was certainly an indication that the judge took a less serious view of the case than his predecessor had done. He had even let Campbell leave court early on one occasion during the trial to give a lecture at the Institute of Physics in Brighton on personal surveillance devices. Campbell had considerable expertise in the area of communications; his book on the microwave system, *The British Telephone System*, had become an Open University textbook. The judge directed the jury to find Berry guilty of the offence under Section 2, of communicating information he had obtained as an office-holder under the Crown to an unauthorised person. Berry had received this information while a serving soldier and clearly had no authority to pass it on to Campbell, whatever his motive. Even so the jury deliberated for an hour as to whether they would, as they had been told to, convict him.

The judge had considered arguments whether acting under a moral duty could be a sufficient defence to a charge under Section 2. He ruled that it could not. In his summing up he directed the jury that, despite the trial's moments of levity, the case was no laughing matter; they should forget the propaganda. It was not about the number of toilet rolls used in a unit, or indeed sausage rolls, but about the undertakings given by honourable men of their own volition to keep secret all they had learned, by having been members of Her Majesty's Signals Regiment, concerning intelligence secrets they must take to their graves.

The jury were out for nearly sixty-eight hours, with three nights in a hotel, before they could agree to convict all three defendants. The judge had been within minutes of discharging the jury, and the Attorney-General had already decided there would not be a retrial, when the jury returned to court with their verdicts.

Berry was given a six-months prison sentence, suspended for two years, and ordered to pay £250 towards his defence costs.

'We will not tolerate defectors or whistle-blowers from our intelligence services who seek the assistance of the press and other media to publish secrets, whatever their motives,' the judge told him. While he considered Berry was a worthwhile fellow, with a strong sense of obligation to the community, what he had done could not be brushed aside. The information would still have been of importance to any enemy, even though it was stale and low-key.

Aubrey and Campbell were both conditionally discharged. They did not, however, escape all penalty, as they each had to pay £2,500 towards the costs of the prosecution as a mark of judicial displeasure at their having continued to contest the case after the clear indication that they would not be sent to prison. The trial cost the taxpayer more than £250,000. Aubrey faced a further bill of £10,000 because the judge ordered that he should pay one-third of his defence costs. He might have expected to have had to pay them all, as he was not receiving legal aid, but the judge considered it would be unjust if Aubrey had to pay all the legal costs of successfully defending the charges under Section 1 and if he was penalized for the indiscretions of LWT, which had necessitated the retrial. Campbell was legally aided but he had nevertheless to pay £2,200 towards his defence costs.

The fact that there had, unusually, been some justification for bringing a charge under Section 2, at any rate against

Berry, was totally obscured by the Crown's insistence on bringing charges under Section 1. The argument as to whether it was in fact right to prosecute the defendants was lost in the attempt to prove that the actions of Aubrey, Berry and Campbell constituted a grave threat to national security. They had started the trial accused of being involved in betraying the country's secrets if not actually spying, and they ended as whistle-blowers who had overstepped the mark. With the débâcle over jury vetting and the ignominious withdrawal of the charges under Section 1, the trial was not Silkin's finest hour, although he at least had the political sense not to exercise his right as Attorney-General to conduct the case in court.

However worthy Berry's motives may have been, the case for prosecuting him was a reasonable one, although the information he passed onto Aubrey and Campbell lacked significance. Berry had had a sensitive posting and he had signed the Official Secrets Act. Yet it was indefensible to charge him under Section 1 when the information he communicated without authority was so relatively unimportant.

It is hard, on the other hand, to justify the decision to prosecute Aubrey and Campbell, who were working journalists. Investigative journalism may be unattractive to the defence establishment, but it is legitimate activity. The decision to use Section 1 to prosecute journalists for the first time in its sixty-six-year history was outrageous. Journalists have to obey the laws relating to national security like any other citizens and have no special privileges under the Official Secrets Act; but the prosecution seems to have lost sight of the fact that it is a journalist's job to collect information and that only in cases of the most exceptional gravity should they be charged with offences carrying fourteen years' imprisonment for doing just that.

The two trials lasted forty-two days and took twenty months to conclude, but they achieved very little. They may have deterred some whistle-blowers. Even an unsuccessful official secrets trial can act as a public warning, and in this case the three defendants were in the end convicted. One can only speculate as to why the case was brought. The government's target seems to have been Campbell after 'The Eavesdroppers' article; the prosecution of Aubrey and Berry was less important. Yet the government apparently failed to understand what Campbell was doing and how he collected his information – not by subverting soldiers but by avidly collecting published material on defence. Observers considered that prosecution counsel John Leonard QC was receiving much of his instructions from the legal adviser to the Security Service, Bernard Sheldon, and that much of the difficulty that confronted the prosecution in this case was the capacity of MI5 to get the wrong end of the stick. At the committal proceedings Campbell's defence counsel, Geoffrey Robertson, told the magistrates that his client was 'a ferret, not a skunk'. The prosecution seems to have viewed him throughout as a skunk, if not a mole. Through its desire to put an end to Campbell's activities and to post a dreadful warning to other like-minded journalists the prosecution was blind to the simple question of discovering where and how Campbell obtained his information. As each piece of information was shown to have a published source, the prosecution was forced back on the argument that Campbell was fitting together the pieces of a jigsaw for the Russians – despite the fact that the Russians had been looking at the picture of the puzzle on the box for some time and that they too perhaps bought *Wire* and *Rose and Laurel*.

The case had one sequel. The Attorney-General brought proceedings for contempt (for revealing the name of Colonel B) against *Peace News*, the *Leveller* and the *Journalist*, which were fined £500, £500 and £200 respectively, at a hearing before the Lord Chief Justice, Lord Widgery. During the hearing, gallant efforts were made by Harry Woolf, counsel for the Crown, to avoid mentioning Colonel B's real name. However, it did occasionally slip out, leading to his being rechristened 'Colonel Oops', and to thoughts of legal history being made by use of a bleeper whenever 'Colonel Johnstone' was mentioned.

There followed considerable competition to find novel ways of naming Colonel B. Red balloons were released

outside the court with the name Colonel H.A. Johnstone
written on them. Johnstone's name was written in letters ten
feet long on the sand of Whitley Bay, a gross contempt of
court until the tide came in. Four MPs – Jo Richardson,
Robert Kilroy-Silk, Ron Thomas and Christopher Price –
named Colonel H. A. Johnstone in Parliament. The question
of contempt was referred to the Director of Public
Prosecutions. The MPs responded as they best knew how by
complaining to the Speaker that the trial judge had
committed a breach of the privileges of the House of
Commons by allowing Hansard to be read out in court
without, as was the rule, first asking permission of the House.
The Speaker ruled that there had been no breach of privilege
and he forbade any further naming of Colonel B in the
House. One consequence of the ABC trial was that the old
rule about obtaining permission to quote from Hansard in
court was abolished.

It was perhaps only a fitting conclusion to the case that the
decision to fine the three journals was overturned by the
House of Lords. *Peace News*, the *Leveller* and the *Journalist*
got their money back on the grounds that there had not after
all been an order by the Tottenham magistrates that Colonel
B should not be named, but merely a direction. It was all very
puzzling, but it is no excuse for radical newspapers to claim
ignorance of the law.

The ABC case was by no means Campbell's last encounter
with the Official Secrets Act. In February 1984 he fell off his
bicycle. While he was receiving treatment for his injuries, the
security authorities interested themselves in the contents of
his saddle-bag and engaged in a six-hour search of his home
during which his address book was photocopied. He had in
his possession a number of official documents, but his
contention was that he had received these in his capacity as
civil-defence adviser to the Greater London Council. He was
not charged, and eventually the documents were returned to
him, with the exception of one entitled *The Army Manual on
Personal Protection*, which contained confidential information including 'Instructions on Defecating in the Arctic',
which it was not felt safe to leave in his possession.

11

Not a Nice Story: Sarah Tisdall

On 23 March 1984 Sarah Tisdall became the first person to be
sent to prison for infringing Section 2 of the Official Secrets
Act since 1970. It was a savage sentence on a young woman of
good character, passed not to punish her for the harm done
but to deter others. The severity of the sentence was
unjustified, and as a deterrent the case was severely
undermined by the trial and subsequent acquittal of Clive
Ponting.

Sarah Tisdall was a junior civil servant aged twenty-three,
employed in the private office of the Foreign Secretary and
engaged principally in clerical duties such as dealing with
mail and incoming telephone calls and assisting the Foreign
Secretary's private secretary. She had joined the diplomatic
service in July 1980 as a Grade 10 civil servant, the lowest
grade in the service. When she had joined the Foreign Office
she had signed a declaration drawing her attention to the
Official Secrets Act and the risk of prosecution if she
disclosed information without authority. She had been re-
vetted when she was posted to the Foreign Secretary's private
office in November 1982. She saw all documents that crossed
his desk except the 5 per cent or so which were marked 'For
the Secretary of State's eyes only'.

Until 21 October 1983 Miss Tisdall was considered a
willing, conscientious and hard-working employee; her work
record glistened with civil servants' comments which would
have done credit to any school report, such as 'absolutely
reliable', 'reliability unquestioned' and 'top marks for

reliability'. It was perhaps no more than her employers expected of a young woman who had an impressive nine O-levels and three A-levels. Her parents were both Plymouth doctors, and she had been privately educated at St Dunstan's School in Plymouth. This settled background had even led in 1976 to the Tisdalls appearing on a television quiz programme, *Ask the Family*.

On Thursday 20 October 1983, Michael Heseltine, then Secretary of State for Defence before falling victim to the Westland affair, prepared two memoranda. The first was entitled 'Deliveries of Cruise Missiles to RAF Greenham Common – Parliamentary and Public Statements'. It was marked 'Secret – UK Eyes A', which was classified at the second highest level of security. It was almost certainly over-classified but it was unquestionably a politically sensitive document. This was a briefing paper from Heseltine to the Prime Minister naming the day the missiles would arrive and outlining the statement to be made to Parliament and at press conferences on 1 November, which would follow the arrival of the much heralded Cruise missiles at RAF Greenham Common.

There was a further minute prepared by the Ministry of Defence and also marked 'secret', which dealt with the security arrangements that were to accompany the arrival of the Cruise missiles. This was an intriguing document, detailing how many police and troops should be kept in reserve to deal with any trouble from the Greenham Common ladies camped outside the base. To avoid demonstrations it was planned to bring the missiles in at first light; it had been noticed that the Greenham Common women disliked getting up early and were not at their best first thing. The memorandum also discussed what might happen if the women stormed the base. It was felt that it would be embarrassing if United States military personnel at the base shot any of the women. The suggestion was that it would be as well if there were a contingent of British troops at the base to reduce the possibility of US servicemen opening fire. The US State Department subsequently confirmed, on 12 November, that there were custodial units at Greenham with orders to shoot if necessary.

Six copies of these memoranda were circulated by the private office of the Secretary of State for Defence to the Home Secretary, the Foreign Secretary, the Lord President of the Council, the Lord Privy Seal, the Secretary of the Cabinet and, as a measure of the politically sensitive nature of the documents, to the Conservative Chief Whip. The memoranda arrived in the Foreign Secretary's office on 21 October; that afternoon Sir Geoffrey Howe left for Brussels, accompanied by his assistant private secretary. Miss Tisdall was able to read the documents and was shocked by what she saw. She later explained to the investigating police officer that she was not against nuclear weapons, but that she just did 'not agree with Cruise because we have no control . . . I am not a spy but I couldn't sit there and let that go through as I felt it was immoral. I felt that this was indecent, sort of doing it by the back door, and I couldn't stomach it. I felt that the public has a right to know what was being done to them.' In a *World in Action* television programme shown immediately after her trial, she said that she thought it was immoral that the Defence Secretary had decided he would not be accountable to Parliament that day.

These emotional if naïve reactions governed the impulsive conduct of Sarah Tisdall. It was, of course, not part of her job to have such thoughts. As Mr Justice Cantley was to observe at her trial after referring to her as a 'silly girl': 'Is not the important thing this, that any individuals in a position of trust should not be permitted to decide for themselves that what has been classified as secret should be published?'

Having read the two documents, Sarah Tisdall decided to make an extra photocopy of each of them. She made photocopies on the machine in her office and put them in her handbag. She does not seem to have given much thought as to how she might avoid detection. The copies she had made and kept bore the numbers and marks of the Foreign Secretary's copies. It was also possible to identify the machine on which her illicit copies were made from the markings on the machine's drums. It does not appear to have occurred to her to transcribe the text of the memoranda on to other sheets of paper, which would have made it more difficult to detect the source of the leak. Instead, she called at

Ryman's the stationers and bought a felt-tip pen, with which
she deleted the identifying marks in the margin of the
memoranda. When the first memorandum was returned to
the government, it was a simple matter to have the document
scientifically examined to see what had originally been
written on it. A pair of scissors would have been a better
investment than the felt-tip pen. Ironically, about the only
skill learnt by Miss Tisdall during her time in prison was the
ability to remove ink signatures from credit cards without
invalidating them. Such expertise might have come in handy
on 21 October 1983.

Sarah Tisdall took her photocopies to the offices of the
Guardian. Such was the degree of premeditation that it took
her some time to discover that the newspaper's offices were in
Farringdon Road and not in Farringdon Street – a difficulty
many have experienced. She had put the memoranda in a
brown envelope addressed to the *Guardian*'s political editor.
Had she been better informed, she would have delivered the
package to his office at the Houses of Parliament. She left it
anonymously with the doorman at six o'clock on Friday 21
October. Had the *Guardian* had any idea who had left it, the
subsequent débâcle might have been avoided, and some steps
might have been taken to prevent the source being disclosed.

On the following day, Saturday 22 October, a large CND
demonstration in London was planned. This made Miss
Tisdall's memoranda all the more topical and controversial.
After checking their authenticity, David Fairhall, the defence
correspondent, wrote an article for the front page, based on
the first memorandum but without specifically quoting from
it, entitled 'Whitehall sets November 1 Cruise Arrival'.

On Monday 31 October the contents of the first
memorandum were published under the headline 'Heseltine's
Briefing to Thatcher on Cruise'. The existence of the second
memorandum was not disclosed by the *Guardian* because of
its short-term security implications. It did however form the
basis of an article on 1 November headlined 'Guard Grows
for Greenham Nuclear Core', which led to questions being
raised in the House of Commons by Roland Boyes MP,
seeking an assurance that the protesters at the Greenham

Common air base would not be shot. Michael Heseltine replied: 'I categorically will give no such assurance.'

Details of the second memorandum appeared in the *Observer* on 18 December under the headline 'New Heseltine Secrets Leak'. Exactly how the *Observer* got the document is unclear. The source was not Miss Tisdall but most likely a *Guardian* journalist concerned at the way his newspaper had been forced by the courts to hand over the first memorandum. The government launched an enquiry into this leak, but the internal Whitehall investigation did not reveal the identity of the mole.

Word reached Peter Preston, the editor of the *Guardian*, through the lobby system of the government's hunt for the source of the leak. In the soul-searching which followed Miss Tisdall's imprisonment, Preston frankly admitted that his paper made a number of mistakes and that there was a failure of concentration on its part which meant it was unable to protect its source. The *Guardian*'s first difficulty was that, because the document had been delivered to the door anonymously, there was no particular journalist who was responsible for protecting his source. Instead three or four copies of the memoranda had been circulated and would be difficult to retrieve at short notice if there was a police raid to seize the documents. In so far as anyone had given the matter any thought, it was felt that the documents would have come from a much higher level than Miss Tisdall and that the source would have taken his or her own precautions. For her part, Sarah Tisdall assumed that the memoranda would be destroyed after use and the editor and his staff would take their precautions. The story sounds no better in Fleet Street than it would in a family planning clinic.

Obviously it would have been far better if these anonymously delivered memoranda had been destroyed after the articles were published. Under the procedures introduced at the *Guardian* after the Tisdall affair they would have been. However, the newspaper's attention was distracted by the United States invasion of Grenada and the blowing up of the US Embassy in Beirut by a suicide bomber.

Having learnt of the government's investigations into the

leak, Preston made what he now acknowledges to be his second mistake, calling in the paper's lawyers, Messrs Lovell White & King. In retrospect it would have been better if he had, of his own initiative, destroyed the memoranda forthwith, instead of taking the lawyers' considered and cautious advice. His concern was what he should do if the police arrived demanding the return of the documents. The advice Preston received was that he should not destroy the documents and that he should contact the solicitors if there were any further developments. He was advised that the newspaper had a defence to a claim for the return of the documents under Section 10 of the Contempt of Court Act 1981, which related to the protection of sources of information. Under Section 10, journalists could not be compelled to disclose their source of information unless it was established to the satisfaction of the court that disclosure was necessary in the interests of justice or national security or for the prevention of disorder or crime.

The issue in this case was whether the interests of national security overrode the fact that the return of the memoranda would reveal Miss Tisdall's identity as their source. It would at that stage – before any proceedings had been commenced – still have been possible for the *Guardian* to tear up the documents. They would no doubt have been criticised, but in retrospect it is a course they would have preferred to take rather than being responsible for Sarah Tisdall's detection and imprisonment.

The police never called at 119 Farringdon Road. On 11 November, three weeks after the *Guardian* had been given the memoranda, the editor received a letter demanding the return of the first memorandum not later than 14 November. Curiously the Treasurer Solicitor did not mention the more sensitive second document, although the government would at the very least have strongly suspected the newspaper of possessing a copy of that as well. Discretion being the better part of valour, the Treasury Solicitor did not ask the *Guardian* for the return of the second memorandum until he had received the first. When he did ask for the second document, he received a reply which could not have been written only by solicitors to the effect that they did not admit their clients had received the document, but that if they had, they make no admission that they did, no such document is now in their possession. No copies would have been made from it and no copies would have been given to any other person.'

In a rare show of defiance, the *Guardian*'s lawyers had not replied to the first request until 17 November, when they indicated that as the handwriting and markings on the photocopy memoranda might reveal the identity of the newspaper's source, the document would be returned with the markings excised. It was a sensible proposal, supported, it seemed, by Section 10 of the Contempt of Court Act 1981. The problem was that the government was not in the least interested in the text of the document, but rather in the opportunity that an examination of the photocopy would give for unearthing the whistle-blower. The government was no doubt encouraged by the success of British Steel in 1980 in its action to discover the identity of the mole who leaked to Granada Television documents alleging inefficiency and waste at the corporation. Granada had acted more boldly than the *Guardian* in that it had cut off all identifying markings on the papers before returning them. The television company was severely criticised by the courts for tampering with and mutilating the British Steel papers and was ordered to disclose its source. The mole owned up at that stage, revealing himself to be in the department responsible for destroying documents and, like Miss Tisdall, not a high-ranking officer as originally thought. Granada was thus spared the *Guardian*'s dilemma as to whether to reveal its source.

It was difficult for the *Guardian*'s lawyers to anticipate the alacrity with which the Court of Appeal would accept that national security would be imperilled if the opportunity to unearth the mole were lost. In fact the newspaper only just failed in its argument in the House of Lords, with the Law Lords ruling against it by the narrowest majority of three to two. By that time, however, Miss Tisdall had served her prison sentence, and the result was of interest only to the legal profession.

The *Guardian*'s suggestion of mutilating the documents did not find favour with the Treasury Solicitor, and on 22 November he issued a writ demanding the return of the first memorandum. Still there was no mention of the second paper. At first the case proceeded at the normal leisurely legal pace. It was not set down for hearing till 14 December, whereupon, most unusually, it was heard the very next day, before Mr Justice Scott. When the *Guardian* appealed against his ruling on 15 December, the case was heard at 2 p.m. that day. The wheels of justice ground exceedingly quick for the government, and the upshot was that the Treasury Solicitor was able to collect the document at 1 p.m. on 16 December. The speed (or, to use the words of the *Financial Times*, 'unseemly haste') at which the process moved was reminiscent of the passing of the Official Secrets Act in the middle of August 1911.

Mr Justice Scott found in favour of the government on the basis that it owned the document and was entitled to have it back. The Court of Appeal took a firmer line and rejected the defence put forward by the *Guardian* under Section 10 of the Contempt of Court Act 1981. The Master of the Rolls, Sir John Donaldson, ruled:

> The maintenance of national security requires that trustworthy servants in a position to mishandle highly classified documents passing from the Secretary of State for Defence to other Ministers shall be identified at the earliest possible moment and removed from their positions. This is blindingly obvious. Whether or not the editor acted in the public interest in publishing the document was not the issue. The Secretary of State's concern was quite different. It was that a servant of the Crown who handled classified documents had decided for himself whether classified information should be disseminated to the public. If he could do it on one occasion he might do it on others, when the safety of the State would be truly imperilled.

Lord Justice Griffiths held that national-security factors overrode the protection of sources: 'The threat to national security lies in the fact that someone probably in a senior position and with access to highly classified material cannot be trusted.'

Although the *Guardian* obtained leave to appeal to the House of Lords, it was given only an hour and a quarter to hand over the document. Having progressed this far down the legal road, the newspaper had no alternative but to give the memorandum back. The time for destroying the evidence had long since passed, and to destroy it at this stage would merely have resulted in large fines for contempt of court and in damage to the *Guardian*'s reputation as a responsible and law-abiding newspaper. In the end, and after much discussion, the prospect of the martyrdom of Peter Preston did not prevail, and support for the rule of law did. The Treasury Solicitor was handed the first memorandum on 16 December. Once the government had the photocopy returned there was not the same degree of urgency about the appeal, which was not heard for seven months – on 23 July 1984. Judgment was not delivered until three months later, on 25 October.

The photocopy was carefully scrutinised by the government investigators. It was soon apparent that it had been copied in the Foreign Secretary's private office. This meant that, with the Foreign Secretary and his assistant private secretary each having an unimpeachable alibi, the likely culprit was amongst the four people working in the registry, including Miss Tisdall. An index card which logged the copies made in Miss Tisdall's department revealed that she had legitimately taken photocopies of the memoranda on 21 October. The question was whether she had run off an extra copy.

On 2 November 1983 Sarah Tisdall had filled in a questionnaire denying that she was the person responsible. When the police came to interview her on 6 January 1984 they were virtually certain that she was the source of the leak. Her interview with Detective Chief Superintendent Hardy of the Serious Crime Squad was not her finest hour. According to the police she lapsed with suspicious ease into police-station jargon: 'What evidence have you got? It is no good just mouthing off about it, tell me what evidence you have got that shows I did it. Others in the office could have done it.' As she then burst into tears, Hardy remained unconvinced.

That weekend Miss Tisdall discussed the matter with her parents, and on Monday 9 January she presented herself at Scotland Yard and admitted that she had made the extra photocopies: 'I have come to tell you about the leak. I know you know it was me who did it but I couldn't tell you about it on Friday because I wanted to talk to my parents about it first. I have felt very guilty about the effect of all this on my colleagues.'

On 9 January, Miss Tisdall was charged with a breach of Section 2: that as a person holding office under the Crown she had on 21 October communicated classified information to a person to whom she was not authorised to communicate such information. That person was not identified, as the government thought better of prosecuting either the *Guardian*'s editor or defence correspondent, or both. As had happened in the Ponting case, news of an impending arrest had reached a right-of-centre newspaper before the defendant was told. On 8 January the *Sunday Telegraph* had run a story that the arrest of the mole was about to take place. Although it described the mole as working in the Cabinet Office, the paper turned out to have had reasonably accurate information, as the arrest took place the next day.

Much was made of Miss Tisdall's failure to own up to what she had done at the outset. Mr Justice Cantley, the trial judge – the man who had created a minor legal legend by referring to one of the defendants in the Norman Scott affair (needless to say not Jeremy Thorpe) as the sort of man who would have a bar in his lounge – criticised her in these terms: 'For two months your department was under suspicion. It is not a nice story.' But one is entitled to ask whether it was incumbent on Miss Tisdall to talk herself into prison. She had acted, however unwisely, out of conscience, and she was not specifically putting the blame on any other individual. As with the Ponting case, the denial of guilt was used as a means of questioning the motives and standards of the defendant.

Miss Tisdall refused offers of assistance from the *Guardian*, which not surprisingly felt some degree of responsibility for her predicament, although the paper paid her mortgage while she was in prison. She was represented on her legal-aid certificate by John Mathew QC. Unlike Ponting she decided to plead guilty – she felt she had committed an offence. This was sensible legal advice, but the prosecution wanted to make an example of Miss Tisdall. Having leaked the memoranda to a newspaper rather than to Tam Dalyell MP, she would have no real defence in law, but she could have defended the action on the grounds that she acted out of a sense of duty and in the public interest. However, her conduct did not bear the same examination as that of Ponting, and it is doubtful whether she had his resolve. She would probably have still been convicted, and might have received a longer sentence. It soon became evident that Mr Justice Cantley intended to send her to prison. He referred ominously to 'the climate of these times' and to the fact that 'people in positions of trust should not flout their obligations in the exercise of their own judgement'. With some justification he did not think much of her admission on 9 January, since it was by then clear that the police were satisfied that she was the person responsible: 'I do not see that she was minded to own up to this until the game was up. In the meantime she was putting her colleagues under suspicion of untrustworthiness – indeed, the whole department.'

Despite a skilful plea of mitigation based on the impulsive nature of her offence, the fact that she acted out of conscience and her excellent character, Mr Justice Cantley decided to send her to prison for six months:

Unfortunately, in these days, it is necessary to make perfectly clear, by example, that any person entrusted in confidence with material which is classified as secret, who presumes to give himself permission but decides that, none the less, it will be published, will not escape a custodial sentence by asserting, however honestly, that he thought it would do no harm, or even that he thought it was a good thing to do.

Following her conviction, Sarah Tisdall appeared on a pre-recorded *World in Action* television programme on 26 March 1984. She gave a remarkably impenitent account of the circumstances that led up to her arrest. She explained why she had sent the document to the *Guardian*:

> I felt it was immoral that the Secretary of State for Defence, who was accountable to Parliament, had decided he was not going to be accountable to Parliament on that particular, the day after the Cruise missiles arrived; he was going to wait until after they were here, and at the end of his allotted question time tell the House that they were here, and then get up and leave before the Opposition had time to react in the House, and go off to Greenham to have photographs taken.

She was equally uncompromising about the *Guardian*, although in retrospect she seems to have acquired some sympathy for the newspaper's dilemma when faced with the court order: 'I think the *Guardian* should have broken the law. Now that's a fairly hairy thing to say on television. I think they should have destroyed the document and then have told the government that they had destroyed it some time previously.'

Miss Tisdall was asked what her feelings were about the prospect of going to prison, and her answer showed no remorse:

> It is a possibility. I think it would be rather absurd to send me to prison for leaking that document which is meant to be a State secret: it was a party political document essentially. I don't feel I damaged national security in any great way by releasing that document. I feel I can cope with prison; it wouldn't be easy but you just have to grin and bear it.

Any minuscule chance she had of the sentence being reduced on appeal must surely have been dispelled by this programme. On 9 April 1984 the Lord Chief Justice, Lord

Lane, dismissed her appeal; he told her that it was dangerous arrogance in civil servants to pick and choose between laws. An immediate custodial sentence was, he said, unavoidable and appropriate. The judge was right to impose a deterrent sentence. It had been a gross breach of trust, and her sentence was not wrong in principle or in length. Miss Tisdall did not hear the words of the Lord Chief Justice, because she was not in court. Her counsel had advised her to sit outside to avoid the risk of the court asking her if she felt any remorse for what she had done!

After she had begun her sentence, her prison warder advised her not to tell the other inmates why she had been sent to prison. This only led them to believe she was a middle-class murderer, but the wide coverage of her case in the press and on television meant that she was more sympathetically treated by her fellow prisoners.

Short prison sentences are normally, as a matter of administrative convenience, served in a closed London prison, rather than a more salubrious open prison. In Sarah Tisdall's case the authorities decided to move her, after three weeks in Holloway, to an Elizabethan mansion at East Sutton Park, Maidstone, which served as an open prison. This was to stem the flow of distinguished visitors arriving at the gaol, the deliveries of flowers (which were filling every available bucket and thereby interfering with the prison plumbing) and the protesters outside the gates. They judged correctly that few if any of these people would travel out of London. Thereafter her only uninvited guest was a journalist from the *Sun* – who posed as a visitor in the hope of negotiating a world exclusive in the form of Miss Tisdall's prison diary, and on another occasion walked into the prison and photographed Miss Tisdall gardening.

For all the muttering about serious breach of trust, Miss Tisdall received considerable sympathy. Of some three thousand letters received by her family only twelve were hostile, and the publicity produced four proposals of marriage. Amnesty International considered but turned down the idea of making her a prisoner of conscience. She even had the doubtful pleasure of a re-enactment of her trial being performed around the country in a play self-consciously entitled *My Name Is Sarah Tisdall*.

The prison sentence was far too harsh a penalty. The argument that it was necessary to send twenty-three-year-old clerks to prison to deter other civil servants from leaking documents to the *Guardian* is surely a sorry reflection on the Civil Service. It is unlikely that this would deter the determined leaker acting on impulse or out of deep-rooted conviction; Ponting (Chapter 12) leaked his documents while Miss Tisdall was still in prison! The only result of the case is that any intending leaker would be likely to act in a more competent way than Miss Tisdall. If such a deterrent sentence was required, it is hard to see what had been happening for the last fourteen years when nobody had had to be imprisoned for such a leak. No evidence was produced to show, if such was the case, that there had been any dramatic upsurge in unauthorised disclosures. The Conservative government has pursued the prosecution of civil servants with some vigour. Between 1974 and 1978 there were no such prosecutions; since 1979 there had been nine.

A more likely conclusion is that the harsh sentence was related to the publicity the leak had obtained and to the politically sensitive nature of the documents disclosed; the speed with which a document sent to the Prime Minister reached the *Guardian* on 21 October had particularly angered the government.

Clearly Miss Tisdall's conduct in sending the memoranda to the *Guardian* entitled her employers to sack her. But was it necessary to prosecute her? Is it necessary for civil servants to be kept in line by the sight of the odd colleague standing in the dock at the Old Bailey or tending the gardens at East Sutton Park? If it is, should not the same principle be extended to ICI, British Telecom and the BBC?

The government's treatment of Miss Tisdall contrasted with that accorded in December 1983 to Ian Willmore, a twenty-five-year-old administrative trainee at the Department of Employment. Willmore leaked to *Time Out* a memorandum in which the Master of the Rolls, Sir John Donaldson, had given advice to Michael Quinlan, the

Permanent Secretary in the Department of Employment, on the future of the law relating to industrial relations. The Attorney-General, Sir Michael Havers QC, decided against prosecuting Willmore, saying that Section 2 should be used sparingly and only when absolutely necessary. There is no justification for the very different treatment of Miss Tisdall and Willmore, except the embarrassment which would have been occasioned at any trial of Willmore.

Even more puzzling was the failure of the government to prosecute the *Guardian*. The newspaper clearly would have known that these documents, marked 'secret', were covered by the Official Secrets Act, and that whoever had sent them to the *Guardian* had done so in breach of the Act. No doubt it made very good political sense not to prosecute the *Guardian*, and someone presumably recollected what had happened in the *Sunday Telegraph* case (Chapter 9). The *Guardian* would not have pleaded guilty; nor, one imagines, would its editor, Peter Preston, have gone quietly to his open prison for six months. Attempts to explain the omission to prosecute the *Guardian* were distinctly unconvincing. Havers told Parliament that there was not the same element of breach of trust in the case of the *Guardian* as there was with Miss Tisdall. But perhaps Sir Michael also remembered from his days as a criminal advocate the judges who justified heavy punishments for receivers of stolen property on the basis that if there were no receivers there would be no burglars. Sir Michael's second ground looked more plausible when he said that such evidence as there was against the *Guardian* was obtained by the compulsory process of a civil action and that it would be unjust in those circumstances to bring a charge based on evidence the *Guardian* had been compelled by the courts to disgorge. While that seems a reasonable proposition, the facts were that the newspaper had published a series of articles based on memoranda which were classified as secret and had reached its offices within forty-eight hours of their leaving Heseltine's desk. The newspaper had published the text of the first memorandum on 31 October, eleven days before the Treasury Solicitor wrote to it for the first time. The *Guardian* had therefore on 31 October itself supplied the

Attorney-General with sufficient evidence that it was in possession of this document in breach of the Official Secrets Act 1911. At that stage it scarcely needed the services of either Sherlock Holmes or a civil action for the recovery of the documents to produce evidence for a charge under Section 2 against the paper. The civil action was concerned with establishing the mole's identity rather than obtaining evidence against the *Guardian* for a possible prosecution.

The last act of bloodletting came in a vitriolic exchange between Peter Preston and David Caute, a writer who attacked the editor (who had rejected his 4,000-word article on the Tisdall affair) for his failure to protect Miss Tisdall as a source and for complying with the court's order to return the documents. His article was published in *Granta*. He referred to the editor as disingenuous, and commented on his attitude of *sauve qui peut*, his betrayal of Miss Tisdall and his naiveté. Preston naturally did not find himself able to agree with this criticism, and he replied in a letter dated 14 May 1984:

> Long ago I made a private vow never to sue in the rough business of journalism; and I'll try to hold to that view now. Others involved, of course, have no such hangups. But if you would like to sue me on my considered view that (in this instance) you are a devious, sloppy and malevolent operator with a rare disregard for fact and a rare talent for obsessed distortion, then that would be a different matter.

Caute did not sue, but that did not prevent a further diatribe from Preston, which took the form of what he termed a fairy tale about a man whose burning political rage had laid a career to waste. This man he described as small and podgy with a crooked grin and a shiny suit, reduced to pursuing random passions. Caute appeared unmoved by this and printed these exchanges in a book he subsequently wrote in close conjunction, it seems, with his publisher's libel laywers, full of such phrases as 'the cool gaze of the young woman in the dock'.

The very last act in the saga was the hearing of the appeal by the *Guardian* to the House of Lords against the decision on 16 December 1983 that it must hand over the first memorandum. In contrast to the unseemly haste of the earlier hearings, judgment was not given until 25 October 1984. While the government was scrupulous about not prosecuting the *Guardian*, it did not seem greatly to care what should happen to Miss Tisdall if it was decided by the House of Lords that the newspaper should not have been forced to hand over the memorandum to the government. She had by then served her sentence.

The hearing in the House of Lords was more academic and less dramatic than those in the lower courts. The issue was whether the right to protect a journalist's source under Section 10 of the Contempt of Court Act 1981 was in this case defeated by the Crown's claim of a threat to national security. Had the evidence put forward by the Crown discharged the burden of proving that disclosure of the document was necessary in the interest of national security?

On the point of law in the appeal the *Guardian* was successful in its wide interpretation of Section 10 of the 1981 Act and in its assertion that the burden of proof of establishing that disclosure was necessary on the ground of national security fell on the government. Only by the narrowest of margins did the *Guardian* fail to establish that the Court of Appeal had been wrong to order it to hand back the memoranda, a result which would have been highly embarrassing because Sarah Tisdall had by then served her sentence. The *Guardian* could perhaps count itself unlucky that in a court of five Law Lords there were not just one but two chairmen of the Security Commission – Lord Diplock and Lord Bridge of Harwich, who both found against the newspaper (with Lord Roskill).

The Crown's case, that the return of the documents was necessary in the interests of national security, was to be found in paragraph 6 of the affidavit of Richard Hastie-Smith, the principal establishment officer at the Ministry of Defence, who was responsible for the security of records and other ministry documents dealing with national security. He stated:

The fact that a document marked 'Secret' addressed by the

Secretary of State for Defence to the Prime Minister on 20 October 1983 which was concerned with a matter of great significance in relation to the defence of the United Kingdom and the North Atlantic Treaty Organisation had, by 31 October 1983, found its way into the possession of a national newspaper, is of the gravest importance to the continued maintenance of national security. It also represents a threat to the United Kingdom's relations with her allies, who cannot be expected to continue to entrust Her Majesty's Government with secret information which may be liable to unauthorised disclosure [the scarecrow as opposed to the jigsaw argument] even though its circulation is restricted to the innermost circles of government. Thus the identity of the person or persons who disclosed or assisted in the disclosure of the above mentioned document to the defendant must be established in order that national security should be preserved.

This affidavit was sworn before Miss Tisdall had been unmasked as the mole and when there was still a possibility that the documents had been leaked by a high-ranking civil servant. It is interesting nevertheless to compare Hastie-Smith's claims about potential damage to national security with the actual damage assessment given to Mr Justice Cantley at Miss Tisdall's trial in March 1984:

The reasons for the memoranda being classified as secret were that the following consequences could have followed from their passing into unauthorised hands:

(1) It had for obvious security reasons been the policy of successive British Governments that plans for the movement of nuclear weapons should be kept secret. Their disclosure on this occasion could have heightened the risk of attempts by people opposed to the deployment of Cruise missiles to interrupt the deliveries, thus heightening the risk of possible violent confrontation between security forces and demonstrators.

(2) There was a potentially major source of embarrassment to Britain in its relations to those allies who had been

consulted about the delivery timetable. In retrospect, it is not thought that the publication of the information contained in the Defence Secretary's minute – and subsequently, of the minute itself – has caused any major embarrassment to our relations with our allies, but it might have involved some erosion in the confidence of our allies in Britain as a partner to confidential exchanges. The position in this respect might have been a good deal worse if the delivery of the Cruise missiles had not, in the end, gone off smoothly.

We do not believe that the revelations proved to be of use to potential enemies, although they might have provided the Soviet Union with an opportunity to try to use the information published in its public campaign against NATO's decision to deploy the new United States missiles in Europe.

Lord Fraser of Tullybelton could not accept that the government had made out its case on national security. If the case was so urgent, why had the government waited twenty-one days from the *Guardian* article of 31 October until demanding the return of the first memorandum on 11 November? He was not particularly impressed by the fact that someone had marked the document 'Secret', nor by the bald assertion by Hastie-Smith that the leak represented a threat to the United Kingdom's relations with its allies. There was no evidence of any such threat. Lord Fraser referred to Lord Justice Griffith's speculation that the leaker was probably in a senior position as an example of the danger of relying on inferences which may have seemed reasonable at the time but were in fact unsound.

Lord Fraser was followed in similar vein by Lord Scarman. He felt that the evidence fell far short of what was required to prove that disclosure was against the interests of national security. He was not satisfied that Hastie-Smith had shown himself qualified to make the assertions in his affidavit on the question of national security. Lord Scarman was particularly unimpressed by the fact that the first memorandum was marked 'Secret':

The memorandum could well have been marked 'Secret' because it would have been politically embarrassing for the government if Parliament or the public were to learn of what was in the government's mind as to the publicity to be given to this politically sensitive matter before a parliamentary statement was made. The judge was offered no enlightenment on these matters.

Although the *Guardian* lost, it had come remarkably close to winning. The Law Lords were prepared to analyse the bald assertions of threats to national security by the government, and two of their number found against the government. No criticism was made of the fact, by then revealed, that the newspaper had destroyed the second memorandum. Indeed, Lord Diplock commended Preston's sense of responsibility in not publishing it and arranging for all copies in the newspaper's possession to be destroyed. There was also further consolation that the paper did not have to pay the government's legal costs, despite technically losing; each side paid its own costs.

No harm was done by Sarah Tisdall's revelations, except that the government felt it expedient to hold up the arrival of the Cruise missiles until 15 November. It would make the task of government very difficult if any civil servant could leak any document of which he or she happened to disapprove. Miss Tisdall's justification of her action – that she was entitled to know why these documents were being kept secret – is unconvincing. A government servant must accept a degree of discipline if she works for the Civil Service. However it is doubtful that it is necessary to throw people like Miss Tisdall into prison; summary dismissal is a severe penalty, and it is not easy to obtain a comparable job – as Miss Tisdall found on her release once the press lost interest in her. She accepted a job with the left-wing Merlin Press.

Profumo without the Sex: Clive Ponting

The Argentinian heavy cruiser *General Belgrano* was built in the 1930s, saw service in the Second World War and survived Pearl Harbor as the USS *Phoenix*. At 8 p.m. on 2 May 1982 it was torpedoed by the British submarine *Conqueror*; 368 of the 1,100 Argentinian sailors perished, and the Falklands war started in earnest. For all the doubts that have subsequently been raised as to the wisdom of sinking the *Belgrano*, there remains a convincing military argument for having taken this action at the time. The *Belgrano* was the largest ship in the southern group of the Argentinian fleet, which had put to sea on 26 April from the port of Ushuaia in Tierra del Fuego. With insufficient air cover the ships in the British task force were very vulnerable, and their margin of error was small. The Falkland Islands were 8,000 miles from Britain but only 500 miles from the Argentine mainland. The Argentinians had installed a garrison of 9,000 men on the Falklands. They had a regular army of 130,000 and no less than 19,500 men in their air force, which was equipped with modern aircraft and Exocet missiles. Pitted against this was the task force of 28,000 men. On 30 April the Argentinians had stated that all British vessels within 200 miles of the mainland and the Falklands would be considered hostile, and on 1 May Argentinian aircraft had flown their first mission against the task force after Port Stanley airfield had been bombed.

On the evening of 1 May, GCHQ decoded an Argentinian signal that the two northern groups should engage the British fleet. It was feared that the *Belgrano* and its group would join in this attack. In fact the attack was cancelled, and at the time that the *Belgrano* was sunk it was still outside the 200-mile total exclusion zone that the British had imposed around the Falklands. It had been steaming away from the Falklands for eleven hours.

The problem for the British government was less the justification of the sinking in military terms than its slightly suspect position in international law and its desire to maintain the support of its allies despite sinking the *Belgrano* outside the exclusion zone and without proper warning. The government's awareness of its predicament led to a series of evasive and on occasions untruthful answers by ministers, which attracted needless suspicion to the government's conduct. It also resulted in an able civil servant, Clive Ponting, sacrificing his career in the Ministry of Defence by leaking confidential memoranda and in his standing trial at the Central Criminal Court on a charge of communicating official information without authority, contrary to Section 2 of the Official Secrets Act.

The intricacies of the *Belgrano* affair are reminiscent of the Schleswig-Holstein Question in the nineteenth century, of which Lord Palmerston said: 'Only three people understood it, and one is dead, one is in a lunatic asylum, I myself was the third and I have forgotten it.' However, although most people have not followed the details, there is a widespread belief that the government's behaviour following the end of the Falklands campaign was discreditable. Michael Heseltine's skilful performance in Parliament after Ponting's acquittal prevented a major scandal, but the government's Falklands image, which had helped it decisively win the 1983 general election, was tarnished. The government's performance as regards veracity earned the affair the accolade of 'Profumo without the sex'.

Five days after the Argentinian invasion of the Falklands on 2 April 1982, the British government had imposed its 200-mile maritime exclusion zone. On 23 April it had issued a warning to the Argentinians that the United Kingdom would take such additional measures as might be required in the exercise of its rights of self-defence under Article 51 of the Charter of the United Nations:

In this connection Her Majesty's Government now wishes to make clear that any approach on the part of Argentinian warships, including submarines, naval auxiliaries or military aircraft, which could amount to a threat to interfere with the mission of British forces in the South Atlantic will encounter the appropriate response. All Argentine aircraft, including civil aircraft engaging in surveillance of these British forces, will be regarded as hostile and are liable to be dealt with accordingly.

This warning was relied upon by the government to justify sinking the *Belgrano*. However, the stance is questionable. On 28 April, John Nott, then Secretary of State for Defence, announced that the maritime exclusion zone for Argentinian warships and naval auxiliaries would become a total exclusion zone, applying 'not only to Argentine warships and Argentine naval auxiliaries, but also to any other ship, whether naval or merchant vessel, which is operating in support of the illegal occupation of the Falkland Islands by Argentine forces'.

On 29 April it appeared that the diplomatic negotiations with the Argentinian government, being conducted through the US Secretary of State, Alexander Haig, had collapsed. At a meeting of the British War Cabinet on 30 April, it was agreed that the airfield at Port Stanley should be bombed – which was done on 1 May – and that the Argentinian aircraft carrier *25 De Mayo* should be attacked outside the exclusion zone – which was not done, because the nuclear submarine *Splendid* was unable to locate it.

Some unease was felt within the War Cabinet, principally by Francis Pym, the Foreign Secretary, and the Attorney-General, Sir Michael Havers, at the general and vague nature of the warning given to the Argentinians on 23 April. There were, after all, 1,200 sailors on the *25 De Mayo*. On 1 May Pym recommended that a specific warning be given. He prepared a document entitled 'Notification to the Argentine Government' in which he pointed out that the British government had decided that the *25 De Mayo* was not to enter what was the exclusion zone and that if it did the ship would be considered hostile and dealt with accordingly.

Pym's document went on to say:

> If any attack anywhere in the South Atlantic is made upon
> British naval or air forces by an Argentine unit, all other
> Argentine naval units operating on the high seas, including
> the carrier the *25 De Mayo*, will be considered, regardless
> of their location, hostile and are liable to be dealt with
> accordingly.

No such warning was sent, but on 2 May the British rules of
engagement were changed at an informal meeting of the War
Cabinet:

> Because of the proximity of Argentine bases and the
> distances that hostile forces can cover undetected,
> particularly at night and in bad weather, Her Majesty's
> Government warns that any Argentine warship or military
> aircraft which are found more than twelve nautical miles
> from the Argentine coast will be regarded as hostile and are
> liable to be dealt with accordingly.

The change in the rules of engagement was signalled to
HMS *Conqueror* at 13.30 on 2 May, six and a half hours
before the *Belgrano* was sunk. Yet no attempt was made until
7 May to communicate this fundamental change to the
Argentinians, by which time it was too late for at least 368
sailors.

The *Belgrano* had first been detected by sonar by HMS
Conqueror at 4.00 p.m. (local time) on 30 April. It was then
sighted at 10.00 (local) the next day. An intelligence analyst at
Northwood Naval Headquarters wrongly concluded from
the GCHQ intercepts that the *Belgrano* had been ordered on
to the attack. This appeared to be confirmed by a further
Argentinian message intercepted at 7.55 p.m. It was thought
that the *Belgrano* would be part of a pincer-movement
attack.

At 00.07 British time on 2 May the Argentinian order
calling off the attack was intercepted at GCHQ, and it was
repeated at 5.19 a.m. The *Belgrano* did not however turn

round and head for port until 9 a.m. The assessment by Sir
Terence Lewin (who became Lord Lewin after the campaign),
Chief of the Defence Staff, of the situation at 9.15 a.m. was
based on the early intelligence reports, which predicted that
the *Belgrano* would turn north and join in the attack on the
British task force. Lewin concluded that 'here was an
excellent opportunity to knock off a major unit of the
Argentinian fleet'. After an early morning session of the joint
Chiefs of Staff he went down to Chequers for a War Cabinet
meeting with his now incorrect intelligence reports and
emerged from this meeting with the authority to sink the
Belgrano. It would have been difficult for the War Cabinet to
disagree with the advice tendered by Lewin.

At 3 p.m. on 2 May *Conqueror* had signalled the
Belgrano's change of course and had earlier communicated
the ship's position to Northwood, by which time it had been
steaming west for six hours. Three signals were sent, at 2
p.m., 4 p.m. and 6 p.m., to sink the *Belgrano*. It was sunk by
two torpedoes at 8 p.m.

This was an understandable decision in the context of a
campaign being waged at a distance of 8,000 miles, with the
attendant risks of a major British vessel being lost as a result
of Argentinian action. Clive Ponting did not criticise the
decision to sink the *Belgrano*. Suggestions that the *Belgrano*
was sunk to scupper the Peruvian peace initiative seem to
belong to the conspiracy theory of history. But having set an
exclusion zone, and with no overtly hostile action by the
Belgrano, it was reprehensible to sink the *Belgrano* outside
that zone without any warning. One can well imagine the
outrage and the demands for bombing Buenos Aires that
would have arisen if the Argentinians had done something
similar to the British. For all the claims of national security
and operational reasons, it would seem that the government's
reticence about what really happened when the *Belgrano* was
sunk was born of a sense of unease at the British behaviour.

The misleading accounts of the sinking of the *Belgrano*
began on 4 May 1982. If the government had wished to
arouse suspicion about its conduct, it could scarcely have set
about it better. First, John Nott said that the *Belgrano* was

closing on the task force when it was sunk. Mrs Thatcher, in the television programme *On the Spot* on 24 May 1983, told a schoolteacher, Mrs Diana Gould (later to write a book, *On the Spot: The Sinking of the 'Belgrano'*), that the *Belgrano* was *not* sailing away from the Falklands when it was hit. In fact, the *Belgrano* had been heading westwards away from the Falklands for eleven hours.

Secondly, Nott told the House of Commons that the *Belgrano* had been spotted by one of our submarines at 8 p.m. on 2 May. He was wrong again. The *Belgrano* had been sighted by *Conqueror* at 2 p.m. on 1 May. Nott was, of course, speaking in the middle of a rapidly changing military campaign. However, his inaccurate statement found its way into the White Paper *The Falklands Campaign: The Lessons*, which was published in December 1982; apparently the error was not corrected because, astonishingly, it was said that such information could have helped the Argentinians. The error also appeared in the official dispatch published in the *London Gazette* in December 1982, by Sir John Fieldhouse, the Commander-in-Chief of the Fleet, in charge of operations in the South Atlantic. However, Fieldhouse complained that the date of the sighting had been changed in the published version of his dispatch from 1 May, which he had originally given, to 2 May. It seems that the change was made at Northwood and it was justified by the Prime Minister as having been done 'in order to protect sensitive operational and intelligence information'. By the time that this false information was published, Admiral Woodward had in a lecture on 20 October 1982 revealed that *Conqueror* had sighted the *Belgrano* before 2 May. Commander Wreford-Brown of HMS *Conqueror* had himself – presumably at some risk of being prosecuted under the Official Secrets Act – disclosed in an interview for the book *Our Falklands War: The Men of the Task Force* by Geoffrey Underwood, which was published in May 1983, that he had been following the *Belgrano* for thirty hours before it was sunk.

Thirdly, John Nott also said on 4 May that the two destroyers which accompanied the *Belgrano* were not attacked in any way, and that only two torpedoes had been fired. In fact the *Hippolyto Bouchard* had been hit by a third torpedo, which did not explode.

Fourthly – not so serious although no less significant – Nott told the House of Commons on 5 May: 'The actual decision to launch a torpedo was clearly one taken by the submarine commander, but that decision was taken within very clear rules of engagement that had been settled in London and discussed by the government.' Although this was literally true the decision had been taken by the War Cabinet. Commander Wreford-Brown said as much when HMS *Conqueror* returned to Faslane in July 1982, sporting, in an exhibition of appalling taste, the skull and crossbones. It seems that the flag was home-made rather than standard naval issue. He was asked by a journalist why he had sunk the *Belgrano* and answered that he had been acting on direct orders from Northwood. This reply appeared to contradict Nott's statement and aroused the interest of Tam Dalyell MP.

Dalyell launched himself on a campaign to discover the truth about the sinking of the *Belgrano*. In March 1984 the newly appointed head of the Ministry of Defence's Secretariat 5, Clive Ponting, was requested to prepare the replies to a letter dated 6 March from Denzil Davies MP, the opposition spokesman on defence. Davies had raised questions about discrepancies between the official accounts of the sinking of the *Belgrano* and those appearing in the books *The Sinking of the 'Belgrano'* by Desmond Rice and Arthur Gavshon and *Our Falklands War: The Men of the Task Force* by Geoffrey Underwood. There was also a letter dated 19 March from Dalyell raising nine questions about the *Belgrano*.

Ponting had been a civil servant for fourteen years. He had been awarded the OBE in 1980 at the unusually early age of thirty-five, in recognition of the work he had done with Sir Derek Rayner, the Prime Minister's adviser on efficiency in Whitehall. Ponting had helped to draw up recommendations which should have produced capital savings of £12 million and annual economies of up to £4 million. He had been invited to attend a Cabinet meeting to make his report. He had discovered, for example, that the armed services employed 175 servicemen to make false teeth for other servicemen at twice the price of commercial laboratories. Despite his evident talents, however, he had succeeded in upsetting the ministry, and found himself on 'gardening leave' – that is, at home without a job but on full pay. This was perhaps due not only to the unwelcome nature of some of his recommendations but also to the intellectual contempt Ponting was said to have for those he did not consider too bright. The fact that the civil servant did not have a job had been brought to the attention of the Prime Minister. Mrs Thatcher, in a decision she no doubt subsequently regretted, interceded for Ponting with Sir Ian Bancroft, the head of the Civil Service, who found him a suitable position within a few days. This decision was no doubt also regretted by John Stanley, Minister for the Armed Forces, on whom Ponting seems to have vented some of his intellectual scorn and whom Ponting has credited with the remark, 'Margaret Thatcher is too good for this country. The country does not deserve such an outstanding person. She is the greatest leader this country has been privileged to have this century, and that includes Winston Churchill.'

Prior to his appointment at the beginning of March 1984 to Defence Secretariat 5, where he advised on current naval operations and short-term future plans for the Navy, Ponting had been head of the Ministry of Defence's Legal Secretariat, DS 15. Ironically, this involved him in advising on whether servicemen should be prosecuted for breaches of the Official Secrets Act. The consent of the Attorney-General was not formally required for prosecutions against servicemen, but as a matter of consistency his advice was sought. Ponting would examine the cases and if they were sufficiently serious would pass them to the Director of Public Prosecutions, who would then refer them to the Attorney-General for his decision. At first it seems that Ponting enjoyed his work in the Defence Secretariat; in his book *The Right to Know* he speaks of this being 'the level at which there is a real interface between higher level policy-making, dealing direct with ministers, and the execution of policy'. However, prior to making the unauthorised disclosures which led to his being charged, he apparently became disillusioned with the Civil Service. He took exception to the wasteful military bureaucracy and disliked the fact that the Civil Service was full of people from Oxford and Cambridge (Ponting had obtained a first-class degree at Reading University).

By March 1984 Ponting's talents were being put to rather unusual use in that he was having to advise the government whether it should give frank replies to the questions raised by Davies and Dalyell. Ponting had been asked to produce two draft replies for the questions raised by Davies: one giving more information and admitting that the *Belgrano* had been sighted on 1 May, and the other maintaining the policy of non-disclosure. In a covering note Ponting said that the revelation of the 1 May date did not breach any operational or intelligence restraints, but it did go against a number of statements already made. If the new date was given it might, he correctly surmised, encourage more questions from Dalyell.

Heseltine did not, at that stage, use either draft answer but on 22 March asked Ponting to produce a chronological breakdown of the events leading to the sinking of the *Belgrano* to see how much information could be published in response to Davies and Dalyell without compromising security. Over a period of four days Ponting produced a full narrative of the events in London and the South Atlantic of the period 7 April to 7 May 1982, based on all the intelligence available at the time.

This document became known as the 'Crown Jewels'. Containing as it did a detailed analysis of the British Government's signals intelligence during the period, the document carried an extremely high security classification and a firm restriction on who could see it. It ran to some twenty-five pages and had eighty-six numbered serials or paragraphs. Originally six copies were produced, and the paper was considered so secret that not even the House of Commons Foreign Affairs Committee was allowed to see it. However, eighteen extra copies had to be made for the trial of Ponting, and in November 1984 the Government relented

and allowed the Foreign Affairs Committee to see a copy –
but on the basis that the committee was forbidden to make
copies and that any notes must be destroyed after each
session of the committee, which had to be attended by
Ministry of Defence officers. There was never any suggestion
that Ponting leaked any part of the 'Crown Jewels', but their
existence enabled the Crown to surround the trial with a veil
of secrecy and to require the court to go into secret session on
four occasions.

On 30 March, Heseltine presided over a three-hour
meeting at which the 'Crown Jewels' were discussed.
Heseltine was said to have brandished a copy of the Gavshon-
Rice book on the *Belgrano* and commented, 'I want to be
quite sure that there is not a Watergate here.' Inevitably it
later became known as Underwatergate. The question of the
Official Secrets Act was raised at that meeting, ironically by
Ponting. In response to Stanley's remark that he thought they
should claim everything was classified and refuse to answer
any of the questions, the civil servant replied that, if this was
going to be the answer, 'What are we going to reply when
somebody asks when are we going to prosecute Commander
Wreford-Brown under the Official Secrets Act for giving out
the date a year ago?'

Following this meeting the Prime Minister wrote to Davies
on 4 April 1984, admitting for the first time that the *Belgrano*
had been detected on 1 May. Ponting then drafted replies to
Dalyell's questions. These were not used by Heseltine, who
sent a curt answer that there was nothing he could usefully
add to the Prime Minister's correspondence. This greatly
upset Ponting. He considered it an abrupt reversal of the
decision taken only a couple of weeks earlier to start telling
the truth. He had 'never come across anything so blatant in
my fifteen years in the Civil Service. It was a deliberate
attempt to conceal information which would reveal that
ministers had gravely misled Parliament for the previous two
years.'

Ponting took the extraordinary step on 24 April of writing
an unsigned note, which later led to the suggestion that he
committed perjury at his trial, telling Dalyell that none of the

information was in fact classified, and that it was Stanley's fault that he had not received a proper answer. His anonymous letter suggested that Dalyell should press for answers to his original questions and ask some new questions about the changes in the rules of engagement, which Dalyell subsequently did, using Ponting's words. The letter ended with the exhortation: 'You are on the right track, keep going.'

Dalyell was encouraged by the note to press for replies to his questions on 1 May. He did not receive them. The excitement seems to have been too much for the MP, who was banned from the House of Commons for five days for calling the Prime Minister a liar. The bizarre position was reached where Ponting was required to draft an answer to a letter from Dalyell based on information he had himself leaked. Ponting's views on the need for disclosure were set out in a minute he sent on 9 May, but on 14 May, Heseltine wrote another curt letter to Dalyell indicating that he saw no purpose in prolonging the correspondence. On 27 May, Dalyell again pressed for replies, on this occasion closely following the wording of Ponting's note of 24 April.

The conduct of the campaign was at the same time being considered by the House of Commons Foreign Affairs Committee. On 11 June 1984, Francis Pym, Foreign Secretary at the time of the campaign, referred to the many changes in the rules of engagement. Although there had been a large number of minor changes, the really significant alteration in the rules of engagement had been that of 2 May 1982, which was not communicated to the Argentinians until 7 May 1982. On 20 June one of the members of the Foreign Affairs Committee, the Labour MP Nigel Spearing, asked Baroness Young, Minister of State at the Foreign Office, to provide details of all changes in the rules of engagement.

A civil servant at the Ministry of Defence, Michael Legge, the head of DS 11, was instructed to reply to his request. He produced a minute dated 6 July 1984. His reasoned advice was that the committee should not be provided with a note listing all changes, but should merely be given a general narrative to avoid the difficulties of security classification and the need to spell out all the rules of engagement. Bearing in mind that hostilities still existed between the United Kingdom and Argentina, it seemed a tenable opinion, which was after all submitted for consideration to the minister answerable in Parliament. The paper was marked 'confidential', but this security classification was later removed. The 6 July minute was the result of co-operation between DS 11 and Ponting's department, DS 15. Ponting did not personally take part in its drafting, but his deputy, Nicholas Darms, did. Ponting's case at court was weakened by the evidence of Darms and a colleague, who asserted that he had been informed of the contents of the document before it was sent. This was disputed by Ponting, who said he had never seen the Legge memorandum, which in any case diverged significantly from the line he had taken at the Ministry of Defence.

What the committee received in July was a short memorandum from Stanley merely indicating that the rules of engagement were changed very frequently during the operation between 2 April and 15 June 1982. This was the breaking-point as far as Ponting was concerned. He felt that this highly selective and slanted memorandum was 'deliberately misleading in an attempt to conceal the information'. Ministers were not involved in blocking an enquiry by a select committee, which had the right to enquire and get fruitful answers. Ministers were also going to provide a misleading memorandum that would at best be 'consistent with previous statements' and had the clear purpose of blocking any further enquiries. The memorandum did not reveal that the attack on *25 de Mayo* was authorised on 30 April, that the changes in the rules of engagement applied not just to the *Belgrano* but to all warships and that the Argentinians were not informed of this 2 May decision to change the rules of engagement until 7 May.

On 16 July 1984 Ponting therefore put in a typewritten envelope addressed to Dalyell at the House of Commons a copy of the confidential Legge minute and the first page of his April 1984 draft answers to Dalyell's first six questions. Even when leaking this document, Ponting still retained some of his civil servant's training, feeling it inappropriate to reveal to

Dalyell the answers to his questions on the tracking of the *25 de Mayo*. He posted the package in Paddington. Ponting does not seem to have anticipated the possibility that Dalyell would hand over the documents and the envelope in which they were sent to Sir Anthony Kershaw MP, the chairman of the House of Commons Foreign Affairs Committee. It was a simple matter of tracing the sender, as the documents had a date stamp of 16 July, which was the date it had gone up to Ponting's department, and the envelope showed that the letter had been posted on 16 July. He would have done better to type out the document on a separate piece of paper; the style and the Whitehall jargon should have persuaded an alert outsider of its authenticity. The leak was also traced to Ponting by a misplaced punch-hole in the memorandum and a horseshoe smudge on the copying paper. When the police came to see Ponting they took him off for a reassuring cup of tea in the Ministry of Defence canteen while a third officer when through his office desk to check Dalyell's copy against Ponting's.

As happened with the 'Crown Jewels' themselves, what had originally been refused was, in the light of subsequent events, granted to the committee. In December 1984 the committee was provided with a complete list of the changes in the rules of engagement.

With Ponting's known opposition to the government's policy, it had been fairly easy to trace the leak to him. Ponting was seen by Detective Chief Inspector Thomas Hughes of the Ministry of Defence police. The first interview was a fairly informal affair; Hughes tastefully illustrated his notes with a doodle of the *Belgrano* sinking beneath the waves. Ponting was seen again on 10 August and shown a copy of the draft letter of April to Dalyell. He said, 'Good God, you don't suspect me?' He was interviewed further that day and allegedly said, 'I can see that there is strong circumstantial evidence against me, but honestly I didn't do it,' although he denied saying this. His denial was weakened by his further comments: 'This country has nothing to hide, so why hide it? Most of the information is unclassified'; and (in a phrase reminiscent of a number of people charged under the Official

Secrets Act), 'The whole thing has blown out of proportion.' He asked to see his wife, Sally, who also worked at the Ministry of Defence, and made a statement to the police: 'I am sorry I have breached the trust the department had in me and that I photocopied and sent the two documents to Tam Dalyell.' Ponting said that he felt that Cabinet ministers were trying to save their political positions because they were not prepared to answer legitimate questions that were being asked about a matter of considerable public interest. He wished to express his regret for his actions and any embarrassment he might have caused the department. Ponting's explanation of his initial equivocation was that he wanted to be sure that the case was being dealt with as an internal disciplinary matter rather than as a breach of the Official Secrets Act resulting in his prosecution.

There was initially some doubt as to what to do with Ponting. Advice was tendered to the Ministry of Defence by the ministry's Chief Constable, John Bailey, that no prosecution should be brought, 'in view of the very limited nature of the potential damage to national security'. Heseltine's view appears to have been that he was shocked at Ponting's flagrant breach of confidence, but that he left it to the law officers to decide whether or not to prosecute. Ponting has said that he was told by senior Ministry of Defence officials that it would be the end of the matter if he was prepared to resign from the Civil Service. He says that he was told by Detective Chief Inspector Hughes in early August that officials had concluded that this was not a case for the Official Secrets Act and that it was not clear that an offence had been committed because the documents had been sent only to the Palace of Westminster. His recollection was that Hughes said that nobody had told the Prime Minister yet; he had been given the impression that if he was prepared to resign, this would be the end of the matter.

On the strength of these conversations Ponting did resign with effect from 10 August. However, following his confession, further consideration was given to his prosecution. Sir Ewen Broadbent, the second permanent secretary at the Ministry of Defence, referred the matter to the Director of Public Prosecutions because of Ponting's seniority and the subject-matter of the charge. The ministry was anxious that there should not appear to be one rule for female clerical assistants such as Sarah Tisdall and another for assistant secretaries with the OBE. At 5 p.m. on 13 August, Sir Ewen went to see Heseltine, who was on holiday at his home in Oxfordshire, to inform the minister of the steps he had taken. The decision to refer the matter to the Director of Public Prosecutions was passed to Mrs Thatcher's private office, which telephoned her on 13 August in Salzburg, where she was enjoying the musical festival. The DPP in turn enlisted the help of the Solicitor-General, Sir Patrick Mayhew QC, as the Attorney-General, Sir Michael Havers QC, was on holiday in France. A report was prepared for the DPP by the Ministry of Defence police. On 14 August, Ponting's resignation was refused. He received a handwritten notification that he could be prosecuted, and he was suspended on half-pay. This had the fortunate result that when he was acquitted he received the balance of his annual salary of £23,194, which meant that his acquittal was worth approximately £5,500 to him in back-pay.

Havers was consulted by telephone on 17 August. He and the Solicitor-General concluded that this was an appropriate case for a prosecution to be brought, as it was a serious breach of duty and trust by a senior civil servant. The Attorney-General did not consult any other ministers as he was entitled to under the Shawcross guidelines. On 17 August the Solicitor-General read the DPP's report and discussed it with the DPP, Sir Thomas Hetherington QC, who took a strong personal interest in the trial, which he attended for its larger part. He then spoke to the Attorney-General, and consent for the prosecution of Clive Ponting was given. When subsequently the Attorney-General was criticised for his decision to prosecute, he said that he had decided to authorise the prosecution because it fell within his published guidelines, and because both the DPP and the Solicitor-General had advised prosecution. He refused to give any undertaking not to use Section 2 in the future where no considerations of national security were involved.

Ponting was charged, at 4.50 p.m. at Cannon Row Police Station, with communicating information obtained by him, or to which he had access, as a person who held office under Her Majesty, to someone other than a person to whom he was authorised to communicate it or to whom it was in the interest of the state to communicate it.

It was perhaps appropriate that even the news of his arrest should be the subject of a leak. He had been charged but was told by the police that they would not reveal details of the charge to the press. The Special Branch, who had wished to interview him, was not allowed to do so. However, by 10 p.m. someone had tipped off the press. Ponting's house in Islington was surrounded by journalists when he returned, and they had even got hold of his ex-directory telephone number.

Richard Hastie-Smith, the head of civilian staff management at the Ministry of Defence, said that there had been no offer of immunity from prosecution and that only the Attorney-General could have given it. However, there was no obligation to prosecute Ponting in the first place. At the outset, the documents had been revealed only to the two MPs, Kershaw and Dalyell. At the trial Hastie-Smith admitted that it had been his personal hope that Ponting's case would be dealt with merely by requiring his resignation. He doubted that he had told Ponting on 14 August, 'This is not going as smoothly as we had hoped. Ministers are jumping up and down,' after the meeting between Heseltine and Broadbent. 'I don't think I said that. I told him that I could not give him an assurance that there would be no prosecution.'

Ponting first appeared in court on 18 August. A week later he publicly announced that he was charged with leaking documents about the sinking of the *Belgrano*, and indicated that he would raise a defence of publication in the public interest. Any chance that he would quietly plead guilty disappeared at that moment.

On 9 November 1984 Ponting was committed to stand trial at the Central Criminal Court, and on 28 January his trial began. The passage to the trial had not been altogether smooth. In September 1984 the Prime Minister's press secretary, Bernard Ingham, had indiscreetly told a private but not leak-proof meeting of Whitehall information officers that he hoped Ponting would get a severe judge, a 'Judge Jeffreys', and he had suggested a few names. He later explained that it was a joke but he apologised to the Lord Chancellor, Lord Hailsham.

The Attorney-General found himself the subject of criticism when, that October, he somewhat unwisely – as the man charged with enforcing the law of contempt of court – allowed himself to be drawn into a discussion of the case on BBC Television's *Law in Action* programme. He said of the case against Ponting: 'In this particular case, it is simply a question of a very senior civil servant who had disclosed matters which I said he had no right to disclose ... It fits rather with Sarah Tisdall and some others.' Havers later explained this was a straightforward description of the basis on which the prosecution had been brought and not any sort of assertion about the facts.

There was one other bizarre occurrence before the trial got properly under way on 28 January 1985. It was brought to the attention of the judge, Mr Justice McCowan, that Channel 4 intended to entertain the public by broadcasting highlights of the day's hearing performed by actors. He immediately made an order forbidding such broadcasts under the Contempt of Court Act 1981. Instead, extracts from the day's transcripts were read each night by retired newscasters.

The case started with the usual jury vetting; a panel of sixty was selected. They were checked to see if they had criminal records or any entries on Special Branch files, but no one was rejected on these grounds. The limited nature of these checks became apparent when one of the jurors, a Ms Lynne Oliver, was revealed by a newspaper to be a left-wing member of Islington council, which apparently was not classified as a subversive organisation and therefore fell outside the Special Branch's remit. Closer investigation would have shown that not only did she live in the same part of south Islington as Ponting, but she had supported a council motion calling for 'the withdrawal of the charges under the Official Secrets Act against Islington resident Clive Ponting, relating to documents about the sinking of the Argentinian cruiser the *General Belgrano*'. It was perhaps odd that, if the prosecution felt it appropriate to vet the jury, it did not check to see where the panel was drawn from.

The case was opened in a fairly low key by Roy Amlot, counsel for the prosecution. He made it clear that the Crown had no wish to see the Falklands war fought again. There was no suggestion that the disclosure of these documents damaged national security; the case involved a breach of confidentiality. He successfully requested that the court go into camera so that the jury could read the 'Crown Jewels', despite a defence offer to agree an edited version, so that the trial could be conducted throughout in open court.

On the face of it, Ponting had no defence to the charge. The fact that he acted out of well-intentioned motives was one that went only in mitigation of penalty. However, the defence turned out to be assisted by what was felt to be the hostile attitude of Mr Justice McCowan towards Ponting's conduct. In his summing up the judge dealt with the fact that Ponting was a Buddhist: 'You heard he had become Buddhist. That is in no way material, you may think, and no one suggests that it is. I am sure that none of you for a moment will hold it against him because he has changed his faith in that way.' The prosecution was further hindered by the fact that, although the government's conduct was not on trial, there was some unease as to the way it had acted and some doubt whether it had acted properly. Furthermore, the prosecution was not assisted by failing to bring to court the two principal figures in the story, Heseltine and Stanley – *Hamlet* without either the Prince of Denmark or Polonius. Instead the civil servants who had been Ponting's colleagues had to give evidence against him, somewhat to their discomfiture. Foremost among these was Richard Mottram, private secretary to Michael Heseltine, who denied that there was any united front to thwart legitimate enquiries by Members of Parliament into the sinking of the *Belgrano*. He was in the witness box for two and a half days. He had to explain that for Heseltine to have answered further questions could have led him into fresh questions and sensitive areas. He told the jury it was Stanley who advised Heseltine to answer that 'it is not our practice to comment on military operational matters, or details of military operations', just as it was Stanley who had been 'cautious about giving information' when Sir John Fieldhouse raised the question as to why the official dispatch had been dated 1 May as opposed to 2 May. When cross-examined about the somewhat equivocal and occasionally hair-splitting nature of some of the suggested draft replies, Mottram produced a suitably Whitehall reply: 'In highly charged political matters, one man's ambiguity is another man's truth.'

Hastie-Smith was left to answer questions about the decision to prosecute Clive Ponting. It was not any part of his duties to decide such matters, but he had to field cross-examination on a subject in which it appeared that he had hoped and possibly expected that there would not be a prosecution before the law officers decided to prosecute. He denied leading the civil servant to believe that he would not be prosecuted. Ponting could, he said, have raised his dis-satisfaction with government conduct with the Under-Secretary Naval Staff (his immediate superior), or, under Civil Service rules, with his civilian personnel director, or with Hastie-Smith himself, or in the final resort with his permanent under-secretary, Sir Clive Whitmore, or the head of the Civil Service, Sir Robert Armstrong. As these last two had been closely concerned with the War Cabinet's sanctioning of the sinking of the *Belgrano*, a complaint to them would have fallen on stony ground. Hastie-Smith also had to explain the rather surprising ministry view that MPs should not receive information graded higher than restricted unless authorised by the responsible minister.

The defence, by way of contrast, called a number of distinguished witnesses such as a former Home Secretary and member of the Franks Committee, Merlyn Rees MP, and Professor Henry Wade QC, Professor of English law at Cambridge University. The central part of the defence case was inevitably Ponting's evidence. Ponting told the jury that he remained of the view that it had been reasonable to send the task force, and there was a military case for attacking the *Belgrano*. He had seen nothing to support the contention that the ship was sunk to put an end to the Peruvian peace plan. However, the Foreign Office had seen fit only to send him two telegrams while he was preparing the 'Crown Jewels'. He explained that the reason he had leaked the documents was that ministers refused to disclose more information about the sinking of the *Belgrano* out of political embarrassment rather than intelligence considerations. He did not believe that Heseltine's arguments for withholding information about the *Belgrano*'s reversal of course were based on sound and sensible grounds, but rather on political considerations. He felt that two years after the sinking of the *Belgrano* the information should no longer be classified.

Ponting denied that he had leaked the documents in a fit of pique because his advice was not accepted. If his methods were underhand, this was because it was the only way he could get the information to Parliament. He did not regret his action beyond the embarrassment he had caused to his colleagues. He agreed that with hindsight it would have been better to have sent the documents and resigned immediately.

One of the major difficulties Ponting faced was that he had chosen to send the documents to Dalyell, who was engaged in something of a crusade about the sinking of the *Belgrano*. He had sent them to him, he explained, because he was a duly elected MP of twenty-two years' standing and a man of considerable integrity: 'Whatever you or I think of his views, Dalyell had been systematically misled.' He had, however, to accept that the only person who could in this instance give authority for a document to be sent to a Member of Parliament was Heseltine, and that under Civil Service regulations he personally would not have that authority. However, he said that he had sent the documents because it was in the wider interests of Parliament to be told that it was being misled and how the government was proposing to mislead it. There was no escaping the point that Tam Dalyell was an unwise choice of MP to whom to send the documents, since he had no official standing and was firmly committed to his *Belgrano* campaign against the government. It was no part of a civil servant's job to feed the opposition with questions to embarrass the government.

Dalyell himself had had problems in the past with leaks. In 1968, while serving on the Commons select committee on science and technology, which was enquiring into defence research, he had sent the *Observer* a copy of confidential evidence taken at Porton Down. He was found guilty of a breach of privilege and a serious contempt of the House and reprimanded.

Ponting's position would thus have been stronger if he had sent the documents to the House of Commons Foreign Affairs Committee rather than to Dalyell. He nevertheless felt that he had some justification for sending the documents to a Member of Parliament, without breaching the Official Secrets Act. He relied on an answer given by Sir Robert Cox, the Permanent Secretary to the Treasury, to the House of Commons Public Accounts Committee in 1978. The question the committee had raised was whether it would be a breach of the Official Secrets Act for an official, who believed that misleading evidence had been given to it by one of the senior officers, to publicise the fact. The Treasury concluded that 'there would, of course, be no such breach if the sole publication were to the committee or to the House, since the publication would in that event amount to a proceeding in Parliament, and would be absolutely privileged'. There was further support from a ruling of the Clerk of the House of Commons in 1938 that 'a person who communicates official information to a person to whom he is not authorised to communicate, commits no offence if the person to whom he discloses it, is a person to whom it is his duty in the interests of the state to communicate it'.

Even if these statements were not a correct summary of the law, they provided an excellent reason for not prosecuting Ponting. They had misled him, and in his work in the Legal Secretariat he had, after all, had some experience of the Official Secrets Act. The decision to prosecute him meant that the leaked documents which had been sent only to Dalyell and Kershaw became public property.

The trial did not prove an altogether happy experience for

Dalyell. He was very nearly gaoled for contempt following a speech he made in Glasgow, when he alleged that Fieldhouse's official account of the sinking had been altered on the instructions of Stanley. He was summoned before Mr Justice McCowan on 4 February 1985. His suggestion to the judge that the matter should be dealt with in the Scottish courts, as he had made his speech in Glasgow, did not go down well; nor did his attempt to mollify him with the comment, 'As a member of one High Court to a member of another, I follow quite clearly what you are saying.' He was required to give an undertaking not to make any public comment about the trial until its end, after being told by the judge: 'If you cannot control yourself for another week even after this warning, I may be driven to put you where you have no option.'

Merlyn Rees gave evidence in support of Ponting's defence that it was not against the interest of the state that he had communicated these documents: 'If I felt there had been a breach of security I would not have come this morning.'

Professor Wade told the jury that though constitutional conventions were not rules of law they could not operate unless ministers gave truthful information to Parliament. If a civil servant is convinced that truthful information is not being given, it might be in the public interest to give that information to Parliament. In his summing up the judge commented a little acidly on this evidence: 'Professor Wade had come perilously close to telling us what the law is; and rightly or wrongly, I am afraid that role is given to me.'

Mrs Ponting said that Hastie-Smith had indicated on 14 August that his clear preference was that her husband's resignation would be acceptable. He might be prosecuted under the Official Secrets Act, but he had said he thought that was not likely.

At the conclusion of the evidence the judge reviewed the case and considered the rulings of law he would give. He concluded that the interests of the state meant the interests of the government of the day. The fact that Ponting honestly believed he had a legitimate public interest in communicating these documents did not afford him any defence. Accordingly the judge indicated that he was minded to direct the jury to convict: 'If the prosecution is right, there is not any scope for an acquittal.' This caused some consternation to the prosecution, who asked for an adjournment to discuss the matter with the Director of Public Prosecutions.

Roy Amlot returned to court asking that the judge should not direct a conviction, which he did not. 'I am very reluctant that in this of all cases you should finish up directing the jury to convict.' This exchange in the absence of the jury gave rise to the final mishap of the trial – apart, that is, from Clive Ponting's acquittal. As the judge failed to make an order prohibiting any publicity being given to these deliberations, as he was entitled to do under Section 4 of the Contempt of Court Act 1981, the *Observer* published the fact that the judge intended to direct a conviction, on the day before the jury retired to consider their verdict. This, as it turned out, was something that worked in Ponting's favour rather than against him. The judge referred the matter to the DPP, who decided that on this occasion the *Observer* could not be prosecuted.

In his closing speech Amlot adopted a moderate tone. The case involved a breach of confidentiality. Unauthorised disclosures were bound to undermine the government process. It did not matter which government was in power. For the defence, Bruce Laughland QC made an altogether more eloquent speech. The case was not about spying, it was a matter of lying to and misleading Parliament. Realising the difficulties that Ponting faced on the law, he appealed to the jury's sense of justice, whatever ruling was given by the judge. The jury's decision, he told them, had more weight because it was the voice of the people. If Ponting was convicted, it was a licence for ministers to withhold information from Parliament with the full acquiescence of tame civil servants, and to infringe our liberties.

Predictably the judge did not care for this approach, and Laughland's knuckles were suitably rapped:

May I say to you quite emphatically, members of the jury, that that would be a wholly wrong approach to your duties and to the oath you have taken. If the case is proved, it is your duty to convict, whatever the consequences. To say to yourself, 'Well, it is proved but I am not going to convict in case it discourages ministers from being forthcoming,' would be false to your oath.

He directed the jury that the words of Section 2, 'in the interests of the state', referred to the policies of the government of the day. The policy of the state meant the policies laid down by the recognised organs of government and authority as they were in July 1984, not what Ponting thought they should be. Ponting was entitled to pass on the *Belgrano* papers only if he was acting in his official capacity in the interests of the state. Dalyell was not an authorised recipient of the information within the meaning of the Act. The jury therefore had only one ingredient in dispute: the prosecution had to prove that Dalyell was not a person to whom it was, in the interests of the state, Ponting's duty to communicate the information. The jury should ignore Ponting's motives, their own political views, their opinions as to whether the Official Secrets Act should be repealed and the fact that the case did not involve issues of national security.

There were those who thought they discerned the judge's view as to whether Ponting's conduct was in the interests of the state. The judge finished his summing up on Monday 11 February, and Ponting, fearing a prison sentence of nine to twelve months, had taken the precaution of having breakfast at the Savoy and filling his pockets with a few creature comforts, in the mistaken belief that he could keep them if he was convicted. The odds against an acquittal varied from 50–1 to 300–1, and the judge's summing up was wrongly thought to have diminished the chances of an acquittal. However, Ponting's choice of Dalyell, who was neither his constituency MP nor a Privy Councillor and had form for leaking, his attempt to remove all identifying marks from the documents, his alleged untruthfulness when first asked whether he was the culprit, his failure to exhuast Civil Service remedies for his grievances, and his attempts to blame others were better explanations of the odds. In the event, he was unanimously acquitted after the jury had retired for no more than three hours. The jury were unhappy with the government's conduct and the way that the prosecution had been mounted. They had no wish to see Ponting sent off to prison. Ponting's acquittal was reported to have cast a shadow over Mrs Thatcher's celebration lunch at No. 10 Downing Street, to mark ten years as leader of the Conservative Party. The jury's common sense was, however, welcomed by Lord Denning.

Although Ponting received the back-pay due to him, the Defence Ministry had very considerable reservations about re-engaging him and confirmed that his security clearance was withdrawn. Steps were taken on 14 February to discourage him from publishing his book, *The Right to Know*. He was reminded that he must conform to the regulations about civil servants' conduct, including the requirement of obtaining permission before entering into any commitment to write and publish in connection with his work or on a matter of public controversy. Ponting solved the government's dilemma by resigning after negotiations about his pension rights. However, his acquittal made the government understandably cautious about taking action to prevent publication of his book. When, at the end of December 1984, he had learnt of Ponting's intention of publishing a book, Sir Clive Whitmore, the Permanent Under-Secretary at the Ministry of Defence, had let it be known that Ponting would be prosecuted, even if he was acquitted at his first trial. After his acquittal, there were clearly second thoughts. To forestall the dangers of a civil injunction being obtained to ban publication on the grounds of breach of contract and confidentiality, no review copies were sent out, and those involved with its publication spoke from public call boxes to avoid the risk of their telephone calls being tapped. Rigorous self-censorship was applied to ensure that no secret material was included in the book.

On 18 February 1985 an opposition motion accusing the government of purveying distorted and misleading inform-ation about the *Belgrano* was defeated by 350 votes to 202. On 19 February, Ponting's behaviour was fiercely attacked by Heseltine and Stanley. Ponting's advice had, they said, been conflicting; first he had suggested that they should withhold the information requested by Davies and Dalyell, then he had advised them to publish it. On 29 March 1984 Ponting had advised that Heseltine should answer Dalyell's letter of 19 March, merely confirming what the Prime Minister had said in her letter to Davies about the sighting of the *Belgrano*; he advised the minister to state that 'the other questions you have raised all concern detailed operational and intelligence matters, on which I am not prepared to comment'. Ponting's recommendations had, he said, changed dramatically between 10 and 12 April. Furthermore, Ponting had written anonymously to Dalyell on 24 April, urging him to press for answers for these questions, which only a few days earlier he had advised ministers not to answer. Heseltine also made the point that the Legge memorandum which he had leaked was the joint work of Ponting and Legge's departments, even though it had gone out in the name of Legge's unit.

Ponting's reply to these allegations was that he had only had four days to prepare the 'Crown Jewels' and only a very short time to draft his proposed reply in March. It was only in April that he fully realised that the answers sought by Dalyell did not relate to classified material. But that as it may, Heseltine and Stanley's performance in Parliament put a swift end to any attempts to beatify Ponting.

It is hard to escape the conclusion that Ponting had no business to leak the documents. The ministers were, after all, elected and answerable in Parliament, and to the electorate. There certainly was a case for dismissing him, but it is difficult to see what purpose was served by prosecuting him. The prosecution was a disaster; it achieved enormous publicity for two not particularly significant documents which had by then been disclosed to only two MPs. It has made the government markedly nervous about bringing prosecutions in controversial cases, and caused it to drop its toy-typewriter prosecution (Chapter 13) for fear of the further ridicule it would bring. No doubt it was also a decisive factor in the decision not to prosecute Cathy Massiter

(Chapter 14). Unwise as Ponting undoubtedly was to leak the documents, there was substance in his complaint about the government's conduct. In July 1985 the House of Commons Foreign Affairs Committee, under the chairmanship of Sir Anthony Kershaw – by then armed with a copy of the 'Crown Jewels', thanks to Ponting – criticised ministers for not correcting without delay errors contained in statements to the Commons made about the sinking during the Falklands campaign by Sir John Nott then Secretary of State for Defence: 'The House remained for too long in ignorance of information which members were entitled to request... To that extent the House was misled.' By a majority the committee concluded that the government's concealment was due 'to excessive caution rather than to a deliberate mendacious desire to mislead'. However, the minority Labour group went on to say that the sinking of the *Belgrano* was unjustifiable, and the sending of the task force was to ensure the life of an administration which had been palpably negligent in failing to deter the Argentinian invasion.

After the case there was the charade of the police investigation as to whether, of all people, the Chief of the Defence Staff, Admiral Lord Lewin, should be prosecuted under the Official Secrets Act for an over-frank interview he had given to Desmond Rice and Arthur Gavshon, the authors of *The Sinking of the 'Belgrano'*, on 29 January 1984. Lewin had described in graphic detail how HMS *Conqueror* would have shadowed the *Belgrano* using hydrophonic towed arrays. The fact that the nuclear submarines were equipped with this new sonar system was thought to be top secret. Lewin explained that the interview was off the record, although the six-hour interview was taped with his consent. Gavshon and Rice, in accordance with normal journalistic ethics, refused to hand over to Commander R. Dawling of Scotland Yard the tapes of that interview. The matter was therefore taken no further by an already embarrassed DPP.

The relations between Neil Kinnock and Margaret Thatcher, which had never been cordial since the former's unworthy remark about the latter's spreading 'guts on Goose Green', took a turn for the worse following the opposition leader's ill-informed accusation about the Prime Minister's personal responsibility for Ponting's prosecution. It was, Mrs Thatcher complained, 'as serious a charge as can be made . . . an honourable man would substantiate or withdraw. Mr Kinnock was steaming in the wrong direction and it was utterly untrue.' Kinnock did not apologise, not did he substantiate his charge, although he did say that he did not believe her and thought her explanation highly unlikely.

In this atmosphere of ill-will there were accusations of perjury against Ponting, which were referred, most unusually, to the Ministry of Defence police rather than Scotland Yard – some indication of where the impetus for the investigation came from. This related to Ponting's evidence at his trial that the first time he had contacted Dalyell was in July, whereas he admitted after the trial that he had sent Dalyell the anonymous note on 24 April. The existence of the 24 April note had been disclosed in the *New Statesman* prior to the trial, but the police never asked Ponting about it. He strongly denied that his evidence was other than truthful on the subject. Denzil Davies spoke darkly about dirty tricks and a vendetta against Ponting. No further action was taken.

Following Ponting's acquittal there were two attempts to reform the law by Private Members' Bills. The first was by Stephen Norris MP, who introduced a Bill seeking to permit a defence of disclosure in the public interest in cases where national security was not involved. The second was by Chris Smith MP, who introduced the Official Secrets Act Amendment Bill, which merely stated: 'Section 2 Official Secrets Act is hereby repealed.' Neither attempt reached the statute book.

13

Tape Cassettes, Buried Notebooks, Sunken Gold, Toy Typewriters and the Romeo of the Nile

The period from 1980 to date has produced a motley collection of trials under the Official Secrets Act. The possibility of raising a defence of publication in the interests of the state after Ponting's acquittal and the government's inept behaviour in the 1986 Westland affair makes it unlikely that there will be many further major cases. However, there is no reason to suppose that the government intends to abolish Section 2 or to replace it by a statute confined to secrets that really matter.

In May 1981 a prosecution that was absurd, even by the exacting standards of the Official Secrets Act, was withdrawn. John Wagstaffe, a low-ranking thirty-two-year-old official at the Ministry of Defence, had taken home tapes containing allegedly highly classified but redundant material. He had not taken them home for the purpose of selling them to the USSR but for the aim of recording pop music on them. Such was the damage done to national security that the absence of these tapes was not noticed for eighteen months. When it was, Wagstaffe was ordered back from West Germany, where he was working as a Ministry of Defence official in a 'humble position'. He was charged with retaining official documents without authority; for good measure his passport was seized, and he was remanded on £5,000 bail. The ludicrous nature of the case was well illustrated by the fact that the government did not know how many tapes he had taken. It originally thought between 50 and 120 tapes were missing, but out of an abundance of caution charged him with retaining only five of them. In the end the charge had to be dropped because the prosecution could not even prove what was on the tapes when Wagstaffe took them.

A good example of the sort of person caught by Section 2 is Martin Hartland. He was a former able seaman, convicted in January 1982 at the Old Bailey of unlawfully retaining a notebook containing confidential information and sent to prison for three months. Hartland's behaviour was misguided and constituted a serious breach of naval discipline, but from the point of view of national security the case was of no importnace. Hartland had a grievance against the Royal Navy following his dismissal after threatening a leading seaman with an iron bar, which had resulted in his serving forty-eight days' detention. He had made notes from an official notebook that contained secret codes on electronic warfare, which was normally kept in a safe, while he was on an electronics course at the Naval Establishment. He copied out this information into his own notebook and buried it in his garden. He had threatened to sell the information to the Russians, but this consisted of telephoning the naval security officer at Portland and saying he would 'approach the Russkies' shortly after he had been let out of Colchester Detention Centre. He was a barman and had been drinking at the time, the day of the Royal Wedding. 'I was cheesed off at being kicked out of the Navy. But I had no intention of disclosing anything to anyone. I have always been loyal to this country.' Hartland was arrested and readily took the police to the spot where the notebook was buried.

In November 1982 Miss Rhona Ritchie, a thirty-one-year-old diplomat, pleaded guilty at the Old Bailey to an offence of wrongfully communicating information to an Egyptian diplomat, Rifaat al Ansari. She was sentenced to nine months' imprisonment suspended for twelve months. She admitted passing to Ansari six telegrams which were all classified as confidential. These related to Middle East policy and included a message from the Foreign Secretary, Lord Carrington, to his United States counterpart, General Haig.

The Attorney-General told the court that Miss Ritchie's conduct was 'more foolish than wicked'. He said that the damage done to British interests was not great. Egypt was a friendly power, and most of the information would have become public knowledge in due course anyway. Her offence lay in breach of confidence and untrustworthiness rather than in the nature of the disclosures themselves. These would have been prejudicial to the conduct of international relations rather than damaging to security.

Although Miss Ritchie's conduct seemed to be a suitable case for prosecution under Section 2, the background to the case raises a question as to whether she should in fact have been prosecuted and whether the government brought the case to court only when a sexual liaison with a foreign diplomat got out of control. Certainly the penalty was severe, when there was no likelihood of Miss Ritchie offending again.

Miss Ritchie had joined the diplomatic service aged twenty-seven, having been a law lecturer. She was positively vetted and, like Miss Tisdall, came from a family where both parents were doctors. In July 1981 she was posted as Second Secretary to the British Embassy in Tel Aviv. After eight months at the embassy, she was promoted in March 1982 to First Secretary. This promotion came shortly after the Military Attaché and the Head of Chancery suspected that she was having an affair with Ansari. Before taking up her posting to the British Embassy in Tel Aviv, Miss Ritchie had been to a kibbutz and a language school in Israel, where she appears to have had a number of lovers. Before she joined the embassy staff, details of her love life became known to her immediate superior, Dr W. G. Harris, then First Secretary at the embassy. He considered her perfectly capable of handling a discreet private life, according to her own judgement, and not allowing it to impinge on her professional work. He did not feel it necessary to make a report to the Head of Chancery. Miss Ritchie asked Dr Harris whether it would be acceptable if a relationship between her and an Israeli government official, with whom she had had a brief affair before joining the staff, continued. Dr Harris advised against it. This advice was passed on to the Head of Chancery at the embassy, although it seems he was not notified about Miss Ritchie's affairs before she joined the embassy staff.

The extent to which members of British embassy staff may have affairs with other nationals is a grey area, giving rise to possible security risks. Conventional wisdom, as outlined in a letter dated 17 September 1982 from Sir Anthony Acland, then Permanent Under-Secretary at the Foreign Office, appears to be that 'emotional liaisons with nationals from foreign friendly countries are unlikely to be a security concern, but that if there were any doubts in the matter the personal particulars of the partners should be sent to the security department'. These equivocal rules were operated ambiguously in Miss Ritchie's case. Although there was no evidence that anyone encouraged her to go to bed with Ansari, the advice she was given, and the attitude of certain of her embassy colleagues, certainly did not make it clear that she risked going to prison if the affair got out of hand.

The Security Commission stated that Miss Ritchie's affair with Ansari was not known to the Head of Chancery, and Dr Harris had left by the time the affair commenced. However, the Security Commission did not consider that it would be profitable to investigate in detail how far the relationship was known to or suspected by more junior members of the staff. As it was, Miss Ritchie was recalled to London, ostensibly to make plans for a trip to Israel by Lord Carrington, when the Military Attaché learnt of gossip at the embassy about her affair with Ansari.

The Security Commission's report does not give the impression of Miss Ritchie being warned, as a relatively inexperienced diplomat on her first posting, of the security risks of such a liaison. Instead one finds her able to seek advice on whether it was acceptable to have an affair with the Israeli official. Furthermore, she was encouraged to develop contacts with Ansari, her counterpart at the Egyptian Embassy – who according to press reports had earned the sobriquet 'Romeo of the Nile' – in terms which perhaps did not make clear the limits of how far Her Majesty's government expected Miss Ritchie to go in furtherance of its interests. She was told that the relationship her predecessor had had with Ansari had been professionally fruitful and that it was very much in the embassy's and Her Majesty's government's interests to maintain contact with Ansari, at a time when complex and sustained negotiations were continuing between the Israelis, Egyptians and Americans on the implementation of the Camp David agreement and on the normalisation of relations between Israel and Egypt. She was therefore encouraged to have the occasional meal with Ansari and to attend the social events of a junior diplomats' club with him at a local hotel.

Although it is clear from the Security Commission's report that the Ambassador and the Head of Chancery did not know and had no suspicion of her affair, a large part of the remainder of the diplomatic community did. Miss Ritchie and Ansari were known locally as 'R and R' (Rhona and Rifaat) and were regularly to be seen at Tel Aviv nightspots evidently not frequented by the Ambassador, such as Café Exodus, Chez Simon and the Red China Restaurant. The more observant would also have spotted a pair of Egyptian CD plates (something of a rarity in Israel) parked at night outside Miss Ritchie's flat.

Unfortunately Ansari proved to be a man of strong character, and persuaded Miss Ritchie to pass official documents to him. When this became known to the Security Service in early March 1982, she was recalled to London.

When Miss Ritchie had been charged under Section 2, the same charade took place as in the Alan Lowther affair (see below). Her case was not to be found on the publicly displayed list of cases to be heard at Bow Street – which would have told the press where the case was to be heard. The charge sheet read out in court stated, no doubt for compelling security reasons, that she was of no known address.

It is essential that diplomats do not pass confidential documents to people working for foreign governments, but this was not a case with any expionage implications. The damage was very limited, and the case arose in unusual and unfortunate circumstances. Whether it was necessary to drag Miss Ritchie through the courts – unsuitable as she had proved herself for the diplomatic service – and whether a prison sentence, albeit suspended, was called for is open to doubt. On 4 June 1985 the Foreign Office admitted privately to the Association of First Division Civil Servants that the prosecution had been handled in a clumsy, unsatisfactory and hasty manner. New procedures were agreed with the Association which would, it was hoped, avoid such prosecutions in the future.

In 1983 a person was convicted for the first time in a civil court for failing to take reasonable care of official documents. This was thought by those concerned to be the first such case under Section 2, but members of the armed forces had been court-martialled on a number of occasions for such conduct. The civil servant who fell victim to this use of Section 2 was a senior information officer at the Central Office of Information, Robin Gordon-Walker. He was the son of a former Foreign Secretary, Patrick Gordon-Walker, who had himself been the subject of some criticism when he published in 1976 his book *The Cabinet* which revealed a number of discussions in Cabinet. No action had been taken against Patrick Gordon-Walker, but in this case there was no question of the sins of the father being visited on the son, as with George Lansbury.

Gordon-Walker had to deliver some Foreign Office briefs to the Foreign Secretary, who was attending a foreign ministers' meeting in Brussels. These briefs contained some highly classified information, including for example how the Foreign Office had anticipated Israel's invasion of Lebanon and how Great Britain was solely responsible for blocking an EEC aid package to Nicaragua. Gordon-Walker had travelled to Heathrow Airport by underground and had put down his briefcase, which bore the NATO logo, on the adjoining seat. When he arrived at the airport the briefcase was no longer there. Someone very thoughtfully passed it to *City Limits*, and the magazine published the documents' contents in its issue of 30 September 1982. The Crown immediately obtained an injunction ordering the documents to be handed back.

Gordon-Walker was prosecuted and fined £500 in the magistrates' court for carelessly handling official documents. He was told by magistrate Ralph Lownie that a short sentence of imprisonment was justified, even if it had been suspended. This was not the most serious of cases, and it seemed that he had been a fool rather than a knave, Lownie commented. The prosecution acknowledged that only very limited damage had been done to the United Kingdom's relations with the EEC. In reality it is difficult to see that any damage was done.

Gordon-Walker was probably unfortunate to be prosecuted; it may have been felt necessary to crack the whip over other careless civil servants. It was no more than an act of negligence, but it did cause embarrassment by virtue of the documents being published in *City Limits*. He did his case no good by falsely – no doubt in a moment of panic – claiming to have destroyed his copies of the documents; shortly afterwards he made an admission.

A prosecution under Section 2 which went wrong was that brought against John Jackson in 1982. Jackson had been employed by the Salvage Association in the City of London for forty years. He had been the manager of its salvage sales and information department since 1973. The Salvage Association is an independent non-profit-making body, founded in 1856 by a group of insurers, shipowners and merchants to protect the interests of the owners of vessels and cargoes lost or damaged at sea. One of its functions is to advise the owners of sunken cargoes on the recovery of their property. The association was incorporated by Royal Charter in 1863 and is independent of any government department.

Jackson was a member of the panel – which included representatives of the Department of Trade, Foreign and Commonwealth Office and Ministry of Defence – convened to consider who, if anyone, should be given the contract to salvage the $5\frac{1}{2}$ tons of gold which lay 128 fathoms down in the Barents Sea in the bomb-room of HMS *Edinburgh*, which had been sunk while on convoy duty from Murmansk to the United Kingdom on 2 May 1942. The gold was being sent by the Russians to the USA via Britain to pay for war supplies. After HMS *Edinburgh* had been sunk, the gold was treated as belonging approximately two-thirds to the Russians and one-third to the British war risks insurance office. At the time HMS *Edinburgh* went down, the gold was worth £1.5 million. In the 1950s a salvor, Risdon Beazley, decided this act of salvage was at that time impractical for technical and financial reasons. Interest revived in 1979 when the gold's value had risen to £40 million, and when it was believed for a time that the wreck of HMS *Edinburgh* was located.

Three companies were interested in salvaging the gold. They had to satisfy the Board of Trade, which had taken over the functions of the war risks insurance office, that they had the necessary technical expertise and the Ministry of Defence that the methods they proposed to use were consonant with HMS *Edinburgh* being a designated war grave. The companies were Risdon Beazley Marine Ltd, Stolt Neilsen Rederei A/S and Jessop Marine Recoveries Ltd. Risdon Beazley had the disadvantage of being a Dutch-owned company in what was seen as a British operation, although its personnel were mainly British. It had successfully brought the SS *Great Britain* from the Falklands to Bristol and had shown an interest in recovering the *Edinburgh*'s gold in 1954. The company's usual method of opening up the ship by explosive charges and salvaging the contents by lowering a grab – known in the trade as 'smash and grab' – was felt to be inappropriate for a war grave. Stolt Neilsen was a Norwegian company which specialized in deep-sea diving and had mounted a search for HMS *Edinburgh* in 1979. Jessop Marine was a firm set up by Keith Jessop, a diving superintendent who had come to the Salvage Association's notice when he recovered the copper from the wreck of the *Joanna Thorden* in the Pentland Firth. Jessop had previously worked in conjunction with Stolt Neilsen. Each company would work for a percentage of the cargo recovered and would receive nothing if it failed to recover any gold. The successful bid, Jessop Marine's, would give the company 45 per cent of the value of the cargo.

Negotiations began early in 1980 between the Department of Trade and Industry and the Soviet government to sign a salvage agreement. The Salvage Association is empowered by its charter to work as agents of the shipping for the owners of the sunken property; when its services were required by the government it would sign a salvage contract with the Department of Trade. It did not get to sign a contract with the department regarding the salvaging of HMS *Edinburgh*, however. The point that the Salvage Association did not in fact have a contract was overlooked by the prosecution when it charged John Jackson with having communicated information, to which he had access as a person employed by the Salvage Association which held a contract on behalf of Her Majesty's Government, to a person (Keith Jessop) to whom he was not authorized to communicate it. The Crown had, as a preliminary measure in proving any such offence against Jackson, to establish that the Salvage Association held a contract with the government. Jessop was charged with receiving the information and counselling and procuring Jackson to communicate it to him in breach of the Official Secrets Act. Neither of them had ever signed the Act.

After assessing the merits of the rival companies, the decision went in favour of Jessop Marine. It was claimed that Jackson passed this information and a number of the relevant documents to David Bona, Jessop's solicitor in Manchester, before the decision was officially announced. Jackson was alleged to have sent Bona a copy of a memorandum of agreement between Stolt Neilsen and the Soviet cargo-owners, and a summary of the interviews of the representatives of the three salvage companies before the assessment panel. A warrant was issued under the Official Secrets Act to recover these documents from Bona's solicitor's practice. At the subsequent trial the judge compared Jackson's behaviour to that of a schoolmaster telling his pupil in advance of his success in his examination. It suitably caught the lack of gravity of this costly and involved prosecution.

The operation to recover the gold was brilliantly successful. In September 1981, 431 bars worth £39 million, representing 90 per cent of the cargo, were recovered before the weather deteriorated and the diving operations had to cease. That however was the moment for recriminations to begin. The behaviour of the divers was criticized; they were accused of placing light-sticks in the skulls of those who had perished on HMS *Edinburgh* – something they denied. An article by Barrie Penrose appeared in the *Sunday Times* which was highly critical of the means used to obtain the salvage contract. The *Sunday Times* had been selected by one of Jessop's colleagues as a responsible newspaper to chronicle the attempt to recover the gold. It was a decision that both Jessop and Jackson came to regret. Jackson later told the police that he himself preferred the *Express* and thought that Penrose, who was following the expedition on the *Stephaniturm* and collecting material for his book *Stalin's Gold,* was a 'bloody nuisance'.

To add to the ill-feeling Jessop parted company with his solicitor, Bona, who presented him with a bill for £285,739.72 which, he subsequently pointed out, did include VAT and disbursements. The return of the expedition was not the triumphant affair it might have been. Further allegations of impropriety appeared in the *Sunday Times*, and a police investigation was launched; two charges under Section 2 were brought against Jessop and Jackson. The judge directed the jury to find Jackson not guilty, as the prosecution failed to prove a basic ingredient of the charges, namely that Jackson's employer – the Salvage Association – held a contract with the government, as at the time of the alleged offences no such contract existed. The charges against Jessop necessarily collapsed and the judge directed the jury to return a verdict of not guilty.

It was difficult to see what purpose was served by the prosecution. Mr Jackson's conduct could possibly have been considered indiscreet but it was certainly flattered by the term 'official secrets'. The real issue was whether the contract had been obtained by any improper means employed by Jessop or Jackson. The jury acquitted Jessop and Jackson of any conspiracy. It is also unclear what the police had in mind when they thought it necessary to arrest Jessop in Yorkshire at 6.30 a.m. and Jackson in Cambridgeshire at 6.40 a.m. in a synchronised operation. The Official Secrets charges seem to have been a makeweight, and it is unfortunate that they were ever brought. Such charges are easy to bring and normally have a high prospect of conviction. In this case the charges failed for lack of evidence and on technical grounds; but the use of the Official Secrets Act in these circumstances could easily have led to the unjust result of the prosecution obtaining a conviction on the minor official secrets charges, while failing to prove that the contract was obtained by improper means.

It is difficult not to sympathize with what Jessop said to the police about Jackson: 'I feel sorry for him. He is just a small man in a small office.'

Some cases brought under Section 2 concern matters which could not by the most charitable standards be said to touch upon national security. The charge brought against Alan Lowther, an accountant in the Prisons Department, concerned nothing more momentous than the manufacture of Lilliput 2000 plastic toy typewriters by prisoners under the organisation of the Directorate of Industries and Farms.

The venture of the Prison Department into the world of manufacturing toy typewriters was a disaster of creditable proportions. At first the prisoners had simply been engaged in making some of the components, but at some stage Home Office officials decided to introduce what was termed the 'whole-product concept'; that is, the prisoners would assemble the entire typewriter. The project was not a success. The problem was a captive workforce rather than a captive market. The work was too difficult for the prisoners, and matters were not helped by the prison officers going on strike. There was insufficient organisational or business acumen at the Prison Department; losses on the toy typewriters amounted to £11 million and on all the Directorate of Industries and Farms projects to £30 million. To add insult to injury, prisoners had originally been making the parts for the typewriters, which were then assembled by a company called Spiralux. When the Prison Department moved to the whole-product concept it found the work too difficult and had to subcontract assembly back to Spiralux.

The Home Office, looking at the size of the losses, felt there must have been corruption and dishonesty for such contracts to have been entered into. It was felt that not all that money could have been lost by incompetence alone. In this, however, the Home Office was wrong; it underestimated its lack of expertise and control over the operation.

In March 1984 the Prison Department set up an internal investigation into commercial dealings between Spiralux and the prison industries. It was headed by Alexander Gold, and accountant Alan Lowther served on the working group. One of the people whose activities was investigated was Alban Connolly, who had been the link between Spiralux and the prison industries. Unknown to Lowther, the Companies Fraud Department had started a separate investigation of the commercial relationship between the Directorate of Industries and Farms and Spiralux. Connolly was a friend of Lowther, and they often lunched together. Connolly wanted to know how the department investigation was going; he had after all been investigated and had been required to hand over all his papers.

The central part of the prosecution's case against Lowther was that Gold had clearly instructed him not to discuss the activities of the working group with Connolly. The prosecution said that Lowther had been told this on at least two occasions in March and April 1984. On 19 June 1984 Lowther was seen by police officers investigating Connolly's activities and was asked by them not to discuss the matter with him. The two friends had lunch together after Connolly had returned from holiday. Lowther was asked whether he had been interviewed by the police, what they had asked him about and what documents they had been interested in. Feeling that Connolly had been made a scapegoat for the losses on the Spiralux contracts, Lowther answered his questions and let him have copies of two documents which were marked 'commercial and management in confidence'. It was, in retrospect, he acknowledged, a foolish thing to have done, but at the time Connolly had not been suspended or charged with any criminal offence. In fact the two documents produced to Connolly were very short and of no particular significance. The whole prosecution case hinged upon two factors. The first was that Lowther had ignored his instructions from Gold, and the second was that he had handed over these two documents. On both points the prosecution case collapsed in some disarray.

At the committal proceedings Gold very fairly conceded that his instruction to Lowther had not been in writing and amounted to an informal request not to discuss the enquiry with Connolly. Gold agreed that Lowther's breach of instructions could have been dealt with under the appropriate disciplinary code. Colin Walsh, another member of the working group, said that with hindsight it was perhaps right to say that when a subordinate was given an instruction, the breach of which could result in criminal proceedings, it ought to be in writing. That disposed of Gold's warnings.

In cross-examination relating to the importance of the two documents which had been found in Connolly's possession, it was shown that these were short and dealt with technical matters relating to typewriters, consisting almost exclusively of material which Connolly would already have known. Connolly would certainly have been no wiser as to how the investigation was going after seeing these papers. The nearest that the prosecution could get to finding some expression of opinion in them, as opposed to a mere recital of technical details, was the scarcely spectacular observation that 'a lot of pertinent questions had been asked about the modification of injection mould tooling' and that 'it would seem possible that this tender [relating to the purchase of assembly jigs and fixtures and modifications] was cancelled and split into two to cover the different aspects of requirements'. On that very shaky foundation the prosecution under Section 2 was launched on 22 October 1984.

The prosecution seems to have been rather in two minds as to what offence, if any, Lowther's conduct amounted to. When he was interviewed on 28 June 1984 the allegation against him was that he might have attempted to pervert the course of justice by having his conversation with Connolly; but when he was charged, it was under Section 2. One rather unusual feature of the way the case was conducted was that – as with the prosecution of the junior diplomat Rhona Ritchie (see above) – it was never properly listed at Bow Street Magistrates' Court on the days that it was due for hearing, as if the prosecution were a little embarrassed by the case. Instead of finding Lowther's name publicly listed for hearing in one of the courts, enquiries would have to be made of the court staff. The case would then be heard in the traffic court, and the clerk would be told that there was an addition to the list in the form of this official secrets case. If there was this initial lack of enthusiasm for the prosecution, it increased considerably after the committal proceedings, which ended on 6 February 1985, about the time that Ponting was acquitted. By then the case was in some disarray.

One month after the committal to the Central Criminal Court, the Attorney-General's office indicated, having considered the matter further, that it would not be in the interests of justice for the case to proceed. The case was therefore listed for hearing on 28 March; it came before Judge Lymbrey QC, who did not dispose of it as quietly as the prosecution would have wished. For the prosecution Allan Green told the judge that the Attorney-General had considered the matter again and had instructed the Director of Public Prosecutions to withdraw the charge. The judge told him that the question of withdrawing the charge was a matter for him, and he required a little detail of the case. The prosecution told the judge that the value of the documents to Connolly was very minor and that they contained information of which he was already aware. Lowther had shown Connolly two documents from a fifty-page report confidentially prepared by the Directorate of Industries and Farms, looking into allegations of irregular dealings between the directorate and private companies.

Having heard these facts, the judge directed an acquittal and awarded Lowther his costs. Lowther's counsel, Geoffrey Robertson, described the charges as trivial and farcical, pointing out that there was no question of any corruption or leaking secret information. Some doubt was cast on whether the excuse for dropping the charges was entirely satisfactory, as the facts surrounding these charges against Lowther had always been well documented. It was some indication of the conflicting sentiments about this case that, only a few days before learning from the Attorney-General that he did not intent to proceed with the case, Lowther had received an indictment setting out the charges that he faced which included by that stage not only the official secrets charge but also a count of attempting to pervert the course of justice.

This was not the only case relating to the unhappy toy-typewriter saga that collapsed. There were no less than three trials at the Central Criminal Court involving three civil servants and an English and an American business man. In each case the prosecution was stopped by the judge as it had failed to produce sufficient evidence to justify the charge. Not a single case of corruption was ever proved by the police. As for Alan Lowther, he should have been dealt with, if at all, by internal disciplinary proceedings. The case was about dis-obeying office instructions rather than disclosing official secrets. There was nothing in Lowther's case to indicate that the law of official secrets had to be imported into the world of plastic typewriters. If Lowther's conduct was unwise he certainly suffered for it. He was suspended from his job for nine months – although curiously on better terms than Ponting's half-pay, in that he received full pay until the authorities illogically reduced him to two-thirds of his pay four weeks before the trial. However, when he was acquitted he was told that the fact that he had been unsuccessfully prosecuted would be revealed to anyone thinking of employing him in the Home Officer; he left to take up a job in the private sector.

The year 1985 was not a good one for the government as regards the Official Secrets Act. Besides Ponting's acquittal, charges brought under Section 1 against a number of service-men serving at the Cyprus Sigint base that had featured in the 'ABC' case (Chapter 10) also failed. In 1984 Paul Davies, a twenty-one-year-old airman, was accused of passing secrets to a Mata Hari called Eva Jafaar. Davies was acquitted after a fifteen-day trial, following his claims that his alleged confession had been bullied out of him by the Royal Air Force police.

Airman Davies was followed into the dock at the Old Bailey by five young RAF men, and three from Sigint. One was discharged at an early stage because the judge was not satisfied that his confession was voluntary. This emerged during a trial within a trial, the purpose of which was that the judge should examine, in the absence of the jury, the circumstances in which the confession was made, in order to determine whether the confession appeared to be voluntary and could then be read to the jury. Before this had taken place, prosecuting counsel, Michael Wright QC, had inadvertently let slip the fact that the defendants had made confessions. This meant that the first jury had to be discharged and a second trial ordered. The remaining seven defendants were all acquitted after a 107-day trial, conducted almost exclusively in camera, with the result that the press were unable to report the allegations of homosexual orgies and splash parties, and a form of drunken horseplay known as 'moonies' (details of which seem to be covered by the Official Secrets Act), in the detail they would have liked. The prosecution claimed that official secrets were passed in return for favours received from Josie, a Filipino dancer, and a lady called Carmelita de Mesa, known on stage as Ning-Ning. To the dismay of the prosecution she appeared at the trial as a witness for the defence and proved to be far from the scarlet lady depicted. She was by then married to an English engineer, who was asked by defence counsel whether his wife had been a virgin when he married her. 'No,' he replied, but seeing the dismay on counsel's face he quickly added, 'but she was when I first met her.' His evidence more than any undermined the prosecution case.

After the acquittal of all the defendants, questions were raised as to how it was that these young servicemen had confessed in such detail to crimes they had not committed. An enquiry into the conduct of the investigations and interrogation techniques was set up under David Calcutt QC. This found that the custody of the servicemen was for part of the time unlawful and that even after they had been lawfully arrested their continued custody was at least improper. He concluded that none of the servicemen had been subjected to any violence or threat of violence or to any form of torture or inhuman or degrading treatment. However, John Stanley, Minister for the Armed Forces, promptly announced that *ex gratia* payments would be made to the seven defendants whose trial had run its full course. Each of the servicemen received back-pay in the order of £13,000. The trial was estimated to have cost £5 million.

14

Defence of the Realm:
Cathy Massiter

The first test of the government's resolve following the
acquittal of Clive Ponting on 11 February 1985 was not long
in coming. A programme called *MI5's Official Secrets* was
produced by Claudia Milne and Geoffrey Seed and their
company 20/20 Vision, for transmission on Channel 4 on
Wednesday 20 February 1985. Under the wide terms of
Section 2 the programme constituted the clearest possible
breach of the Official Secrets Act. It made no attempt to
disguise the fact that it was based on information supplied by
an MI5 officer, Cathy Massiter, who had worked for the
Security Service for thirteen years until she resigned in 1983.
The programme was also based on information supplied by
an anonymous and recently retired MI5 clerk, who was not
identified in the programme. Both the former MI5 employees
were prohibited under the terms of their employment and by
declarations they had signed on their retirement from the
service from disclosing information they had obtained in the
course of working for MI5.

In May 1984 Miranda Ingram, herself a former MI5
officer, had written an article in *New Society* about the
Michael Bettaney case, following his being convicted and
gaoled for twenty-three years on spying charges. The *New
Society* article was considerably more sympathetic to
Bettaney than the reports which had appeared elsewhere in
the press. Miss Ingram had worked with him in K Branch, the

counter-espionage arm of MI5. She wrote of 'the obsessive secrecy surrounding the Security Service which creates an aura of glamour among those who belong to it', and argued for public accountability, which she said would benefit both the service and the public. This led Miss Massiter to write a letter to *New Society* expressing some sympathy for Bettaney's predicament. She indicated that there were a number of officers who were disillusioned with some of the activies of MI5. As a result, Seed contacted Miss Massiter, and the interview with her became the centre of the Channel 4 programme.

This interview contained a number of sensitive and politically embarrassing allegations. These included assertions that MI5 tapped telephones of trade unionists such as miners' leaders Arthur Scargill and Mick McGahey, as well as the phones of leading members of the fire brigade union and the shop stewards' committee of the Ford Motor Company during the strikes in which they had been involved. In the case of Ken Gill, an alleged Communist, general secretary of the appropriately named TASS – the white collar section of the engineering union – and a member of the TUC General Council, MI5 had even burgled his house in order to plant a bug.

The revelation that the Security Service kept a close eye on the goings-on of the trade unions was nothing new. Barbara Castle had written in her diaries (published in 1980 as *The Castle Diaries 1964 to 1970*) on 6 May 1968:

> One of my discoveries in my new job is that the Minister of Labour has always been furnished with security reports on the Trade Unions. The first on my desk was about the inner Communist clique in the engineering unions. Say security, of the fifty-two members of the AEF National Committee, ten are Communist members and nine more are sympathisers. They have been holding secret meetings under the Chairmanship of Ramelson, the Communist Party's Chief industrial organiser. All very James Bond but I gather Denis Barnes doesn't take these security boys very seriously.

On 22 March 1969 Castle reported:

> Another Security Service report on the Ford dispute. The more I read these reports the less confidence I have in our intelligence. To begin with the material is always mighty thin and most of it would be obvious anyway to an informed politician.... Take Jack Jones: I don't need a Security Service to tell me that he succeeded in giving the impression that he was more militant than Scanlon or that he hadn't been in touch with the Communist Party during the dispute, or that Harry Unwin is Jones's protégé. It is mildly interesting, if true, that Unwin has a record of Communist Party membership, though he isn't currently a member. But it is a blinding bit of the obvious to say that the Communist Party is finding it difficult to counter its critics on the left who will contend that it has conceded every point of principle – the inclusion of 'penal' clauses – on which it supported the strike in the first instance. Altogether I really wonder what we pay these people for. I bet I could find out more myself in a few weeks, if I were given the job, than they do in a lifetime.

Barbara Castle was not prosecuted under the Official Secrets Act, nor was any attempt made to prevent publication of her memoirs.

Channel 4's *MI5's Official Secrets* also alleged that the Security Service was persistently disregarding the rules as to when it was permissible to tap telephones. There is no statute governing the operations of the Security Service; the nearest one gets to any form of charter is the directive sent in September 1952 by Sir David Maxwell-Fyfe, then Home Secretary, to the Director-General of the Security Service. The rules relating to telephone tapping can be found in the Birkett Report in October 1957, in a statement by Lord Harris of Greenwich in the House of Lords on 26 February 1975, in a White Paper on the interception of communications of April 1980 and in Lord Diplock's report in March 1981. Despite the number of rules the principles are perfectly clear, and according to the television programme they were being ignored.

Maxwell-Fyfe's directive had said:

The Security Services' task is the defence of the realm as a whole from external and internal dangers arising from attempts at espionage and sabotage and from the actions of persons and organisations whether directed from within or without the country which may be judged subversive to the state.

The directive went on to make it clear that the work of the Security Service was strictly limited to this task, that it must be kept free from any political bias or influence and that it should conduct no enquiry unless it was satisfied that it had an important bearing on the defence of the realm. However, paragraph 6 of the directive provided that ministers should be provided with detailed information obtained by the Security Service only when they asked for it and then only such information as was necessary for the determination of the matter upon which the minister was seeking guidance. The worthy aim of this document was to ensure that the Security Service could do its work without political interference; but the effect, if Miss Massiter was right, was that the Security Service could take advantage of the fact that it worked without effective supervision of a minister answerable in Parliament.

The television programme described the surveillance of leading members of the Campaign for Nuclear Disarmament. It alleged that the Security Service had succeeded in infiltrating the ostensibly left-wing treasurer of the Institute for Workers' Control, Harry Newton, into CND's London headquarters, when in fact he had been on the books of MI5 since the 1950s. The programme also contained an interview with Ronald White, a Jewish pharmacist in Leeds. White had infiltrated the National Front on behalf of the Special Branch and, to maintain his cover, had reluctantly to participate in the odd beating-up of members of the black community. When he had left the National Front he had been beaten up by them for his pains. There were also allegations that MI5 had opened files on those associated with the National Council for Civil Liberties, such as its general secretary

Patricia Hewitt and its legal officer Harriet Harman. By the time the programme was transmitted, early 1985, both had moved on from the NCCL into mainstream politics – Hewitt as adviser to Neil Kinnock, and Harman as a Labour MP.

The allegations in the programme were more topical and politically sensitive than the activities in the 1940s and 1950s of senior civil servants who were now either very elderly or dead. The people who were the subject of the activities of MI5 were very much alive, many of them in positions of some political influence. The fact that MI5 kept a close watch on political extremists and on trade union activities was known, but its extent and the way MI5 operated had never been publicised in this manner. Even if the programme was inaccurate, it contained official information which the two MI5 employees had no authority to communicate to television journalists.

The producers of the programme were advised at an early stage that it was more likely than not that they would be prosecuted. A prosecution would almost certainly have led to the programme not being shown. There was an equal risk of an injunction being obtained in the civil courts, which would also have stopped the programme. *MI5's Official Secrets* had therefore itself been produced in conditions of some secrecy.

Some benefit was obtained from the fact that the producers had originally intended to make a programme about the Special Branch, to coincide with the investigation of its activities by the House of Commons Home Affairs Select Committee. The problems that could arise in making a programme about the Special Branch soon became apparent. The producers had seen one of its former officers, who had introduced them to another former colleague, who reported back to Scotland Yard about the proposed programme. Shortly afterwards the original officer was visited by Special Branch, interrogated for five hours and warned in unambiguous terms of the risk of being prosecuted under the Official Secrets Act and of losing his pension rights. Both the producers soon found that their telephones at home went out of order, with the result that they were compelled to use the office telephone, which they suspected was being tapped.

Word reached Geoffrey Seed of a request by telex for background information about him from the police force in his home district in Wales, and of enquiries being made by a company search agency used by the Special Branch about companies with which he was connected. These events had the advantage that they emphasised the need for secrecy in the production of the programme and diverted attention from the fact that the programme was about the revelations by two MI5 employees rather than the Special Branch.

The production was moved out of the company's London office to the depths of the country. It was not until the day the programme was to be transmitted, 20 February 1985 – when it was submitted to the full Independent Broadcasting Authority for approval – that it became known outside the immediate circle of the producers and the IBA officers who had earlier seen the programme that it even mentioned Cathy Massiter. The programme was merely billed as a documentary from 20/20 Vision. By that time the producers had a completed programme scheduled for transmission and a much stronger base for fighting to have it shown.

On 20 February the film was shown to the Chairman and Deputy Chairman of the Independent Broadcasting Authority and to the other ten members of the IBA. The authority's lawyers also watched the programme and they advised that there was a clear breach of the Official Secrets Act and that the IBA ran the risk of being prosecuted, although they correctly advised that this was unlikely. This advice placed the IBA in some difficulty as it had not itself produced the programme. It was a statutory body set up to carry out the law under the Broadcasting Act 1981, and however unsatisfactory the terms of Section 2 were, it was considered no part of its function to court a prosecution. Accordingly the IBA decided that it should stop the programme being transmitted until it became clear whether the government was going to prosecute either Miss Massiter or the producers.

It would have been easy for the government to bring a prosecution under Section 2. 20/20 Vision was a very small company without the resources to fight costly legal battles. The main problem would have been deciding whom to prosecute. The dock would have filled quite nicely. There were the two producers, Claudia Milne and Geoffrey Seed, the two former MI5 employees and the programme's presenter, Hugo Young, a columnist for the *Guardian*. Had Channel 4 shown the programme its executives could also have been prosecuted. There was thus the risk that if a prosecution were brought the defence would be backed by the *Guardian* and by Channel 4. The thought of all these defendants could have been a factor in not prosecuting, but the real reason for not bringing a prosecution under Section 2 was the acquittal of Ponting earlier in February 1985. This showed that, even where there appeared to be clear breach of the Act, where much of the case could be heard in camera and where the judge came close to directing the jury to convict, it was still possible for the defendant to raise a successful defence of public interest and to question the policy he had been asked to implement.

Following closely upon the post-mortem on the sinking of the *Belgrano*, the prospect of a dissection of the murkier activities of MI5 was too awful to contemplate. There were clearly in the revelations of Miss Massiter issues of considerable public interest, arising out of the lack of accountability of MI5 and MI6, with their 5,000 employees and budget of £300 million per year. Furthermore, any prosecution would have taken place at the same time as the government would be shepherding the Interception of Communications Bill through its last stages in Parliament. This Bill had been introduced without any noticeable enthusiasm by the government to bring Britain into line with the European Convention, following the decision of the European Court of Human Rights, in a case brought by James Malone (who had been acquitted on a charge of receiving stolen goods), that the United Kingdom was in breach of its obligations under the European Convention. The Interception of Communications Bill was to provide for a tribunal and a commissioner to supervise the powers of authorising telephone tapping.

The producers of *MI5's Official Secrets* had made plans to obtain the maximum publicity for their programme to prevent the film being quietly buried and never seeing the light of day. Within three and a half hours of its being banned at 12.30 on Wednesday 20 February, a video of the programme was being shown to a group of journalists at the Russell Hotel in London. It was shown to MPs at the House of Commons at 7 p.m. For those who missed the first screening it was repeated the following evening. A copy of the film was placed in the House of Commons library and a copy was thoughtfully sent to the Director of Public Prosecutions and to Lord Bridge of Harwich, Chairman of the Security Commission. Several hundred cassettes had been produced as a precaution against the programme being banned, and the video rights in these were acquired by Richard Branson of Virgin Records. He marketed these in a slightly garish pack entitled *MI5's Official Secrets – The Programme That Couldn't Be Shown*. Lively trade was done in the cassettes until the ban was lifted and the programme was televised in March.

In addition, copies of the script of the programme went on sale, and a large extract was published in the *Guardian*, on 1 March. Sixteen-millimetre versions of the film were shown in cinemas in Oxford, Brighton and London. Plans had been made for a screening at the premises of the Bath Labour Party, but, in a spirit not altogether reminiscent of the Tolpuddle Martyrs, they decided after legal advice not to show it. The event took place instead, with standing room only, at Walcot village hall. Clips from the programme appeared on West German, United States, Australian and Dutch television.

The producers had also anticipated that steps would be taken to discredit Miss Massiter. To combat this she was produced at St Ermine's Hotel in London, where she met John Cartwright, Steven Norris and Alf Dubs, MPs belonging to Social Democratic, Conservative and Labour parties respectively. Attempts were made to discredit Miss Massiter by revealing that she had written to Bettaney while he was in prison awaiting trial and that prior to her leaving MI5 she had been asked by them to consult the service's psychiatrist. Unlike Ponting she had voiced her misgivings

about what she was being required to do. The meeting with
the MPs enabled them to form their own view as to whether
Miss Massiter really was a neurotic betrayer of trust.

With this publicity and the government's distaste for an
MI5 Official Secrets Act case after Ponting's acquittal, it not
surprisingly took the Attorney-General, Sir Michael Havers
QC, little time to decide that there would not be a
prosecution. He announced his decision on 5 March; this had
been well leaked, and newspaper reports that Sir Michael had
decided against prosecution had started appearing on 27
February. On 6 March the IBA lifted the ban on the
programme, and on 8 March it was transmitted unaltered.

The Director of Public Prosecutions ordered a police
investigation of the claims made in the programme that the
Security Service had broken the law and that Ronald White
had, while acting as an agent for the Special Branch, joined in
assaults on members of the black community. As with the
police investigations of the allegations concerning Lord
Lewin following the Ponting trial, the enquiry was of a
perfunctory nature. The producers were merely asked to
produce a cassette copy of the broadcast. As the film had now
been televised, cassettes of 'the programme that could not be
shown' were in plentiful supply, and the request was readily
complied with. The producers were not interviewed further
by the police, and there were no enquiries into the question of
official secrecy.

Miss Massiter herself was seen by the police, but their
interview with her lasted only a few minutes; no one even
mentioned her pension rights. The police did not trouble
themselves to interview the other MI5 employee, although it
could have taken no more than four or five hours to establish
her identity from the operations of MI5 which she had
discussed in the programme. Following the television
screening, Lord Bridge was requested to investigate that the
necessary formalities for obtaining a warrant to tap a
telephone had been complied with and that the criteria for
phone tapping were being observed. Over the last fifteen
years 6,129 such warrants have been issued, and it would have
been an enormous task to investigate them all. As it was,

Lord Bridge began his enquiry on 28 February and reported on 6 March, despite having sat as a judge in the House of Lords for two of those days, that nothing was amiss and that all the authorised taps were in fact authorised. The findings of Lord Bridge were widely criticised. Roy Jenkins, a former Home Secretary, wrote to *The Times* expressing the view that the time and scope of the investigation made Lord Bridge appear a 'poodle of the executive', a view with which Lord Bridge was quick to point out that he disagreed. The *Daily Telegraph* found his report distinctly 'hasty and bland' and called it 'the Bench's answer to fast food, a juridicial Big Mac'.

The pre-publicity for the programme ensured that it was seen by many more people than would otherwise have tuned into Channel 4. The political reasons for not bringing a prosecution under Section 2 are understandable, but the failure to do so will make it very much more difficult to defend prosecutions on less important matters. The anxiety of the government not to prosecute an MI5 officer like Miss Massiter was underlined by the fact that a blind eye was turned to the interview she gave on 10 March 1985 to Nick Davies on the *Observer*. This interview set out in far greater detail than the television programme her work in F Branch, the industrial desk of MI5, but no action was taken against the newspaper or her as a consequence.

15

Question of Judgement?
Cecil Parkinson

The unsatisfactory state of the law regarding the extent to which ministers can authorise themselves to disclose information was illustrated by the experiences of two Cabinet ministers, Leon Brittan MP (Chapter 16) and Cecil Parkinson MP. Parkinson had in 1983 been driven from office at the Department of Trade and Industry by the revelations by Miss Sara Keays about their affair, their near-marriage and their impending love-child. These were aired at the time of the 1983 Conservative Party Conference and led to Parkinson's resignation. Until September 1985 it looked as if Parkinson might, despite some opposition from within the Cabinet, be brought back into government by Mrs Thatcher. What lingering hopes there might have been for his rehabilitation were shattered by the announcement by Miss Keays that she was publishing her memoirs with the inappropriate title *A Question of Judgement.* Worse still, she was serialising them in the *Daily Mirror*, whose proprietor, Robert Maxwell, was able to achieve record sales of the newspaper at a Conservative Party Conference by beginning serialisation on the opening day.

It was an unhappy and uninteresting account of the break-up of their affair, which succeeded in filling six pages of the *Mirror* on its first day of publication and continued to run on through the week. It was distinctly flattered by the banner headline 'The Story That Had to Be Told'. Some attention was attracted by Miss Keays's claim that, during the Falklands war, Parkinson had told her about the discussions which had taken place as to whether Lord Carrington should resign, and had even asked her views on the subject. Parkinson was a member of the War Cabinet, and Miss Keays told us that she 'felt it a great privilege to know so much of the events behind the scenes'. She watched 'the official news bulletins on television avidly, with my awareness of the dangers heightened by what Cecil told me of the background of these momentous events'. Perhaps the other members of the War Cabinet did not breathe a word to their spouses as to what was happening, but it must be a regular occurrence for Cabinet ministers, like other people, to give some indication to their wives (or husbands) of what they have been doing that day. The fact that Miss Keays was not Parkinson's wife but rather his girlfriend of twelve years' standing made no difference to the quality of what was done. It was inevitable that someone should raise the question whether, if Miss Keays's account was correct, there had been a breach of the Official Secrets Act – the suggestion being that Parkinson had imparted this information to her in her capacity as something other than his amanuensis.

Tam Dalyell MP raised the question as to why there was not a prosecution. One MP said that what was sauce for the goose should be sauce for the gander, but it seems he was rather more interested in the gander than in this goose's sauce. No one appeared much interested in the question of whether Miss Keays herself should have been investigated for receiving information which it might equally have been said she knew was passed to her in breach of the Official Secrets Act. However, in fairness one wonders what she could have done, other than placing her hands over her ears. Such is the scope of the Official Secrets Act that she could have been charged with the offence of harbouring a person suspected of breaching the Act when she allowed Parkinson to stay the night!

According to Miss Keays, Parkinson committed another possible offence under the Official Secrets Act when he left his red dispatch boxes overnight in a car outside her house and the car was stolen. Fortunately the boxes were recovered intact; dispatch boxes should remain in a minister's sight or be locked up in a safe at night. All these matters had to be fully investigated by the police, yet the entire charade was probably no more than a waste of time. Des Wilson, Chairman of the Campaign for Freedom of Information and no supporter of the Conservative Party, wrote on 17 October 1985 in a letter to *The Times*: 'The investigation and the prosecution of Mr Parkinson would be even more absurd and frivolous than the absurd and frivolous prosecution of Clive Ponting.'

The disagreements between Parkinson and Miss Keays related to their private lives. To wheel in the apparatus of the Official Secrets Act to deal with a conversation in a private place between two law-abiding individuals graphically illustrates the absurdity of the Official Secrets Act.

16

A Genuine Difference of Understanding:
Leon Brittan

If proof were needed that the question of prosecuting under the Official Secrets Act is essentially a political matter, it is to be found in the government's handling of the leak in the Westland affair in January 1986. Whether there should, at the least, have been a proper outside investigation of the case by the Director of Public Prosecutions rather than the unsatisfactory internal enquiry by Sir Robert Armstrong, the Cabinet Secretary, depends on where the truth of the matter lay and the extent to which Mrs Thatcher directly or indirectly sanctioned the leak. A full-scale investigation would certainly have been politically embarrassing, and the government was better served by Sir Robert Armstrong's enquiry, which proceeded on the very doubtful proposition that if a minister authorised the disclosure there could be no prosecution.

The leak was an unusual one in that it was made to the Press Association on the specific authority of one Cabinet minister, Leon Brittan QC, the Secretary of State for Trade and Industry, seemingly to discredit one of his ministerial colleagues, Michael Heseltine, the Secretary of State for Defence. It arose in the context of the attempt at the end of 1985 to rescue Westland Helicopters. Heseltine favoured the European bid, whereas Brittan preferred what turned out to be the winning combination of Sikorsky/Fiat. Brittan authorised the leak of part of a letter from the Solicitor-

General, Sir Patrick Mayhew QC, to Heseltine. Such letters from law officers to Cabinet ministers should never be disclosed; even the fact that a minister has received legal advice from a law officer should be kept confidential.

Problems had arisen when Heseltine wrote, on 3 January 1986, extolling the virtues of the European proposals to David Horne of Lloyds Merchant Bank, which was advising Westland on the merits of the rival bids. The following day Mrs Thatcher referred Heseltine's letter to the Solicitor-General for his advice. He wrote on 6 January to Heseltine, querying a number of his assertions in the letter. Heseltine subsequently replied to the points raised by Mayhew. The Solicitor-General's letter was drawn to Brittan's attention during a luncheon engagement at 1.30 p.m. on 6 January. Brittan was being lunched by Sikorsky's merchant bankers, Morgan Grenfell, where the former Permanent Secretary of the DTI, Sir Peter Carey, was a director – Carey was later to become a director of Westland when Sikorsky took over. Brittan took particular note of the Solicitor-General's phrase at the end of his letter that Heseltine's letter 'does in my opinion contain certain material inaccuracies in the respects I have mentioned, and I must therefore advise that you should write again to Mr Horne correcting the inaccuracies'.

Brittan arranged through his private secretary, John Mogg, for the Director of Information at the Department of Trade and Industry, Miss Colette Bowe, to have highly selective extracts from Mayhew's letter made public. Miss Bowe seems to have been a little more worldly-wise than her boss when it came to leaking; in 1981 she had had a letter marked 'strictly confidential' – which she had written to the Society of Motor Manufacturers about the steps being taken by the government to prevent the import of cheaply priced cars from the Continent – disclosed to the *Sunday Times*. She now wanted specific authority from her minister before she leaked extracts from Mayhew's letter to Heseltine. This she obtained and she then checked the position with 10 Downing Street before making any disclosure. What happened at 10 Downing Street is far from clear, but it gave rise to the immortal phrase 'a genuine difference of understanding between officials' in a saga in which Mrs Thatcher was to declare truth stranger than fiction. Mrs Thatcher, it seems, did not get involved at that stage. Nevertheless Brittan – normally a shrewd political operator – was under the impression that he did have the authority of the Prime Minister to disclose the letter's contents.

Precisely what transpired between Thatcher and Brittan appears to be the one impenetrable official secret of this saga. Dr David Owen, the SDP leader, was moved to comment: 'The affair is a spider's web, and as each strand of the web is unravelled we get closer to the spider's nest, which is No. 10, and the spider herself is the Prime Minister.' The Prime Minister was later to say that if she had insisted upon becoming involved she might have subjected herself to the criticism of being 'Mrs Bossy Boots'. However, the Press Secretary at 10 Downing Street, Bernard Ingham, was consulted before the document was released to the press. It seems that the principal concern of 10 Downing Street was to ensure that the leak emanated from the Department of Trade and Industry rather than from No. 10 – surely an interesting insight into the approach of No. 10 to the matter. Ingham advised that the contents of the letter (or such extracts as were to be released) should be passed to Chris Moncrieff of the Press Association, but should not be seen as coming from No. 10.

At 3.30 p.m. on 6 January extracts from Sir Patrick's letter were duly leaked to the Press Association – that is, within two hours of a copy of it being received at the Department of Trade and Industry. The official reason for this urgency was a laudable worry that commercial judgements might have been based on Heseltine's 'material inaccuracies' at an important meeting at Westland being held at 4 p.m. that day. However, that meeting was not a shareholders' meeting but merely a press conference. The obvious person to whom to flash this information was Sir John Cuckney, the chairman of Westland, but all that happened was that a copy of the Press Association release was passed to the company's public relations officer, Bob Greig, who merely mentioned it to Sir John when he arrived for the meeting.

On 7 January the Solicitor-General gave vent to his feelings about his private and confidential letter being leaked to the press. Sir Patrick wrote to Heseltine of his anger at the impropriety of the disclosure:

> I want to express my dismay that a letter containing confidential legal advice from a law officer to one of his colleagues should have been leaked, and apparently leaked in a highly selective way.
>
> Quite apart from the breach of confidentiality that is involved, the rule is very clearly established that even the fact that the law officers have tendered advice in a particular case may not be disclosed without their consent, let alone the content of such advice.
>
> It is plain that in this instance this important rule was immediately and flagrantly violated.

One can only speculate as to whether Mayhew would have written in such forthright terms if he had known that the source of the leak was his fellow minister and QC, Leon Brittan.

On 6 January, Heseltine had had enough. He resigned by walking out of a Cabinet meeting. As a result of the controversy surrounding this leak, the Prime Minister set up a commission of enquiry under Sir Robert Armstrong, the Cabinet Secretary. It subsequently transpired that Mrs Thatcher had learnt of the source of the leak a few hours after the letter had been released by the Press Association, and in such circumstances many wondered why the whole panoply of a commission of enquiry was set up. It was apparently the government's view that if the leak was authorised by a minister there could be no breach of the Official Secrets Act; therefore there should have been no need for an enquiry. It showed a strange lack of judgement on the Prime Minister's part.

Brittan lost the support of many Conservative back-benchers when on 17 January he was thought to deny the existence of a letter sent by Sir Raymond Lygo, the chief executive of British Aerospace. Brittan did not, of course, say anything that was untrue, but he adopted a lawyer's skirting round the truth that those of his parliamentary colleagues who were not lawyers found distinctly unattractive. He was asked whether he had received any letter from Lygo giving his account of the somewhat stormy meeting Brittan had had with British Aerospace, at which he had allegedly warned of the dire consequences for British Aerospace if the European bid for Westland was successful. Brittan replied that he had not received any such letter, meaning (as was the case) that he *personally* had not received a letter from Sir Raymond. He subsequently added that he was not aware of any letter from Lygo to anyone else either. However, a letter in such terms *had* been received by Mrs Thatcher from Sir Austin Pearce, the chairman of British Aerospace, and Brittan had been told about this before he went to the Commons. A number of Members of Parliament misunderstood Brittan's replies to be a denial of the existence of such a letter, although he had not made any such denial. Nevertheless Brittan felt sufficiently embarrassed by the incident to return to the House of Commons at 10.30 that evening to apologise unreservedly for any inadvertent misleading of the House. The text of Sir Austin's letter was published the next day. Brittan's explanation of why he had answered the questions as he had was that Pearce's letter was marked 'strictly private and confidential', and he had accordingly felt bound to give answers that concealed its existence.

Admiration for Brittan's laudable aim of protecting the confidentiality of this correspondence was tempered as a result of his apparent amnesia that only one week before he had flagrantly violated the confidentiality of correspondence between Sir Patrick Mayhew QC and Michael Heseltine. Even those who subscribe to the view that a week is a long time in politics found this hard to swallow. Indeed, there were those who looked for precedents in the case where the Attorney-General, Sir Rufus Isaacs KC, on being asked in 1912 in Parliament whether he had purchased any shares of the English Marconi Company, had replied in forthright terms, 'Never from the beginning have I had one single transaction with the shareholders of that company.' It transpired that the wrong question was asked. Sir Rufus's answer would have been very different if he had been asked whether he had bought shares in the American Marconi Company!

On 23 January 1986 the Prime Minister announced the result of the leak enquiry. She informed the House of Commons that she personally learnt of the leak only some hours after it occurred. Mrs Thatcher said that she regretted that there were a number of matters which could have been handled better; she went on to say that she deeply regretted the fact that the document had been disclosed without reference to the Solicitor-General. Her statement had a distinctly depressing effect on Brittan's job prospects, and he resigned the following day.

The criticisms of Brittan's conduct by the Prime Minister seemed to be supported by Sir Robert Armstrong when he gave evidence for two and three-quarter hours to the House of Commons Select Committee for Defence. He said he regretted the discourtesy, impropriety and unwisdom surrounding the Westland leak – language to be flung back in Sir Robert's face by the committee, despite its built-in Conservative majority.

The leaking of Mayhew's letter was a disaster for Brittan and cost the Prime Minister the services of a very able minister. The loss of office was a cruel blow, but one is left with the impression that if the leaker had been in a more lowly position, he or she might have been prosecuted. If the fault had lain with Miss Bowe, which it did not, she might well have ended up in the dock of the Old Bailey. She had wisely obtained the permission of her minister to disclose the document and had insisted on being given immunity from prosecution before she co-operated with the Armstrong enquiry.

Brittan had been responsible (or so it seemed) for leaking a letter whose existence he had no conceivable right to make public, in view of the statement of the Solicitor-General that not only the contents of a law officer's advice, but even the fact that a law officer had advised, should never be revealed. The fact that he was a minister of the Crown did not give him *carte blanche* to make disclosures of this kind, particularly when they concerned a highly confidential letter, written by one government colleague to another. It was not a document emanating from his department. Section 2 does not provide any guidance as to the meaning of the words 'a person to whom he is authorised to communicate it'. In practice ministers are, as the Franks Committee pointed out, self-authorising; they decided for themselves what to reveal. But, as the Franks Committee also made clear, this does not mean that a minister can reveal anything to anyone. Had that been the case there would presumably have been no investigation at all of Parkinson, as he was a minister at the time he was alleged to have passed information to Miss Keays.

The only person who could validly have authorised this leak was the Prime Minister. She denies having done so; it would appear however that Brittan was under the impression that the publication of the extracts from Mayhew's letter was approved by the Prime Minister if not expressly authorised. Brittan had reported back to Mrs Thatcher at 7 p.m. on 4 January after he had spoken to Mayhew. He was under the impression that he had the Prime Minister's approval. She later told the House of Commons that she 'did not know about Leon Brittan's role'.

The Franks Committee's view was that 'ministers largely authorise themselves to disclose information. Nevertheless, ministers have the same public duty to protect official information as their civil servants and should continue to be subject to the law as at present. It would be wrong to place them in any special position.' Doubtless Brittan considered that he was entitled to act as he did but equally clearly he was not, and ignorance of the law is no excuse even for government ministers or QCs. The judge's ruling in the Ponting case indicated that the offence of communicating information without authority was an absolute offence and did not depend on proof of criminal intent.

No minister has ever been prosecuted for breaching the Official Secrets Act, and this was clearly not the case in which to start considering prosecuting ministers. However, the automatic assumption that Brittan's conduct could not have been a breach of the Official Secrets Act is questionable. It would, of course, be most undesirable for errors of judgement by ministers to lead to their prosecution, and apart from anything else it would clog up the courts, if not actually filling Her Majesty's prisons. In Brittan's case there was the additional reason for not contemplating taking proceedings of a genuine question as to whether he could be said to have been authorised by or on behalf of the Prime Minister. If he had been authorised to leak the document by the Prime Minister, there would have been no question of his being prosecuted under Section 2. Nevertheless, lesser people are prosecuted for such errors of judgement. The uncertainties as to what constitutes an authorised leak that can arise with ministers in Brittan's position is yet another reason for abolishing Section 2.

The final episode of the Westland saga consisted of the hearings before the Defence Select Committee of the House of Commons – proceedings as remarkable for who was prevented from appearing and for the reluctance of certain witnesses to answer the questions put to them as for the evidence actually given. The committee found itself unable to form a view on Mrs Thatcher's responsibility for the leak. It nevertheless criticised Brittan for acting improperly and Heseltine for provoking the crisis by his one-man guerrilla campaign against his Cabinet colleagues. Sir Robert Armstrong did not escape criticism for his decision to conduct the Cabinet enquiry into the leak when he must have known that ministers were involved. His subsequent refusal to discipline any of the civil servants directly involved was regarded as wholly unsatisfactory. It is to the Head of the Home Civil Service that all civil servants have to look for an example and a clear lead in such things. In this case, the committee observed, that lead had not been given.

The committee recommended that the two jobs held by Armstrong – head of the Civil Service and Cabinet Secretary – should henceforward be separated. Prior to the publication of the report, Armstrong was requested by the Prime Minister to stay in both posts after he had passed the normal Civil Service retirement age.

17

Paranoia about Ancient Secrets:
the Law of Confidence

When it comes to unauthorised publication, the government has an even stronger weapon than Section 2: the law of confidence. As it is part of the civil law, success does not depend on conviction by a jury, which, as the Ponting case had shown, is not always predictable. The law of confidence has the added advantage that it gives the government the opportunity of obtaining an injunction against a book by going before the judge *ex parte* – that is, privately and without any public hearing, and very often in the first instance without any notice to the other side. The result is that the publishers and author may be prohibited from publishing the book anywhere in the world and may even be ordered to collect their manuscript from any foreign publishers if it is still within their power to do so. Instead of having to prove its case beyond reasonable doubt, therefore, the government can compel the publishers and the author to reveal the contents of their book and possibly the source of their information, if they wish to have the injunction lifted. The way the government has taken advantage of the law of confidence has been erratic and at times contradictory. It is possible nevertheless to draw some principles from the practice of the government in this area.

In the 1920s and 1930s considerable latitude was given to those who wished to write about their experiences in the Security Service. No one seems to have been particularly concerned when Sir Basil Thomson, who had been assistant commissioner in the Special Branch and Director of Intelligence, wrote about his experiences, devoting a chapter to the Special Branch, only a year after he left Scotland Yard in 1922. His bland book, *Queer People,* was perhaps most noticeable for its contention that the Russian Revolution was the work of a number of Russian Jews. Karl Marx was dismissed as 'a Prussian Jew'. As there was a degree of anti-Semitism in the Security Service at the time, the book may have fallen on receptive ground.

There was some flexibility about the publication of Cabinet papers. In November 1919 the Cabinet decided that ministers could keep such documents as they wished, but attempts were made by the Cabinet Secretary, Sir Maurice Hankey, to restrict this rule. The prosecutions of Compton Mackenzie (Chapter 3) and Edgar Lansbury (Chapter 4) were intended to discourage the writing of memoirs based on official government papers. Ironically, Hankey was himself to fall foul of his own rule (see below).

After the Second World War a number of people wished to write about the success of British intelligence during the war. The British succeeded in breaking the Abwehr cipher with the result that a substantial proportion of the German agents sent to spy in this country were captured and controlled by the British. The British also succeeded in breaking the German military ciphers generated on a machine known as the Enigma, which was read by the Allies throughout the war and provided most of the important intelligence that was intercepted.

There was very considerable reluctance to allow books about such subjects to be published. The government appeared to operate a rule that those who had worked for the Security Service in whatever capacity should not be allowed to publish their memoirs, particularly if they happened to have signed the Official Secrets Act. There were, however, exceptions to this rule. In 1955 Sir Percy Sillitoe, who had been the head of MI5 from 1945 to 1953, was permitted to publish his memoirs, *Cloak without Dagger*. This was a time when the activities and the very existence of the Security Service in peacetime were a closely guarded secret. Yet in the foreword to the book the former Prime Minister Clement Attlee had written: 'A Director-General of MI5 needs very special qualities.' Sillitoe's views on the need for secrecy about his activities differed markedly from those of his predecessors and successors. He was the only head of the Security Service who listed in *Who's Who* his job as Director-General, Security Service, 1946 to 1953; usually there would be an entry such as 'attached to the War Office'. He was probably right to take a slightly more relaxed view about the need for secrecy. Shortly after he had been appointed to his post as Director-General of the Security Service his son arrived at Victoria Station only to discover that he had mislaid his father's office address. He therefore had to ask the taxi driver to take him to MI5. Without hesitation the cab driver replied, 'That will be at 11 Curzon Street,' and took him there.

Sir Percy had been appointed Director-General at the insistence of Herbert Morrison, the Lord President of the Council in the Labour government, in preference to MI5's candidate Guy Liddell. Morrison viewed Sir Percy Sillitoe as 'an honest copper'. He had had a successful police career in the colonies and latterly was Chief Constable in Glasgow, where he broke up the razor-gangs and had set up the C Division specials to combat the IRA. Among his many successes was an incident when one of his specials was able to observe one of the nuns accompanying a coffin from Dublin to Glasgow shaving in her cabin. A closer examination of the coffin showed that it was full of arms, ammunition and grenades.

Sillitoe's police background did not make him universally popular in MI5. Professor Hugh Trevor-Roper referred to him as 'a self-advertising policeman'. Sir Percy in his turn criticised a number of employees of MI5 as 'book-learned intellectuals'. No doubt he did not have the noble professor in mind. Sir Percy's first attempt at writing his memoirs was ghosted by his personal assistant, Russell Lee, but was vetoed by the government. Eventually he was able to negotiate the necessary cuts with the Home Office, and an officially acceptable version of the book was published; subsequently a departmental committee was set up to devise more stringent rules to prevent such books being written. Sillitoe appears to have been less than happy with the cuts he had to make, complaining that 'the government tore the guts out of the book and completely emasculated it'. That was the extent of Sir Percy's writing, although he had the curious distinction of being mentioned in Ian Fleming's book *Diamonds are Forever*, having been hired after his retirement from the Security Service by De Beers Consolidated Mines as its adviser on security matters.

In February 1955 attempts were made to prevent Colonel Alexander Scotland from publishing his book *The London Cage*, so named after the house in Kensington Palace Gardens known as the London District Cage, where he had assisted as an intelligence officer in the interrogation of important German prisoners of war. The case illustrates the close interrelation between the Official Secrets Act and the law of confidence as well as the confusion and over-reaction that bedevil such cases. Colonel Scotland had in 1951 been threatened with prosecution by the War Office when he wrote a book called *The Kesselring Case,* in which he suggested that the Field Marshal should not have been sent to prison as a war criminal. In July 1954 he had sent the War Office a copy of the typescript of *The London Cage* and had been told by the public relations officer that it was 'a very good book'. However, difficulties arose when it reached the Army security branch, and Scotland was interviewed at the War Office in November 1954 and told that he could not publish the book. In the best tradition of such cases, the War Office would not tell him what was wrong with the book, but questions raised in the House of Commons revealed that it had been banned because it was thought to be in breach of the Official Secrets Act. So matters remained until February 1955, when Special Branch officers led by Superintendent G. C. Smith raided Scotland's flat in Paddington and removed all documents connected with the book. The reason for that action appears to have been a fear that his book was to be published in the United States.

Colonel Scotland was a man of some character, having

been associated with British intelligence since 1915, and with the unusual distinction of having served in both the German and British armies. (He had fought under the name of Schottland for the Germans in the Hottentot Wars between 1903 and 1907.) He contested the government's attempts to suppress his book, and eventually it was published in 1957 with the disclaimer: 'The War Office wishes to make it clear that the views stated in this book are the author's own responsibility. Further, the War Office does not in any way vouch for the accuracy of the facts and does not necessarily accept any opinions expressed in the book.'

The rule that intelligence officers could not publish their memoirs was further breached in 1966 when a book called *British Agent* by John Whitwell was published. John Whitwell was the pseudonym of Leslie Nicholson, and this was a full account of his life as a spy, first in Czechoslovakia, then in Latvia in its days of independence from 1934 to 1940. His publishers, William Kimber, had negotiated clearance for this book with the assistance of Graham Greene and Malcolm Muggeridge, both of whom had been connected with the Secret Service. The book itself did not reveal many secrets but it did constitute an exception to the general rule against British agents publishing their memoirs. Nicholson had operated under the cover of an import-export business. When he was in Warsaw a senior London colleague in the Secret Service came out to see him by train. The telegram warning him of the agent's impending arrival ended: 'Will be wearing Old Etonian tie.' Nicholson resisted the temptation to reply: 'Regret unfamiliar with OE colours.' Fortunately the MI5 officer was perfectly distinctive as he emerged from the train surrounded by peasant women and wearing his black tie with blue stripes.

There was increasing resentment among those who had worked for the Security Service on Ultra and Enigma at the fact that they were not able to give an account of what had unquestionably been a great triumph for British Intelligence, at a time when publication would have done no damage to national security. A number of such books did slip through the net, such as, in 1955, *The Man Who Never Was*, by Ewen

Montagu QC, describing how German intelligence had been fooled by the planting of documents on the corpse of a British officer which was washed up in Spain. The enormous success of such books increased the feelings of frustration.

A number of people wished to write about Enigma. These included an American writer, Anthony Cave Brown, who, having begun his book in 1962, learnt of the Ultra secret in 1969. He was reminded of the Official Secrets Act and rather less formally was told by certain intelligence officers that, if he published and went too far, his gizzard would be slit or at best he would be horsewhipped. After Group Captain Winterbotham had published his book, *The Ultra Secret*, Cave Brown was able to publish his account in 1975, under the title *Bodyguard of Lies*, without any damage to his gizzard or being horsewhipped.

A further inroad came with Sir John Masterman's *The Double Cross System* in 1972. He had been Chairman of the XX (20) Committee, which had been involved with the work of the Radio Security Services (RSS) in intercepting incoming radio signals from the Germans generated through their Enigma machines, and with the work of the Government Code and Cipher School (GCCS) at Bletchley. The activities of RSS and GCCS were subsequently combined in GCHQ. Masterman had also been concerned with the operations of BI(a), which took charge of German agents who had been unmasked by the interception of their messages and encouraged to work for the British. He felt strongly that these matters could then be written about and he was in a good position to judge. Like a number of intelligence officers, he found himself increasingly irritated at what he considered to be the inadequate and often inaccurate books published following the war by people who had not been in the Security Service.

At the end of the war Masterman wrote an account of the XX Committee's activities running double agents, whose performance he had monitored for the committee. A hundred copies were printed, but it appears that someone thought better of it and destroyed seventy-five of those copies. Sir John kept one for himself. He approached three successive heads of the Security Service – Sir David Petrie, Sir Dick White and Sir Roger Hollis – for permission to publish his report. All these attempts failed. Although he received a more sympathetic hearing from the next Director-General, Sir Martin Furnival Jones, the question of publication became bogged down in various Whitehall committees. It was referred for consideration to the Cabinet Secretary, Sir Burke Trend, and to the Permanent Under-Secretary of State at the Home Office, Sir Phillip Allen. By this time Sir John was aged eighty, and the government perhaps hoped that *anno Domini* might resolve the problem of publication. However, Sir John's determination was not to be underestimated; with the assistance of his literary agent, A. D. Peters, his book was accepted for publication by Yale University Press in the United States.

As a matter of courtesy Masterman informed the Home Secretary, Reginald Maulding, of the forthcoming publication. This information produced a dramatic reaction in comparison to the inactivity over the last twenty-five years: the problem emerged with the speed of light from the departmental committee which had been considering the question at the Home Office for many months. Sir John received a telegram from the Foreign Secretary, Sir Alec Douglas-Home, inviting him to lunch before going on to see the Home Secretary.

When Sir John saw the Home Secretary he found him very much more sympathetic to the project now that the government was faced with the prospect of the book being published in the United States. The government wished to have some control over what was published in the USA, and Sir John wished to have his book published in Britain. A compromise was therefore reached whereby the government would be able to inspect the typescript of the American edition and request that any matters threatening the national security be removed. In the event, relatively few changes were requested, and these were readily agreed; it was a very sensible solution. The book was published with an unusual copyright notice in view of earlier government behaviour: 'Copyright © 1972 by Yale University – Crown Copyright

Reserved'. Once it had been agreed that this book could be published Her Majesty's Stationery Office appeared on the scene to demand all the royalties receivable by Sir John, although ultimately HMSO settled on 50 per cent! If the government hoped that this was the last it would hear of Masterman, it was again disappointed. He described his difficulties in publishing *The Double Cross System* in his memoirs, *On the Chariot Wheel*, but no attempt was made to prevent their publication.

There was some precedent for having published material contained in a report originally prepared for the Secret Service. Professor Trevor-Roper had been permitted in the early 1950s to publish his book *The Last Days of Hitler*, which was based on a report he had produced as an MI6 officer. The justification may have been to dispel any myth that Hitler had survived the war.

The next major breakthrough as regards restrictions on publication came in Group Captain F. W. Winterbotham's book *The Ultra Secret*, published in 1974. It was immensely successful, selling more than four million copies worldwide, and it established a precedent for publishing books about intelligence work in the Second World War. *The Ultra Secret* highlighted both the interest that there was in such books and the commercial rewards for their authors.

Winterbotham had been the first head of the air section of the Secret Intelligence Service. He had had the unusual experience during the First World War of meeting the German pilot who had shot him down, who looked at the bullet-ridden seat cushion on which Winterbotham had been sitting and commented, 'Just one more inch and you would have been a soprano.' During the Second World War, Winterbotham had worked at Bletchley, and his book dealt with the breaking of codes used by the German Enigma machines. Although this had been an outstanding triumph for British intelligence, which a number of those involved wished to publicise, the problem was that the British government had after the war sold a number of these Enigma machines to unsuspecting developing countries, including Indonesia, without informing their governments that the

British could now read their coded messages. This had proved very helpful during the Malaya campaign, when the Indonesians were supporting Communist rebels against British rule.

Winterbotham's book took nearly two years to pass through the D-notice committee, and was also submitted for inspection by three committees at MI6, GCHQ and the Foreign Office. Curiously it was the Foreign Office that caused the trouble, where it seems to have been the official historians who were responsible for the objection. This meant that the book had to be referred to the Prime Minister, Harold Wilson. Having recently written his own memoirs, Wilson passed the book. The information about the Ultra system was by that stage very elderly, and Winterbotham agreed not to disclose details of how the code had been broken. The book was a good example of how publication is permitted when the account in question shows the intelligence service in a good light. Even so, difficulties were placed in the way of Winterbotham in that he was not allowed access to any of his records to assist in writing his book. Subsequently the thirty-six tapes that he gave to the Imperial War Museum of his experiences in the First World War and in MI6 from 1930 to 1945 were withheld by the Foreign Office, despite the fact that there was nothing in them of a secret nature that has not already been published. The Imperial War Museum is thus not even able to disclose them to approved researchers and historians.

A similar approach was adopted by the government on the question of restricting the availability of official documents when Sir Stuart Milner-Barry sought access to a report he had compiled on the wartime activities of Hut Six at Bletchley, which had been engaged in deciphering messages transmitted on Enigma machines. Unlike Masterman and Professor R. V. Jones he had not kept a copy. Milner-Barry wished to look at his report in order to determine whether a book could be written about the activities of Hut Six, to set the record straight against claims made by Polish refugees in the United States that all the credit was due to them. On five occasions Milner-Barry was refused permission to see what he had himself written. Then, in 1982, *The Hut Six Story* was published in the United States by a leading wartime cryptanalyst, Gordon Welchman, who was one of the group of mathematicians who had worked at GCCS at Bletchley Park on the Ultra programme. This account was written without reference to either GCHQ or the CIA and it gave Welchman's version of how Enigma was broken. Its publication caused considerable resentment at GCHQ, which surfaced when an article written by Welchman shortly before his death, entitled 'From Polish Bomba to British Bomb: The Birth of Ultra', was published in the magazine *Intelligence and National Security* in 1985. This passed the D-notice committee on 8 July 1985, when it appeared that GCHQ had no objection. However, on 12 July, Sir Peter Marychurch, the director of GCHQ, wrote an astonishing letter to Welchman in the United States, who was now dying from cancer, asserting that the article could inflict direct damage to national security: 'We do not expect outsiders to show any great sense of responsibility in what they publish, but you can perhaps understand that it is a bitter blow to us, as well as a disastrous example to others, when valued ex-colleagues decide to let us down.'

This outburst was severely criticised by Milner-Barry – himself a former senior intelligence officer. He wrote a letter to the *Guardian* containing an unusual public dressing down for the director of GCHQ:

As one of Gordon Welchman's oldest friends and colleagues from Hut Six I feel bound to record an emphatic protest at the slur cast on his memory by the letter from Sir Peter Marychurch, quoted in your issue of 15 October as having been sent to Welchman within a few months of his death. Even had there been substance in Sir Peter's complaint, he might, I should have thought, have refrained from writing to a man of Welchman's distinction, twenty years his senior, in terms more appropriate to the rebuke of an erring subordinate.

But in fact the complaint is a prime example of the lengths to which GCHQ's paranoia about the preservation of ancient secrets will carry them. To talk of 'direct damage to security' in the context of Welchman's article in *Intelligence and National Security* is surely moonshine. The secrets of the Enigma and how it was broken are of fascinating interest historically, and it is a sad pity that the authorities still prevent the story being properly told. But to suppose that the battles which we had to wage before the birth of the first electronic computer (which must seem to present-day cryptanalysts rather like fighting with bows and arrows) could be relevant to security now is just not credible.

Milner-Barry's book was never written. Winterbotham's *The Ultra Secret* was followed in 1978 by *Most Secret War* by Professor R. V. Jones. Jones was a physicist who had joined the air section of the SIS under Winterbotham. He was the former scientific adviser to MI6, and his book was an account of British scientific intelligence from 1939 to 1945. Jones had avoided the difficulties that faced Winterbotham and Milner-Barry by taking the sixty reports he had compiled during the Second World War with him when he left the service. In fact nearly all of these had become available in the Public Records office following the publication of Winterbotham's book, but they remained safely intact and away from the file weeders at Aberdeen University.

When the government learned of Jones's intention to publish the book, he was reminded that no MI6 officer should ever discuss his work. However, he was determined to proceed. Despite the age of his material it contained an important amount of technical historical matter dealing with radio navigation, the system whereby the British had been able to deflect the navigational beams of the German night time-bombers and the use of radar intelligence in connection with the German VI and V2 rockets. After much haggling with the Cabinet Office, MI6 and the D-notice committee, Jones was able to negotiate an acceptable text with Sir Leonard Hooper, the former head of GCHQ, by then attached to the Cabinet Office and by chance a fellow governor of Alleyns School in Dulwich. As with the Masterman case the government after its initial objections sought a copyright fee, and Jones had to pay about £600 for the photographs he had used.

Section 2 and the law of confidence were used not only against those who had worked in the Security Service. Sir Maurice Hankey, later the first Baron Hankey, who had created the Cabinet Secretariat in 1916 and remained Cabinet Secretary until 1938, found himself in 1957 being threatened by Harold Macmillan and Norman Brook, his successor as Cabinet Secretary, with prosecution under Section 2 if he published his memoirs. There was some irony in the fact that he nearly fell victim to Section 2 and the law of confidence, when he had been responsible for so rigidly enforcing such rules in the 1930s when he had taken a firm line against J. H. Thomas. In recognition of his outstanding service as Secretary of the Cabinet during the First World War, the government had made him a grant of £25,000. From this grant he had been able to reward the services of his own private secretary, who received a box of small cigars. Hankey had been a member of the Cabinet in the Second World War until Churchill sacked him in 1942. He had kept a diary of his experiences covering his period as Cabinet Secretary, and found that politicians such as Lloyd George and Churchill were consulting his diaries in order to write their own memoirs. Lloyd George had relied heavily on Hankey's diary in his six volumes of war memoirs, published from 1933 to 1938, as had Churchill in relation to his *The World Crisis 1911 to 1918,* published between 1923 and 1929.

Hankey had the dubious distinction of having his application to write his memoirs turned down by three successive Prime Ministers: Attlee, Churchill and Macmillan. Hankey had some cause for grievance as regards Churchill; not only had the latter referred to his diaries, but he had liberally used War Cabinet and other government papers for his book *The Second World War,* published from 1949 to 1952. When Macmillan wrote to Hankey in 1957 congratulating him on his eightieth birthday, Hankey took the opportunity to apply once more to be allowed to publish his memoirs. In May 1957 Macmillan told him that to publish a book 'laying bare the inner workings of the central government machine would impair, for the present and future, relations between Ministers and their most intimate official advisers'. Hankey had a protracted correspondence with Downing Street that resulted in an extraordinary letter from Macmillan dated 11 July 1958, which was a thinly veiled threat of prosecution under Section 2:

> I enclose an extract from Section 2 of the Act: you will not, I think, need a lawyer's interpretation to realise that this makes it an offence for any person who has held an official position to publish any information which he has acquired by virtue of holding that position and it cannot be contested that your book would be publishing such information.

Hankey had pointed out in correspondence that a number of memoirs had been permitted to be published without complaint under the Official Secrets Act, such as the diaries of Field Marshal Viscount Alanbrooke.

Notwithstanding his many years in Whitehall, Hankey felt so incensed by the refusal of the government to allow him to publish his memoirs that he decided, in the best tradition of enraged senior civil servants, to proceed without permission. He deleted a number of passages which he thought might possibly give rise to difficulty. In fact his memoirs were sufficiently cautiously written and so devoid of sensational content that he experienced some difficulty in finding a publisher. His book was published in 1961 by Allen & Unwin in two volumes, under the title *The Supreme Command 1914–1918*. No action was taken either under the Official Secrets Act or to restrain publication of these memoirs as a breach of confidence.

It is at times difficult to discern any consistent principle in the attitude taken by the government towards the use of the law of confidence to restrain the publication of potentially secret material. On occasion the guiding principle appears to be to prevent embarrassment to the government. In 1956 Tom Driberg, a Labour MP and a double agent for MI5, sought to publish his book *Portrait with a Background*, which was based on conversations with the defector Guy Burgess in Moscow. Publication took place after Guy Burgess and Donald Maclean surfaced in Moscow on 11 February 1956. As Burgess had checked the proofs of the book in Moscow, there was little doubt that the Russians knew exactly what was in it. Nevertheless, when it came before the D-notice committee the point was taken that in the book Burgess described attempts made by the British intelligence to overthrow the government of Albania in 1949. As far as the British government was concerned, this SIS operation did not officially exist. The Russians, however, knew about it; Kim Philby had told them. Driberg pointed out to Admiral Thomson, the secretary of the D-notice committee, that no doubt Burgess had told the Russians everything that was in the book, to which he received the reply: 'Good heavens, old boy! – It isn't the Russians we worry about; it's the British public we don't want to know about it.' Equally, with very much the same motives, attempts were made by means of the D-notice procedure to prevent details of the trial of George Blake in 1961 being given, and even to restrict references to foreign newspapers which did give such details.

The extraordinary way in which these laws were administered is well illustrated by the government's behaviour in relation to the publication of details in the case of the traitor Kim Philby. Following Philby's defection to the Soviet Union in 1963 the fiction had been maintained that he was no more than a low-ranking diplomat who had subsequently become a journalist with the *Observer* and the *Economist*. The *Sunday Times* assembled a team of reporters to try to discover more about Philby's position. They encountered a wall of silence from his ex-colleagues, but dark hints from former Security Service officers that Philby was a blackguard encouraged their enquiries. Their breakthrough came when Leslie Nicholson told Phillip Knightly over his second glass of brandy that Philby had been made head of the anti-Soviet section of British intelligence in 1945.

Word reached the government of the enquiries being made by the *Sunday Times*. In an attempt to forestall embarrassing revelations of Philby's spying activities, two D-notices were delivered to all newspapers, saying that no reference should be made to the names of British secret departments or their responsibilities or past actions. No mention should be made even of people who had worked for such departments. Philby was not named as such, but the D-notices were designed to cover him. The *Sunday Times* took the view that, since Philby had been a serving officer of the KGB for more than twenty years, there was little that it could publish that was not known to the Russians. The article duly appeared, and no action was taken against the newspaper.

These events encouraged Philby to write his autobiography, published in 1969 as *My Silent War*. By this time the government was seemingly resigned to the book's publication, and no attempt was made to stop it. There was, if anything, a stronger case for stopping this book than for issuing the D-notices against the *Sunday Times*, even though everything Philby wrote was known to the Russians. His account laid out in some detail how MI5 and MI6 worked and were organised. He named a number of retired and serving MI5 officers. There was probably little point in trying to prevent publication; but it is interesting that, whereas the government tried to stop loyal officers of the Crown from publishing their memoirs, it was prepared to allow traitors to write books at considerable profit to themselves. The *Sunday Times* subsequently published a book in 1977: *Philby: The Spy Who Betrayed a Generation*, written by its Insight team – Bruce Page, David Leitch and Phillip Knightley. Nor was objection taken to an essay written by Professor Trevor-Roper, 'Espionage, Treason and the Secret Service', published in 1968, where he described in some detail Philby's work in the Secret Service from 1941, when he started work for MI6 in the counter-espionage section.

It is a curious feature of the government's approach to the law of confidence that the objections raised to books on security matters disappear when a proposed book records a triumph of British intelligence over its enemies. No one then says that such a book would help the USSR to piece together its jigsaw of British intelligence. In 1947 Alexander Foote, who had spied for the Russians in Switzerland during the

Second World War, defected to Britain. Not only was he permitted to write a book on his experiences when it could very logically have been argued that the Russians should not be told how much the British had discovered about their methods, but the government even provided the head of MI5's Russian counter-espionage section, Courtney Young, to help write the book. As the intelligence matters concerned were considered to be Russian ones, they could be described in detail. The book described how signal plans worked, how messages were enciphered and deciphered and how 'one-time pads' were used. The object of such pads was that a particular code should not be used more than once. After they had been used, the sender and receiver would each tear off the top page of the pad so that they would have a different code for the next message. At the time of Foote's book, one-time pads were still in use; and when the spy Gordon Lonsdale was arrested in 1961 he was found still to be in possession of them. The extent of British knowledge about these pads was then still highly secret, in that during and immediately after the Second World War the USSR had economised on the use of the pads, so that particular pads were being used on a number of occasions. This had enabled the West to break the Russian codes and to read the radio traffic coming in and out of various Russian embassies. This was known as the Venona material, which unmasked Burgess and Maclean as spies. However, because we had put one over on the Russians different considerations applied. In Foote's book there was an appendix, 'Notes on my W/T code with Moscow', written by Courtney Young with the assistance of Peter Wright – the same man who nine years after his retirement announced his intention of writing his memoirs in Australia and was served with a writ by Her Majesty's government.

One major means whereby the government seeks to restrain the publication of books which it feels might damage the national interests is by relying on the fact that people have signed the Official Secrets Act. This produces a number of artificial distinctions which have little, if anything, to do with national security. A demonstration of this was the attempt of Joan Miller to publish her memoirs prior to her death in

1984. She had worked for MI5 during the war in a lowly position. Her main distinction was that she had had an affair with Maxwell Knight, probably one of MI5's most successful agent-runners of all time and the model for Ian Fleming's 'M'. Her story was published in the *Sunday Times* colour supplement, and there had been no problem about its publication because on that occasion the article was written by a journalist. Publishers Weidenfeld & Nicolson commissioned Joan Miller's book, but felt it prudent to engage the services of a ghost-writer. The manuscript was completed and submitted to the D-notice committee, where Rear-Admiral Ash indicated that although the account gave rise to no security problem it could not be published because Miss Miller had signed the Official Secrets Act. The government could not be moved from this stance, and the book was published in Ireland after her death and after litigation which the government lost. As a result of the litigation, the book sold many more copies than its publishers could originally have hoped.

Similar tactics were used in 1980 when Madeleine Clanmorris, the wife of John Bingham, Lord Clanmorris, was due to have her book *Smiley's Wife* published. This was an autobiographical account of her life and her husband and family. In the book she tried to answer some of the criticisms that were made of MI5 and to explain the problems which arose for the wife of a man whose job in the Security Service was surrounded in secrecy. The title came from the fact that the author David Cornwell – better known as John le Carré – had based the character Smiley on her husband, for whom he had worked in MI5. John le Carré's name was considered by the Clanmorrises to be a private joke of David Cornwell's, for when translated from the French 'John the Square' was a dig at her husband. It did not however prevent le Carré complaining through his publishers about her using the name Smiley in the title of her book.

At an early stage in the preparation of the book, Lady Clanmorris had spoken to the deputy head of MI5 to ensure that there was no official secrets problem. He informed her that MI5 could not see anything wrong in the book, but requested that she take out the real names and substitute false ones. Her publishers, Hamish Hamilton, then edited the manuscript, prepared it for the printers and assembled the photographs that were to be included in the book. It was featured in the firm's catalogue for the following spring.

However, the secretary of the D-notice committee, Rear-Admiral Ash, then approached Hamish Hamilton and persuaded the publishers that it would be a most unfortunate precedent if this book were published. It was contrary to the national interest because Lady Clanmorris had signed the Official Secrets Act when she had worked as a secretary for MI5 in 1940. The government could not be dissuaded, and the book was never published.

A book on Maxwell Knight, *The Man Who Was M*, was published in 1984 written by Anthony Masters. Masters had not signed the Official Secrets Act, and accordingly the government did not feel that it could directly prohibit publication of the book. However, it did its best to wreck the book. Masters obtained some considerable assistance from Knight's widow, who was upset at the allegations of homosexuality which had come out in Joan Miller's *Sunday Times* article. At the time, Mrs Knight was in a hospice suffering from terminal cancer. Masters conducted correspondence with Mrs Knight through a mutual friend, and this exchange of letters came to the attention of MI5. An employee of MI5 – inappropriately called a welfare officer – visited Mrs Knight at her Sue Ryder Home, warning her that her widow's pension could be removed if she co-operated with Masters (not such a threat for the terminally ill). Ever mindful of Mrs Knight's welfare, the MI5 officer instructed the staff to refuse Masters entry. Mrs Knight decided nevertheless that she would see Masters and wrote through the mutual friend telling Masters that she would see him. This letter also came to the attention of MI5; this time an establishment officer wrote to Mrs Knight reminding her that she had signed the Official Secrets Act and that she must on no account talk to her husband's biographer. Before she was able to do so, she died. However, her sister, aware of her feelings, did give Masters some assistance. She too had signed the Official

Secrets Act, when she had worked for GCCS at Blenheim as a secretary during the Second World War. This led to her also being threatened with the loss of her minuscule pension, a threat she ignored.

The practice of the Security Service of threatening to remove what tend to be fairly small pensions is of doubtful legality. The theory is that pensions paid to members of the service are entirely discretionary, but the better view appears to be that they are entitled to their pension like any civil servant. On 2 February 1982 Baroness Young was asked in the House of Lords whether it was the practice to continue to pay index-linked pensions to former members of the foreign or other public service who had admitted to acts of treachery and disloyalty but who had not been prosecuted. Lady Young replied that, as the law stands, Civil Service and other public service pensions can be forfeited only if a person is convicted of treason, of serious offences under the Official Secrets Act or of offences in connection with their employment which a minister has certified to have been gravely injurious to the state or to be liable to lead to serious loss of confidence in the public service.

This policy has meant that a man like Dick Ellis, who admitted in 1966 that while working for the Security Service before the outbreak of the Second World War he had betrayed to the Germans the fact that their secret telephone between Berlin and their embassy in London had been tapped for three years by the British, was able to keep his pension. This may be the price of living in a free society, but it contrasts strangely with the threats that are from time to time issued by MI5 to its former officers that they will lose their often paltry pensions if they fail to do what they are told. MI5 must be one of the few organisations in the world that finds it appropriate to begin letters to its former employees – when for example warning them in November 1982 not to speak to the author Nigel West – with the formula 'Dear Pensioner'.

18

Mr Kane's Campaign and
Other Breaches of Confidence

In 1983 publishers Robert Hale were poised to publish
GCHQ, the Negative Asset: The Failure and the Cover-Up
by Jock Kane. Kane described breaches of security at GCHQ,
both at home and in offshoots abroad. He alleged that the
interests of the West, particularly of the United States in
Vietnam and of the British in Aden and the Falklands, had
been severely damaged because of GCHQ's failure to supply
accurate and up-to-date intelligence to the British Cabinet.
The book also contained a chapter on Geoffrey Prime, the
spy who was convicted in 1982, and on how conditions at
Cheltenham enabled him to do what he did. Kane's thesis was
that Prime was basically an amateur spy who was able to
cause enormous damage to the security of the West but who
had been caught coincidentally because of his proclivity for
very young girls. Kane claimed that lax security and
corruption had made GCHQ a fertile breeding-ground for
spies, giving a detailed account of incidents at GCHQ bases in
Hong Kong, Aden and Cyprus.

Kane had been employed as a radio operator and
subsequently as a radio supervisor at GCHQ in Cheltenham,
and had worked for GCHQ in Hong Kong, Cyprus, Aden
and Turkey. He was appalled by the breaches of security and
evidence of corruption he found, particularly abroad. He
made allegations against a former Ministry of Defence
official who had an interest in a hotel at which all GCHQ staff
had to stay, which resulted in a prosecution for corruption.

He drew attention to the security problems that existed in Hong Kong; for example, a Chinese radio operator, Chang Tak Sei, had been arrested in 1961 and a spy-ring had been uncovered at GCHQ's base at Little Sai Wan; in 1973 two Chinese had defected from Little Sai Wan. The problems of espionage in Hong Kong were very considerable because of the proximity of Red China – nearly 150 people had been arrested in Hong Kong for spying in the period 1970–76. One of the problems that Kane highlighted was the failure to take proper care of classified documents. They tended to be left out where they could be examined by the Chinese cleaners. Kane made the point that employing Chinese cleaners from a deaf-and-dumb school near the base was scarcely a solution to the problem, as they could still read and write. Indeed, such was the unquestioned loyalty of the staff in Hong Kong that on one occasion 1,700 feet of copper wire were stolen from the antennae of the transmitters.

From 1973 Mr Kane sought to expose what he considered to be the security weaknesses and corruption in GCHQ. He pursued every channel open to him in the Civil Service; he had approached the Special Branch, the Director of Public Prosecutions, the Security Commission and his Member of Parliament, Kenneth Warren. Warren had brought the matter to the attention of the Prime Minister, James Callaghan, who requested a former Under-Secretary at the Home Office, Sir James Waddell, to see if the allegations had been properly investigated. Waddell's report in April 1978 was never published, and the enquiry was limited in its scope, dealing only with internal security problems.

In November 1975 Kane pointed out to the GCHQ authorities at Cheltenham the security regulations regarding photocopies were not being observed. These required that an officer should be appointed by the head of station to ensure that proper records were kept of the photocopies made. He followed this up in January 1978 by writing to the head of E Division about the number of photocopies being made without proper records being kept. He made the point that a large number of documents were missing, and it was difficult to know whether they had been unlawfully removed by a spy or merely thrown away without the procedure for the certification of the destruction of secret documents being followed.

The trial in 1985 of eight soldiers attached to GCHQ's base in Cyprus raised the same question of the whereabouts of a number of secret documents (Chapter 13). No one seemed sure whether the missing documents had been thrown away or handed over to the Russians.

In 1978 Kane took early retirement. In June 1980 he appeared in the *World in Action* television programme 'Mr Kane's Campaign'. Until then the work of GCHQ had not been publicly admitted. In May 1980 the *New Statesman* had published two articles about Kane's allegations in anticipation of the broadcast. The Independent Broadcasting Authority at first banned the film but on further consideration allowed it to be transmitted after a short sequence showing the antennae of Little Sai Wan had been removed (by that time the copper had been replaced). The relief of the producers at being able to show their programme was such that they thought it might be tactless to point out to the IBA that from Little Sai Wan you could see Russian trawlers some two hundred yards offshore, and presumably they could see the aerials.

In July 1982 Geoffrey Prime was arrested for child molesting and was subsequently discovered to be a spy, for which he was sentenced to thirty-five years' imprisonment.

Prime had been spying for the USSR since 1968: first as an NCO in the RAF engaged as a Russian linguist in signals intelligence work; and subsequently, from September 1977, as a civilian employee of GCHQ. He had been able to photocopy thousands of pages of top-secret material relating to spy satellite projects, and had for example compromised project Sambo – a detection system used to locate Soviet ballistic missile submarines when they surfaced. Such was the security at GCHQ that Prime was able to photocopy these documents during his lunch-break. On 16 May 1980 Geoffrey Prime had handed no less than five hundred films to his Soviet controllers in Vienna. Nevertheless in May 1982, just before Prime's arrest, the Prime Minister had informed Parliament that a Security Commission enquiry had found that security in the intelligence services including GCHQ appeared to be satisfactory. When asked about Kane's allegations, Mrs Thatcher indicated that for the most part they were without substance; in so far as they had any foundation, they had been attended to.

Shortly after Kane's book was submitted by his publishers to the D-notice committee, all copies were seized by the Special Branch, who interviewed the author for seven hours and threatened him with prosecution under the Official Secrets Act. Kane had signed the Act in the course of his GCHQ employment. However, he was not prosecuted; instead, the Treasury Solicitor obtained an ex-parte (that is to say, without giving Kane any notice of the hearing) injunction from a High Court judge, preventing him from publishing the book anywhere in the world and requiring him to hand over all copies of the manuscript which he had in Britain, and to collect any copy which he might have sent abroad. Two Special Branch officers went to the United States to collect the copies of the manuscript there. This was done in an interesting way. A visit was paid to Kane's agent in England, Jolie Mulvany, an American, who was led to believe that her UK resident's permit might be withdrawn if she did not sign a form asking the US publishers to hand over their copies of the manuscript to the Special Branch. Kane was granted an emergency legal aid certificate, but his fairly modest capital assets took him above the limits for legal aid in a civil case. He must be the only milkman in Hampshire ever to fight, out of his own resources, a breach-of-confidence case against Her Majesty's government.

The case is still before the courts, albeit somewhat becalmed. The government's assertion is that publication would damage GCHQ, national security and the security of Britain's allies, it might provoke foreign counter-measures, endanger the lives of overseas personnel and disclose top-secret information about certain overseas operations.

The interesting feature of the government's case is that it took the view that it was under no obligation to consider what part, if any, of Mr Kane's manuscript could be published without damaging the national interest. Asked to spell out which parts of the manuscript constituted a particular threat to the public interest, the government's lawyers replied that this was a matter purely for the Crown to judge. Surprisingly but conveniently the government had taken the view that the question as to whether or not criminal proceedings should be instituted against Kane under the Official Secrets Act should be deferred until the resolution of the civil proceedings. The case illustrates the overlap between the Official Secrets Act and the civil law of confidence. Criminal proceedings would normally take precedence. The civil proceedings are unlikely to be resolved in the near future, and accordingly the question of Kane's prosecution looks likely to be postponed for some years. The government has no intention of prosecuting Kane; the civil law has provided it with the required remedy. If the case does come to trial, Kane's contention that it was in the public interest to disclose that GCHQ was not subject to proper supervision and control, and that there was evidence of corruption, inefficiency, misuse of public funds, breaches of security, misconduct and mismanagement on a large scale, will be tested. His contention is that it is not the existence and physical location of signals intelligence installations but their successes which require protection. If the USSR can find out what we have learnt through Sigint, it can change its frequencies or put out disinformation such as fictitious technical problems relating to satellites or the wrong location of supply depots – as happened in the Vietnam War, when as a result the United States B52s bombed the wrong targets.

Despite the injunction obtained by the British government and the efforts of the Special Branch officers, the *Washington Post* obtained a copy of Mr Kane's manuscript and published extracts from the book in November 1985 under the front-page headline 'Laxness Cited at British Spy Agency, Secrets Act Invoked to Seize Manuscript'.

No action was taken to prevent the publication of Michael Straight's book *After Long Silence* by Collins in 1983. Straight was a wealthy American who had been approached at Cambridge University by Anthony Blunt and asked to spy for the Soviet Union. He became a member of the Apostles, being, as his name would suggest, one of its few heterosexual members. Blunt asked him to join the banking house of J. P. Morgan in Wall Street, so that he could provide information about the financial markets to the Russians. Straight did not do so, but instead became a speech-writer for the Roosevelt administration. According to an analysis of 'The Cambridge Comintern' by Robert Cecil, Straight continued to meet his Soviet control and to make political assessments for the USSR until 1941.

Straight's importance in the world of counter-espionage was not so much what he may or may not have done in the early years of the war for the Russians, but rather that he provided British intelligence with the first hard evidence of Blunt's treachery and of his links with Burgess. The way in which this matter came to light was rather curious. In 1963 Straight was offered the job of Chairman of the Fine Arts Commission by the Kennedy administration. This meant that his background would be investigated by the FBI and that it would be revealed that he had been a Communist at Cambridge. He therefore withdrew his name and made a full statement to the FBI about his connection with Blunt. What then happened is fully described in his books; he was asked to repeat what he had told the FBI to Arthur Martin, then MI5's leading mole-catcher. In his books he describes in detail meetings with British intelligence officers, culminating in a confrontation with the traitor Blunt (then Keeper of the Queen's Pictures) at his flat. Straight tells how he was in part responsible for Burgess defecting in 1951, as he had been horrified to find him still working for the British government and had threatened to report what he knew about his activities to the FBI.

Although Straight deserves some credit for extricating himself from the Russians and denies that he passed over any secret material, his meeting with his control while working for the White House was bound to give rise at the very least to some misunderstanding, and his failure to report what he knew about Burgess harmed the security of the West. Despite the fact that he was also revealing secret details of the debriefing of Blunt, he was permitted to publish his book. It may well be that the government felt that since he was a US citizen there was not very much it could do about the book anyhow.

Much the same had happened with the book written by Goronwy Rees, *A Chapter of Accidents*, in 1972. Rees worked for a short time for the Russians but had ceased doing so in 1939. Burgess had told him that he was a Comintern agent. Like so many of that group, out of a misguided sense of loyalty he felt an obligation to keep this to himself, but he did tell MI5 what he knew about Burgess after his defection in 1951. Pressure was put on Rees not to publish his book, and two MI5 officers were sent to interrogate him and to examine his manuscript at Aberystwyth, where he was principal of the University College of Wales. Following these gentlemen's visit and the publication of extracts from his book in a Sunday newspaper, he found himself confronted at the university with false accusations of homosexuality, corrupting students by offering them glasses of sherry and general hostility to Welsh aspirations! This did not deter him, and the book was published.

An example of the more liberal attitude in such cases in the United States is to be found in the book *Wilderness of Mirrors* by David Martin. Martin worked for *Newsweek* in Washington. His book was about two men – James Angleton, the head of counter-intelligence in the CIA, and William Harvey, described as a gun-toting, hard-drinking FBI agent who masterminded the bizarre scheme to assassinate Fidel Castro. The book was published in the United States in 1980 and without difficulty in Britain the following year.

Wilderness of Mirrors makes an interesting contrast with the attitude of the British government (particularly in relation to Peter Wright – Chapter 22), in that Martin was allowed to publish a wealth of technical detail about the Berlin Tunnel, which enabled the West to tap into Soviet High Command. This operation was later betrayed to the Russians by George Blake. Martin's book also explained how codes could be broken and how cables could be tapped in such a way as to intercept messages *en clair* going into a building before being enciphered. He described in detail the breaking of the Russian codes by the use of the Venona material, when the Russians used their one-time pads more than once, which had led to the unmasking of Burgess, Blunt and subsequently Philby. The book also discussed for the first time the possibility that a number of defectors to the West were planted by the USSR to mislead Western intelligence. Because the book had been published in the United States no action was taken against it; had it been written by an Englishman, attempts would undoubtedly have been made to stop it. Much of what Martin discussed was dealt with by Peter Wright in the Granada Television programme and presumably would be in his proposed book (see Chapter 22).

It is often difficult to detect why certain publications are banned and others are allowed. Robert Cecil, who from 1946 to 1950 had been personal assistant to Sir Stewart Menzies, the head of MI6, was permitted in 1984 to publish a very detailed account of the activities of the Cambridge spies in an essay called 'The Cambridge Comintern'. Cecil provided details of the dealings of Straight and Rees with the Russians and how Blunt, Burgess, Maclean and Philby were recruited, where they worked and even what their finances were. Burgess and Blunt, it seems, benefited from the fact that the MI5 head of personnel's file of character-defects consisted only of 'A' for adultery and 'D' for drink; 'B' for buggery was not apparently included in the list. Cecil dealt with the recruitment of Blake into the SIS and with such matters as the steps taken by MI5 regarding Maclean's drunken conduct before his defection. Maclean had told Rees in 1950, 'You used to be one of us but you ratted.' Cecil criticised MI5 for its failure to apprehend Burgess and Maclean, and MI6 for its reluctance to accept that Philby was a spy. He concluded that the contest between Soviet intelligence and British counter-intelligence resembled, at least until the late 1950s, a football match between Manchester United and Corinthian Casuals in the decline of amateurism.

David Mure who wrote *Practice to Deceive* and *Master of Deception* received assistance from other MI5 officers in writing his books about the Ultra deception and the activities of an agent called Triangle and Derek Tangye, author of *The Way to Minak*, worked for MI5 until 1950. The latter writer made no secret of the fact that he had been an MI5 officer and gave his view of Philby when he was working as chief of the Soviet section of MI6, known as Section V. An MI5 officer called Nigel Clive was able to publish his book, *The Greek Experience, 1943*–48, on his experiences in Greece during World War II. The way that the government operates the law of confidence is by no means always successful. A series of books were written by Nigel West: *MI5: British Security Service Operations 1909-1945,* published in 1981; *A Matter of Trust: MI5 1945-1972,* published in 1982; and *MI6 British Secret Intelligence Service Operations 1909-1945*. In 1985 West published a book jointly with a former secret agent, Juan Pujol, called *Garbo*. The book which gave rise to the problems was *A Matter of Trust*. It seems that a copy of the manuscript made its way to MI5's offices and was photocopied before being returned the next morning, although exactly how this happened is a mystery. An ex-parte injunction was obtained in October 1982 in conditions of such secrecy that not only was Nigel West not told, but neither was the secretary of the D-notice committee, Rear-Admiral Ash, to whom West had earlier offered his manuscript for inspection, as he had done with his previous book. When Ash sought to take up the offer he was told that he could now no longer have a copy, because to supply even the head of the D-notice committee with one would be in breach of the injunction!

The government proceeded to submit affidavit evidence that merely enhanced West's reputation. The Attorney-General's legal secretary, James Nursaw, deposed that

The manuscript contains previously unpublished information classified as secret, and identifies present members of the Security Service who have not been previously identified. There are many references in the manuscript to incidents, operations and investigations which are said to have taken place since the end of the Second World War and which can only have been related to Mr West by past or present members of the Security Service. Some of these references relate to incidents, operations, investigations and other matters which have not been previously made public.

Negotiations followed. It was politely but firmly pointed out that the manuscript was already in the United States, where Stein & Day were preparing it for publication. The point was also made that the government's action in photocopying the manuscript constituted a breach of copyright in respect of which West intended to sue. Up till then the Security Service had indicated that it objected to the whole book; but it had taken care not to threaten to prosecute under the Official Secrets Act, even though the book acknowledged that there had been assistance from a number of former SIS officers. When it appeared that, in addition to the problem of publication in the USA, the *Sunday Times* was offering to support West in defending any action that the government might take, the authorities decided that discretion was the better part of valour. The government then sought to persuade West to remove the names of certain agents and to use his best endeavours that they were also removed from the US edition. This was agreed after the list had been reduced by removing those whose names West pointed out had already been published.

The action was not particularly successful as far as the government was concerned. Some indication of the government's strong feelings on the matter can be gauged from a remark made by the genial deputy Treasury Solicitor, J. B. Bailey, to the *Sunday Times*. 'This is a very important and serious matter. It's pretty clear that some of the things have not come from the imagination of an author. To use the vernacular, it looks like an inside job.'

When *Garbo* was published in 1985, jointly written by West and the Spanish double agent Juan Pujol about his activities during the war, the book was sent to the D-notice committee and was passed without problems. Pujol, being a Spaniard, had not signed the Official Secrets Act.

An example of the over-sensitivity of the government in this field is to be found in its treatment of Geoffrey McDermott, following the publication in 1973 of his book *The New Diplomacy and its Apparatus*. McDermott had spent twenty-seven years in the diplomatic service and had been the Foreign Office adviser to the chief of SIS, Sir Dick White. He was one of the first people to refer to GCHQ, which was then officially a secret. He did so very discreetly: 'GCHQ works near staid Cheltenham. Here the staff consists largely of boffins, mathematicians and first-class chess players. It is described as a department of the Foreign and Commonwealth Office, engaged in research, development and production of communications equipment.' The problem arose when McDermott appeared on a *World in Action* television programme in 1980, where he was filmed outside GCHQ saying of the place no more than, 'They invent machines, they keep them up to date, they make codes and break codes.' This was too much for the government. Through the secretary of the D-notice committee, Rear-Admiral Kenneth Farnhill, a cut in the programme of any reference to GCHQ was demanded. In vain it was pointed out that the address and telephone number of GCHQ were listed on page 387 of the current *Whitaker's Almanac*, and that the address was frequently to be found in advertisements in radio magazines for radio operators. A sixty-second cut had to be made in order to remove the offending thirteen seconds so that the film could be shown.

The intervention of the government to claim that a book breaches national security can on occasion provide helpful publicity. An example of this was *MI5*, by a journalist named John Bulloch. Published in 1963, this was a modest history of the operations of MI5 up to the end of the Second World War. Bulloch's publisher, Jim Reynolds of Arthur Barker, hoped that book would sell 3,000 copies. Two weeks before publication Reynolds was surprised to receive a request from Colonel Lohan, the secretary of the D-notice committee, to see an advance copy, and to be reprimanded for not having submitted proofs to him 'in case the book might contain a breach of the Official Secrets Act'. Reynolds sent him a copy with a covering note, explaining that he had not submitted the proofs because there was nothing in the book that had not in his view been published before.

Reynolds thought it prudent nevertheless to consult his solicitors, who confirmed that there had been no contravention of the Official Secrets Act and that the book need not be withdrawn. However, a few days before publication Lohan returned the book, which by this time was a mass of blue-pencilled deletions indicating what had to be removed before the book could be published. Three days before publication Reynolds received a telephone message that the Home Secretary, Henry Brooke, wished to see him urgently. Publisher, author and solicitor duly presented themselves at the Home Office the next day.

Among those present were Sir Roger Hollis, the head of MI5, who they were told had to be referred to as 'Mr Rogers'; on no account should his real name by used. The Home Secretary, who did not appear to have been fully briefed, opened the proceedings by warning them that publication of the book would be a very serious breach of the Official Secrets Act. He was immediately corrected by 'Mr Rogers', who said that the publication was not in breach of the Act but would be against the public interest.

'Quite, quite,' said the Home Secretary. Would Mr Reynolds agree to amending the text in a manner to be approved by 'Mr Rogers'?

Meanwhile, Reynolds protested that everything in the book had been published before, to which Brooke replied, 'Ah yes, but you see from a Russian point of view obtaining our secrets is rather like putting together the pieces of a jigsaw puzzle. The book of Mr Bulloch is doing the Russians' work for them.'

Reynolds asked how much the Home Secretary wanted taken out of the book and was told that a good number of pages would have to come out. At this stage his solicitor said that, if there was no question of illegality, he assumed that the Home Office would pay all the costs. The minister, who did not appear to be expecting the question, murmured that he supposed some accommodation could be made.

Publication was therefore postponed, and reviewers who had received advance copies were advised that the book had been withdrawn in order to make some deletions 'for security reasons' and were requested to return their copies. Few came back, as people hunted in vain for breaches of security in the text. In consequence the book received publicity beyond the publishers' wildest dreams – nearly 10,000 copies were sold. A few new pages were inserted, and the legal costs and costs of rebinding were met by Her Majesty's government.

The government has sometimes tried to lock the stable door long after any horse may have bolted. *Beneath the City Streets* by Peter Laurie was published in 1970 and reprinted in 1972. Problems did not arise until a much later reprint in 1978. The book, which followed a *Sunday Times* article by Laurie of 11 December 1967, contained fifty pages in chapter 9 describing the British government's preparations for a nuclear war. Laurie was a researcher and had held no government post. He had pieced together his information in very much the same way as Duncan Campbell (Chapter 10) was to do. *Beneath the City Streets* contained a detailed account of underground centres where the government could continue to function in the event of a nuclear attack and how the telephone system was linked with civil defence. The book contained maps of London and the British Isles, pinpointing the locations of radar stations, sub-regional controls and possible regional seats of government, RAF stations and defence communication network sites. The author took the precaution of including a footnote (no doubt inserted by his lawyers) to the effect that 'Unlike the last two chapters, this one owes nothing to official information given to me personally.'

At the time of the original publication, some concern existed as to whether the book could constitute a breach of the Official Secrets Act, and as a precaution it was referred to as 'Project A' while it was being prepared for publication. The manuscript was sent to the Home Office. On 16 March 1970 Tom McCaffrey (James Callaghan's adviser in such matters) wrote, saying:

We do not wish to ask for any changes in the text we have seen, but you will, of course, understand that the Home Office, while not wishing to comment, cannot accept any responsibility for the statements, whether of fact or of opinion, in the book. I should be very glad if you could find the time to let me know the actual date of publication, when it is fixed.

Subsequently the Central Office of Information asked for a copy after publication. However, upon reprinting in 1978, the D-notice committee became interested and requested alterations on the grounds of prejudice to national security, without specifying which pages it objected to. The author was left to guess what the committee disapproved of and to try to make such deletions as he thought would satisfy it.

It seems that in the period since publication the government had become concerned at the possibility of the underground and other sites being used as terrorist targets. But if it was going to take the unusual step of objecting to what had been written eight years earlier, it would have been sensible for the government to be specific. It may be that official interest was aroused by a review reprinted in the blurb of the 1972 edition, which ran:

Although it might be possible to interpret this book as a contravention of that all-embracing piece of legislation, the Official Secrets Act, it is hard to see what damage it can do. It is true that even the KGB can be inefficient at times but probably the Russians know already most of the contents of Chapter 9.

The Cabinet Secretary, Sir Burke Trend, wanted to excise almost everything except the last twenty pages of the memoirs of Anthony Nutting, a former Minister of State at the Foreign Office, which were published in 1967 under the title *No End of a Lesson*. In the end, the names of certain civil servants were deleted, and some Cabinet material was removed. During a lunch between the Prime Minister, Harold Wilson, and Nutting's publisher, George Weidenfeld, enough was said to convince the publishers that they could proceed, which they did.

Even the official histories of the activities of MI5 and of British counter-intelligence in the Second World War, written by Anthony Simkins and Professor Michael Howard, were affected by the uncertainty as to what can and cannot be published. The authors were respectively a former deputy Director-General of the Security Service and the Regius Professor of History at Oxford University. Simkins's book, dealing with events of nearly forty years before, was commissioned in 1970 by the Cabinet Office on the understanding that there was no commitment to publication. When he submitted his manuscript in 1980, MI5 favoured its publication but there was some resistance from MI6, supported by the Prime Minister. Consequently the book was not published, although presumably it had been commissioned with a view to publication, to counteract inaccurate official histories rather than as a limited edition for the Cabinet Office library. A three-volume study of British intelligence in the Second World War, by Professor Harry Hinsley of Cambridge University, had been published; but the difference there was that the first volume was published during the time that James Callaghan was Prime Minister, and Mrs Thatcher did not feel able to prevent publication of the subsequent volumes. Professor Howard's manuscript was submitted for publication in 1980, but it too suffered the same fate, although objections have now been waived.

Publication has been allowed of more recent accounts of the activities of MI6 on the rather specious grounds that they were not written by intelligence officers, although assistance was evidently obtained from at least former intelligence officers. An example of this is Anthony Verrier's *Through the Looking Glass: British Foreign Policy in an Age of Illusions*. This book deals with SIS operations in Kuwait, Argentina, Northern Ireland and the Nigerian civil war. It also describes what are still considered the highly secret operations of the SIS in Albania in 1949, about which the government allows no access to the Russian committee papers – although the

USSR has known all about this operation since Philby betrayed the facts in 1949. *Through the Looking Glass* also deals with SIS involvement with the Soviet defector Colonel Oleg Penkovsky, with the defection of Anatoli Golitzin, a KGB officer, in Helsinki, and with the question of how MI6 was involved in foreign policy from the time of Suez – when consideration was given to assassinating Nasser – to the Falklands. The book includes a description of operations in Northern Ireland by the SIS. The names of agents are not given, but there might have been more valid objection to discussion of the opening of an SIS office in Belfast, and the description and probable identification of the pipe-smoking head of station in Northern Ireland, than to the histories of forty-year-old operations.

Equally, when books dealing with security matters are published by left-wingers, there seems to be a reluctance to take action. *British Intelligence and Covert Action*, by Jonathan Bloch and Patrick Fitzgerald, was published in 1983, first in Ireland and then in Britain. Some indication of the authors' sympathies can be found in their descriptions of an SAS officer, Robert Nairac, who was tortured and killed by the IRA, as having been 'executed'. The book sets out to describe MI5 , MI6 and SAS operations and concludes, for reasons about which one can only speculate, with an appendix of members or former members of MI6, GCHQ and the Information Research Department and of those who have served as overseas security advisers or liaison officers of MI5. It is a nasty little book that comes equipped with a foreword by Philip Agee. It could be argued that little could be done after the book had been published in Ireland, and that the government should not give respectability to such an account by trying to ban it. However, such latitude makes nonsense of banning the publication of books by loyal citizens, who would be only too happy to remove any passages which would jeopardise security if only the government would approach the question of such deletions fairly and without seeking blanket cuts.

It is always open to the government to request a disclaimer. This happened in the case of a book published in 1967 by

Greville Wynne, who after being convicted by the USSR of spying wrote his memoirs, *The Man from Moscow*. The Foreign Office arranged to insert at the front of the book: 'Certain passages would almost certainly have been objectionable on security grounds, had they been true.' At the request of the D-notice committee Wynne deleted the names of certain people to whom Col. Oleg Penkovsky had been introduced in Britain.

A series of articles was published in the *Guardian* in April 1984, entitled 'The Watchers' (the name for the MI5 operatives who keep certain targets under observation). The articles described in considerable detail the various branches of MI5 – such as A Branch, with its sub-classification A1, the technical operations or 'dirty tricks' department; and F Branch, which dealt with subversion and had a number of departments including F7, which dealt with, amongst others, MPs, teachers, lawyers and journalists. Names were not given, but a brief résumé of the work done by junior serving officers was included; this presumably enabled them to be identified by those with a reasonably detailed knowledge of the subject. The articles also described how telephones were tapped, mail was opened and agents were infiltrated, and how trade unions and the peace movement were kept under surveillance. Publication of 'The Watchers' followed the conviction for spying of Michael Bettaney, recruited from Oxford University by MI5. The *Guardian* articles caused the Security Commission, which looked into Bettaney's conviction, considerable concern; the commission suspected that the ultimate source of this information must have been Bettaney. There was a dilemma in official circles as to whether or not to take action to discover the source of this alleged leak, which would presumably have involved an exercise of powers under Section 6, but the Security Commission concluded that its efforts would have been a cumbersome and profitless exercise.

The sometime head of 'the watchers', Jim Skardon, is one of those MI5 officers who wish to write their memoirs but have been prohibited from doing so. Skardon made his reputation as the interrogator of the spy Klaus Fuchs. He learnt his techniques from the monocled Tin-Eye Stevens. The public is unlikely to be able to read of Skardon's techniques for the watchers, which themselves became legendary. Each MI5 car required no less than three watchers: one to drive, one to read the map and the third to keep a look-out. Women were not allowed, because it was thought they would be depraved by the amount of time that watchers had to spend in pubs and cafés. On one occasion a watchers' car skidded near Buckingham Palace and collided with the KGB car it was following. With some humour the chief watcher got out and agreed with his Soviet counterpart that they would exchange false names and addresses.

19

Looking out at St James's Park

The law of confidence has not been confined to what might loosely be termed national security. In 1975 the government tried but failed to obtain an injunction against the literary executors of Richard Crossman, who had permitted the publication of his diaries for the years 1964 to 1966 under the title *The Diaries of a Cabinet Minister*. Crossman had been Minister of Housing and Local Government in the Labour government and had, like a number of his colleagues, spent his evenings recording the events of the day. He wanted the diaries published not because they showed him in a rosy light but because he felt that they would show how the Cabinet worked. His choice of literary executors was a shrewd one, consisting of Michael Foot, who was Secretary of State for Employment in Harold Wilson's Cabinet, Graham C. Greene, managing director of Jonathan Cape (the publishers of the diaries), and his widow, Anne Crossman. This had resulted in the curious spectacle of the Cabinet Secretary, Sir John Hunt, seeking to obtain an injunction against one of the members of a Cabinet he served.

The first step taken by the executors was to involve a national newspaper to assist in the defence. Serial rights were sold to the *Sunday Times* for £17,000, and its editor, Harold Evans, eagerly entered the fray. There was a clear risk of prosecution under the Official Secrets Act; Brian Neill QC advised that an action under the Act would succeed, and this opinion was supported by Lord Lloyd of Hampstead QC and Lord Goodman. The government itself took the view that a prosecution under the Official Secrets Act would fail. Somewhat surprisingly it took this view on the basis that, as Crossman had died (on 5 April 1974), the chain had been broken, and the necessary link between the person disclosing the information and the publisher could not be established. It is doubtful whether this view was correct, but it saved an embarrassing prosecution.

The initial reaction of Hunt was nevertheless that the book could not be published in its proposed form during the closed period for Cabinet records – that is, until 1996. This he said was based on the inherent needs of the government and the mutual trust that should exist between ministers, their colleagues and their senior advisers.

Lord Goodman embarked on negotiations with Hunt to see what could be published without breaching the Official Secrets Act or the law of confidence. Sir John indicated that he was prepared to look at the material, provided that no details were given of Cabinet discussions, or of advice given by civil servants to ministers, or of discussions about senior appointments in the Civil Service, or about the conversations which various members of the government had had concerning the policy of the administration. These parameters, as they came to be called, would have ensured that the Crossman diaries were stripped of any possible interest. There then followed lengthy negotiations between Lord Goodman and Hunt, which resulted in Goodman, in a moment of exasperation, asking Hunt:

'What *can* we say? Can we say that Crossman sat at his Cabinet table and looked out at St James's Park?'

Hunt replied, after reflection, 'Yes, provided you don't indicate who else was sitting with him.'

Matters came to a head when Hunt wrote to Evans seeking an undertaking that the *Sunday Times* would not publish extracts from the Crossman diaries that had not been cleared with him, without giving him at least seven days' clear notice. Overlooking momentarily the fact that the *Sunday Times* was a Sunday newspaper, Sir John asked for this undertaking to be given to him by Monday 27 January 1975. The result was that the serialisation started on 26 January and ran until

23 March 1975. The policy of the *Sunday Times* was to publish the less sensitive material at the outset, introducing the more controversial extracts as the series progressed. The serialisation was completed without any action by the government in the courts. However, when it was announced that the book would be published, the Attorney-General indicated that he would seek an injunction to ban it, even if nearly 100,000 words of the book had already been published. Rather than let the government exert pressure on the more financially vulnerable publishers, in an act of defiance the *Sunday Times* published further Crossman material which had not been submitted to the Cabinet Office, in an extract called 'The Jigsaw of Truth'. This analysed the material that had appeared in the Crossman diaries and compared it to the differing accounts given by Harold Wilson of the same event in his memoirs.

A writ was immediately issued, and a temporary injunction was granted on 26 June by Mr Justice Ackner. The case was heard on 23 July before the Lord Chief Justice, Lord Widgery. He heard evidence from a large number of witnesses, including two former Lord Chancellors. The court's attention was drawn to the evidence of Sir Burke Trend to the Franks Committee that in practice a distinction was drawn between matters of national security, which ministers would delete from their memoirs on request, and other items, which could properly be drawn to the ministers' attention but were left to their own discretion. Hunt sought to clarify the situation by explaining that this was an off-the-cuff supplementary answer by his predecessor, with which he did not happen to agree.

The Lord Chief Justice ruled that the expression of individual opinions by Cabinet ministers in the course of Cabinet discussions was a matter of confidence, the publication of which could be restrained by the Crown when this was clearly necessary in the public interest. However, a time would come, and in this case had come, when the confidential character of such information would lapse. Lord Widgery – not known as the most liberal of judges – indicated that advice given by senior civil servants and observations made by ministers on the capacity of individual civil servants and their suitability for specific appointments need not necessarily be protected by confidence. In other words, he did not uphold Hunt's parameters, but he did indicate that they were capable of being protected by the law of confidence. The government failed to obtain an injunction because the information concerned was already at least eight years old and not particularly confidential, and much of it had already been published.

The government did not appeal, realising that it was unlikely to succeed in the Court of Appeal and feeling that, to some extent, it had established the principle that such matters could be protected by the law of confidence. Instead, a committee of Privy Councillors was set up under Viscount Radcliffe to consider the rules relating to the publication of ministerial memoirs. This reported on 22 January 1976, and laid down the rules that manuscripts should be submitted to the Secretary of the Cabinet, and that anyone keeping a diary should leave instructions in his will, to ensure that its publication would be dealt with in the same way as it would have been if he were still alive.

There were some crumbs of comfort for the government in the Crossman diaries case, in that the defence lawyers conceded that different considerations might have applied if there had been any question of national security. It was therefore to this that the government turned its attention in subsequent cases.

20

D-Notices

The D-notice system acts as a further restriction on the publication of unwelcome material. It has the advantage of not requiring any legal action on the part of the government but relying merely on persuasion. The D-notice committee, the Defence, Press and Broadcasting Committee, is a body consisting of eleven representatives of the armed forces, civil servants and the media. Its purpose is to secure voluntary compliance by the media with government rulings as to what can and what cannot be published on defence matters. The committee meets once or twice a year. The fact that the press co-operates on this basis with the government is a source of some astonishment in foreign countries; it would not be lawful in the United States, for example.

The D-notice system was set up in 1912, when it was known as the Admiralty, War Office and Press Committee. There had since 1909 been strong pressure for controls over the press in security matters, and the committee was established under the auspices of the Newspaper Proprietors' Association. The committee did not meet from 1923 to 1946. From 1939 to 1945 it was replaced by the Press Censorship Department at the Ministry of Information. In 1945, when censorship was abolished, it was decided nevertheless to keep the D-notice system. The secretary was no longer from the Press Association, but was normally a retired member of the services. The existence of the D-notice committee was not publicly revealed until 1952. In 1962 its functions were reviewed by a committee chaired by a leading judge, Lord Radcliffe, which recommended that the system be retained on a limited basis, and that the notices should warn editors that certain defence-related items were regarded as highly confidential.

For a time the D-notice system served a useful purpose in enabling editors and publishers to determine what could be published without causing damage to national security. Editors and defence correspondents became adept at framing stories in such a way as to avoid infringing D-notices. One popular technique was to head the story that it was based on United States sources, since the D-notice committee's jurisdiction did not extend to the USA.

The D-notice system was used to try to prevent publication of the location of underground headquarters intended for use by the government in the event of nuclear war, which had been revealed by an anti-nuclear group in 1963 in a book called *Spies for Peace*. The attempt to prevent this information being revealed was weakened by the fact that the CND's Aldermaston march had been specifically diverted to one of the headquarters at Warren in Berkshire.

When it became apparent that D-notices were being issued for reasons other than the protection of defence, the system fell into disrepute. This was particularly illustrated by the Labour government's handling of the Lohan affair. Colonel Sammy Lohan, the handlebar-moustached and monocled secretary of the D-notice committee, was consulted in 1967 by Chapman Pincher, defence correspondent of the *Daily Express*, regarding a story that he intended to, and did, publish about the fact that the Secret Service monitored all cables leaving Britain, whether they were diplomatic or commercial. Pincher's information came from a telegraphist at Commercial Cables and Western Union, Robert Lawson. The article was published in the *Daily Express* on 21 February 1967 under the headline 'Cable Vetting Sensation'. The Prime Minister, Harold Wilson, told the House of Commons that the newspaper article was utterly unfounded and contravened two D-notices. This was disputed by Pincher. He said that he had lunched with Lohan in a restaurant on 20 February, and that during the course of the meal Lohan had produced two D-notices – one dated 27 April 1956 and the other 27 April 1961 – saying that one did not apply to cables and the other was so bloody marginal that he could put it away, which he then did. Lohan's account of what had happened at the lunch differed in that he said he had warned Pincher against publication. Lohan asked the editor of the *Daily Express* not to publish, but the editor decided to proceed with publication. The Prime Minister was furious at the newspaper story, which caused considerable embarrassment to the Americans because of their association with the cable vetting, which was illegal in the United States. Wilson spoke of Lohan's over-close relations with journalists, particularly Pincher.

An enquiry into the matter was set up under Lord Radcliffe, which exonerated the *Daily Express* and Lohan – a conclusion that the government was most reluctant to accept. No action was taken against the *Daily Express*. The government's behaviour in this matter, and the way that Lohan was treated – he had to resign and subsequently became the restaurant correspondent of the *Evening Standard* – did much to discredit the D-notice system. The government's conduct meant that what was a minor affair that would have blown over within a few days lasted for about six months.

The *Spectator* published one of the D-notices produced by Lohan at the lunch with Pincher. In consequence its editor, Nigel Lawson (later Chancellor of the Exchequer), together with his columnist Alan Watkins, had to appear before the committee of Privy Councillors and had his knuckles rapped for having done so. Lawson had been under the misapprehension that the *Spectator* did not participate in the D-notice system. The Radcliffe Report emphasised that D-notices should be issued only where the secrets were genuinely military and were likely to prejudice security.

The system was further tarnished by its use in the attempt by the government to suppress embarrassing details of the treachery of George Blake in 1961 and Kim Philby in 1967. The *Sunday Times* ignored the two D-notices aimed at preventing any mention of Philby. Yet more damage was done by the *Sunday Telegraph* case of 1970 (Chapter 9), in which the newspaper had, before publishing the Scott report, contacted Vice-Admiral Sir Norman Denning, the secretary of the D-notice committee, and had been informed that the proposed article did not infringe any D-notice. The *Sunday Telegraph* was nevertheless prosecuted under the Official Secrets Act. Another example of a notice operating to save government embarrassment can be found in the experience of Tom Driberg in connection with his book on Guy Burgess (Chapter 17).

Twelve D-notices were in force until 1982, ranging from the first – defence plans, operational capability and state of readiness – to the twelfth – the whereabouts of Mr and Mrs Vladimir Petrov, he being the Russian who defected to Australia in 1954. This did not recently prevent the publication in Australia of a photograph of Petrov in a Melbourne hospital. D-notices have not been revised since 1981. There was then a recommendation that the twelve should be reduced to five. In 1980 the House of Commons Defence Committee was highly critical of the system, pointing out that major newspapers had stopped consulting the D-notice committee, that the D-notices had not been amended during the previous ten years, that some categories of sensitive information were not covered by D-notices and that the notices were not received by foreign or fringe members of the press. In 1980 the *New Statesman* published a series of articles by Duncan Campbell on telephone tapping, despite being warned by Rear-Admiral Ash, the secretary of the D-notice committee, that they contravened a D-notice, but no action was taken.

In September 1984 Rear-Admiral Ash complained to the *New Statesman* after it had named one man as 'MI5's burglar-in-chief' and another as 'in charge of organising the infiltration of left-wing organisations'. No action was taken against the *New Statesman*.

A new set of D-notices was introduced in 1982, reducing the number to nine. The new D-notices cover defence plans, operations, readiness, training, equipment, radio and radar transmissions and communications, the British security and intelligence services, war precautions including civil defence, and photography of defence establishments and installations.

There is a marked contrast between the attitude of the British and the United States governments. Action had been taken by the British government to prevent Peter Wright from publishing his book on the Security Service (Chapter 22), whereas in the United States a very similar account has been published, David Martin's *Wilderness of Mirrors*. Publication of Miles Copeland's *The Real Spy World* was permitted in the United States. Copeland was head of the CIA's London station, and the book dealt with the techniques of espionage used not only by the CIA but also by the British. He described the operations of the CIA through its station chief, HQ desk officer and case officer, also discussing the various types of agent – talent-spotted, 'walk-in' and long-term agents. There is also the agent known as a 'willie', who in fact works for a Soviet agency but believes himself to be working for something else, like a credit investigation organisation or a newspaper. This book would not, under normal rules, have been passed for publication in Britain if it had been written by a member of the British Secret Service. Once it had appeared in the United States, however, it could then, in 1974, be published here. Stansfield Turner, the head of the CIA, was permitted to write his memoirs, entitled *Secrecy and Democracy: The CIA in Transition*. These were published in Britain in 1986. In July 1985 the head of the Australian Security Intelligence Organisation (ASIO) appeared on Australian television and discussed his work. It is inconceivable that the Director-General of the British Security Service would appear on television in Britain in such circumstances. The ASIO has also introduced a public relations officer; he must be unique among public relations officers in that his name cannot be published, as by convention only the head of the ASIO is named.

It is hard not to feel uneasy about the British practice, and the position is well illustrated by Andrew Boyle's *The Climate of Treason*, published in 1979. The problem in this instance was not the Official Secrets Act as such, but libel. In his book

Boyle unmasked Anthony Blunt as the fourth Cambridge University spy, but in the first edition he had to use the name 'Maurice' to reduce the risk of being sued for libel. Fortunately Blunt's threat to issue libel proceedings through his solicitors resulted in his identity becoming publicly known. Whereas Boyle was able to obtain files on Blunt and Maclean under the United States Freedom of Information Act, and to obtain assistance from the CIA, he could not have access to such files in Britain and could – at some risk to himself – receive only informal assistance from certain former MI5 and MI6 officers. It was the public unmasking of Blunt as a traitor in Boyle's book that prevented the Protection of Information Bill becoming law in November 1979. This would have enabled ministers to produce a conclusive certificate that such matters could not be published, and Blunt's treachery would not have been known to the public. Blunt had admitted working for the USSR to the security authorities in April 1964, following the revelations of Michael Straight. This was announced by Margaret Thatcher in a parliamentary answer on 15 November 1979, although the misleading impression was given that he had worked for the Soviets merely between 1940 and 1945.

For all its imperfections the D-notice system works as a system of self-censorship based on the British art of compromise. Nevertheless in 1987 the BBC found its Glasgow offices were raided by the Special Branch (no prosecutions ensued) over its proposed programme on the Zircon satellite system, despite the contents of the programme being discussed with the D-notice committee. Thereafter the BBC programme on the Security Service, *My Country Right or Wrong*, was injuncted. On that occasion, not only had the programme been discussed with the D-notice Committee, but its secretary, a retired admiral, had agreed to appear on the programme!

21

Reform

It is surprising that Section 2 has survived for so long. The attempts in 1920 to expand the powers under the Official Secrets Act 1911 met with considerable criticism (Chapter 2), and the use of the powers under Section 6 of the Official Secrets Act 1920 led to further dissatisfaction with the Act and to the passing of a modest reform of the Act in 1939 (Chapter 5). There has been a long line of critics. Lord Strabolgi described Section 2 in 1939 as 'capable of indefinite expansion to all manner of communications and information which may have been received from anyone who holds or has held office under His Majesty'. Richard Crossman called the Act 'a mangy old sheep'. The first genuine attempt to reform Section 2 came in 1965 from the organisation Justice, which produced some sensible, if modest, proposals. It suggested that the Act be confined to information relating to such matters as the security of the state and the disclosure of information prejudicial to the national interest or in breach of an assurance given to the supplier of the information that it would be treated as confidential. Significantly the Justice committee recommended that it should be a defence to a prosecution under the Official Secrets Act to show that the information was disclosed in good faith, in the public interest and without harming the essential security of the state.

During the twenty years since the Justice report, some faltering steps have been taken to amend Section 2, but successive governments have failed, for not very convincing reasons, to reform the law. The line between the citizen's right of access to the background to government decisions and the need for secrecy in certain sensitive areas may not be an easy one to draw, but such a political decision is no more difficult than many that any government faces in implementing its legislative programme.

The reform or abolition of Section 2 and the introduction of freedom-of-information legislation are represented by certain pressure groups as being closely interlinked, but they need not be so. There is no reason why a government could not merely reform Section 2 and not introduce any measure for greater access to information, although it has often been said that the reform of Section 2 should lead inexorably to a greater degree of information freedom. Appendices 4–6 show that Australia, the United States and Canada, which have all introduced freedom-of-information legislation, have still retained statutes with powers similar to those under Section 2. Certainly the reform of Section 2 should not be delayed by arguments as to the time that it would take to set up the necessary apparatus for a system of freedom of information. There is unfortunately no reason to suppose, as the present Prime Minister does, that Whitehall will put its own house in order and that the citizen will be sufficiently protected by procedures voluntarily introduced by government departments for great consultation with, and access to information for, the public. The attitude of the Civil Service is well illustrated by the reply given by Sir Burke Trend, then Cabinet Secretary, to the Franks Committee: 'Once you embark on the strip-tease of government, where do you stop?' Any British freedom-of-information legislation should draw on the experience of other countries. It is reasonable to introduce such an Act, avoiding creating in a moment of over-exuberance a freedom-of-information bureaucracy with large numbers of civil servants with nothing else to do than to process endless freedom-of-information applications or to sit waiting for some member of the public to show interest in their esoteric acitivies. It would also be useful to avoid creating a machine that becomes even more costly each year and itself undermines the move towards greater freedom of information. Any government thinking of introducing such legislation should bear in mind the Canadian approach, which involved a review of the operation of its legislation after three years.

In 1968 a committee under Lord Fulton, Vice-Chancellor of Sussex University, reported on the state of the Civil Service and made recommendations for a more open system of government:

> The administrative process is surrounded by too much secrecy – the public would be better served if there was a greater amount of openness. We suggest the government should set up an enquiry to make recommendations for getting rid of unnecessary secrecy in this country. Clearly the Official Secrets Act would need to be included in this review. There are still too many occasions when information is unnecessarily withheld and consultation is merely perfunctory.

The response to the Fulton recommendations was a White Paper produced by the Labour government in June 1969 called *Information and the Public Interest*. It recommended that there should be progress towards a system of greater consultation of the public and proposed that the government should expand in every possible way the practice of widening the range of information whose release could be authorised. However, the White Paper revealed no particular enthusiasm on the part of the government for reforming Section 2 because it claimed, wrongly, that the Official Secrets Act did not conflict with that practice since it affected only the disclosure of *unauthorised* information. The labour government was defeated in the 1970 election before the matter could be put to the test.

In 1970 the Conservatives came to power under Edward Heath, having stated in their manifesto, *A Better Tomorrow*: 'We will eliminate unnecessary secrecy concerning the workings of the government and we will review the operation of the Official Secrets Act so that the government is more open and more accountable to the people.' After the conclusion of the proceedings against Jonathan Aitken and the *Sunday Telegraph* (Chapter 9), a committee was set up under Lord Franks, which produced a report in September 1972 stating that Section 2 was a mess. Franks produced a draft Official Information Bill which would have repealed Section 2 and replaced it by narrower and more specific provisions relating to such matters as defence, internal security, foreign relations, the maintenance of law and order and the protection of information supplied confidentially by the citizen. The Franks Committee felt that a number of cases which were prosecuted under Section 2 could be dealt with under specific legislation such as the Prevention of Corruption Act, and it proposed that the mere receipt of official information by a private citizen should not amount to an offence. The committee did not, unlike the Justice Committee, accept that there should be a defence to a charge brought under the Act of disclosure in the public interest. In 1973 the Home Secretary, Robert Carr, said that the Conservative government accepted the essential recommendations of Franks but required more time to consider the categories of protected information. However, Heath's confrontation with the miners put an end to his proposals for a greater freedom of information, as he was defeated in the February 1974 general election.

In its October 1974 manifesto the Labour Party undertook to replace the Official Secrets Act by a meaure placing the burden on public authorities to justify withholding information. These proposals were based on the Swedish Freedom of the Press Act, which gives a legally enforceable right to the citizen to see government information unless it falls within a particular exempt category. It was however nearly five years before the Labour government took any positive step to legislate for the abolition of Section 2 and for the introduction of a greater freedom of information, and even then this consisted of no more than supporting a Private Member's Bill introduced by the Liberal MP Clement Freud.

In 1975 the Queen's speech stated that proposals would be prepared to amend the Official Secrets Act to liberalise the practice relating to official information. In November 1976

Merlyn Rees, a member of the Franks Committee and by then Home Secretary, made a statement of government policy based on the Franks recommendations. Rees said that Section 2 was too broad and he envisaged an Official Information Act following the lines recommended by Franks but widening the categories of information whose disclosure would remain an offence. His aim, he told the House of Commons, was to change the Official Secrets Act from a blunderbuss into an Armalite. The Queen's speeches of 1977 and 1978 made further promises of legislation, but it was not until July 1978 that the government produced a White Paper on the reform of Section 2. This predictably followed the lines of the Franks Committee, although interestingly it rejected the proposal for criminal sanctions against the disclosure of Cabinet documents – an understandable decision in view of the number of members of the government writing their memoirs. Rees's approach to the question was pragmatic; on one occasion he allowed himself to become sufficiently exasperated by a member of the freedom-of-information lobby to comment, 'See if you can find two or three people in your constituency who give a damn about more open government.'

The debate on the 1978 White Paper was interesting for the comments of the Conservative opposition, whose opportunity to introduce such legislation was less than a year away. Sir Michael Havers QC welcomed the reforms proposed by the White Paper and what he termed the government's second thoughts about freedom of information in the form of Rees's announcement that the government would carry out a detailed study of overseas experience to see how the flow of information to the public could be increased. Leon Brittan QC, later Home Secretary, observed: 'Section 2 is simply indefensible – yet it is still there. Why is that? It is there in spite of the government's assurances – they have not the courage to fight and overcome the strenuous rearguard action of Whitehall.'

In the meantime, the Croham directive (so named after the then head of the Civil Service) had been sent to fifty-one heads of department in July 1977. It advised all permanent secretaries that 'Henceforth the working assumption should be that all background material will be published unless the responsible minister or ministers decide otherwise.' However, in the best traditions of Whitehall, this important directive itself became an official secret, and its existence became known only through a leak to *The Times*. A subsequent audit carried out by *The Times* showed that the directive had been largely ignored. When Mrs Thatcher's government came to power in May 1979, the Croham directive was found a suitable pigeon-hole; it was announced in a confidential letter to the heads of department, which was also leaked, that the government did not intend to introduce public-access legislation. The Civil Service minister, Paul Channon, indicated in 1979: 'It will be the practice of this government to make such information as is possible available to the public including background papers and analytical studies relevant to major policy decisions.' There is no evidence that this statement has proved much more than a platitude.

In October 1978 a Freedom of Information Bill was prepared by the national executive committee of the Labour Party. It was followed in March 1979 by a Green Paper entitled *Open Government*, which examined overseas practice on freedom of information. The government stated that it saw the reform of Section 2 as an essential step in creating a climate in which greater openness could prevail. It would replace Section 2 by provisions to restrict criminal sanctions for unauthorised disclosure of official communications to a strictly limited range of information. However, there was still no government legislation as the Labour government moved towards the end of its five-year term. In March 1979 Clement Freud MP introduced the Official Information Bill, having won first place in the Private Members' ballot in the House of Commons. His Bill was based on the draft by the Outer Circle Policy Unit; it would have abolished Section 2 and introduced public access to government information. The Labour government indicated that it would not oppose the Bill on the second reading, but the Bill was unable to reach the statute book when Callaghan's administration lost a vote of confidence. The

Labour Party manifesto of 1979 gave an undertaking to introduce a freedom-of-information Bill to provide a system of open government and to enact the proposals made by the government in its White Paper of July 1978 to reform Section 2.

In February 1979 a Council of Europe report emanating from its legal affairs committee invited the governments of member states which had not done so to introduce a system of freedom of information involving access to government files, the right to seek and receive information from government agencies and departments, the right to inspect and correct personal files and the right of privacy, with the right to rapid action before the courts in these matters. Various European countries had in the meantime moved towards a system of greater freedom of information without too much difficulty. In France, for example, where there had been considerable restrictions on public access to government information, legislation was enacted in July 1978 permitting public access to government records with an independent commission to monitor the law. A French court of state security decides what ought to be kept secret in the interests of the defence of the nation.

The Conservative government that came to power in June 1979 showed no particular enthusiasm for abolishing Section 2 and even less for a system of greater freedom of information. The views of the Prime Minister had moderated since 1960 when, as a newly elected MP, she had introduced with these words a Private Member's Bill expanding the right of the public to attend council meetings: 'The paramount function of this distinguished House is to safeguard civil liberties rather than to think that administrative convenience should take first place.'

Nevertheless in October 1979 the Conservative government introduced a Protection of Information rather than a Freedom of Information Bill. This would have replaced Section 2 by a fairly restrictive piece of legislation enabling information relating to matters of security and intelligence to be protected whether or not they were common knowledge. The Lord Chancellor, Lord Hailsham, described it as a code which was 'more liberal, more intelligible and even capable of enforcement'. One of the more satisfactory features of this legislation was that a stricter test would be applied in deciding whether to prosecute in that the test would be whether the disclosure of the information would be likely to cause serious injury to the interests of the nation or to endanger the safety of the citizens of the United Kingdom. However, the Bill had many shortcomings and it was mauled on its second reading in the House of Lords. One particularly unattractive feature of the Bill was that the minister could have issued a conclusive certificate under the Act that the disclosure of information relating to security matters would lead to serious injury to the interests of the nation. That certificate could not then be challenged in the courts. The Act might have passed through Parliament had not the parliamentary debates coincided with the fortuitous revelation that the traitor who could be named only as 'Maurice' in Anthony Boyle's book *The Climate of Treason* (because of the danger of libel actions) was in fact Sir Anthony Blunt. Under the Protection of Information Bill the government could have prohibited the discussion of Blunt's identity on the ground that it related to national security. Blunt's foolishness in threatening to sue for libel anyone who claimed that he was Maurice cleared up any residual doubts as to Maurice's identity. The Bill was abandoned. There was some irony in that the exposure of Blunt's activities had been possible only through the access Boyle had had to British government papers in Washington under the US Freedom of Information Act. The Conservative administration there-after took the view that having tried and failed to reform the law there was little more it could do about it. In a debate in the House of Lords on 20 March 1985 Lord Elton, Minister of State at the Home Office, said that the government did not favour legislation either to introduce a general right of access to government information or to reform Section 2.

In its 1983 election manifesto the Labour Party had promised to 'introduce a freedom of information Bill providing a genuine system of open government and placing the onus on the authorities to justify withholding inform-ation.' The SDP/Liberal Alliance proposed to introduce an

Act along the lines of Freud's Bill with a public right of access to government and official information and with the aim of reducing the unreasonably broad criminal sanctions of the Official Secrets Act so that they would apply only to the protection of compelling interests of the state and its agencies. The Labour, Liberal and SDP leaders indicated support for the Campaign for Freedom of Information, while Mrs Thatcher remained unenthusiastic:

> I welcome any moves that will help to ensure that public demands for information are heard and as far as possible satisfied – but I firmly believe that major constitutional changes such as your campaign is proposing are in-appropriate and unnecessary. We already have a clear policy to make more information available and the necessary machinery to do so... but above all ministers' accountability to Parliament would be reduced and Parliament itself diminished.

There is some reason to doubt that the policy of making more information publicly available is achieving significant progress. The arguments about damage to ministerial accountability in Parliament have been rejected in Australia and Canada without visible ill effects.

There is no doubt that Section 2 should be abolished. The question is, what should be put in its place? I would favour the enactment of a law restricted to the protection of certain limited and clearly defined categories of information where the national interest would require that such information should not be disclosed. Such a law should be severe in its application (being confined only to essential national interests) but used only very sparingly. Government in Australia has survived without the comparable provision in its law being used, and until very recently the equivalent legislation in the United States was virtually never used. Much of the political criticism relating to prosecutions under Section 2 could be removed by replacing the need for obtaining the Attorney-General's permission for proceedings to be taken by cases being prepared by the Director of Public

Prosecutions and then placed before a High Court judge, or preferably a divisional court of three judges, for authority to issue a summons under the Act. There is precedent for such a procedure in relation to the law of criminal libel, where a High Court judge must give his consent before prosecution can be started. The advantage of having a divisional court of three judges would be the greater degree of independence, a reduction of the likelihood of prosecutions depending on the idiosyncrasies of particular judges, and less opportunity for court administrators to place such applications before judges who could be relied upon to give the government a smoother ride.

The criminal law against the disclosure of official information should be restricted in its scope but should at the same time be capable of being enforced without the difficulties that now beset prosecutions under Section 2. It should be confined to the protection of secrets that really matter. Precisely what these are is a matter on which there is considerable scope for disagreement. In a number of areas the Franks Committee would have been prepared to allow prosecutions where the Labour government in 1978 felt that it was not necessary to introduce the criminal law. Broadly speaking, the criminal law should be confined to the disclosure of documents relating to defence secrets, relations with foreign countries, security and intelligence matters, what could loosely be termed a law-and-order category and the protection of the confidences of the citizen. The law-and-order category would relate to the disclosure of information which assisted in the commission of criminal offences or the escape of prisoners from lawful custody or the prevention of arrest of offenders. Many of these offences could be dealt with by specific legislation, and I would hope that any judge, before giving consent to such a prosecution, would require to be satisfied as to why a charge under this new law was necessary. Very often such offences would amount to corruption or could be punishable under specific legislation relating to the police or the prison service. There have been far too many cases where a charge under Section 2 has been chucked in to nail the defendant if the main charges fail. It is generally accepted by those in favour of the reform of the law that the criminal law should continue to apply to the disclosure of information given in confidence by the citizen. People who provide, often under compulsion from the government, personal information about their families and homes or about their health or themsevles in their income tax returns or their social security applications should be satisfied that this information will not be leaked to third parties. The inclusion of this category is, I suspect, largely a political matter because it will in practice be very seldom possible to establish that the disclosure of such information would be likely to cause serious damage to the national interest. The citizen is surely better protected by specific privacy legislation, and officials who breach their obligation of confidence are probably better dealt with by specific legislation which would, for example, punish the errant social security officer, Inland Revenue official or census collator.

'It would not be sufficient merely to show that someone who worked in the area of defence or foreign relations had leaked information without authority. For there to be a successful prosecution the government should have to show that the disclosure of such information would be likely to cause serious injury to the national interest or to endanger the safety of the public. Mere administrative inconvenience or embarrassment to the government should be insufficient. The prosecution would therefore have to show that the disclosure of such information would be likely to cause significant damage to the defence of Britain or to the enforcement of the criminal law or to the exchange rate. If the disclosure fell short of that, the leaking civil servant would still be liable to instant dismissal with the loss of status and financial benefits, which are certainly considered to be a severe deterrent in the private sector. The number of jobs open to a civil servant who has betrayed the trust placed in him is not great.

If one has a system where, by the very terms of the legislation, only serious cases can be prosecuted and no one can be put on trial until the alleged offence has been examined by a judge or a panel of judges, it is then possible to curtail the circumstances in which the accused can raise a defence of public interest. No doubt in many cases the public is interested by documents that are leaked, but that is rather different from saying that there was a public interest in disclosing the documents. It seems to be at least a fear of the present government that a defendant accused under Section 2 can 'do a Ponting' – that is, put the particular aspect of government policy on trial. In 1979 the proposal was that a minister could produce a conclusive certificate that a particular document was likely to cause serious damage to the national interest. That was a monstrous proposal, removing as it did from the jury their right to decide on one of the essential ingredients of the offence. The proposal was rightly attacked in the House of Lords. Why was the government so frightened of juries deciding such matters? There appears no reason other than a purely political one for the government's reticence. After all, juries can properly be vetted so as to remove political undesirables, and particularly sensitive parts of the evidence can be heard in camera. This is regularly done in espionage trials, of which that of Bettaney was one of the most recent examples. In the Ponting case the prosecution allowed the jury to read (albeit in camera) the 'Crown Jewels', arguably one of the most secret documents disclosed in a court and much more significant than any document which has been the basis for a prosecution under Section 2.

If the criminal law is confined to very serious cases the argument for a stricter law becomes stronger. Whereas there are very good reasons for not throwing into prison filing clerks who do no more than leak politically embarrassing documents, there are stronger arguments for enforcing the law against those who are indisputably handling secret material and who have chosen to work in the area of defence secrets, foreign relations or the prevention of crime. If there are these restrictions on the circumstances in which a prosecution for unauthorised disclosure of information could be brought, the circumstances in which a defence of public interest could be raised could be clearly and closely defined. If a civil servant finds himself in fundamental disagreement with the policy of his department, he is under no obligation to continue working in that area of government, nor is he obliged to ventilate his grievances in a newspaper. The defence of claiming that disclosure of the document was in the public interest should be a very limited one. The defendant should have to establish that there was conduct exposed by the disclosed document which merited its revelation, that the means adopted by the civil servant in disclosing the documents were themselves reasonable and that in all the circumstances of the case the conduct of the civil servant in disclosing the document was itself reasonable.

It should be a defence for a civil servant to establish that he had no reason to believe that the document was classified. I would hope that the replacement of Section 2 would be accompanied by a complete revision of the practice relating to secrecy. Far too many people find that the Official Secrets Act and the declarations they have to sign are surprisingly unclear in view of the dire criminal consequences that can ensue. The declarations under the Act were criticised by the Franks Committee, although it did not produce a substitute. In April 1985 the Earl of Gowrie, Chancellor of the Duchy of Lancaster and Minister for the Arts and thus as suitable a spokesman on the matter for the Conservative government as anyone else, told the House of Lords that the government was considering the Official Secrets Act declarations with a view to reducing the number of forms wherever possible and making those that remained clearer and more intelligible. At the same time the procedures relating to and the guidelines for classifying documents into particular categories of secrecy should be clarified and the practice made more uniform. This was envisaged by the 1978 White Paper. There is general agreement, shared even by the Security Commission, that documents are, as a matter of practice, over-classified. The classification of documents is often a matter of administrative convenience rather than secrecy.

The statute that would replace Section 2 should be divorced entirely from the law relating to espionage. Spies and leakers are different animals, and the distinction between leakage and espionage has been unnecessarily blurred. The new law should prima facie be restricted to those in government service and government contractors. Mere receipt by a private citizen of official information should not be of itself an offence unless that person took it upon himself to communicate the information to a third party well knowing that it was highly classified material. The catch-all nature of Section 2 should be abolished entirely and replaced by a law confined to important secrets, where the law can be easily enforced. This is not to propose that any dissatisfied or corrupt official should have a licence to leak documents. They should where appropriate be prosecuted under the general criminal law for corruption or theft or under specific legislation relating to their occupations. A telecommunications engineer who assists in the tapping of telephones, or a police officer who passes a friend information from the police computer, or a prison officer who reveals classified information about plans to move prisoners, should be dealt with by the legislation that covers those individuals' activities.

Measures to permit a greater degree of public access to official information are also desirable. The overlap with the abolition and replacement of Section 2 is that certain categories of information require either absolute or limited exemption from public access. In practice the categories which would be kept for prosecutions under the replacement for Section 2 would be broadly similar to those where there would not be unfettered freedom of information. It is even more important in this area that confidential information given by citizens, whether in tax returns or census forms, cannot be inspected by inquisitive neighbours. Appendix 6 shows that in Canada the right to privacy and the right to freedom of information are dealt with in the same statute.

The framework for a Freedom of Information Act is relatively simple, although it would in practice be the subject of considerable political discussion and argument. The first step is for the government to decide which departments of government should be exempt from the freedom-of-information legislation. Although there would doubtless be those who would want unfettered access to every government department, in practice it is likely that, at least for a certain number of years after the particular document came into being, agencies dealing with national security such as MI5, MI6 and the Special Branch, the departments of the Foreign Office dealing with sensitive relations with foreign governments and departments of the Treasury dealing with financially sensitive information regarding the country's reserves or exchange rate, would be exempt. The alternative approach is to look at each request on its merits, but without some untouchable departments the business of government would become very difficult and there would be considerable reluctance to commit certain matters to paper. The number of such untouchable agencies should be strictly limited, and the opportunity should be seized to cut down the thirty-year rule that applies to public documents. The Official Information Bill in 1979 proposed a period of five years. That might not be sufficient for all government agencies, but a slightly longer period could be fixed for those departments. The wide discretion that at present exists in the hands of the Lord Chancellor, who has responsibility for public records, to withhold documents even after the expiry of the thirty-year period should be severely curtailed.

There would be certain government departments where some activities should be exempted from a general right of access. How this works in practice is examined in Appendix 4, which deals with the operation of such legislation in Australia. An example would be the protection of the commercial operations of a government corporation such as British Airways. It would not be right for all the competitors of British Airways to discover, under the guise of a freedom-of-information enquiry, the corporation's commercial secrets.

There should in addition be a residual right on the part of the government to certify that the release of certain documents would be harmful to the national interest. Most government agencies are likely from time to time to have a highly sensitive or secret document in the course of their activities even though there might normally be nothing particularly secret about their work. I would oppose the right of the government to have an unchallengeable veto on access to particular documents. A balance has to be struck between the government's need to keep certain of its activities secret, at least for a few years, and the citizen's right to know what the government is doing. A sensible compromise would appear to be to use the existing machinery of the Ombudsman. He is answerable to Parliament and independent of the executive, and he has been there for nearly twenty years. If the government refuses to produce a document on the grounds of its particular secrecy or sensitivity and the applicant presses for its disclosure, the Ombudsman should adjudicate the matter. He should have the right to call for and inspect the document or, as the case may be, the data bank and to question the witnesses in private as to the reasons for non-disclosure. He would then decide whether the document should be produced, without its contents having in the meantime been publicly revealed. As a senior lawyer with experience of the government process he seems a preferable choice to the Conservative Party's proposals in 1978 (not implemented when it came into government) of 'three wise men'. In practice such men tend to be retired civil servants and trade union officials with knighthoods who are perhaps not the best panel to decide these matters.

It is not the purpose of this book to draft a freedom-of-information law. That is in fact a relatively simple process after the decision has been taken as to what categories of information are to be exempt from a general right of access. Any government introducing such legislation would do well to examine carefully the experiences in Australia, Canada and the United States, which are briefly dealt with in the appendices to this book. The procedure relating to freedom of information is almost as important as the question of what matters are completely or partially exempt. It is essential to make the system cheap, quick and easy to understand. Government departments would be required to provide a simple statement of their activities and of where members of the public would be likely to find the documents relating to those activities. Forms applying for access to government information should be designed to be intelligible, straightforward and not matters that would require legal advice. The experience of countries that have had freedom-of-information legislation is that the overwhelming majority of applications under the Act are individuals wanting to find out about records kept about them or why a government department made a particular decision about them. The experience of those countries is that the number of people trying to discover goverment secrets, and of companies trying to uncover information about their competitors' commercial activities, is very small. The procedures of the Act should therefore be geared to its consumers.

Equally, the experience of countries with freedom of information and with the very worthwhile right of the citizen to apply to have inaccurate records kept about him corrected – a power that already exists in Britain under the Data Protection Act 1984 – is that when people have seen the papers relating to their case they very rarely ask for their records to be corrected. A cynic might say that this was merely the result of their ignorance about their rights, but there is evidence in Australia that the disclosure of papers has resulted in the settling of a number of grievances. Clearly there will be cases where it will not be appropriate to reveal a person's papers; for example, it would almost invariably be inappropriate to show a mentally disturbed person his medical records. However, the proposition that good administration would be hampered by the fact that the general public might at some stage have access to the papers is open to doubt. The experience in Australia, where the tendency is to allow access, does not bear this out. Further, there is much to be said for civil servants not putting down on paper comments of which they would be ashamed if they were seen by the person about whom they are written.

The fees for application under the freedom-of-information law should be modest. The experience of countries with such legislation shows that the fees recovered from information research are likely to produce only a very small fraction of the cost of the operation. To introduce fees that reflect the underlying cost of the whole structure of the freedom-of-information system would put the benefit of the legislation beyond the reach of most of the people who would wish to use the Act.

It is likely to be only a matter of time before Section 2 is abolished and replaced by a workable law. All political parties appear to be agreed on that, and in due course the Conservatives will no doubt stop wringing their hands and, given the opportunity, abolish Section 2. Sooner or later they will probably also be converted to the need for freedom-of-information legislation and will recall the moves made by their party in this direction when Edward Heath was at the helm.

In January 1988, the Protection of Information Bill of November 1979 was resurrected in a Private Members Bill of the same name by Richard Shepherd, a Conservative MP on the right wing of the party. His Bill would have replaced the catch-all nature of Section 2 and would very sensibly have restricted the criminal law to protecting official information relating to defence, international relations, security and intelligence where disclosure would be likely to cause serious injury to the interests of the nation or endanger the safety of a British citizen. It would also have protected certain categories of information which were necessary for the maintenance of law and order and the protection of confidentiality where citizens were compelled under existing legislation to supply personal information about themselves. Where there was a dispute as to whether information was likely to cause serious injury, this would have been decided by the Judicial Committee of the Privy Council rather than by a branch of the executive, which had caused the fall of the 1979 Bill. There were two principal defences, one was that the information had already been disclosed in the sense that it was publicly available and the other was that disclosure was in the public interest in the sense that it would reveal the existence of crime, abuse of authority, neglect of official duty or other misconduct, provided that the person disclosing the information could show that he had taken reasonable steps to draw such misconduct to the attention of the responsible authorities.

Under this change of the law, Sarah Tisdall (p. 157) would have had a defence on the basis that her disclosure would not have caused serious injury to national interests. Clive Ponting (p. 177) probably would have had a defence (provided that he had gone through the appropriate complaints procedures) on the grounds that he was exposing an abuse of authority or misconduct on the part of the government.

Shepherd would also have de-criminalised the trivial breaches of the Official Secrets Act of which examples abound in the appendix of this book. Civil servants who were found to have old government documents in their attics at home would only be prosecuted if they had acted in a way which was in intentional or reckless disregard of their official duty.

Despite its earlier statements about the shortcomings of Section 2, the government, in what many felt was part of an increasingly authoritarian and arrogant attitude to its exercise of power, took the virtually unprecedented step of imposing a three line whip to vote the Bill down. It revealed that, unknown to the majority of the population, it was in fact two-thirds of the way through its proposals to reform the law. It declined to say what was wrong with the Shepherd Bill. There were no realistic attempts to discuss with Shepherd the contents of his Bill or to reach any form of compromise with him as to the orderly introduction of what was admitted to be necessary legislation. In consequence, the government's majority fell from 101 to its lowest of the Parliament, thirty-seven, with nineteen Conservative MPs voting for the Shepherd bill and approximately fifty others also defying the whip and abstaining or deliberately absenting themselves. The government failed in the debate to specify what were its proposals. The suspicion must remain that the government will introduce a tougher and more enforceable law of official secrecy without permitting a public interest defence in the criminal law, although it is available in the civil law of breach of confidence. The government may also make a breach of a newly defined duty of confidentiality on the part of some government servants a matter not just of civil law but also a criminal offence. The impression the government gives is of being more interested in tightening up the law relating to official secrets so that it can start using the law again and have a reasonable prospect of obtaining convictions rather than in any relaxation of the criminal law. A number of MPs complained about the government's high-handed treatment of Parliament. It was significant that a number of Labour MPs who had had experience of security matters in government felt able to vote for Shepherd's Bill, as did the former Prime Minister, Edward Heath, who had set up the Franks Committee, as well as certain former cabinet ministers in the Thatcher administration.

22

The Wright Case: A Tale of Perversity

Although I had been introduced to *Spycatcher* some months earlier, the Peter Wright case started for me in Abergavenny. It was there that I heard of the letter which the Treasury Solicitor John Bailey, knighted later in the case, had sent to Heinemann in London. Bailey had chosen the middle of August 1985 to threaten court proceedings within seven days against Heinemann unless they gave an undertaking not to publish Wright's book (this threat had already deterred one publisher). It was a strange time to choose as the government would have known of the possibility of Heinemann publishing the book from an article that appeared in the *Observer* four months earlier. In fact, Heinemann had already decided not to publish in Britain. (Subsequently, in February 1986, they did give an undertaking that they would not publish in Great Britain without giving fourteen days notice to the government.)

Heinemann Australia received a similar ultimatum in a letter dated 20 August 1985 from Australian lawyers acting on behalf of the Attorney-General for the United Kingdom. It was perhaps indicative of the accident prone nature of this litigation that this letter was not only sent to the wrong address but also to the wrong State. Heinemann Australia carry on business at Richmond Victoria, whereas the government had tracked them to a former office at Denistone East in New South Wales. This initial mistake appears to have led the British Government to commence proceedings in September 1985 in New South Wales rather than the more conservative courts of Victoria, where they might have fared a little better. In view of the mistake as to the location of Heinemann Australia's offices, it was uncharitable of the Australian press to blame the British government for an unexplained fire at the time at the Richmond offices! In those proceedings, the Attorney-General sought an injunction to prevent publication of any book by Wright, an account of any profits he might make and reimbursement of their legal costs. Wright had retired to a farm in Tasmania; he could not by law be extradited to the United Kingdom to face a charge under Section 2 of the Official Secrets Act 1911. He had been told by Sir Anthony Kershaw MP, who had discussed the matter with the Attorney-General, that he would be arrested if he set foot in England. This may have been merely to discourage him from returning. The Massiter affair (p. 222) reveals that the government is most reluctant to risk a contested prosecution of former intelligence officers. Certainly the government has shown no enthusiasm for proceedings against any other participants in the Wright case. It has conducted investigations under the Official Secrets Act 1911, but decided there was insufficient evidence to proceed – despite what must have stared it in the face. Consequently the government had to proceed against Wright and his publishers under the civil law of breach of confidence.

In July 1984 Heinemann Australia had approached Wright to write a book a few days after they had read in the Melbourne *Age* about his appearance on the Granada *World in Action* programme, *The Spy Who Never Was*. They felt, accurately as it turned out, that an Australian court would take a more critical view of British claims of damage to national security than would be the case in England. They declined to be deterred from publishing the book and in September 1985 an interim injunction (later replaced by a voluntary undertaking) was granted to restrain publication pending the trial.

Wright had worked from 1940 to 1955 as a scientist for the Admiralty before joining the Security Service (MI5) and

serving as a principal scientific officer. He provided scientific
and technical support for MI5's counter-espionage operations. His last post had been as a personal consultant on
matters of counter-espionage to the Director General, Sir
Michael Hanley. He was awarded the CBE in 1972 and left
the service with the praise of many of his colleagues. He was,
however, convinced that Sir Roger Hollis, head of MI5 from
1956 to 1965, had been a Soviet spy. Wright had been
chairman of the Fluency Committee, which had investigated
Soviet penetration of MI5. The evidence Wright had
examined while serving on the Committee had reinforced his
view of Hollis's treachery. He was appalled at the cover-up
which had taken place and felt that it was his duty to place on
record the extent to which the USSR had subverted British
intelligence.

As is now well-known, the result was *Spycatcher*, which
Wright wrote with the assistance of Paul Greengrass, a writer
and television producer, whose detailed knowledge of the
intelligence service proved invaluable at the trial in Sydney.
Among its allegations were that MI5 had plotted to de-
stabilise the Wilson government in 1974 and that Hollis, the
Director General of MI5, had been a Soviet spy. The book
detailed the bugging of foreign missions and described how
diplomatic conferences at Lancaster House, including the
Zimbabwe negotiations, had been bugged. When the Russian
leader Krushchev had visited England, his suite at Claridges
had likewise been bugged. The book even chronicled the
unsuccessful attempt made by Burgess on Soviet orders to
seduce Churchill's niece despite his sexual proclivities.

In view of the welter of litigation to which the book gave
birth, it is worth noting that, with the exception of the Wilson
plot, all the material in the book was at least twelve years old.
What renders of dubious validity the government's determination to litigate the Wright case to the last appellate court in
any country where it believed it had a worthwhile prospect of
success is the fact that Wright's allegations were for the most
part already widely publicised. He had been the main source
for Chapman Pincher's book *Their Trade is Treachery*
published in March 1981. No action had been taken to stop

that book. Despite what was said at the trial in Sydney the government clearly did have legal grounds for stopping *Their Trade is Treachery*. The suggestion that there was insufficient time to determine who was Pincher's source was untrue. The government had had more time to find this out than apparently it chose to reveal to Sir Robert Armstrong and by the time of publication it knew very well that Wright indeed was Pincher's source and certainly that Pincher had been assisted by a Fluency Committee member. At the trial in Sydney, Armstrong admitted that it was known to the British government from checks made of lists of airline passengers that Pincher had visited Wright in Tasmania in 1980. The fact that Pincher travelled as Dr Chapman does not appear to have fooled Her Majesty's government. Furthermore, in 1981 Wright had remarked, in a letter to a former colleague, that he might write a history of his time in MI5, but that he did not intend to publish it during his lifetime. This had produced a stinging rebuke from the Ministry of Defence that if this was meant seriously, he should be in no doubt that action would be taken against him under both the criminal and civil law.

Wright's connection with Pincher came about as a result of an introduction by his friend, Lord Rothschild. Rothschild had written to Wright in August 1980 expressing concern about the Blunt affair and the false allegations being made against him and his wife because of their long standing friendship with Blunt and Burgess. Rothschild sent Wright an airline ticket and the two men met at Rothschild's flat. Wright felt that Mrs Thatcher had been inadequately briefed by MI5 on the Blunt Affair in November 1979. He wanted the 154 page dossier that he had written entitled *The Security of the United Kingdom against the Assault of the Russian Intelligence Services* to be brought to the Prime Minister's attention and not to be sat on by MI5. As Wright explained at the trial, Rothschild suggested he use Chapman Pincher to ghost write the material he had put together. Pincher had, he told Wright, the advantage of good contacts in the intelligence world and he should be able to ensure that the book was published without official interference.

Wright felt that this venture at least must be tacitly

approved by the authorities even if it were to proceeed as part of a 'deniable operation'. Pincher signed a contract with his publishers, Sidgwick and Jackson on 12 December 1980; Rothschild arranged for payment of royalties through a Netherlands Antilles company, Overbridge International. In a book Pincher has written about the Wright Affair, entitled *A Web of Deception* Pincher claims that Rothschild's only involvement with the matter was instructing a colleague in his bank to make a payment of the 50 per cent of the royalties of *Their Trade is Treachery* which were payable, after expenses, to Wright in Australia. Thereafter, Pincher tells us, Rothschild had no connection with the affair. Curiously, Pincher gave a somewhat different account in the course of the seventy or so letters that he wrote to Wright in the period from 1980 to 1983 using a somewhat crude code about horse trading for his literary activities. At that time he wrote in rather greater detail about what he then said was Lord Rothschild's involvement in the matter, such as 'our mutual friend (meaning Lord Rothschild) has just confirmed the deposit for the mares (code for the book money) is on its way to you... I had a session with our horse-coper (meaning Rothschild) who says he cannot safely change the arrangements in the foreseeable future... I have talked with our intermediary and he will see what he can do about our Swiss venture, but rather regards himself as having completed his contribution'. There were a number of other letters to similar effect.

Whatever the extent of Rothschild's involvement, it is puzzling that as a man with considerable intelligence experience and with a name that is almost a byword for discretion, he should have contacted Wright in the first place and that he should, in however peripheral a manner, have been party to ensuring that Wright should be paid for providing Pincher with the information that enabled him to write *Their Trade is Treachery* – a book liberally scattered with official secrets. Pincher attributes the failure of the government to take action against *Their Trade is Treachery* to the good offices of an intermediary whom he calls the Arbiter but refuses to name. Although Pincher says that he was willing to give evidence for the government against Wright, it seems that this information about the role and existence of the Arbiter was not communicated to Sir Robert Armstrong. If Pincher's account is correct, this is a further instance of the truth being concealed from Sir Robert Armstrong when he gave evidence at the trial in Sydney.

Perhaps no less odd than the failure of the British government to take action against *Their Trade is Treachery* was the fact revealed by Pincher to Wright in a letter dated 27 January 1983 that Pincher had, in the course of a New Year's day shooting party with 'a very friendly' Sir Michael Havers QC, the then Attorney-General, and a lunch with Dickie (Sir Arthur) Franks, the head of MI6, gleaned sufficient information to be able to ensure Wright that 'there is no intention whatever of taking action against me, *which means you too*'. No less surprising was the fact that Pincher told Wright that Havers had discussed the possible prosecution of Nigel West for his book, *A Matter of Trust*, with Pincher. He wrote to Wright explaining that Havers had told him that the problem was that West had been adopted as a Tory candidate. 'Mrs T is furious with him (West).' The authority of what Pincher told him was, in Wright's view, increased by the fact that notwithstanding the publication of *Their Trade is Treachery*, Pincher had been appointed paid specialist adviser to the Parliamentary inquiry into positive vetting and a member of a Ministry of Defence Committee to study censorship problems arising out of the Falklands War. Pincher had, in the past, done such errands for the security service, such as reporting back to MI5 on his meetings with the Russian press attaché, Anatole Strelnikov.

In *A Web of Deception*, Pincher tells us that he was sufficiently appalled by Wright's behaviour in writing a book that he volunteered after the trial in Sydney to give evidence for the government. 'My own view, as a citizen and tax payer, is that the government had no alternative (to taking action against Wright) and that it would have happened even if Labour had been in office at the relevant time. The principle of confidentiality could hardly be more important and not just regarding secret service officers, but all former servants

of the Crown who have had access to secret matters.'
However, Pincher's views seem to have changed radically
since 1982 when he was seeking Wright's assistance and
obtaining information not only for *Their Trade is Treachery*,
but also for his next book *Too Secret Too Long*, and while he
was in fact encouraging Wright to write a book. He wrote 'the
only solution, short of your TV project, is a book. Clearly if
you could write one under your own name you could
probably make a killing. A book under a pseudonym would
not have the same impact and its contents would no doubt
reveal its author. What is the position about your book? Is it
for posthumous publication, by which time (I hope) interest
will have waned still further? Would you like soundings
made, without mentioning your name, about a publisher?
Have you thought about an American outlet?' It is a matter
for conjecture why Pincher, with all his experience in this
field should have executed such a U-turn and produced a
book such as *A Web of Deception* that must have been so
welcome to the government.

When Wright appeared on 16 July 1984 on the *World in
Action* programme he had made a number of detailed
allegations concerning his time as a security service officer.
He described an operation called 'Party Piece', when MI5
officers had burgled the Mayfair flat of a wealthy Communist
in 1955 and had removed for microfilming a list of 55,000
members of the Communist Party. He said that it was 99 per
cent certain Hollis was a spy and described the working of the
Fluency Committee. He said that a number of the successes
claimed by MI5 were part of a KGB disinformation campaign.
He also dealt with some of the more bizarre activities of MI5,
such as the fact that the former Prime Minister, Lord Wilson
of Rievaulx, had been investigated three times between 1964
and 1974 and that MI5 had looked into the possibility that
Hugh Gaitskell, Wilson's predecessor as leader of the Labour
Party, had been poisoned by the Soviets.

Despite what was said at the trial in Sydney to the contrary,
the fact that Wright was intending to appear on the Granada
programme was well-known to MI5. No less that twenty
former MI5 and MI6 officers as well as Hollis's son Adrian

had been approached by the programme's producers, John Ware and Paul Greengrass. At one stage it looked as if a former director of counter-espionage would be prepared to contradict what Wright had said on television. Wright's hope of a proper enquiry into Soviet penetration of British intelligence came to nothing. He had hoped *Their Trade is Treachery* would produce such an inquiry. Pincher did not show him the synopsis (although it was sent to MI6); nor did Wright see the complete manuscript. More surprisingly, Pincher's conclusion that there was no need for an inquiry was the opposite of Wright's. The Prime and Bettaney spy trial convinced Wright that Soviet penetration continued as before. It was after the arrest of Bettaney, an MI5 officer, that Wright had agreed to give an interview to Granada Television.

After Wright had appeared in July 1984 in the *World in Action* programme he had forwarded a copy of his dossier to Sir Anthony Kershaw MP, Chairman of the House of Commons Foreign Affairs Committee. Contrary to Wright's wishes, Kershaw had fowarded it to Sir Robert Armstrong, who referred it to the Prime Minister. Following a meeting with the Director General and Deputy Director General of the Security Service, Sir Anthony was persuaded not to raise the matter in Parliament and he returned the dossier to Granada. Notwithstanding the fact that it contained many of the allegations which formed the basis of *Spycatcher,* no attempt was made by the government to impound it or threaten proceedings, if its contents were disclosed. In contrast to the letters which subsequently flowed from the law officers of the Crown, no action was taken by the Treasury Solicitor or the D-notice committee to prevent newspapers using information contained in the dossier. Nor was Wright, in the discreet phrase used by Armstrong at the trial, 'reminded of his obligations'. No steps were taken by the authorities to investigate the matters in the dossier.

The British government's objections to Wright's book emerged from three increasingly finely tuned affidavits that were to be sworn by Sir Robert Armstrong and to form the basis of his evidence at the trial in Sydney. The material in

Wright's book, Armstrong maintained, would damage liaison between the British security service and foreign intelligence agencies; it would cause a loss of confidence among those with whom the service co-operated; it might encourage other people to write their memoirs; it might assist terrorists and, by a process of collateral verification, it might enable the Russians to confirm one set of facts by reference to another set of facts in Wright's book. Throughout the case the government declined to specify any particular passage which gave rise to a particular risk or to avail itself of the defence offer to remove any passages which might endanger national security. The government preferred to rest on these somewhat tenuous and ingenious generalisations.

One interesting feature of the Wright litigation was that although certain appellate judges were prepared to accuse Wright of being a traitor – which he certainly was not – the judges who have actually examined the contents of *Spycatcher* in detail and have had to preside over the trials where the government's contentions have been tested, have unquivocally rejected the government's claims. Mr Justice Powell considered that the British obsession for secrecy bordered almost on paranoia. He considered that the British government had failed to establish its claim, as much of the information in Wright's manuscript no longer retained the quality of confidentiality and that the publication of such information as might still be regarded as confidential would not cause any detriment to the British government or MI5. Mr Justice Scott, who conducted the case brought by the Attorney General in England against the *Guardian*, the *Observer* and the *Sunday Times* and who saw Sir Robert Armstrong being cross-examined, commented that he could not escape the reflection that the absolute protection of the security service, for which Sir Robert Armstrong was contending, could not be achieved this side of the Iron Curtain.

The case against Peter Wright has been misrepresented. It has been suggested that there is something inherently wrong in someone like Peter Wright, who had worked for MI5, writing such a book. However, there are intelligence officers who have written books with some degree of government authority, such as Sir Percy Sillitoe, who had been head of MI5 and who even included a photograph of a serving MI5 officer in his book, Jim Skardon. In addition, Sir John Masterman and Professor R. V. Jones wrote books about their intelligence experiences with the, albeit reluctant, approval of the government. There are also a number of distinguished intelligence officers who have written their memoirs in the hope that they will be able to publish them. In the case of Anthony Cavendish, he went one stage further by having 500 copies of his memoirs, *Inside Intelligence*, privately published and distributed to various friends and Sunday newspapers of his acquaintance. Somewhat bizarrely, the government took no action against him although it did proceed against the Sunday newspapers when they failed to give undertakings not to publish extracts from the book. Cavendish did agree not to distribute any further copies. The government did appear to have a change of heart in that they did agree to blue pencil the parts of the book to which they objected – something they resolutely refused to do in Wright's case. Intelligence officers in other countries such as the United States, France and Australia have written their memoirs without difficulty. Clearly such memoirs need to be vetted to ensure that they do not betray operational secrets. The problem that Wright faced is that in this country we have a government which has a policy of invariably refusing to give consent to such memoirs insofar as they touch on details of life in one of the intelligence agencies irrespective of content and operational significance. In Wright's case, the high moral position for which the government seemed to be contending was weakened by the fact that it appeared that part of its objection to Wright was that he had, through Pincher, already had his say and the time had now come to shut him up. The government would never say to which parts of the book it really objected. I suspect that that was because it was not possible for the government to produce any convincing example of damage to national security. If it were the government's case that, notwithstanding the antiquity of the operational and technical matters discussed by Wright, there were matters of interest in the book to the intelligence agencies of third world countries as opposed to the Russians who probably knew it already, it seems that the choice of the British government to go for all or nothing will itself have damaged national security. What may have upset the intelligence agencies as much as anything about Wright's book was its questioning of the worth of much of their activities and its depiction of their personnel as not particularly attractive bureaucrats, with MI5 spending much of its time sniping at MI6. Among some of Wright's enemies it was possible to gain the impression that they disliked Wright more for having broken the rules of a gentleman's club and for standing to make money out of his book (an aspiration of a number of authors) than for traitors like Blunt, who had spied out of conviction and were, after all, from the right side of the track.

In any event, and for whatever reason, the government decided to pursue their case against Wright no matter how long it took and what it cost. The proceedings were brought in the name of the then Attorney-General, Sir Michael Havers. It seems that he was something of a figurehead in the litigation and that the real impetus for the litigation came from No. 10 Downing Street and from the legal adviser to the security service who, on the instructions of the D-notice committee, but notwithstanding the fact that he had been extensively named in the press in relation to other cases, became known as Bernard X.

The first legal team Heinemann Australia engaged proved numerous and costly and in December 1985 produced a pessimistic prospect of success. Bad as things had got, Heinemann had had no hesitation in sending an obscure Soviet publisher packing who had offered to publish Wright's manuscript! I happened to be visiting Australia at the time, so I took the opportunity of reviewing the situation with those involved. I went to see Wright in Tasmania. I was shocked at the straitened circumstances to which he was reduced, living in a three room pre-fabricated house. After my visit he wrote, 'David Hooper appeared to understand what it is all about. It is a battle against the deliberate suppression of facts which should be exposed in the national interest. It is a battle against the use of Australian civil law to achieve a purpose which could not be achieved under British criminal law. It involves a gross denial of natural justice for myself. It is a *political* case which *must* be fought and *can* be won.' (Receiving a letter from Wright is an unusual experience. I found myself rebuked by him for not sealing every edge of my airmail letter and being told that, despite my sellotaping efforts, the letter could still be read. His was sellotaped all round, and the return address was – perhaps by way of a joke against his former employers – T. Rout, Waterfall, New South Wales.)

A friend at the Bar introduced me to Malcolm Turnbull, a thirty-two-year-old solicitor, who had practised initially as a barrister and then as Kerry Packer's lawyer. He was prepared to act for Heinemann and Wright, whose fortunes then changed dramatically. Without the restrictive practices that afflict the legal profession in England, Turnbull was able to appear as a solicitor in all the courts which heard the case. Turnbull's strategy for fighting the case was simple. Wright should come to Sydney to give his evidence, as should Sir Robert Armstrong to be cross-examined on his affidavit. The British government should be compelled to specify to which parts of Wright's book they really objected.

On 24 March 1986, the government was ordered by Mr Justice Powell to state which parts of the manuscript it wished suppressed. The government, after due reflection, answered all parts. Later it was said that only the three chapters dealing with Wright's early life before formally joining MI5 could be published. Without apparent irony, counsel for the British government, William Caldwell, said of the remaining twenty chapters that the odd sentence possibly could be picked out which might be unobjectionable, but even they could not be published. In fact the selection of the three chapters did not make much sense. Wright had worked part-time for MI5 in the period 1950–55, but he was nevertheless allowed by this somewhat arbitrary decision of the government to recount his first job for MI5; to show the Americans how the Satyr microphone, thoughtfully implanted by the Soviets in the Great Seal which they had supplied for the Ambassador's office, worked!

When Turnbull came to London in April 1986, I took him to see the Treasury Solicitor John Bailey. The meeting was not a success. Bailey lectured Turnbull on the law, unwisely underestimating his opponent. He turned down flat any proposal to negotiate cuts in Wright's manuscript. He was sufficiently moved by Turnbull's broadside: 'You'll be in a rather special position after everyone has blamed you for this disaster. I would get to work covering my backside if I were you, Bailey. You will wish you never heard of Peter Wright by the time I'm finished with you', to reply, 'Well, you tell Wright he had better seek some medical advice before he comes to Court. He'll get no quarter in the witness box on account of his ill-health.' Bailey's parting shot was: 'Well Mr Turnbull, we will have to see what you are like on your feet.'

Turnbull's next step was to produce extensive particulars showing which information in *Spycatcher* had already been published and which pages disclosed criminal, treasonable or illegal conduct on the part of the security service or its officers. Thereafter, Turnbull settled some 150 interrogatories – questions which the British government had to answer on oath. It would be asked specifically if an allegation of misconduct made by Wright on a particular page was true or false. The government believed that it could fight this case without indicating which parts of the book were true or showing what real detriment it would suffer if Wright's book were published. The government seems to have been under the impression that no Australian judge would order it to answer such questions. Only after two days of the hearing in August 1986 did the government realise that this was exactly what Mr Justice Powell had in mind. After consultations late into the night, it decided to admit that, for the purposes of these proceedings only, all the allegations in Wright's manuscript – and for that matter in the *20/20 Vision* programme featuring Cathy Massiter (p. 222) – were true. Mr Justice Powell considered the admission 'quite dramatic'. The British government avoided answering all but five of the interrogatories – relating to the circumstances of publication in which West's book, *A Matter of Trust*, and Pincher's *Their Trade is Treachery* were published and the Granada and Massiter programmes were broadcast.

This admission was a mistake. It dealt with the short-term problem of answering the interrogatories, but it made it very much more difficult for the British government to argue that it was contrary to the Australian public interest to read about the criminal activities which it had now admitted. These included admitting that Sir Roger Hollis, who had helped set up ASIO (the Australian MI5) was a Soviet spy and indeed that the man who assisted setting up ASIS (their MI6), Dickie Ellis, was also a spy. These were matters of considerable interest to the Australian public. The British government had made it much more difficult for itself to meet the test laid down in the judgement of Mr Justice Mason in *Commonwealth of Australia* v. *John Fairfax & Sons Ltd* in 1980:

> The court will determine the government's claim to confidentiality by reference to the public interest. Unless disclosure is likely to injure the public interest it will not be prohibited. The court will not prevent the publication of information which merely throws light on the past workings of the government, even if it be not public property, so long as it does not prejudice the community in other respects.

Despite the greatly reduced number of interrogatories the government now had to answer, it unwisely did so with a certain economy of the truth. In relation to West's book, *A Matter of Trust*, Armstrong was asked whether the proceedings taken to restrain publication of that book were settled on the basis that the book could be published. A simple answer of Yes did not find favour with the government's lawyers and Sir Robert was compelled to reply 'The proceedings were stayed by consent following discussions between the parties to the proceedings, the (Attorney-General) being satisfied that those matters contained in the manuscript which (he) believed had been obtained by (West) in breach of a duty of confidence would be removed.' The problem here was that West's book when published still contained significant details about MI5's organisational charts and its internal structure.

In relation to Pincher's book, *Their Trade is Treachery*, Armstrong was asked whether consideration was given by (the Attorney-General) or any other servant or agent of the British Crown to restrain the publication of the said book prior to its publication. Again Armstrong appears to have been advised against answering Yes, but replied, '(The Attorney-General) was advised that it had no basis to restrain the publication of the said book.' The position here was that it emerged at the trial that the Attorney-General had not even been party to any such discussion. It was an answer that disclosed a surprising lack of familiarity with the law of confidence on the part of the Attorney-General's legal advisers – if true – but it was not true. At the trial on 18 November Armstrong insisted this was the decision of the Attorney-General personally. Only ten days later, after heated exchanges the day before in the House of Commons, did Armstrong correct his evidence, apologising for unintentionally misleading the court. He had been repeatedly asked to check the facts, but only when Havers threatened to resign did anyone see fit to correct the facts. Armstrong had spoken to a colleague in the Cabinet Office and had learnt, that 'Sir Michael Havers (the Plaintiff in the case) was unhappy with the answers I have given'. Despite the presence of a number of British advisers in court who ought to have known the true facts, the matter seems only to have been corrected when Havers threatened to resign if the record was not put straight.

Turnbull was also interested to know when the government first saw a copy of *Their Trade is Treachery* prior to its publication on 25 March 1981. The answer was 'in or about February 1981'. The longer before publication the government had a copy of Pincher's book, the more inexplicable became their failure to take action to stop the book being published. In fact the government had known about the book longer than it cared to admit.

Turnbull: Did anyone else in the service of the government

to your knowledge know in late 1980 that Pincher was writing this book about Hollis?

Armstrong: Not to my knowledge.

In the course of the trial the government was ordered to disclose a number of secret documents it had in its possession about these matters, but had not disclosed to the defence. It had to admit that, contrary to what Armstrong had said, the security intelligence agencies had received a two page synopsis of *Their Trade is Treachery* on 15 December 1980. These agencies apparently had decided that there was no point in trying to encourage specific deletions or changes in the text.

It was extraordinary that Armstrong, as the Prime Minister's principal official adviser on matters of security and a man who had had very close liaison with MI5 for at least ten years, should have given the court an untrue answer. Either he was being distinctly economical with the truth or he was not being told the truth by the security service. One would have expected Armstrong to be fully briefed on the circumstances of the publication of Pincher's book by the time of the trial, even if he had not known about it in early 1981. As a result of all the preliminary manoeuvring before the trial, he would have been well aware that this was a live issue on which he was likely to be extensively cross-examined. It was odd therefore that he could not give a true answer and that his answer remained uncorrected despite the presence in court of a security service representative, who would have been aware that the government, unknown at that time to the defence, was sitting on a document that contradicted Armstrong's answer. I believe that the truth was not told to Armstrong by the security service. It was disgraceful conduct on the part of the British government not to tell the truth and to try and deceive an Australian court.

The government turned out to be equally reticent in admitting that they knew that Wright was going to participate in the *World in Action* programme shown on 16 July 1984. Again, the truth seems to have been kept from Armstrong and the Australian court was misled. Initially

Armstrong said that it was not known until the morning of 16 July what Wright would say when Whitehall read an article in *The Times* headlined 'Security Head Was Soviet Agent' and this meant that the government could not 'get the act together' in sufficient time to stop the programme – itself a somewhat surprising assertion as they still had eleven hours in which to bestir themselves. He said that they had probably learnt about the programme some days before this. It was put to him that in fact they had known months before. Armstrong answered 'I don't know about "months", weeks possibly'. He did not think it was as long as months although it might be. In fact the government was once more sitting on documentary evidence which contradicted Armstrong's evidence: MI5 knew by 4 May 1984 that there were plans for a *World in Action* programme in which Wright was assisting and might take part. Far from learning about Wright's allegations over their breakfast tables on 16 July, MI5 had known by 3 July that Granada intended to show an interview with Wright in which Wright would re-open the allegations against Hollis and in effect present the case against him and had so advised the Treasury Solicitor in a letter of that date. The Treasury Solicitor was present in court when Armstrong gave his erroneous evidence as to the events leading up to the broadcast. However, this document was only revealed when an order for discovery was made at a later stage in the trial.

The government having decided not to make any compromise and to cling to the Admiral Byng principle at all costs – and the exercise might well end by costing the British government well over £3 million – the case started in Sydney on 17 November 1986. This was fifteen years to the day that Armstrong had written to Wright telling him that he had been recommended for a CBE. The government's underlying anxiety in the case was brought home when we heard that the normally unflappable Armstrong had crowned a photographer at London Airport with his brief case. He attended the trial with the government's two top lawyers, the Treasury Solicitor John Bailey and his assistant David Hogg, an MI5 officer, a cypher clerk and a foreign office press officer, Ivor Roberts, who gave daily briefings on how well the Cabinet

Secretary was faring. It was no doubt an unintended irony that when Sir Robert Armstrong flew back to London at the first available opportunity, Roberts dispensed champagne to the press corps! The British government was anxious to obtain the assistance of the Australian government to testify that publication of Wright's book would be contrary to the Australian public interest. It seems that to achieve this, the British government had reminded the Australian government of the transient nature of the assistance given to the Australian Defence Signals Department by GCHQ. There was some opposition in the Australian Cabinet to assisting the British and a compromise was reached which consisted of a weak affidavit from their Cabinet Secretary, Michael Codd, and the presence in court of the Australian Solicitor-General, Dr Gavin Griffith. The securing of this assistance led the British Attorney General in the course of a necessary, if unauthorised, leak to inform a representative of Heinemann that Bob Hawke had agreed to help out Mrs Thatcher. This led to some successful political lobbying by Turnbull of various members of the Australian Cabinet.

In the course of the five week trial, it became apparent that the British government was not at its best in away fixtures. It appeared that the government was running the case as it felt best and without proper consultation of the leading firm of solicitors Stephen Jacques Stone James in Sydney whom it had engaged and who appeared to be excluded from much of the decision making process. It was, on the whole, unwise to criticise the judge, Mr Justice Powell, in the course of the trial. Nevertheless, on 3 December certain lobby correspondents were briefed that the British government considered Mr Justice Powell had grossly mishandled the trial. On 8 December the *Mail on Sunday* reported in best lobby jargon, to the evident displeasure of the judge, that intelligence chiefs feared that highly secret documents in the hands of the Australian judge in the Sydney law case over the Wright book would eventually be leaked. It was needlessly insulting to a judge who had served as an intelligence officer in the Australian Army Intelligence Corps and who might have hoped for greater respect than being treated by the

British like a Pakistani umpire. A similar whispering campaign could be heard about the government's very able Counsel, Theo Simos QC.

When the government was ordered to disclose the secret documents it had been withholding, the difficulty of running such a case from London became apparent. The hearing in Sydney had to be suspended for three hours, while the British team had trans-oceanic telephone conversations, which ended at 2.00 a.m. London time. One could only speculate who in London was telling the British team what to do, but in all probability the telephone call had been to No. 10 Downing Street.

The trial attracted worldwide publicity, batteries of television crews and scores of journalists. The trial was even re-created on television. It was memorable for the ruthless breaking down of Armstrong's generalisations in cross-examination by Turnbull and the undermining of the claims of consistent policy regarding publication of intelligence matters. Eventually Armstrong was forced to the qualification that 'the policy is consistent with practice; it does not have to be invariable'. No doubt it made sense in Whitehall – in Sydney it was pure Sir Humphrey.

Armstrong provided no satisfactory explanation as to why the government had taken no action against two recently retired MI5 officers, Miranda Ingram and Cathy Massiter, who had disclosed the counter-espionage operations of MI5 nor in 1981 against Tony Motion, a former MI5 officer, who had appeared on *Panorama*, nor why accounts of security operations far more detailed and up-to-date than Wright's had been allowed to appear unchallenged in the *Guardian* and the *New Statesman*.

The most memorable piece of cross-examination arose when Armstrong was asked why he had, on 23 March 1981, written to the Managing Director of Sidgwick & Jackson, indicating that he had read extracts of *Their Trade is Treachery* in the *Daily Mail* and that the Prime Minister would need to have a copy to make a statement in Parliament, when in fact they had had a copy for more than six weeks. Armstrong agreed he had misrepresented the facts.

Turnbull: So it (his letter) contained an untruth?

Armstrong: Well, it does not contain that truth... it is a misleading impression, it does not contain a lie.

Turnbull: What is a misleading impression?

Armstrong: It is perhaps being economical with the truth.

The British Cabinet Secretary was followed into the witness box by his Australian counterpart, Michael Codd. Codd was there only a few hours, but his evidence scarcely helped the British government. His evidence that the Australian public interest would be damaged by the publication of Wright's book was dismissed by Mr Justice Powell as 'complete and utter moonshine', 'ridiculous' and 'totally without foundation'. Mr Justice Powell did however prefer not to adopt Turnbull's pun of 'codswallop'.

In the meantime, a vigorous Parliamentary campaign was run by the British authorities for domestic consumption, principally by means of anonymous press briefings. These were sometimes of dubious veracity, such as the claim that Neil Kinnock had a mole in the defence team – an outright lie – and that as a result of Wright's book, twenty-six agents had to be moved. This was a somewhat surprising assertion, since all but one of the MI5 and MI6 officers mentioned in Wright's book were either dead or retired. The one exception was about to retire from a senior post. It seemed a curious thing to get into the papers, while the government was making an application to the New South Wales Court of Appeal in the course of the trial. Perhaps it was thought that it would advance the government's case. As reference was made to former security services officers, who had spoken to authors such as West, Pincher, Penrose and Knightley, so the rather improbable list of people such as Lord Rothschild, Sir Arthur Franks, Arthur Martin, Nigel West and Chapman Pincher considered for possible investigation for criminal conduct grew. If there had been evidence of breach of the Official Secrets Act, action could have been taken many years before. It was as if the government's actions were conditioned by the need to act in what it considered a manner most likely to help it in the Wright case. A case in Australia should not determine the British government's reactions and thinking. The Wright litigation, which was born out of an obsession, became an obsession in itself. Interestingly the tightening up on confidentiality and secrecy did not prevent the publication of two books during the course of the trial. One was *The Second Oldest Profession* by Phillip Knightley and the other *Conspiracy of Silence* by Barrie Penrose. Both explicitly indicated that a large number of former MI5 and MI6 officers were sources of the information appearing in this book: forty-six former intelligence officers were named in *Conspiracy of Silence* and twenty-six were quoted as sources. Nevertheless no action was taken to suppress either book – possibly because they both contained a chapter that was highly critical of Wright as the government has come under greater pressure in the Wright case, so it has retreated from this distinction about not taking action against 'outsiders' books'. When Sir John Bailey learnt of plans by Michael Joseph to publish a book about Sir Stewart Menzies, the head of SIS from 1936 to 1952 entitled *The Secret Servant* by Anthony Cave Browne. Cave Browne was never a member of the intelligence services, but that did not stop Bailey writing to the publishers saying that it is possible the book contained information obtained from members of the security or intelligence services in breach of their duty of confidentiality to the Crown.

Wright gave his evidence in the form of a thirty-two page affidavit of which he read two thirds in open court. He explained why he had written the book and how he had been approached by Rothschild. He felt that MI5 was still covering up the truth about the extent of Soviet penetration and that these matters should now be brought into the open. The briefs MI5 had prepared for the Prime Minister concerning Blunt and Hollis were untrue. To say that Blunt had done no damage was poppycock and it was wrong to say that there was no usable evidence against Blunt. The Prime Minister's statement to the Commons concerning Hollis was substantially false, and its errors must have been known to those in MI5 who prepared it.

Wright could not give evidence in open court as to the

contents of his book, but he did deal with the suggestions that his book was causing continuing damage to national security and with the claims made by Armstrong in his evidence as to the potential harm of the book. The book, he said, was mostly very old stuff, of historical interest only. It would compromise no operations, prejudice no sources and expose no secrets. It was rubbish to say that the book would undermine national security; what the government and the security service were worried about was the embarrassment it would cause them. It was complete nonsense to claim that his book would lead to the identification of terrorist targets. Dealing with Armstrong's evidence he made the point that most of his information was at least twenty years old. What he said about the tradecraft of counter-espionage was out of date, and one could find much more up-to-date material in such publications as Security Commission reports and even in the works of John le Carré. The technology he described was long out of date and where there was any doubt about the matter, he had taken care not to give technical details. In order not to damage national security, Wright said he had not described in any detail his time in Northern Ireland. There was no prospect of the CIA being offended by his book – they themselves allowed similar books to be published and it was scarcely likely they would break off liaison relations with Britain over his book, when they had not done so after the treachery of the various MI5 and MI6 officers. Wright's defence was that he was not precluded from publishing the material in his book by any obligation of confidentiality either because it was already in the public domain or because it exposed criminal or illegal acts or conspiracies or because it was no longer confidential since it had been betrayed to the Soviets.

As he neared the end of his evidence, the emotions which had brought Wright to court became evident. He said that his patriotism remained undiminished and quoted in English the words of Gregory VII that he has framed in his house, '*Dilexi iustitiam et odi iniquitatem. Propterea morior in exilio*'. ('I have loved justice and hated iniquity. Therefore I die in exile'.) Perhaps for fear of what he might say in court, the

British government chose not to cross-examine him in any detail.

The defence's first witness was Gough Whitlam, Australian Prime Minister from 1972 to 1975. He had read Wright's book but like other witnesses could answer questions about its contents only hypothetically. Whitlam's evidence was that until 1972 ASIO had acted in the same way as MI5: it would burgle and bug diplomatic premises and adjoining buildings. MI5 might have a licence to break the law, ASIO did not. It would be offensive to Australian Greeks if there had been any attempt to assassinate General Grivas. If there had been any plot against Wilson, he believed it would be a travesty of democracy if the security service was lending itself to the undermining of a government or the leader of a government. If there had been a plot to assassinate Nasser, there was a very strong Australian interest in that the Prime Minister of the day, Mr R. G. Menzies, was at the time negotiating on behalf of the Western Powers with Nasser. Either he had condoned the plot or he had been deceived by the British. Whitlam felt it was important for Australians to know if Hollis was a spy. Hollis had advised the Chifley government on the establishment of ASIO. Hollis's influence would continue beyond his death, and with some sarcasm he commented that it was not even for Mr Codd – 'with his intense experience extending over, I think, nine months' – to say that there can be no validity in that assertion. It was essential, he contended, that a country of the location and size of Australia abide by international agreements. He clearly had little sympathy for a country that did not adhere to such obligations. He was also unimpressed by some of MI5's actions, such as bugging Patricia Hewitt's telephone. She was then a leading figure in the National Council for Civil Liberties but latterly a member of Neil Kinnock's staff. Whitlam was asked by Turnbull if he thought her to be likely to be plotting the violent overthrow of the British government: 'I have never felt myself at risk in her company,' was his reply. He considered there to be nothing in the book which would hinder Australian intelligence practices. There was nothing in the book which referred to counter-terrorist practices in the last twenty-five years.

The defence's next witness was Bill Schaap, a New York lawyer and director of the Institute for Media Analysis, whom I had met in New York while researching the American practice in relation to the memoirs of former CIA officers. He explained how US intelligence officers in the equivalent position of Wright have to submit works to the Publications Review Board. In the period January 1977 to March 1983, 170 authors had submitted 430 items for approval. No item had ever been prohibited in its entirety and the changes requested were generally modest. The board would list such deletions as it thought appropriate, and these could be the subject of negotiation. CIA officers have to sign a secrecy agreement, but if they want to write about their experiences – and many very recently retired senior officers have, including the director and several deputy directors of the CIA, chiefs of station and covert action specialists – they submit their books to be considered on their merits. The insider/outsider distinction on which Armstrong relied did not exist in the United States. Former intelligence officers could write their books provided they followed the proper procedures.

Mr Justice Powell took twelve weeks to prepare his 286 page judgement. The judge had made a detailed analysis of thirty-three books written on intelligence matters and of the circumstances in which a number of them had been published. It was a scholarly and carefully considered judgement that lacked the caustic Australian asides that had punctuated the trial. Clearly the judge had a considerable interest in the subject matter and he observed that Fort Monkton, MI6's office at Gosport was the basis of John le Carré's Sarratt Nursery in *Tinker, Tailor, Soldier, Spy* and that Sai Wan, GCHQ's post in Hong Kong, was the model for High Haven in le Carré's *The Honourable Schoolboy*.

His judgement was a savage indictment of the way the British government had conducted its case and an outright rejection of its legal contentions. He rejected its argument that Wright was employed under a contract, which would have made the enforcement of an obligation of confidentiality easier. He was employed under the royal prerogative, although subject to an obligation of confidentiality. The government had had some difficulty in formulating the terms of Wright's supposed contract, having amended their Statement of Claim no less than seven times, until they ended up with (or so they thought) a contract which not only prevented the making of any authorised communication but required Wright not to make any unauthorised statement relating to his service which was likely to cause detriment to the security service irrespective of content, whether true or false and whether or not previously published.

Mr Justice Powell would have none of this. He criticised the British government's tactics ('serpentine weaving') and its apparent unwillingness to abide by decisions of the Court and its apparent wish perpetually to change its grounds in search of some obscure, tactical advantage which only it could perceive. He was critical of Armstrong's qualifications as the witness to give evidence on the matters which the government had to prove to establish its case. He felt that Armstrong had no personal knowledge or expertise in matters of security and intelligence and that his knowledge of operational matters and matters relating to the technology of intelligence gathering appeared to be virtually non-existent. Much of his evidence on matters of importance had to be treated with considerable reserve, the judge felt. In fact Armstrong had appeared to have little enthusiasm for the thankless task of appearing as the government's chief witness, though as a loyal civil servant and as a man committed to a very high level of confidentiality, he had undertaken the task as best he could. 'I do not know why I was chosen for this job,' he had told Turnbull at the trial. The Attorney-General, Sir Michael Havers QC, who had not attended the trial, was rather more blunt after the trial; Armstrong was, he said, echoing a phrase of Turnbull's, 'the natural fall-guy'.

Mr Justice Powell's approach to the government's claim was markedly different from the English judges who had, by that time, dealt with the injunctions obtained against the *Guardian* and the *Observer* arising out of publication of material in Wright's book in June 1986. He commented that Sir John Donaldson, the Master of the Rolls, was rather more likely to have felt a need to suppress Wright's evidence that MI5's headquarters may, at one stage, have been at Leconfield House in Curzon Street (a fact extensively publicised) than he personally would have. He found as a fact that the British government had, either by express authorisation or by acquiescence in earlier publications, surrendered its claim to the confidentiality of most of the information in Wright's book. Publication of such information in *Spycatcher* which might still be regarded as confidential would not cause any detriment to the British government or MI5. Insofar as it was necessary for him to decide the issue, he felt that it would have been in the public interest for matters in Wright's manuscript to be the subject of public discussion.

Mr Justice Powell accordingly ruled that Wright and Heinemann Australia could be released from their undertaking not to publish and could recover damages for any loss they had sustained as a result of publication of the book being delayed. However, publication remained injuncted until the appeal in the New South Wales Court of Appeal was heard.

Since July 1986 the *Guardian* and the *Observer* had been injuncted in the English Courts on the grounds of breach of confidence from disclosing any or the contents of Wright's book. At the end of April 1987 a copy of the manuscript had fallen into the hands of the *Independent*, who published some of the more striking allegations made by Wright. The Attorney-General commenced proceedings for contempt of court against the newspaper, together with the *London Daily News* and the *Evening Standard* which had regurgitated the *Independent*'s article. Similar articles had appeared in the Melbourne *Age* and Canberra *Times* and in the *Washington Post* – the government was unable to prosecute them for contempt. The contempt proceedings against the *Independent* constituted what was generally thought to be a radical extension of the law of contempt of court, because the *Independent* was being accused of contempt of court by not obeying an injunction made against other newspapers in litigation to which it was not a party. On 7 May 1987 the Vice-Chancellor Sir Nicolas Browne-Wilkinson ruled that the *Independent* and the other papers could not, in those circumstances, be guilty of contempt. However, on 15 July 1987 the Court of Appeal overruled the decision of Sir Nicolas and held that the *Independent*'s article was capable of constituting contempt. It remained therefore for another judge to conduct a trial to see if the *Independent* was in fact guilty of contempt. This, it was decided, should wait the decision of yet another judge to see whether the *Guardian* and the *Observer* were in fact guilty of a breach of confidence when they published their original articles in June 1986, which had been injuncted and in respect of which injunctions the *Independent* was said to be in contempt of Court. It was an unholy tangle with the Treasury Solicitor firing off letters to newspapers threatening proceedings for contempt if they published certain articles and to booksellers who were likewise warned of the possibility of contempt proceedings being taken against them if they sold *Spycatcher*. These were unpleasant threats to be making involving, as they did, a possibility – albeit a remote one – of imprisonment. It was perhaps symptomatic of the government's case that these threats were made on what appeared to be somewhat shaky foundations. The uncertainty in the law did not prevent the government threatening prosecutions for contempt. The Wright litigation had therefore spawned an extended use of the law of confidentiality against the press backed up with threats of contempt against all other newspapers tempted to stray down the same path as the originally injuncted newspapers. In this time the arrogance of the government knew no bounds with newspapers being asked to give assurances in advance to the Treasury Solicitor as to what they would print and finding, if they declined, that injunctions were obtained at hearings they could not attend – often on flimsy evidence. The government found this type of pyjama justice – so called because it could involve getting a High Court judge out of bed – preferable to the D-notice system.

It was an alarming and unprecedented sight to see six newspapers prosecuted for contempt of court with two others being proceeded against for breach of confidence. The *Sunday Telegraph* and the *News on Sunday* had joined the *Independent,* the *London Daily News* and the *Evening*

Standard in the dock in respect of articles they had written which referred to the contents of Wright's book. The issue was fast moving from a case about Wright's alleged breach of his lifelong duty of confidentiality to one of the suppression of freedom in the press.

The attempt to prevent publication of the Wright book suffered a terminal blow when on 14 May 1987 Viking Penguin Inc. of New York announced its intention of publishing *Spycatcher* in the United States. Viking was a subsidiary of the Pearson Longman Group. Strenuous pressure was put on the main board to order its subsidiary not to publish. The government had been advised that it had no prospect of stopping Wright publishing *Spycatcher* in the United States or even of making him account for the profits he made on the book in America. It tried nevertheless to cajole the board of Pearson plc to instruct the directors of its subsidiary, Viking Penguin Inc., not to publish *Spycatcher* on pain of dismissal. When Lord Blakenham, the chairman of Pearson, explained to David Hogg, the Assistant Treasury Solicitor, that his legal advice was that there was nothing effective which he could do to prevent publication, Hogg remonstrated: 'It is indeed hard to conceive how the power which your company has to remove the directors of the American subsidiaries is not "effective"'. Persuasion having failed, the government took no action in the courts to try to stop the Viking edition.

On 13 July 1987, *Spycatcher* went on sale throughout the United States and Canada. It monopolised the No. 1 position in the United States and Canada for non-fiction hardback books for over eleven weeks. The rate at which it sold broke all records. Well over 750,000 copies were soon sold in the United States and over 100,000 in Canada. Thousands of copies were brought into the United Kingdom. The government, no doubt mindful of their obligations under the Treaty of Rome and the European Convention of Human Rights, took the view that they could not ban *Spycatcher* as a prohibited import. Copies were shipped and flown into the United Kingdom in substantial quantities from the United States and Europe.

To coincide with publication in the United States the

Sunday Times had, on 12 July, published the first part of its serialisation of *Spycatcher,* having acquired the rights from Heinemann Australia. Knowing that the first edition of the newspaper went to No. 10 Downing Street, from where orders would have been given immediately to injunct all later editions, Andrew Neil, the editor, in the melodramatically named Operation Eagle, ordered that serialisation be omitted from the first editions. The strategy worked so well that not only was the newspaper able to carry the serialisation in later editions, uninjuncted, but the reviewers of the papers on the radio who also worked from first editions made no mention of the serialisation in their reviews of the papers. The next day proceedings were taken against the *Sunday Times* for contempt of court and breach of confidence.

After these extensive sales of *Spycatcher*, the *Guardian* and the *Observer* sought to have the injunctions imposed on them in June 1986 lifted. They were successful before the Vice-Chancellor, Sir Nicolas Browne-Wilkinson on 22 July 1987. He rejected the suggestion that the newspapers could not publish details of what the rest of the world knew to be in *Spycatcher:*

> Once the news is out by publication in the United States and importation of the book into this country, the law could, I think, be justifiably said to be an ass and brought into disrepute, if it closed its eyes to that reality and sought by injunction to prevent the press or anyone else from repeating information which is now freely available to all.

His decision was reversed immediately by the Court of Appeal. The question of whether there should be a temporary injunction preventing the newspapers reporting the contents of *Spycatcher* when they were so freely available elsewhere in the world was considered by the House of Lords at the end of July.

That hearing produced scenes of unparalleled judicial discord and by a decision of 3–2 the House of Lords upheld and widened the scopes of the injunctions on the newspapers restricting what the press could report of the proceedings in Australia. The majority did so on the basis that Wright had, in their opinion, acted in flagrant breach of his duty of confidentiality and that it was right that the *status quo* should be preserved, so that there should be no further publication of the Wright allegations pending the full hearing of the breach of confidence case against the *Guardian* and the *Observer*. Particularly remarkable was the strength of the language of the dissenting judgement of Lord Bridge of Harwich, a former Chairman of the Security Commission, 'freedom of speech is always the first casualty under a totalitarian regime... the present attempt to insulate the public in this country from information which is freely available elsewhere is a significant step down that very dangerous road. The maintenance of the ban, as more and more copies of the book *Spycatcher* enter this country and circulate here will seem more and more ridiculous'.

The government suffered a further reverse in December 1987 when Mr Justice Scott held that the *Guardian* and the *Observer* had not after all been guilty of a breach of confidence when they published their original articles in June 1986. He lifted the injunctions against them, but the government appealed. The government simultaneously lost proceedings it had brought in New Zealand against the *Dominion* newspaper for serialising extracts of *Spycatcher*. The government was more successful in similar litigation which it brought in Hong Kong against the South China *Morning Post* in respect of its serialisation of *Spycatcher* where it succeeded by a majority decision in obtaining an interim injunction restraining publication pending the full trial. Copies of *Spycatcher* continued to be sold in Hong Kong in significant numbers.

In Australia the Court of Appeal of New South Wales by a majority upheld Mr Justice Powell's decision, but on somewhat different grounds that as there was no contract governing Wright's terms of service, the courts of New South Wales could not entertain an action by a foreign government to enforce a purely equitable obligation of confidence. Leave to appeal to the High Court was granted but on 29 September 1987 the injunction restraining publication was lifted by Mr Justice Deane.

145,000 copies of *Spycatcher* were printed in Australia and sold – *Spycatcher* again breaking records and once more far exceeding the most optimistic expectations that the publishers could have entertained before the government legal artillery was trained on the book. *Spycatcher* was simultaneously published in Ireland where 40,000 copies were published and the millionth copy of *Spycatcher* was sold. The British government was advised it had no prospect of restraining publication in Ireland after the decision of Mrs Justice Carroll in the Joan Miller case (p. 258–9). A distribution network for people in England to buy *Spycatcher* was set up through Easons in Dublin. An increasing number of retailers in England felt inclined to defy the government threats of contempt of court and sell the book which was in such demand.

Spycatcher was now available worldwide except for its natural market, the United Kingdom. It was translated into many languages, Japanese to Finnish, Catalan to Cantonese. The *Spycatcher* case had shown how to publish a book which the British government wished to suppress. The government may have reduced Wright's earnings in respect of sales in this country, although with the scale of importation of the book even that is unlikely. However, they have done so at vast cost to the taxpayer and to the reputation of this country as a haven of good sense and liberal traditions and have along the road converted a probable hardback sale of 50,000 into 1,250,000 by dint of this litigation. It is difficult to see what the government will have achieved at the end of the case and what value it would have given the taxpayer for his £3 million. It will have learnt how not to conduct such cases and of the need to give such people as Wright a proper contract of employment whose terms foreign courts will be prepared to enforce. On the debit side, it has shown people in Wright's position how and where such books can be published and the profits that can be made. My criticism of the government would be not so much for bringing an action against Wright, but for running the case abroad for domestic political advantage and not taking the advice of their local lawyers. The government should have had the good sense to settle the Wright case on the basis of negotiated deletions from the book either shortly before or in the early stages of the Sydney hearing, when it would not have needed a crystal ball to see that the defence was prepared to fight the case through to the end and that the government was likely to lose. That way any material in the book which might damage British national security could have been removed. Indeed it is arguable that the government was negligent in not obtaining such cuts and thereby protecting national security against the damage it said Wright's book would cause.

At the heart of the enforcement of Section 2 of the Official Secrets Act 1911 has been the proposition that we should rely on the good sense of the Attorney General in deciding whether proceedings are justified. The Wright case must call that good sense into question. Just as Section 2 needs to be reformed, so a proper system for allowing people like Wright to write their memoirs needs to be devised. The Crossman case (p. 280) shows that the limits of what can be written do change from time to time. No well-intentioned person, and certainly not Wright, suggests that an agent retiring on 31 December should, on 1 January, be allowed to publish a book on everyone and everything he knows about the security service. The proposition that such books as Wright's can never be written has as much sense of reality as the attempt to enforce prohibition in the 1920s in the United States.

The Americans have produced a workable system with books being submitted to the Publications Review Board. There would have been no problem about Wright writing his book, if he had worked for the CIA rather than MI5. The proposition advanced on behalf of the British government that by our policy of blanket secrecy we have a better security service than the CIA seems questionable. It seems to have lost sight of the fact that Philby, Blunt, Burgess and Bettaney worked for our intelligence agencies rather than the Americans. The instinctive reaction of the British authorities in such circumstances is to cover up. The implications of the defection of Burgess and Maclean were not admitted until 1955, when a White Paper was published. Philby's treachery was concealed in Macmillan's statement to the House of

Commons in 1956, giving the spy a seven year remission before he too fled to the Soviet Union in 1963. No action was taken against the traitor. Blunt, despite the suspicions against him which arose in 1951. Even when firm evidence of his treachery was produced by Michael Straight in 1963 (p. 267), this was kept from the public until 1979 (p. 289). All that one can conclude from this is that cover-ups are getting longer. It was Wright's view that such statements about security matters which have been made concerning Blunt in November 1979 and Hollis in March 1981 were misleading.

On past form, and in the absence of any discernable inclination by the present administration to release information on the subject, it will not be much before the year 2000 that we discover the truth about the matters that the government has been trying to cover up about the material in Wright's book. A clearer picture will then emerge about how a dissident section of MI5 tried to interfere in domestic politics to influence and probably reverse the result of the 1974 election. Light may also be cast on the circumstances in which Lord Rothschild assisted Wright in his project of writing *Spycatcher* and the extent to which the government acquiesced in this. If they did not do so, we will no doubt learn why it decided not to prosecute Lord Rothschild under Section 2 of the Official Secrets Act. We will probably also learn more about the identity of the Fifth Man, the undisclosed spy in the higher echelons of British intelligence. Wright has stated that of the twenty-one intelligence officers who investigated Soviet penetration of the security agencies, sixteen believed there had been a spy at a high level. Eight of those believed Hollis was the spy.

The government has, by its appointment of Sir Philip Woodfield, already realised the need to have an official outside the security service to whom officers and ex-officers can turn if they feel that matters of concern to them are not being dealt with properly. Such a person, depending on the powers he has given in practice, might have led Wright to believe that the matters which troubled him could have been dealt with internally rather than by publication of a book such as *Spycatcher*. Such a person could perhaps have dealt more pragmatically with Wright's dissatisfaction about his pension. Wright's contention was that he was given assurances on joining MI5 that his existing pension rights would be taken over by MI5 – a not unreasonable matter for a man of forty to raise when changing job. This assurance was not honoured and Wright only received a pension for the time he spent in MI5, twenty-one years of a full working life, and 60 per cent of the pension he might have expected to receive. Wright was told before his book was published that Mrs Thatcher had suggested that he should be paid £1,000 extra a year only to be told by her Whitehall advisers that there would be problems with the auditors. As reported to Wright, an exasperated Mrs Thatcher replied that the security service did not know what audits were. In any event, Wright was not paid the extra money.

As the Wright case was fought principally in Australia, it is to be hoped that the government's time and money spent in Australia was not totally wasted. It will have seen that intelligence officers such as R. H. Mathams (*sub rosa: Memoirs of an Australian Intelligence Analyst*) and M. Thwaites (*The Truth Will Out*) have been permitted to write their memoirs. Mathams performed a job for ASIO that was very similar to that of Wright. The activities of the security service were the subject of a royal commission set up in 1972 under Mr Justice Hope, which led to a clearer definition of what ASIO could and could not do. The overall conduct of ASIO is supervised by the joint Parliamentary ASIO Committee. The activities of ASIO are further monitored by the Inspector General of Intelligence and Security who reports to the Australian government.

There is something here for the British government to learn, but I am not optimistic that those lessons are likely to be learnt in the near future.

Appendix 1

Selected Official Secrets Acts Cases

Government statistics given on 18 February 1985 show that, since 1955, fifty-one people and one company have been prosecuted under Section 2 of the Official Secrets Act; thirty-six have been convicted, nine have been acquitted, four charges have been withdrawn and one was withdrawn after magistrates discharged the accused on all except one charge and the prosecution decided not to proceed further. There follows a selection of the cases brought under Section 2 and similar legislation.

Defendant	Date	Occupation	Official secret involved	Charge
Emile Dupurs	July 1915	Language teacher	Information acquired in censor's office	Communicating information to unauthorised person
Two Irishmen, names unknown	March 1916	IRA members	Information relating to Portsmouth dockyard	Unlawfully communicating and receiving information
Thomas Maude and Charles Mattocks	May 1916	Clerk in War Office and journalist	War Office documents	Communicating information to unauthorised person and receiving official information
Alfred Gibbings	Jan. 1918	Engineer	Weapons documents	Communicating information to unauthorised person
Joseph Jonas and Charles Vernon	July 1918	Managing director of steel manu-facturers and company director	Trade secrets	Communicating information to unauthorised person

Brief facts	Sentence on result
A Belgian language teacher who worked in the censor's office of Neutral Countries Mail told a London schoolmistress that her mail was under observation as a result of her having received a letter from a friend in Germany. He tried to obtain payment for this information.	12 months' imprisonment with hard labour
Details unknown	15 and 18 months' imprisonment respectively
A clerk in the War Office communicated contents of War Office document critical of senior officer to a journalist working for the *Military Mail*	4 months' imprisonment each
An engineer in the machine tool department of the ministry of munitions sent a confidential document relating to a weapon to some Swiss tool manufacturers, hoping to make some money. The letter was intercepted by postal censors.	4 months' imprisonment
Sir Joseph Jonas was a managing director of a firm of steel manufacturers and the former Lord Mayor of Sheffield. He was a naturalised citizen of the Grand Duchy of Hesse. He was charged with a number of other defendants of German origin with conspiring to contravene Section 1, Official Secrets Act, as well as under Section 2.	He and fellow defendant fined £2,000 and £1,000 respectively and had to pay costs of prosecution; acquitted of the charge under Section 1

Defendant	Date	Occupation	Official secret involved	Charge
Michael Simington	June 1920	Civil servant	Office of Works plans	Unlawful retention of official documents
Lionel Ballard, Frederick Budgen	June 1932	Probate clerk and reporter	Contents of wills	Communicating and receiving official information without authority
William Burger	Jan. 1935	Employee at Woolwich Arsenal	Unknown	Communicating official information to unauthorised person

Brief facts	*Sentence or result*
Simington was a member of the Irish Self-Determination League of Great Britain and in sympathy with the IRA. He had removed plans of such places as the Irish Office from the Office of Works and of buildings used by the explosives departments of the Ministry of Munitions, where he was employed. These plans were found in his lodgings, together with an Irish Republican flag. He was also charged with larceny.	15 months' imprisonment; conviction was upheld by the Court of Criminal Appeal, which ruled that the word 'plan' in Section 2 was not merely confined to prohibited places
For a payment of £8, a probate clerk at Somerset House disclosed details of the wills of three leading figures to a *Daily Mail* reporter before probate was granted. In fact, the wills would have been made public a few hours later.	Ballard was sentenced to 6 weeks' imprisonment, despite being terminally ill. Budgen was sentenced to 2 months' imprisonment, despite an exemplary war record. The Attorney-General successfully persuaded the deputy-chairman of London Sessions, Sir Herbert Wilberforce, not to reduce these sentences on appeal
Employee at Woolwich Arsenal tried to sell ICI highly confidential information.	12 months' imprisonment

Defendant	Date	Occupation	Official secret involved	Charge
Albert Fulton	March 1935	Bookmaker	False address	Furnishing false information in an accommodation register
James Goodrich and Sidney Norris	Sept. 1937	Freelance journalist and Post Office telephonist	Telephone message	Theft and Telegraphy Act
Wilfred Vernon	Oct. 1937	Civil servant	Air Ministry documents	Unlawful retention of official documents relating to a prohibited place

Brief facts	*Sentence or result*
For reasons which one can only guess at, a bookmaker gave a false accommodation address for replies to his advertisement in the *Daily Telegraph* seeking a lady with 'modern ideas, vivid imagination... smart, refined and docile'.	The magistrate dismissed the charge on the basis that the wide powers conferred by Section 5 related only to accommodation registers prescribed by the Official Secrets Act. The Lord Chief Justice, Lord Hewart, directed a conviction despite having told the House of Commons that these measures were only necessary to guard against spying
A telephone operator was caught passing information he learnt in the course of his job to a journalist by means of the police using a trick message about the theft of registered letters from van from the post office at Driffield. Even the facts of the case are very similar to that of Atkinson and Appleyard (page 91), but the prosecution in this case did not find it necessary to resort to Section 2 but used the specific legislation under the Telegraphy Act instead.	Norris was fined; there was a separate case against Goodrich, which was dismissed on 9 September 1937
While on holiday a civil servant who was employed in the technical publication section of an RAF establishment at Farnborough had his house broken into by four men. They persuaded the court that they were only searching for political literature and for evidence of the civil servant's Communist activities. They were bound over in the sum of 40 shillings for 12 months.	Fined £30

Defendant	Date	Occupation	Official secret involved	Charge
Edward Edwards	May 1939	Clerk and Territorial Army soldier	War Office circular	Retaining documents without authority and communicating them to an unauthorised person (the Communist Party)
Walter Moore	May 1939	Design engineer	Shipping plans	Retaining documents without authority
Montagu Fyrth and Hubert Fyrth	April 1940	Members of the Royal Naval Reserve	Letter from the French government	Defence regulations: communicating information to an unauthorised person (a Communist newspaper)
Roy Day	Oct. 1940	Fascist	Report of secret session of House of Commons	Communicating information which might be useful to an enemy and publishing an unauthorised report
William Hipwell	Oct. 1942	Election candidate	Shipping information	Defence regulations: communicating information which might be useful to an enemy

Brief facts	*Sentence or result*
A 37-year-old clerk who was a member of the Communist Party and International Brigade was unlawfully in possession of Territorial Army documents in code. The judge considered that he had the documents in order to subvert His Majesty's forces.	18 months' imprisonment with hard labour
Nine plans valued at 9 shillings belonging to the British Power Boat Company in Southampton had been found in the attaché case of the 25-year-old design engineer. Much of the case was heard in camera.	Bound over in the sum of £5 for 2 years
Two members of the Naval Reserve communicated details of a 'not particularly secret letter' from the French government, seeking the co-operation of the British Expeditionary Force in carrying out a decree, to the *Daily Worker* (a Communist newspaper). The letter was of little military significance.	12 months' imprisonment and 6 months' imprisonment respectively
A young Facist supporter was found guilty under the defence regulations of publishing an unauthorised report of a secret session of the House of Commons and publishing details of air-raid damage and the broadcasting times of the pro-Nazi British broadcasting station in Germany in a pamphlet called *Uncensored British News Bulletin.*	18 months' imprisonment
During the Salisbury by-elections he made a remark about the condition and location of one of His Majesty's ships.	Fined £50 with 12 guineas costs

Defendant	Date	Occupation	Official secret involved	Charge
Stuart Morris and Arthur Williams	Feb. 1943	Pacifist and civil servant	Civil service waste documents	Conspiracy to contravene the Official Secrets Act
William Fowler	Feb. 1943	Drinker	Aircraft parts	Defence regulations
Violet Van der Elst	March 1943	Campaigner	Post-mortem records	Unlawful retention of official information
Aristed Hulrich	Dec. 1943	Student	Military pass	Defence regulations: unlawfully having an official document in his possession and receiving information about Army units
Albert Coombs	May 1944	Telephonist	Telephone message	Defence regulations
Name unknown	1945	Civil servant	Shipping information	Communicating official information to an unauthorised person
Arnold Chapman and William Macartney	Sept. 1946	Military intelligence officer and journalist	Military information	Communicating official information to an unauthorised person

Brief facts	Sentence or result
Instead of destroying secret documents Williams had given them to Morris, who was general secretary of the Peace Pledge Union as well as being a former honorary canon of Birmingham Cathedral.	9 months' and 12 months' imprisonment respectively
Careless talk about aircraft parts in a public house.	2 months' imprisonment with hard labour
She was a campaigner against the death penalty. She worked at Wandsworth Prison and had in her possession post-mortem records concerning the health, between the time of their sentence and execution, of people executed at the prison. She claimed to have received them from an ex-convict.	Fined £10 with £10 costs
This 17-year-old was found guilty of recording information about units in Britain and unlawfully having an official document, namely a pass, in his possession. He was presumably saved from more serious penalty by his youth.	3 months' hard labour
He passed on information he had learnt in the telephone department of the General Post Office to his wife, who had told someone else.	Fined £20
A civil servant gave a shipping broker official information about the disposal of tanker tonnage by Allied governments during the war.	Fined
This case came to light after a publication had said that one of the two men was employed by military intelligence. The hearing at Bow Street was in camera.	Fined £50 each with 25 guineas costs

Defendant	Date	Occupation	Official secret involved	Charge
Christopher Hutton	June 1951	Air Ministry employee	Air Ministry sketches and documents	Failure to comply with a direction by the Deputy Director of Intelligence in the Air Ministry
Patrick Murray	June 1951	Bankrupt	Furnished accommodation register in Hammersmith boarding-house	Giving false information about his name and address to a keeper of furnished accommodation and causing false entries to be made in books kept under the Official Secrets Act 1920
William Hoggett and James Reid	Nov. 1952	Prison officer and journalist	Information regarding prisoner	Attempting to persuade a prison officer to communicate information in breach of Official Secrets Act

Brief facts	Sentence or result
Hutton was writing a book on wartime escape aids with a title uncomfortably similar to the present book: *Official Secret*. He failed to comply with a direction given in April 1951 to hand over his sketches, documents and manuscripts. He was charged, but he then handed the documents over, and the charge was dropped. There was no suggestion that he acted for any purpose prejudicial to the state, and the prosecution accepted that he had acted in all innocence. The magistrate commented that the prosecution had acted properly in bringing the prosecution and then dropping it. However, the effect of the prosecution was that criminal law was used in place of the civil law where the government could perfectly well have obtained an injunction. It was totally unnecessary to use the criminal law. Mr Hutton's book was published in 1960 without further difficulty.	Case withdrawn when the documents were returned
In a case very similar to the Fulton case (page 350) and with no apparent link with any official secrets, Murray, an undischarged bankrupt, was charged with causing his landlord, Arthur Nixon, to make a false entry in the record he had to keep under the Official Secrets Act 1920 relating to furnished accommodation. The real complaint against Murray was that he was running a business while an undischarged bankrupt. The proper charge was under the Bankruptcy Act.	Charge was dropped, but he was proceeded with under the Bankruptcy Act
A journalist employed by the *Sunday Despatch* and a Leeds prison officer tried to obtain information from the superintendent of weaving at Wakefield Gaol regarding Dr Nunn May, an atomic scientist doing ten years' penal servitude for spying. The defence was that the questions asked of the superintendent were perfectly legal.	Acquitted

Defendant	Date	Occupation	Official secret involved	Charge
Tony Dewick	Jan. 1953	Trooper	Reports on defects of Centurion tank discovered in Korea	Communicating information to unauthorised person (the Communist Party)
Louis McGurn	June 1953	Trooper	Unreported	Communicating information to an unauthorised person
Christopher Cobbs	March 1954	Squadron leader	Documents setting out the organisation of station personnel and events at RAF fighter station and a letter from the headquarters of Middle East Air Force	Failing to take proper care of official documents
Richard Lessingham Edmund and Richard Bailey	April 1954	Commander and Lt-commander	Naval documents	Causing secret documents to be lost

Brief facts	*Sentence or result*
A naïve 18-year-old trooper in the Royal Armoured Corps who was also a member of the Young Communist League felt he wanted to 'do something for the organisation to which he belonged'. He tried to communicate the information to the district secretary of the Hampshire and Dorset Young Communist League. He confessed he had made a stupid blunder. He was also charged under Section 1 and it is difficult to see what purpose was served by the charge under Section 2.	Court-martialled; 1 year's imprisonment and discharge with ignominy
He was a trooper in the Royal Scots Greys. The case was held in camera on the grounds that the disclosure of the facts would be against the national interest and security.	Court-martialled; 2 years' imprisonment; dismissed with ignominy
This RAF officer was unfortunate in that a customs officer found a few documents concerning his work which he should not have taken with him but had in fact sent back in his unaccompanied baggage from Iraq. It was said that the documents should have been stamped 'secret' but they had not been.	Severely reprimanded at a court martial
These naval officers were perhaps even more unfortunate in that their briefcases were stolen in a Trafalgar bar	Reprimanded

Defendant	Date	Occupation	Official secret involved	Charge
Michael Andrews	July 1955	Able seaman	Unreported	Failing to heed a warning that he should not reveal 'certain information' which had come to his knowledge in the course of his official duties
Thomas Fawcus	August 1957	Flight lieutenant	RAF documents	Neglecting secret documents in his care
Robert Oakes	Sept. 1958	Assistant test manager	Munition contracts and tests	Retaining documents used in a prohibited place and attempting to communicate them to an unauthorised person

Brief facts	*Sentence or result*
Andrews was an able seaman attached to HMS *Dolphin*. The court martial on HMS *Victory* was held in camera, and the details were not published.	3 months' detention
He was attached to an RAF unit in Ruislip and mislaid a sealed envelope containing 86 documents, of which 11 were secret and 6 confidential, when in the waiting-room at Putney Bridge Station. The documents were subsequently recovered in a parcel wrapped in brown paper which was returned to the railway station. The case is a good example of the practice of prosecuting when such documents fall into the hands of a third party.	Severely reprimanded at court martial; 6 months' loss of seniority
Following his dismissal, a twenty-year-old employee at a defence establishment tried to sell details of munition contracts and tests for the ridiculously large sum of £50,000 to someone he met at the Farnham labour exchange. The evidence showed Oakes was immature and in need of medical treatment.	2 years' imprisonment. This was the maximum sentence under Section 2, although the judge could have gaoled him for 2 years consecutively on each charge. Observing that he would have passed a longer sentence but for Oakes's immaturity, Mr Justice Slade said, 'I find it difficult to understand how anyone who had the good fortune to be born a British subject could be prepared to sell his country's secrets for money.'

Defendant	Date	Occupation	Official secret involved	Charge
Michael Brown	Dec. 1958	Senior aircraftman	Weapon test documents	Wrongfully retaining official documents
Bryan Scott	Jan. 1961	Former naval radio operator	Confidential waste material	Communicating official information without authority
John Palmer	July 1961	Admiralty clerk	Admiralty documents relating to defence installations	Unlawfully retaining 89 classified and 6 secret documents
Christopher Chamberlen	Dec. 1964	Lt-commander	Documents relating to the atomic submarine HMS *Dreadnought*	Losing secret documents
Name unknown	1964	Radio supervisor	Secret signals book	Failing to take proper care of official documents

Brief facts	*Sentence or result*
A 21-year-old senior aircraftman had been searched in relation to another matter and some documents showing by how far two Red Duster missiles had missed their targets were found in a suitcase belonging to him. The prosecution accepted that the documents were not terribly important and that there was some evidence of personal inadequacy.	Also charged with escaping from arrest; this probably led to apparent severity of 12 months' imprisonment
This 19-year-old Walter Mitty figure met a Mr Gunther Rains in a cafe on Chelsea's King's Road. He told Rains his name was Nicholai Brownovitch and that he was a freelance spy and killer. He tried to offer information to the Russian embassy before being marched at gunpoint into Chelsea police station.	Fined £40 with 10 guineas costs. His counsel described the case as something out of a penny novelette
A 19-year-old clerk took papers home with him to catch up on his work. He had the misfortune to work in the underwater department of the Admiralty and to be caught up in the spy scare after the discovery of the Lonsdale and Kroger spy ring. He was observed by MI5 to be taking documents home and seems to have been punished as much as anything for breaking the rules and putting MI5 to the trouble of keeping him under observation for 6 weeks.	Fined £20 and £10 costs
His briefcase was stolen at a time when it contained secret documents which should have been kept in a safe. The briefcase was subsequently recovered on a building site. Because the documents had temporarily fallen into the hands of some third party, Chamberlen was prosecuted.	Reprimanded at court martial
A radio supervisor lost a secret signals book when supervising a bonfire of outdated secret papers.	Court-martialled and lost 2 good-conduct medals

Defendant	Date	Occupation	Official secret involved	Charge
Brian Parselle	May 1965	RAF officer	Secret bombing attack log and confidential weapon amendment list relating to Vulcan, Victor and Valiant bombers and some plan position photographs taken over Hull	Retained secret documents without authority
John Curtis	Sept. 1965	Flight lieutenant	Two classified documents which he had retained while working for Middle East Command education centre	Retaining two classified documents which were inadequately secured, without authority, and communicating information without authority
Victor Donne	August 1966	Police constable	Police information	Communicating information to unauthorised persons without authority

Brief facts	*Sentence or result*
He was found by a zealous member of the RAF police to have left secret documents relating to Vulcan, Valiant and Victor bombers in the glove compartment of his car, which was parked outside RAF married quarters rather than in the security area. It was a breach of the disciplinary rules. When his house was searched three further secret documents which he had failed to return were found. His treatment is in marked contrast to that accorded to Richard Crossman two weeks earlier when he had left his documents in Prunier's restaurant and no action had been taken.	Court-martialled in Aden and dismissed from the RAF; there was also a complaint about the dishonouring of five cheques he had written totalling £119
As the case was heard in camera, the facts are obscure, as are the origins of the case, which came about as a result of letters addressed to Dominic Elwes being found in his suit at a dry cleaner's.	Court-martialled and dismissed from the RAF; acquitted of communicating documents to Elwes
A Huntingdon policeman passed information to Ronald Toseland, a nightwatchman and police informant, about police enquiries into a garage owner, and offered to supply further information for £500. Could have been dealt with as a police disciplinary matter or for corruption. He apparently resented being transferred from CID to uniformed duties.	Fined £50 with 3 guineas costs, and dismissed from the police force

Defendant	Date	Occupation	Official secret involved	Charge
Peter Reen	Nov. 1966	Squadron leader	Air Force documents and necktie	Retaining official documents without authority
Helen Keenan and Norman Blackburn	Oct. 1967	Typist and surveyor	Cabinet Office documents	Communicating information to unauthorised person without authority
Keith Borst	August 1968	Police constable	Police information	Disclosing official information to an unauthorised person
William Daves	Nov. 1968	Former postman	Information regarding mail train and route of prison van	Communicating information without authority

Brief facts	*Sentence or result*
He had been senior radar officer on Christmas Island when the first British atomic bomb was exploded. He had some 70 official documents, one of which was marked secret and all of which were very old. The documents were stored in his loft as he did not know what to do with them. His tie was seized because it had a buffalo motif, and the project was code-named 'Buffalo'.	Fined £10 with £20 costs. The Security Commission subsequently made recommendations making it easier for people like Reen to return official documents.
A shorthand typist in the Cabinet Office passed details of secret Cabinet documents to a man who purported to be an intelligence agent	She received six months' imprisonment; he received on four charges a total of five years – said on appeal to be 'not a day too long'
A Grimsby policeman had been trying to catch some local villain for 6 years and thought that he could succeed where the regional crime squad had failed. He therefore gave the criminal a map on cellulose tape showing the route of the mail van and details of its escort. The criminal, contrary to the habits of a lifetime, grassed to the police, and PC Borst was immediately caught. After his conviction he left the police to set up a private detective agency. It is difficult to see why the prosecution felt it necessary to add three charges under Section 2 unless they were there as long stop in case the main charges failed.	Also convicted of two charges of incitement to rob; 2 years' imprisonment suspended for 3 years
While in Swansea Prison he was said to have disclosed information to fellow inmates about the delivery of high-value packages to Narbeth railway station. He was acquitted after a sparkling performance by Geoffrey Howe QC: 'Any observant Boy Scout could have seen the van arrive and the mail-bag being left on Narbeth platform.' The case was based on the uninformed gossip of gaolbirds, he claimed.	Acquitted

Defendant	Date	Occupation	Official secret involved	Charge
Clive Bland	Feb. 1968	Photo-printer	Spoilt Royal Aircraft Establishment documents	Communicating documents to unauthorised person (the Soviet Embassy)
Name unknown	1968	Police cadet	Police information	Communicating official information
Henry Jackson	Nov. 1968	Prison warder	Prisoners' files	Communicating documents to unauthorised persons
Name unknown	1969	Postman	Post office information	Communicating official information without authority

Brief facts	*Sentence or result*
A 20-year-old photo-printer at the Royal Aircraft Establishment at Farnborough and a former cinema projectionist sent a number of documents which were acknowledged by the prosecution to have been of no real importance, although two of the secret documents were part of a document which gave the result of tests on components of guided missiles. The Soviets appear to have thought that Bland was not intelligent enough to be an agent. The Security Commission concluded that his low pay (£11.9s.6d. a week) and poor prospects could have involved a security risk, but the harm done to national security was not substantial; arguably it was non-existent.	Fined £50 with £10 costs; had to spend 7 weeks in custody prior to the hearing
A police cadet passed confidential police bulletins to a criminal.	Suspended sentence of imprisonment
Roy Fontaine of C-wing, Parkhurst, said that he had given Jackson, a prison officer, £30 to produce documents from his own personal file and files relating to other prisoners, including the spies, the Krogers. The case is memorable for the answer given by another resident of Parkhurst, Algernon Watson, who was asked if he had been given any sort of encouragement to make his statement against this prison officer: 'If you call "you are going to get a bloody good kicking" encouragement then I was encouraged.'	Acquitted
A postman gave information enabling criminals to rob a post office.	12 months' imprisonment

Defendant	Date	Occupation	Official secret involved	Charge
Clive Robinson	May 1969	Police constable	Police information	Communicating official information without authority
Edward Collins	April 1973	Political activist	Sketch-plan of Catterick Army camp	Having in his possession a sketch-plan likely to be prejudicial to the safety and interest of the state
Paul Thompson	Nov. 1973	Apprentice joiner	Royal Navy armament depot	Entering prohibited place for purposes prejudicial to the interest of the state

Brief facts	*Sentence or result*
A CID officer attached to the Sheffield and Rotherham police force gave information to a man who entered premises to steal to enable him to enter premises for the purpose of stealing. He was also convicted of incitement to steal and of charges under the Prevention of Corruption Act. Again the charges under Section 2 appear to have been added as a makeweight.	5 years' imprisonment in all
Collins was thought to be connected with the political wing of an extremist organisation. However, it turned out that the plan that he had of Catterick Army camp had been copied by some unknown person from a freely available plan.	Charge dropped on advice of DPP, as was a charge of stealing a wallet containing £3; Collins had been in custody for 4 weeks
An 18-year-old pacifist caused a full-scale alert with 50 police officers called out when he was found inside the perimeter of the Royal Navy armament depot at Broughton Manor. The Official Secrets Act charge was subsequently dropped, and like a number of other cases in this appendix it does not appear in the Official Secrets Act statistics given from time to time in Parliament.	DPP decided not to proceed with the Official Secrets Act; but Thompson pleaded guilty to various offences, e.g. possession of a jemmy and a knife, for which he was fined £25; for damaging the wire fence he was put on probation for 2 years, enabling him to resume job as apprentice joiner; spent 4 weeks in custody

Defendant	Date	Occupation	Official secret involved	Charge
John Russell and Mila Caley	Jan. 1975	Researchers	Ministry of Defence manual	Unlawful possession of official documents
Alastair Smith	Jan. 1975	Soldier	Three Army training pamphlets	Retaining documents without authority and conducting himself so as to endanger the safety of such documents
Name unknown	1975	Post Office engineer	Post Office information	Communicating information without authority
Name unknown	1979	Senior examiner in bankruptcy	Bankruptcy file	Communicating official information without authority
Demetri Demetriou	Sept. 1979	Estate agent	Special Branch files	Inciting a police inspector to commit an offence under Section 2

Brief facts	Sentence or result
Two *Time Out* researchers arrested and charged under Section 2 when found in unlawful possession of volume 3 of *Counter-Revolutionary Operations*, after a photograph of volume 3 had been published in *Time Out*. Photo had in fact previously been published in the *Dublin Sunday World*.	Charged under Section 2, but Attorney-General decided not to proceed; proceedings withdrawn at the magistrates' court
A soldier in the Royal Highland Fusiliers became involved with a revolutionary group called the Scottish Army of the Provisional Government whose activities ranged from breaking into explosive stores to robbing banks. This was one of the minor charges but seems to be the only case brought under Section 2 in Scotland.	Unknown
A Post Office engineer used confidential Post Office information to assist a private detective to tap a telephone line.	Fined
A senior examiner in bankruptcy, examining the affairs of a professional criminal, allowed him to see a confidential report and make copies from it.	3 months' imprisonment suspended for 1 year
A Greek Cypriot estate agent offered £5,000 and holidays in Greece to a police inspector to hand him information on Turkish activists in Britain from Special Branch files. He claimed to be working for Greek intelligence but was considered to be a Walter Mitty rather than a James Bond.	18 months' imprisonment

Defendant	Date	Occupation	Official secret involved	Charge
John Groves	Dec. 1979	Detective chief super-intendent	Police information	Communicating official information without authority
Michael Emary	June 1980	Naval commander	Ministry of Defence documents	Failing to take care of official documents
Edward Dodsworth	May 1981	Police officer	Police information	Communicating official information to an unauthorised person (a journalist)
Name unknown	1981	DHSS employee and private detective	Information on DHSS computer	Communicating and retaining official information

Brief facts	*Sentence or result*
A detective chief superintendent, third in command at the criminal intelligence unit of the Metropolitan Police, passed confidential information including 154–page dossier on Judah Binstock to Sir Eric Miller of Peachey Properties (later to shoot himself). Sir Eric was interested in learning the whereabouts of Binstock so that they could discuss the small matter of a debt of £150,000. Bistock had retired to Spain complaining that Sir Eric was a 'bloody maniac'.	Also charged with corruption, Groves was acquitted on both charges; the prosecution succeeded only under the Official Secrets Act; fined £500
Commander Emary took some work home with him in a folder (which he should not have done) and it fell off his bicycle. It included one secret document. He reported the loss to the police and the Ministry of Defence. The folder was found outside Lavender Hill Police Station. As the documents had clearly fallen into the hands of a third party, he was prosecuted.	Court-martialled and reprimanded
During the hunt of the Yorkshire Ripper, Det-Sgt Dodsworth offered to sell a freelance journalist a a list of suspects, which included a well-known actor, for £1,000. The laws of libel prevented these documents being published, and the journalist reported the matter to the police. Although this conduct was reprehensible and went beyond a matter of police discipline it is questionable whether Section 2 is the appropriate part of a criminal law where police information is sold for private gain. Dodsworth had been commended 13 times in 20 years for his police work. It was claimed on his behalf that these events were a result of overwork.	Fined £750 plus £400 costs
An employee of the DHSS communicated personal information about members of the public stored on the DHSS computer to a private detective	Each had to do 180 hours' community service and pay £25 costs

Defendant	Date	Occupation	Official secret involved	Charge
Name unknown	1981	Retired Army captain	Orders for use in the time of war or civil emergency	Failing to take care of official documents
Name unknown	1982	Police officer and enquiry agent	Police information	Communicating and receiving official information without authority
Ronald Cox	Sept. 1982	Registry clerk	Diplomatic mail	Retaining official information without authority

Brief facts	*Sentence or result*
A retired Army captain failed to take reasonable care of secret orders for use in the time of war or civil emergency.	12 months' imprisonment suspended for 2 years; also convicted of offences of theft, for which he was fined
A CID officer allegedly passed details of criminal convictions on the police national computer and criminal records office to an enquiry agent so that he could compile reports for his clients. The enquiry agent perhaps unwisely pleaded guilty to 5 offences before the magistrates under Section 2, whereas the CID officer elected to be tried at the Crown Court, only to find that the magistrate decided that he had no case to answer on all but one of the summonses against him. The prosecution then decided not to proceed on the remaining summons and it was withdrawn.	The enquiry agent was fined £500 for receiving the information from the police officer, but the police officer was acquitted of passing it to him
A junior clerk at the Foreign Office working as a filing clerk in the British Embassy in Bangladesh had been unable to deal with all diplomatic mail. At the conclusion of his tour of duty, he took them home, and they were found years later by the person who bought his house. The documents were relatively unimportant, and the offence was brought about by his inability to cope with his work. Some 400 documents were found of which 141 were classified confidential and 53 restricted. All but one of the items were still unopened and had been dumped into cardboard boxes. He had already resigned from the Foreign Office. Had he burnt these documents no one would have been any the wiser.	Fined £600 on each of 2 charges, £1,200 in all – a harsh penalty for a trivial offence

Defendant	Date	Occupation	Official secret involved	Charge
Ewan Dear	August 1983	Warrant officer	Royal Engineers documents	Retaining official information without authority
Name unknown	1983	Police officer	Police information	Communicating official information without authority
Eric Loat	August 1984	Police computer operator	Police information	Disclosing official information without authority and doing an act preparatory to such an offence

Brief facts	*Sentence or result*
While working as a chief clerk at the Army air centre in Middle Wallop he took home 74 classified documents and stored them in his caravan. 10 of these were secret, 25 confidential and the remainder restricted. He admitted he had been a bit silly and explained he had done this to cover up his own inefficiency. He had intended, he said, to return them but never got round to it. It seems that he had drink and marital problems.	6 months' imprisonment; this also took account of the fact that he was charged with dishonesty in relation to a rail warrant and expense allowance totalling £294
A police officer passed information concerning motor vehicles obtained from the police national computer which was then used in connection with criminal offences. He was charged with three offences but convicted on only one.	Fined £100
A police computer operator employed by the West Midlands County Council passed on to a burglar alarm company information which he had obtained about the roads and areas where burglaries had been committed so that they knew where they could best make their sales drive. He appealed on the basis that he was not employed as a person who held office 'under her Majesty' on the basis that he was employed by the West Midlands County Council even though most of his work was concerned with operating a terminal of the police national computer. This argument was rejected by the court, which showed no inclination to narrow the scope of the Act, saying that as he was employed exclusively at a police station he worked 'under' a police officer.	Fined £400, conviction upheld on appeal

Defendant	Date	Occupation	Official secret involved	Charge
Richard Lea	April 1985	Army officer	Military documents	Retaining documents without authority
Jeff Dennis	May 1985	Filing clerk	Foreign Office memorandum	Arrested but not charged
John Jack	Sept. 1985	Retired lieutenant commander	Plans for Home Defence	Retaining documents without authority

Brief facts	*Sentence or result*
A colonel in the SAS who had been in the army for 32 years and had been awarded the DSO and MBE had his house burgled while he was military attaché in Oman. He was found to have 153 official documents in his house and he admitted having a further 7 in Oman. These documents were of a sensitive nature giving the names and dates of top-secret SAS operations. Colonel Lea faced 6 charges at his court martial at Chelsea Barracks. Initially he claimed he was entitled to retain the documents by virtue of his rank but after taking legal advice he pleaded guilty. All but 15 minutes of a 6-hour hearing was held in camera.	Severely reprimanded at court martial
A filing clerk in the Foreign Office leaked a memorandum from the Mexico and Central American Department of the Foreign Office to an MP, who sent it to the *Guardian*. This indicated that the British would continue their covert support of the steps being taken by the US government to wreck the economy of Nicaragua. The memorandum stated that the British government should claim that its opposition is based on technical grounds, to which someone had added, 'if we can find them!'	Although this was very similar to the Tisdall case the DPP decided not to prosecute following the acquittal of Clive Ponting
The lieutenant commander found secret plans for Home Defence in an old briefcase on the top of the cupboard at his home when he was spring-cleaning and he handed them in to the authorities.	Severely reprimanded at court martial

Defendant	Date	Occupation	Official secret involved	Charge
Peter Galvin, Derek Bonfield, Richard Tucker, Colin Bain	Dec. 1985	Company directors and civil servants	Information from Rolls-Royce aircraft engine manuals relating to spares for obsolete Vulcan bombers	Using Ministry of Defence documents for the benefit of a foreign power and receiving documents communicated without authority (the first time this part of Section 2 had ever been used)

Brief facts	*Sentence or result*
The charges related to the possible supply of Rolls-Royce aircraft engines to Argentina. The first two defendants were cleared by the examining magistrates after a three-day committal hearing on a charge of using Ministry of Defence documents for the benefit of a foreign power, Argentina. The other two defendants were acquitted of receiving documents in contravention of the Official Secrets Act. They were accused of receiving two engine manuals, one of which was obsolete, relating to spares for Vulcan bombers. The British had recently sold a Vulcan for scrap for £38,000. The defendants persuaded a friend to obtain an obsolete manual out of the Ministry of Defence library. The magistrates threw the case out when they were told the Argentinians had earlier been supplied a manual in Spanish. The charges were reinstated at the Crown Court against Galvin and Bonfield.	Discharged at magistrates' court, but Galvin was given two years' imprisonment under Section 2 of the Act and on a charge of receiving a parts manual stolen from the Ministry of Defence; he and Bonfield admitted other charges including bribery, and Bonfield was given 12 months' imprisonment. Galvin's conviction under the Act was quashed on appeal, as his defence that the Ministry of Defence had either expressly or implied the authorisation of the communication of this information, was not properly put to the jury.

Defendant	Date	Occupation	Official secret involved	Charge
Raymond Williams, The *Observer* Limited	April 1986	Civil servant and national newspaper	Ministry of Defence documents	Prevention of Corruption Act 1906
Alan Hobbs	June 1986	Naval officer	Naval documents	Negligent performance of his duties
Stephen Kirkham	Feb. 1987	Former County Councillor	Social Security Files	Unlawfully obtaining details of Social Security claims files
John Lee	April 1987	Journalist	Police files	Obtaining police records about a convicted criminal without authority

Brief facts	*Sentence or result*
In December 1983, Williams, who held a senior position in the directorate of naval weapons, resources and programmes at the Ministry of Defence, provided the *Observer* with documents for an article, 'The Black Hole of Whitehall', exposing waste in the Ministry of Defence. These allegations were found to have some substance by the Auditor-General and the Defence Select Committee of the House of Commons. The *Observer* paid Williams £1,500 for a freelance consultancy. Williams was convicted of corruption in January 1985. The *Observer* was not charged until July 1985 and was acquitted in April 1986. Although there might appear to be something to be said for bringing a specific charge of corruption rather than a nebulous official secrets charge, the paper was not charged until 20 months after the article and 6 months after Willams's conviction. The Crown seemed keen not to bring an official secrets charge even when it emerged in the trial that Williams had given the paper secret information about the Spearfish torpedo.	Williams was sent to prison for 6 months for being corrupted by the *Observer*. The *Observer* was acquitted of corrupting him
A 24-year-old naval lieutenant left classified documents in a cardboard box in his unlocked cabin on HMS *Hermione*.	Court-martialled; fined £400 and severely reprimanded
A former Liberal councillor was accused of obtaining details of claims files to smear a Labour party rival.	6 months imprisonment suspended for 2 years; £200 costs
A crime reporter obtained documents about a convicted rapist's previous convictions left in a hotel bar.	Acquitted on the judge's direction as the prosecution failed to prove he knew the documents were covered by the Act

Appendix 2

Section 2 of the Official Secrets Acts 1911

WRONG COMMUNICATION, etc., of information
(1) If any person having in his possession or control any secret official code word, or pass word, or any sketch, plan, model, article, note, document, or information which relates to or is used in a prohibited place or any thing in such a place, or which has been made or obtained in contravention of this Act, or which has been entrusted in confidence to him by any person holding office under His Majesty or which he has obtained or to which he has had access owing to his position as a person who holds or has held office under His Majesty, or as a person who holds or has held a contract made on behalf of His Majesty, or as a person who is or has been employed under a person who holds or has held such an office or contract, –

(a) communicates the code word, pass word, sketch, plan, model, article, note, document, or information to any person, other than a person to whom he is authorised to communicate it, or a person to whom it is in the interest of the State his duty to communicate it, or,

(aa) uses the information in his possession for the benefit of any foreign power or in any other manner prejudicial to the safety or interests of the State;

(b) retains his sketch, plan, model, article, note, or

document in his possession or control when he has no right to retain it or when it is contrary to his duty to retain it or fails to comply with all directions issued by lawful authority with regard to the return or disposal thereof, or,

(c) fails to take reasonable care of, or so conducts himself as to endanger the safety of, the sketch, plan, model, article, note, document, secret official code or pass word or information:

that person shall be guilty of misdemeanour.

(1A) If any person having in his possession or control any sketch, plan, model, article, note, document, or information which relates to munitions of war, communicates it directly or indirectly to any foreign power, or in any other manner prejudicial to the safety or interests of the State, that person shall be guilty of a misdemeanour.

(2) If any person receives any secret official code word, or pass word, or sketch, plan, model, article, note, document, or information, knowing, or having reasonable ground to believe, at the time when he receives it, that the code word, or pass word, sketch, plan, model, article, note, document, or information is communicated to him in contravention of this Act, he shall be guilty of a misdemeanour, unless he proves that the communication to him of the code word, sketch, plan, model, article, note, document, or information was contrary to his desire.

Appendix 3

Official Secrets Act Declaration

Form E.74

OFFICIAL SECRETS ACT

Declaration   To be signed by members of Government
                Departments on appointment and, where
                desirable, by non-civil servants on first being
                given access to Government information.

My attention has been drawn to the provisions of the Official
Secrets Act set out on the back of this document and I am
fully aware of the serious consequences which may follow any
breach of those provisions.

I understand that the sections of the Official Secrets Act set
out on the back of this document cover material published in
a speech, lecture, or radio or television broadcast, or in the
Press or in book form. I am aware that I should not divulge
any information gained by me as a result of my appointment
to any unauthorised person, either orally or in writing,
without the previous official sanction in writing of the
Department appointing me, to which written application
should be made and two copies of the proposed publication
be forwarded.

I understand also that I am liable to be prosecuted if I publish
without official sanction any information I may acquire in
the course of my tenure of an official appointment (unless it

has already officially been made public) or retain without official sanction any sketch, plan, model, article, note or official documents which are no longer needed for my official duties, and that these provisions apply not only during the period of my appointment but also after my appointment has ceased. I also understand that I must surrender any documents, etc., referred to in Section 2(1) of the Act if I am transferred from one post to another, save such as have been issued to me for my personal retention.

Appendix 4

'I Want to See my File and Personal Documents': Australia

Australia provides a good example of a system of freedom of information in a Westminster-style government, without noticeable ill-effects. In 1972 a Labour government was returned for the first time in Australia in twenty-seven years, under Gough Whitlam, on a platform of open government. Work started under the then Attorney-General, Lionel Murphy, to prepare the necessary legislation, and in December 1974 an inter-departmental committee reported. Murphy himself later became a judge and fell victim to an unwelcome degree of openness when his telephone was tapped by New South Wales police. He was convicted of attempting to pervert the course of justice, but subsequently his conviction was quashed and a retrial was ordered, when he was acquitted. He was accused of trying to interfere with the course of justice by telephoning the New South Wales chief magistrate regarding committal proceedings against a Sydney solicitor, Morgan Ryan, who was alleged to have been involved in an immigration racket. Murphy was said to have attempted to win favourable treatment for Ryan, who was subsequently convicted, although his conviction was quashed on legal grounds and a retrial was ordered.

The New South Wales chief magistrate in question, Clarrie Briese, should not be confused with his predecessor, Murray Farquhar. Farquhar was sentenced to four years' imprisonment for seeking to influence another magistrate, who was determining a case brought against a friend of his, a well-known figure in the rugby-league world who was facing a charge of fraud. Farquhar did not qualify for a retrial, but he had to serve only eight months in prison.

Murphy's case revolved upon the telephone transcripts and what exactly he had meant when he said, 'What about my little mate?' The tapes also revealed a slightly more relaxed attitude to life among certain of the Australian judiciary than might be the case with English judges. When Murphy was taped asking his solicitor friend if he had had a good weekend, having been told by the solicitor that he could fix the judge up with some girls, he had received the reply: 'If you call getting tired and drunk and fucking everything in sight a good time – Yeah.' Murphy caused some surprise in legal circles at his second trial when he chose not to give evidence on oath, on which he could be cross-examined, preferring to make an unsworn statement from the dock, on which he could not be questioned.

The Whitlam government was dramatically dismissed from office in November 1975 by the Governor-General, Sir John Kerr, before it could enact its freedom-of-information legislation. It was succeeded by a Liberal government under Malcolm Fraser. The Attorney-General in the Fraser government, Senator Durack, produced a draft Freedom of Information Bill in June 1978. This was considered at length by the Senate Standing Committee on Constitutional and Legal Affairs, which produced a report in November 1979 that led to the Freedom of Information Act 1982 in substantially narrower terms than had been recommended by the Senate committee. A Labour government under Bob Hawke was returned in 1983. It slightly widened the Freedom of Information Act, though not by as much as it had promised.

This legislation relates to the federal or Commonwealth government of Australia rather than to the state governments. The only state that has enacted its own freedom-of-information legislation is Victoria, which did so in 1982 when a Labour government was returned to power there for the first time for twenty-six years. Under its leader, John Cain, it was committed to freedom of information on the basis that a government open to scrutiny is more accountable to the people who elect it, and that where people are informed about government polices, they are more likely to become involved in policy-making and in government itself.

There is, overall, less of an atmosphere of secrecy in Australia than in Britain. The Australians do have an equivalent of Section 2 of the Official Secrets Act 1911 – i.e. Sections 70 and 79 of their Commonwealth Crimes Act 1914, which punish, in similar terms to the Official Secrets Act, government contractors and servants who leak official documents. The offence is likewise punishable with two years' imprisonment. However, although it is from time to time brandished this law is never used. There was not, for example, a prosecution either when the book entitled *Documents on Australian Defence and Foreign Police 1968–1975* was published, or when extracts from it appeared in the *Sydney Morning Herald* and the *Melbourne Age* in October 1980. This was a collection of top-secret Australian papers relating to such matters as the East Timor crisis and the cables that passed between Canberra and Jakarta, the negotiation of the agreements regarding United States bases in Australia, an outline of the United Kingdom and US intelligence services, and the Anzus Treaty. In marked contrast to what would have happened in England, not only was no one prosecuted, but the government even failed to obtain an injunction on the grounds that publication constituted a breach of confidence. The judge, Mr Justice Mason, was not prepared to assume that publication of any of the documents would prejudice national security. In any event, a number of copies had already reached the Indonesian and United States embassies. The case was particularly striking for the approach of the judge:

> The court will not prevent the publication of information which merely throws light on the past workings of government, even if it be not public property, so long as it does not prejudice the community in other respects. The disclosure will itself serve the public interest in keeping the

community informed and in promoting discussion of public affairs.

The government did in fact obtain an injunction on the basis of breach of copyright, but that was something of a consolation prize.

There have been recent suggestions in Australia that the Commonwealth Crimes Act should be used. A demand was made that it be invoked against a Cabinet minister, Mick Young, special Minister of State in the Hawke government, in 1983. This was a colourful case that arose out of the Australian security and law-enforcement agencies' practice of tapping the telephones of leading figures to keep abreast of the peccadilloes of judges, stipendiary magistrates, politicians, trade union leaders and commissioners of police. The Australian Security Intelligence Organisation (ASIO – the equivalent of MI5) had detected a close association between the former secretary of the Australian Labour Party, David Combe (a successor of Young in the job), and a Soviet diplomat and KGB officer, Valeri Ivanov, who was trying to cultivate him as a contact. The ASIO reported meetings between Combe and Ivanov where they hit the vodka with some gusto. After the matter had been discussed in Cabinet and the security reports were evaluated, it was decided that Ivanov should be expelled from Australia and Combe should be denied access to ministers – a disaster for Combe in his then role of lobbyist. For reasons that are not altogether clear, Young felt it necessary to confide news of the impending expulsion to another Canberra lobbyist in the carpark of the Nineteenth Hole Motel after a convivial dinner. When this revelation was itself publicly disclosed, Young had to stand down while the matter was considered by a Royal Commission under Mr Justice Hope.

The leaking of this information by Young was criticised as improper, unauthorised and damaging to national security; it was accepted that there was no question of Combe being a spy. However, as the revelation was purely accidental and merely led to the disclosure of the information a few days early, Young was allowed to return to his post, until he became involved in another mishap, which came to be known as the Paddington Bear affair. This arose out of a series of genuine misunderstandings when a number of items were brought into Australia by Young, of which the most innocuous but most eye-catching was a Paddington Bear on which the proper duty had not been paid. The dispute related to a customs declaration made on behalf of Young. He again left the Cabinet while the matter was resolved, during which time no opposition platform was complete without a Paddington Bear. When the matter was resolved, Young returned to the Cabinet. Combe was also rehabilitated; in 1985 he became Trade Commissioner to Vancouver.

It may be that the authorities felt that Young's revelation was purely accidental, like that of J. H. Thomas (Chapter 4). In any event, the question of prosecuting him was not apparently seriously considered, and it is unlikely that there will ever be any more prosecutions under Section 70 or 79 of the Commonwealth Crimes Act.

In introducing freedom-of-information legislation the Australians paid tribute to the English theory, although not its practice. The Senate committee quoted with approval statements by Lord Croham, a former head of the British Civil Service, that greater openness of the public service to the general electorate would 'lead to a strengthening of Parliament in relation to the executive . . . in that members of Parliament could be expected to be better placed to scrutinise the government's performance on openness, obliging ministers to explain refusals to release documents on request'.

As to the argument that the Westminister-type system would be undermined by a system of freedom of information – a view recently enunciated by Mrs Thatcher, who spoke of ministers' accountability to Parliament being reduced and Parliament itself being diminished – the Australian Senate committee felt that the term 'Westminister system has been used as a smokescreen behind which to hide and with which to cover up existing practices of unnecessary secrecy'. The Senate committee supported the remarks made by a US President, James Madison, as long ago as 1822 when he wrote: 'A popular government, without popular information or the means of acquiring it, is but a prologue to a farce or a tragedy; or perhaps both. Knowledge will for ever govern ignorance: and a people who mean to be their own governors must arm themselves with the power which knowledge gives.'

The introduction of freedom-of-information legislation in Australia was part of a move both in the courts and in Parliament towards greater openness in government. When in 1978 a Mr Sankey brought an unsuccessful conspiracy action against the ministers of the former Whitlam government in relation to an A$4 billion loan for temporary purposes, the acting Chief Justice, Sir Harry Gibbs, took a firm line on the question of disclosure of government documents. He said: 'It is in all circumstances the duty of the court and not the privilege of the executive government to decide whether a document will be produced or may be withheld.' Equally, in the Combe/Ivanov affair the Cabinet notes were provided to the Royal Commission; and when a former Liberal Cabinet minister, Peter Howson, followed the example of Richard Crossman and published his diaries in 1984, no attempts were made to stop him doing so.

At the same time, the machinery for reviewing administrative decisions was overhauled. This helped break down the traditions of secrecy in the Australian Public Service, which had been imported from Whitehall. The Ombudsman Act 1976 set up an Ombudsman to deal with complaints about maladministration. The Administrative Appeals Tribunal Act 1978 established a tribunal to review administrative decisions on their merits. The Administrative Decisions (Judicial Review) Act 1977 amended the law relating to the circumstances in which one could appeal to the courts on questions of law regarding decisions taken by the executive.

Various administrations have shown themselves capable of a considerable degree of secrecy. When HMS *Melbourne* and HMS *Voyager* collided in 1964, with the loss of eighty-four lives, such was the reticence of those connected with the Navy in the evidence that they gave to the first commission of enquiry that a second commission was required to unravel the cover-up. In 1970 questions were asked about the number of draft-dodgers who were resisting being sent to Vietnam.

On 30 June 1970 the government said that 2,416 were being investigated. The government's lack of candour in the matter led Senator Cavanagh to complain in an unguarded moment that 'the only way we can get the figures is by theft'. The duly stolen figures showed that as at 30 December 1970 there were in fact 10,164 draft-dodging cases being investigated.

The Australian freedom-of-information legislation is an example of clarity which could well be followed by other governments. Before the legislation came into operation on 1 December 1982, explanatory literature had been produced for the general public explaining how the Act worked. Because many of those who might want information about government decisions would be immigrants, this literature was translated into eight ethnic languages including Croatian, Turkish and Vietnamese. Government departments received detailed guidelines from the Attorney-General as to how they should apply the Act; although on occasions somewhat restrictive these guidelines were useful in making the Freedom of Information Act work. Considerable thought was given to making the procedure simple. All that has to be done is for an Australian citizen, or someone entitled by right to reside in Australia, to make a request in writing to the prescribed address for the production of the documents. No reason for wanting the documents need be given, and to assist in making such requests, many agencies have produced a number of easy-to-understand forms such as those headed 'I Want to See my File and Personal Documents' and 'I Want to Change my File.'

Under the Freedom of Information Act Section 2, each government agency has to produce a statement which describes the organisation and function of that agency and the categories of documents in its possession, where they can be inspected and the person to whom a freedom-of-information request should be addressed. For example, the Department of Ethnic Affairs states in its Section 8 statement how the various departments work, which brand would, for example, deal with applications for resident status, refugee problems or deportation matters, and what legislation it operates under. Section 9 of the Act requires a department to list its internal memoranda and the procedures under which it operates, together with details of where they can be inspected. For example, the Department of Defence lists how you can find the defence force rules relating to the assistance that it would give to the civil authorities by way of counter-terrorist operations; it also lists a serviceman's conditions of service, the rules relating to living in sin and gambling, compensation for accidents, funeral arrangements and naval dentists' instructions. It is therefore a relatively simple matter for an individual, with assistance if need be, to trace where he should go for the document he requires.

Once the agency concerned has received a valid request, it has forty-five days within which to produce the documents or a reason why it will not produce the documents. From 1 December 1986 this period is reduced to thirty days. The agency is bound to produce only documents created since 1977 unless the applicant can satisfy the agency that documents prior to 1977 are reasonably necessary to understand a document produced since that date.

There are twenty-four untouchable agencies whose documents cannot be requested under the Freedom of Information Act. These range from the Australian Security Intelligence Organisation to the Snowy Mountain Engineering Corporation. There are nineteen agencies that are partially exempt, where the documents relate to sensitive commercial operations of that agency. This could cover, for example, the Australian Canned Fruits Corporation and the Australian Wine and Brandy Corporation.

If the agency is not excluded from the operation of the Act, it can nevertheless decline to produce the documents if they fall within one of the fourteen exempt categories. Four of those categories – including documents which could affect national security, defence or international relations, or relations between the Commonwealth government and the various state governments, and Cabinet documents – can be prohibited from disclosure by the issue of a conclusive certificate of exemption by the minister or principal officer in charge of the agency. In practice the issue of such conclusive certificates is rare. The Administrative Appeals Tribunal can rule whether there are reasonable grounds for the certificate. It cannot compel the minister to produce such documents, but if he decides to retain the certificate he must give his reasons to Parliament within five sitting days for not producing the documents. Documents can also be exempt from production if they might prejudice the enforcement of the law for the protection of public safety, or if they relate to matters of personal privacy, or are documents obtained in confidence, or are documents produced under a statute which stated that the information given would remain secret.

If an exemption is claimed on those grounds, the agency must state the reason. Then, if the applicant is dissatisfied, he can either return to the agency within twenty-eight days and ask it to review its decision, or complain to the Ombudsman if the matter has not been properly handled, or appeal to the Adminstrative Appeals Tribunal; or, if there is a question of law, he may go to the federal court for a ruling.

In the year 1 July 1984 to 30 June 1985 there were 32,956 requests made under the Freedom of Information Act. The vast majority of these related to the applicants' personal files and were directed to five principal agencies. Thirty-one per cent of the requests related to veterans' affairs, dealing with such matters as allowance benefits and medical treatment; 15 per cent related to social security problems, and 21 per cent to tax matters. In addition, many immigrants wished to see their change-of-status files, and a number of applications related to an examination of police and/or medical records. Although the Act provides for inaccurate or incomplete records to be amended, out of the 19,227 requests in the corresponding period 1983 to 1984, only 163 applications to change a file were made, of which 105 were granted. It may be that people are unaware of this right to amend, but it does suggest that a surprisingly small number were dissatisfied by what they found in their files.

In 1984 to 1985 access was allowed in full in 69 per cent of the cases and in part, with deletions being made, in 25 per cent of the cases. Only in 6 per cent of the cases was access refused altogether. Where access was refused entirely or in part, the reason in 25 per cent of the cases was that the documents concerned the personal privacy of another citizen, or in 7.8 per cent of the cases that production of the documents would be a breach of confidence. In 20.5 per cent of the cases exemption was claimed on the grounds that the information had been supplied under one of the 200 statutes which provide that the information given may not be disclosed to any third party. Another significant ground of exemption was that the information requested, in 19.4 per cent of the cases where exemption was claimed, was information the disclosure of which could hinder the enforcement of the law. Only in 1.4 per cent of the refusals was it suggested that questions of national security arose. The Freedom of Information Act is overwhelmingly used by private individuals to discover information about themselves. Some journalists use the Act to obtain information about the activities of the government, and foremost among these are those employed by the *Canberra Times,* the *Melbourne Age* and ABC Radio; one newspaper made 500 requests in the period 1984 to 1985. A number of applications have been made by lawyers engaged in litigation, and questions of general government policy have been the subject of requests by the Public Interest Advocacy Centre, a body largely funded by the interest earned by solicitors on their trust accounts, which raises matters of public interest at no cost to an applicant.

In 1984 to 1985 the administration of the Freedom of Information Act cost A$19 million, a slight increase on the corresponding period 1983 to 1984 of A$17.2 million. This can perhaps be set against the A$100 million spent by the government on its own publicity. In Victoria the cost in 1984 to 1985 was A$2 million, whereas that state's government spent A$26 million on its publicity. The figure of A$17.2 million corresponds exactly with the sum spent in two years in providing VIP flights, overseas travel allowances and the like for the twenty-seven ministers in the Hawke government and their retinue. A further comparison can be made with the A$6 million that the government is prepared to spend on the defence of the Americas Cup.

On average, each request for information cost A$584,

which represents a drop of 36 per cent against the comparable period 1983 to 1984. This may suggest that the government is becoming more efficient in dealing with requests, or it may merely be an economy of scale. More than 250 Australian civil servants are engaged wholly or in part in operating the Freedom of Information Act; but this may be contrasted with the 405 apparently required to run the government's benefits office, which looks after pensions and allowances paid to government employees. On average, a request is dealt with in thirty days. Of those cases that do give rise to disputes, 60 per cent are resolved before any hearing takes place.

The Freedom of Information Act was amended and slightly extended by legislation in 1983, which gave greater power to the courts to examine claims of exemption by way of conclusive certificate, and introduced a rule that the federal Commonwealth government had to establish that it was in the public interest to withhold documents regarding its property and financial assets. It would nevertheless be wrong to believe that the Australian government's enthusiasm for freedom of information was unbounded. Inevitably it was concerned about the cost of the Act. One of the problems was that the charges did not begin to make any inroads into the cost of administering the system. In 1983 to 1984, when the Freedom of Information Act cost A$17.2 million, only A$13,000 was recovered by way of fees – less than 0.1 per cent. (This did not prevent the authorities from seeking to charge a member of the House of Representatives A$2,000 before they undertook the research he had requested.) A proposal was therefore introduced in May 1985 by the federal government that charges should be increased by 150 per cent and, perhaps more seriously, that applicants should be required to deposit 50 per cent of the estimated cost of the searches without any guarantee that any particular document would be found. This legislation, which would have severely restricted the use of the Freedom of Information Act, was thrown out by the Senate.

Rather the same thing happened in Victoria in that state legislation was introduced to counteract decisions of the courts that they could examine and rule upon claims of conclusive certificates. The legislation also sought to widen the categories of document which could be called Cabinet working documents and were therefore exempt, and thus once more to undo the inroads made into this by the courts. The second chamber, the Legislative Council, rejected the legislation.

The agencies subject to the freedom-of-information legislation have, on the whole, welcomed it. They have stated that it encourages the maintenance of accurate records and a general awareness of the role of the agency. One of the agencies most used by applicants under the Freedom of Information Act, the Department of Veteran Affairs, acknowledges that the production of documents very often goes some way to resolving grievances and avoids time-consuming correspondence. Not all agencies have been unstinting in their praise of the legislation, however. The Commonwealth Scientific and Industrial Research Organisation complained that the publication of certain of its documents has merely led to demonstrations by animal liberation groups!

Now that the legislation has been operating for three years it is possible to gain some indication of who used the Act and what results have been obtained. People have requested to see their police records and documents dealing with the question of whether they should be granted parole. An exception has been made in the case of psychiatric records. Students have been able to see their exam results and assessments made of them. Wards of state, that is, those who have been adopted or placed in the care of the state, have been able to trace their families. Immigrants have been able to look at the policy documents that form the basis of immigration policy. Plaintiffs in product liability cases, such as those concerning the drug Debendrox and the Dalkon contraceptive shield, have been able to examine documents which set out the claims made by the manufacturers regarding products' efficacy and safety.

A number of cases exist where injustices have been remedied by virtue of the aggrieved party being able to see the relevant documents. In 1981 Fred Silvester, the head of the

Australian Criminal Bureau, was accused of an association with the wife of a known criminal. Although documentary evidence was said to exist, he was refused access to it because of its 'sensitive' nature. However, the federal police admitted subsequently that the document was so sensitive that it did not in fact exist! Silvester resigned after clearing his name and began an action for libel.

Dr Frank Peters, an Australian government analyst, lost his job in 1977. He was able to examine the relevant documents and discovered that the reason for his dismissal was nothing more substantial than that someone with the same name and initials as his wife had written to newspapers opposing government policy – something she would not have been allowed to do because of his post.

A ward nurse was able, following an application under the Act, to correct a false allegation made about him by a patient to the psychiatric superintendent that he had been seen engaging in sexual misconduct with an elderly patient.

The Freedom of Information Act has also uncovered instances where it would appear that the Executive had failed to cover itself in glory. Suspicions arose of social security frauds perpetrated principally by Greeks, who allegedly claimed invalid pensions when they were perfectly fit. The response of the government was to withdraw such benefits from a large number of Greeks (usually on no more substantial ground than that they were Greek), although subsequently it was acknowledged that in 90 per cent of the cases there was no basis for doing so. An examination of the relevant documents under the Freedom of Information Act revealed why the government was acting as it did; it also produced an interesting communication between the magistrate considering cases against certain doctors accused of complicity in the alleged fraud, and prosecuting counsel, indicating that he did not think very much of the case and suggesting that it proceed no further. The documents revealed catalogued the very unsatisfactory way in which the matter had been handled by the government, which resulted in one of Australia's longest running trials, at the end of which virtually no one was convicted.

The Act uncovered instances of bad administration, such as the great Australian desiccated coconut factory fiasco, where a project for the Tongans that should have cost A$1.5 million was ultimately scrapped after the expenditure of A$2 million with nothing achieved.

Freedom-of-information documents enabled Victorians to discover that a toy that had been banned on safety grounds in New South Wales continued for nine months to be on sale in their state. Perhaps the most extraordinary thing about this case was that anyone should have wished to buy the toy in the first place. It was called the Sweet Suzie Toy Vacuum Cleaner, and its objectionable feature was its 'play dirt', which children inevitably swallowed.

The Act has enabled the residents of the farming district of Cobar in New South Wales to fight a scheme for the Australian army to acquire compulsorily 963,000 hectares of farming land. Proceedings to obtain the relevant documents under the Freedom of Information Act turned up a report by the Defence Facilities Policy Committee which showed that, contrary to assertions being made in support of the scheme, there was only a low priority for obtaining this land. The disclosure of this material led to an enquiry being set up by the House of Representatives.

Relatives of the victims of asbestosis at a factory in Baryulgil were assisted in their litigation by obtaining under the Freedom of Information Act the reports that the factory owner was making to government factory inspectors. These showed that the true level of asbestos dust was being concealed by the factory owner's practice of cleaning his machinery each time the inspectors were scheduled to call. The true level of asbestos dust was in fact 500 times the permitted maximum.

When questions have arisen in the courts as to the interpretation of the Freedom of Information Act, the Australian courts have shown themselves willing to interpret the statutes liberally. They have, for example, been prepared to look into the question of whether documents have been properly certified as exempt from production, rather than feeling themselves bound to accept the minister's certificate.

When the Victorian Special Branch inadvertently destroyed
no less than two thousand Special Branch files after the
announcement of its disbandment, but after having been
ordered to preserve them, the court, as a mark of its
disapproval, ordered the Chief Commissioner of Police to
pay the costs of this matter being reported to the court. The
Australian courts have also shown a refreshing willingness to
examine each case on its merits and to weigh up the policy
implications of their decision. Whereas the court would not
allow a solicitor to see details of a complaint made about him
to the Victorian Law Institute, since to do so might
discourage future complaints, it was prepared to permit a
man who claimed he was wrongfully convicted of murder to
have access to the police records of an interview with the chief
prosecution witness when she retracted her retraction of her
evidence against him. He was also allowed to see the notes of
the police doctor's assessment of the witness's mental
condition. The court there decided that on balance disclosure
was desirable as it would help clear the air and remove the
suggestion that there was a cover-up.

On the question of clearing the air, it is a matter of some
regret that those involved in establishing the truth about the
Marralinga nuclear tests carried out in the 1950s and 1960s by
the British government found that they could not see a
number of the relevant documents, because the British
government had prohibited access under the thirty-year rule.
Eventually a number of positively vetted Australians were
permitted to examine most of those documents, but the case
highlights the difference between the Australian and the
British approach to access to government information.

The Australian experience with freedom-of-information
legislation seems to have been a success, even if the
government is reining back on its initial enthusiasm and is
concerned at the cost of operating the Act. These are,
however, matters that can be adjusted relatively easily.
Australia's experience should afford useful guidance to any
British government contemplating introducing a Freedom of
Information Act.

Appendix 5

Up to his Keister with Leaks: the United States

The United States of America has been one of the leading exponents of the principle of freedom of information. The US Freedom of Information Act was passed in 1966 despite an attempt by President Johnson to have it killed off in Congress. This imposed an obligation on the federal government to allow access to most documents in its possession. However, in practice the Act was cumbersome and subject to delay. The Act was strengthened in the post-Watergate era by the Freedom of Information Act 1974. The 1974 Act's most striking feature was that it enabled the courts to consider whether particular documents were properly classified as exempt from disclosure. Once more the legislation did not meet with full presidential approval, and President Ford tried to veto the Act.

The Freedom of Information Act gives any person the right to require access to information held by any executive department, military department, government corporation, government-controlled corporation or any other establishment in the executive branch of the government, including the executive office of the President, or any other regulatory agency, including the CIA and FBI, and internal revenue. The National Security Agency is however exempted from the Act. The department must reply to the request within ten days, and if access is refused, the applicant has twenty-eight days within which to appeal. The burden is on the agency to justify its refusal to grant access.

US freedom-of-information legislation is supported by a number of other statutes, which make for a freer system of government than in Britain. The Privacy Act 1974 gives individuals an opportunity to inspect their files and correct them. It covers nearly all government agencies, although not the CIA and the FBI (which are nevertheless subject to the Freedom of Information Act). It runs in parallel with such legislation as the Fair Credit Reporting Act, which gives citizens a right to see the records held on them by credit reference agencies. Acts have been passed to allow access to the meeting of certain government bodies, such as the Federal Advisory Committee Act 1972 and the Government in the Sunshine Act 1976. There is also the Whistleblowers' (Civil Service Reform) Act 1978, designed to protect civil servants from any retribution from the government if they disclose government wrongdoing or malpractice. This extends to information which the employee reasonably believes shows a violation of any rule or regulation, mismanagement, gross waste of funds, or an abuse of authority. It would have provided a defence for Clive Ponting.

As elsewhere, there are matters in the USA which require to be exposed and which the government would undoubtedly prefer to keep covered up. Edgar Hoover, when the head of the FBI, himself provided many examples of government misbehaviour. He was shown by documents revealed under the Freedom of Infomation Act to have engineered a fraudulent letter sent to a Hollywood gossip columnist in which the fictitious writer of the letter claimed to have been at a rally where Jane Fonda and leading Black Panther figures had led a chant urging the killing of President Nixon. Hoover also bugged the room of Martin Luther King at the Willard Hotel, Washington; he played the resulting nineteen tapes to his cronies, adding to King's alleged Communist sympathies the further crimes of moral impropriety and interracial sex.

The Freedom of Information Act showed that ten patients at a Philadelphia nursing home had died in the 1960s because they had been subjected to experiments with the drugs Haldol and Nacton.

The CIA had to disclose under the Act how it had trained

police officers from three Washington departments to crack safes, engage in burglaries and repair walls after breaking through them to enter buildings.

The Freedom of Information Act has been particularly useful to researchers, and a number of English authors have benefited. Andrew Boyle was able to obtain evidence from CIA files of the treachery of Anthony Blunt. William Shawcross gained access to CIA and National Security Council documents which were classified 'confidential' and 'top secret – eyes of addressee only – no forn' (that is, they should not be seen by foreigners such as him) for his book *Sideshow: Kissinger, Nixon and the Destruction of Cambodia*. Ludovic Kennedy was allowed to examine FBI evidence of the framing of a German-born carpenter, Richard Hauptmann, by the New Jersey state police under Colonel Norman Schwartzkopf, which resulted in his going to the electric chair in 1936 for the murder of the Lindbergh baby; this consisted of altering Hauptmann's work timesheets to destroy his alibi and cutting out a piece of wood from his attic which was used to link him with a home-made ladder found near the site of the kidnapping. Such records would not be made available in the United Kingdom for seventy-five years from the date of the trial.

Not all United States Presidents have been opposed to the principle of greater freedom of information. President Kennedy indicated in retrospect that he wished that the *New York Times* had not bowed to his administration's request not to publish a story indicating that a US invasion of Cuba was planned, shortly before the Bay of Pigs fiasco. President Kennedy had made a personal approach to the newspaper's publisher, Orvil Dryfoos, not to publish because it would gravely damage the interests of the state. Dryfoos responded to this by severely toning down the story, and Kennedy later acknowledged that, if the *New York Times* had stuck to its guns, the disastrous enterprise might have been abandoned. However, for the most part the traffic is in the opposite direction, and this has been particularly so in the case of President Reagan. Reagan has been assisted by certain decisions of the US courts and he has supported legislation being passed which reduces the effect of the Freedom of Information Act. Even in the USA, then, there are concerted attempts to restrict what can be published; but with the existence of the Freedom of Information Act it has sometimes been possible to uncover the behaviour of the government or its security agencies in trying to suppress publications of which they disapprove. Some of the claims made for the protection of national security, as for example in the Marchetti case (see below), illustrate the absurd claims of secrecy that from time to time are made by security agencies.

In theory the USA does not have an equivalent of Section 2 of the Official Secrets Act 1911, although a more strictly defined National Defense Act prohibiting the communication of military secrets, based on the British Official Secrets Act 1889, was passed on 3 March 1911. But it has unfortunately come rather close to it with the use made of the Espionage Act 1917. This Act was passed when the USA entered the First World War, to prevent the transmission of defence secrets to the enemy, and it has been used to punish those who leak defence-related information. A similar Act, called the Comint Act, was passed at the beginning of the Korean War to prevent the disclosure of communications intelligence. The first attempt by the government to use the Espionage Act in such cases was against Daniel Ellsberg, who had been engaged in 1967 by the Secretary of Defense, Robert McNamara, to give an account of US involvement in Indo-China since the 1950s. This study became the 47-volume *History of US Decision-Making Process on Vietnam Policy*, better known as *The Pentagon Papers*. Ellsberg was utterly shocked at the record of ineptitude, deceit and concealment in such matters as the US complicity in the plot against President Ngo Dinh Diem and the engineering of the Tonkin resolution, which formed the justification for US intervention in Vietnam. Ellsberg decided to send twenty of the volumes to the *New York Times* on 3 March 1971. Despite the advice given by the newspaper's lawyers of forty years' standing, Lord, Day and Lord, that it would be committing a criminal offence in publishing extracts from the papers, the *New York Times* began to publish on Sunday 13 June under the headline 'Key Texts from Pentagon Vietnam Study'. There was no reaction from the government until the evening of Monday 14 June, by which time the second instalment had been published. The newspaper then received a telegram from the Attorney-General, John Mitchell, that publication of the papers constituted a breach of the Espionage Act and should cease forthwith. The *New York Times* sent a telegram in reply, respectfully declining to do so. In the event, no attempt was made to prosecute the newspaper in the criminal courts for any breach of the Espionage Act, or to imprison its editor. It was in fact the Attorney-General, John Mitchell, who found himself going to prison a few years later as a result of the Watergate scandal.

The US government did seek an injunction against the *New York Times* and twenty-two of its executives and employees to restrain any further publication of *The Pentagon Papers*. The newspaper found that its lawyers were unwilling to defend it because of the view that they, and particularly their senior partner, Herbert Brownell Jr, a former Attorney-General, had taken of the law. This left the paper's chief counsel, James Goodale, without the benefit of any outside legal representation against the government law machine in court the following day, and holding the brief himself, although his court experience was at that stage limited to two undefended divorces. Fortunately, at midnight he was able to engage the services of Professor Alexander N. Bickel of Yale Law School. The government obtained an interim injunction while the case was prepared for a full trial. However, on 18 June a copy of *The Pentagon Papers* reached the *Washington Post*; the government failed to obtain any injunction at all to prevent publication in the *Post*. The government then failed to obtain an injunction against the *New York Times* after a hearing by Judge Gurfein. The judge, who was a Nixon appointee and a former intelligence officer, refused to take the government's claims of damage to national security at face value. It seems that he was right to do so, and it is probable that his UK counterparts would not have stood up to the executive. In secret sessions the government's chief witness, Vice-Admiral Francis J. Blouin, the deputy chief of naval operations, testified that it would be a disaster to continue to publish *The Pentagon Papers*. Blouin was asked ten years later what specific harm the publication of the papers might have caused; he replied, 'Looking at them today, I don't think there was any great loss in substance.' Looking at the matter in retrospect, former Secretary of State Cyrus Vance believes that publication helped end the Vietnam War and that none of the dire consequences of publication foreseen by the government or the three dissenting members of the Supreme Court came to pass. The US government was more successful against the *New York Times* in the US Court of Appeals for the Second Circuit, in that it obtained an injunction against publication, but this was discharged by the Supreme Court by a majority of six to three at a hearing beginning on Saturday 26 June 1971. The *New York Times* was able to resume publication on 1 July after sixteen days of frantic litigation. The newspaper was held by the Supreme Court to be acting within the terms of the first amendment to the constitution: 'Congress shall make no law abridging the Freedom of Speech or of the Press.'

The Pentagon Papers were of a highly classified nature, ranging from 'secret' to 'top secret – sensitive', but the government failed to make out its case that publication would damage national security. Giving evidence in camera, Dennis Doolin, Deputy Assistant Secretary of Defense for Internal Security Affairs, contended that the revelations in this study and in the documents 'would have a very, very serious, tremendously serious impact on current military operations, on existing plans, contingency plans and so forth'. However, it proved possible to show that a considerable amount of the material had already been published. For example, the government's claim of potential damage to its security operations by the revelation of its capacity to intercept messages relating to the Gulf of Tonkin incident was undermined by the fact that this evidence had been published three years previously to the Senate Foreign

Relations Committee on 20 February 1968.

Ellsberg was nevertheless prosecuted under the Espionage Act, but the prosecution collapsed when the extent of government misbehaviour in the case, with its peculiarly American flavour, became apparent. The Watergate 'plumbers', Egil Krogh Jr and Howard Hunt, had arranged for Ellsberg's psychiatrist's office to be broken into on 4 September 1971. There was also some evidence that the government had offered the trial judge the job of director of the FBI. The trial was stopped, and Ellsberg was acquitted.

The Espionage Act was used in circumstances which were only marginally less outrageous against Samuel Morison, an employee at the Naval Intelligence Center in Maryland, in December 1985. With the knowledge and approval of his employers, he worked as the US editor of the British publication *Jane's Fighting Ships*, at a salary of $5,000 per year. In an apparent error of judgement he sent three US satellite photographs, classified as 'secret', of a Soviet aircraft-carrier under construction, to the weekly publication, *Jane's Defence Weekly*. Morison may have been under the impression that US national security would not be damaged, as the Soviets in all probability knew that they were building this aircraft-carrier and that the United States regularly flew spy satellites over the USSR. In any event, he was prosecuted under the Espionage Act, and for theft of government property. He was accused of having acted in the hope of obtaining a full-time job with the magazine, and of revealing the sophistication of US spy satellites. He faced a maximum of 400 years' imprisonment and a fine of $40,000. The sentence passed on Morison was two years' imprisonment. This was due in some part to the exertions of the federal prosecutor, who had demanded a sentence of four years and a fine of $4,000 and who had described the defence plea for probation as 'ludicrous and astounding arrogance – without a jail term ... other government employees are going to think that what he did was not very serious, that the court does not think that it was very serious, and that it is okay to do it'.

In the Ellsberg case the arguments in favour of freedom of information had prevailed, but the Morison case showed that the courts were prepared to enforce a law somewhat similar to the Official Secrets Act. Cases relating to attempts by former employees of the CIA have shown the extent to which the US courts are prepared to intervene to prevent the publication of books by those who have served in the security services. However, the existence of a Freedom of Information Act has enabled the claims made of damages to national security to be examined.

In 1972 the US government obtained an injunction against Victor Marchetti, who was employed in the CIA for fourteen years, until his resignation in 1969, in a post that could exist only in a security service: Executive Assistant to the Deputy Director. Marchetti had signed a secrecy agreement not to reveal anything about his service unless he was specifically authorised in writing by the Director of the CIA. Initially the government tried to have 339 passages cut from his proposed book. Some of these cuts were patently absurd, such as the attempt to prevent him describing how, at a meeting of the National Security Council, the head of the CIA had mispronounced the name of the Malagasy Republic. Marchetti's book was eventually published in 1974, in association with John Marks, entitled *The CIA and the Cult of Intelligence*. The book had 168 blank passages where the government had demanded cuts. In 1982, when a further edition of the book was published, objections to twenty-five of the cuts disappeared. These reinstated passages revealed the fatuous nature of some of the objections. Where the first edition of the book had had to read that 'Henry Kissinger talked in relation to the problems of Southern Africa about the general posture the US could maintain towards the.......', the US public were now permitted to know that the deleted words were nothing more sinister than 'white regimes'. Details of some of the other 143 cuts were obtained under the Freedom of Information Act. Some of these, in the best tradition of such cases, seemed to relate to matters more of political embarrassment than of national security: for example, the description of Henry Kissinger speaking to the Forty Committee, which directed CIA covert activities, and saying, in relation to Chile, 'I don't see why we need stand by and watch a country go Communist due to the irresponsibility of its own people.'

By contrast, when in 1980 Kissinger wrote his extremely profitable account *The White House Years* he acknowledged the assistance of Dr Zbigniew Brzezinski, National Security Advisor, in working out the treatment of classified material in the book. Enquires showed that only a very small part of the manuscript had in fact been delivered to Dr Brzezinski. One intriguing device of Dr Kissinger's book was that, when he quoted from secret documents, just that part of the document became declassified and not the whole document.

The experience of Frank Snepp, the CIA's principal analyst in South Vietnam of North Vietnamese political affairs, was very different. Unlike Dr Kissinger, he was ordered to pay to the government every cent he had made, even before the deduction of three years' expenses, from his book *Decent Interval* and to submit everything he wrote in future to the CIA for its prior written approval, whatever its subject-matter. When the government won its case in the Supreme Court, Snepp had to produce $116,658.15 immediately and a further $24,000 within a short period, which he had to borrow. The Supreme Court decided the case without the benefit of the submission of full written briefs or oral argument. By 1985 Snepp's debt to the government had increased to $200,000. It was a result that other security services, including Britain's, have looked at with envy.

Frank Snepp was no Philip Agee. He had no wish to expose the activities of the CIA with the consequent risk of endangering the safety of its agents. He was the son of a North Carolina district court judge and was conservative in outlook. He was appalled at the blunders, dishonesty and hypocrisy of US policy in Vietnam, particularly at the time of the US withdrawal in April 1975, and at the way that their South Vietnamese allies had been treated. The book was dedicated to a South Vietnamese, Mai Ly, who killed herself when the US Embassy refused to help her leave Vietnam. Snepp was particularly critical of the incompetence of US policy and of the failure to appreciate the extent of the North

Vietnamese threat. When he failed to obtain any enquiry into these matters he resigned from the CIA in 1976 and started to write his book. He was taken to court by the CIA in 1978 because of the secrecy agreement he had signed in 1968, that he would not publish any material relating to the agency or its intelligence activities during or after his term of employment, without the specific prior approval of the agency.

No one except the judge who tried the case claimed that Snepp had been other than very circumspect in the way he dealt with intelligence matters. However, Snepp had the misfortune to have his case heard by the eighty-year-old Virginian Judge Oren Lewis, known as 'Roarin' Oren' because of the way he treated people who appeared in his court. Lewis rejected Snepp's claim for a jury trial and on twenty occasions stopped government witnesses answering questions from defence lawyers by sustaining the objections which he anticipated would have been made by the government lawyers had he allowed them the opportunity to do so. When Admiral Stansfield Turner was asked if any source had stopped co-operating with the CIA because of his book, Judge Lewis would not allow Turner to answer. The CIA's case rested not on the damage it was anticipated that Snepp's book might do, but on the very dubious scarecrow argument that, if this book were published, British intelligence would cease co-operating with the CIA.

Roarin' Oren had little doubt about the matter. He found that Snepp had wilfully, deliberately and surreptitiously breached his position of trust with the CIA and his 1968 secrecy agreement. He had deliberately misled the CIA into thinking he would clear the book with the agency. The book, the judge found, despite Turner's evidence, had caused the United States irreparable harm and loss; and Snepp had, he said, written the book predominantly for financial reasons. He ruled that Snepp therefore held the money he had received under a constructive trust for the government and thus that it all belonged to the state.

This ruling was reversed by the Court of Appeals, which said that the judge had been wrong to disallow Snepp's application for a jury trial and that the government's remedy was, if at all, in damages for any harm done to it, rather than for every cent he had earned. The Supreme Court in 1980, however, upheld Judge Lewis by six to three. There was a strong dissenting judgement by Justice Stevens against the idea of the constructive trust. He even cast doubt on whether such a harsh covenant as that signed by Snepp should be enforced. Nevertheless, the government had won and had by this ruling come one step nearer the stricter law of confidence applied in the United Kingdom.

Admirable though the Freedom of Information Act is, there are a number of instances in which the United States administration under President Reagan has attempted to reduce its scope. In 1983 Reagan tried to broaden four of the nine exempt categories and to add two more on the cosmetically attractive grounds of helping law enforcement, protecting businesses' proprietory information and safe-guarding personal privacy. However, he failed to get this legislation passed through the House of Representatives. Likewise he failed in his attempts to increase charges so that they not only covered the time spent searching for documents and costs of copying but would reflect the overhead administrative costs of the freedom-of-information legis-lation, and to limit the circumstances in which such charges could be waived. The differing approach by various government departments on costs has been a source of concern to users of the Freedom of Information Act. Copying charges can vary from five cents for one copy to one dollar depending on the agency producing the documents. The US Department of Health and Education is prepared to carry out freedom-of-information research for a bargain-basement fee of $3 an hour, whereas the Department of Justice charges $188 an hour. The FBI wanted a payment of $37,607 before it was prepared to access the 150,000 papers it had relating to the trial and execution of the Rosenberg spies. With even less justification the Union of Concerned Scientists was asked for a fee of $30,000 before it could see three Nuclear Regulatory Commission documents.

Some amendments restricting the scope of the Freedom of

Information Act have been passed, exempting certain 'operational' CIA files, and the defence and energy departments have been authorised to withhold unclassified information which can have military or space application or unclassified information relating to the design of nuclear weapons. In 1983 Congress passed a law making it a crime to publish the names of intelligence agents.

Hard on the exclusion of the press from Grenada for the first two and a half days after the United States invasion in October 1983, President Reagan announced that he had 'had it up to his keister with leaks'. Reagan's remedy was twofold. Firstly he took advantage of the Supreme Court decision in the Snepp case and required all government employees with access to 'sensitive compartmented information' to sign agreements to submit anything that they wrote to government censors, even after they left government service. There are 100,000 federal employees with access to such sensitive compartmented information. Secondly, under the terms of his 1984 National Security Decision Directive, Reagan granted authority to request employees to take polygraph, that is, lie-detector tests. The Defense Department has already been authorised to test 3,500 of its employees, and it has been stated that 'as a minimum adverse consequences' will follow an employee's refusal to co-operate with a polygraph examination.

The record of the United States in the area of freedom of information is impressive, and a model of how a country with secrets to keep can allow its citizens access to decisions affecting them and to information about the processes of government. However, even in the US system there are devices to restrict freedom of information and an unfortunate tendency to look longingly towards some of the restrictive rules in the United Kingdom, regarding breach of confidence and the Official Secrets Act.

Appendix 6

Freedom of Information in Canada

In 1982, despite its Westminster-style government and almost British tradition of secrecy, Canada introduced its freedom-of-information legislation. Like Australia, it had its equivalent of Section 2 in the form of Section 4 of the Official Secrets Act 1970; but unlike the practice in Australia, the Official Secrets Act had been used in Canada fairly regularly to punish cases where information was leaked. The Canadian Access to Information Act 1982 is hedged with a number of exceptions to its scope, but the Act has an unusual but sensible provision for its operation to be reviewed after three years. The Act came into force on 1 July 1983; it has made a cautious start in the area of freedom of information but it can serve as a useful example for countries considering introducing such legislation.

Not only does Canada have a wide Official Secrets Act but government secrecy is well enshrined. The practice is hallowed by a number of bureaucratic rules, such as that documents with low-level security classification can be protected by nothing more than a $4 padlock, whereas secret documents require safes costing at least $820. Security-classified documents going through the post must be sealed in an internal envelope, and no such documents must be read over the telephone.

The high water mark of prosecutions in Canada was reached in 1978, when the Act was used for the first time against journalists – the publisher, editor and distributors of the *Toronto Sun*. The consequences of the failure of that prosecution are in many respects reminiscent of the position in Britain after the débâcle of the Ponting prosecution. Those working at the *Toronto Sun* had been incensed by Prime Minister Pierre Trudeau's statement to the Canadian Parliament that, although it might be true that the KGB was an enemy of Canada, it was not true that the Soviet Union was an enemy of Canada. Trudeau sought to support his point with somewhat doubtful logic by arguing that, although the CIA might have agents operating in Canada, the United States was not an enemy of Canada. The *Toronto Sun* decided to publish extracts from a report by the Royal Canadian Mounted Police into Soviet espionage activities in Canada entitled *Canadian-related Activities of the Russian Intelligence Services*. This had been printed in 1976 under the authority of the chairman of the Intelligence Advisory Committee. It had, it was true, been marked 'top secret – for Canadian eyes only'; but by 1978 sixty-seven inter-departmental copies had been made, the report had been mentioned in Parliament on three occasions by Tom Cossitt MP, who for these purposes played the role of Tam Dalyell MP, and it had been the basis of a Canadian television programme, appropriately called *Code Blue*. This programme had described how the wife of the KGB spy chief had a hotel liaison with an Ottawa cabbie and how the wife of a KGB officer had successfully seduced a Canadian professor into smuggling an advanced laser out of the country in a duffel bag. It was scarcely surprising that the provincial court judge who heard the case, Judge Waisberg, referred to the report as 'shop-worn'.

The decision to prosecute the *Toronto Sun* was widely suspected of being a political one. It was said that the Minister of Justice was not in favour, and that his view was supported by the Commissioner of the Royal Canadian Mounted Police. The editor of the *Edmonton Journal* went as far as to describe the decision to prosecute as being based on 'vindictiveness'.

This was not the first time that the activities of the *Toronto Sun* had displeased the Canadian government. In March

1976 its offices had been searched by the Mounties armed with a warrant under the Official Secrets Act, following the publication of leaked documents showing that the Security Advisory Committee was no longer screening Quebec separatists joining the federal Civil Service, allegedly on the orders of Premier Trudeau. This had led to lively scenes in the Canadian Parliament, when the Solicitor-General had replied to demands for an enquiry monosyllabically: 'Nuts.' When Trudeau was approached by reporters who asked him if he was responsible for the order to search the offices of the *Toronto Sun*, he told them to 'shove it'. He described the accusation regarding his responsibility as 'scurrilous, inaccurate and venomous'.

The 1978 prosecution against the *Toronto Sun* was thrown out by Judge Waisberg, without the defence having to call any evidence. He ruled that the government had to prove that the document was secret, that it contravened the Official Secrets Act and that those who were accused of receiving the document had to be shown to have had reasonable grounds to believe that the information was communicated to them in contravention of the Official Secrets Act. This, he said, the government had failed to do, and the fact that the document was stamped 'top secret' had no official meaning. It was a matter of administrative and inter-departmental convenience.

In taking this liberal view of the significance to be attached to the marking 'top secret', Judge Waisberg was following the same line as Mr Justice Marchand in the case brought against Boyes in 1946. In marked contrast to the approach of the English courts from the time of the Crisp and Homewood cases (Chapter 2), Mr Justice Marchland had ruled that the Official Secrets Act, by its very title, did not apply to what had been published or publicised or had fallen into the public domain.

In 1979 Peter Treu, who had been working under a Canadian government contract on secret air communications systems, was convicted of unlawfully retaining classified documents and failing to take reasonable care of them. Despite the fact that he was tried no less than four years after his house had been searched, he was sentenced to two years' imprisonment. His conviction was then quashed by the Quebec Court of Appeal because of doubts as to the quality of the evidence against him. The court appears to have accepted Treu's claim that in good faith he believed himself to be properly cleared for the possession and use of the secret documents. His evidence was that he had read the security manuals governing his work and had been cleared by a designated security officer to handle most of the documents in his possession.

There has been strong pressure in Canada for relaxing the Official Secrets Act. In 1969 a Royal Commission was set up under Mr Justice David MacDonald to investigate police misconduct. It reviewed the operation of the Official Secrets Act 1939, which MacDonald had criticised as an 'unwieldy statute couched in very broad and ambiguous language'. The Royal Commission advised that the Official Secrets Act should be confined exclusively to espionage cases, rather than applying to the unauthorised release of government information in general. It commented that the draconian penalties for leakage fostered an unnecessarily oppressive climate of administrative secrecy, and ought to be reduced. However, the Official Secrets Act 1970 substantially re-enacted the 1939 Act, and Section 4 of the 1970 Act substantially follows the line of Section 2 of the Official Secrets Act 1911, even to the extent of its anachronistic terminology such as 'apparatus for wireless telegraphy'. While the freedom-of-information legislation was being considered, two government reports were published, one entitled *Security Information* in 1979, and the second *Freedom and Security under the Law* in 1981. The latter stated that the Official Secrets Act was an anachronism and should be substantially revised. The Access to Information Act 1982 and the Privacy Act 1982 were the product of those two reports but there was no attempt to repeal or amend the Official Secrets Act.

The Canadian Access to Information Act 1982 had a ten-year gestation period. Various provincial states had previously passed freedom-of-information legislation, such as Nova Scotia in 1977, New Brunswick in 1978 and

Newfoundland in 1980. A Green Paper had been published in 1977 to consider the introduction of a federal Freedom of Information Act, and this had led to a Bill being introduced by the Conservative Prime Minister Joe Clarke in 1979. His government had fallen, but the Act was shepherded through Parliament by the Liberal leader, Trudeau. The purpose of the Act is spelt out in Section 2:

> There should be access to information and records under federal government control in accordance with the principles that government information should be available to the public, that necessary exceptions to the right of access should be limited and specific and that decisions on the disclosure of government information should be reviewed independently of government.

A Canadian citizen or a person permanently resident in Canada can therefore make a request to examine any federal government document which is not specifically exempted under the Act, by making a request in writing for its production. The procedure is simple and inexpensive. In making his application he would be assisted by background information provided by the government such as the index to federal programmes and services, which lists the government instructions applied by a particular agency in decision-making, and the access guidelines, which give a breakdown of the records kept by a particular department. A fee of $5 will cover five hours' searching and preparation of documents by government employees. The government has to reply within thirty days. If it refuses to produce the documents, the applicant can complain to the Information Commissioner, whose job it is to investigate complaints by individuals who believe that their rights under the Access to Information Act have been denied. The present Information Commissioner, Inger Hansen QC, has been appointed for seven years; independent of the government departments she investigates, she is an officer of the Canadian Senate and House of Commons, to whom she reports annually. The commissioner has wide powers to review a government decision concerning access to government documents. She can call witnesses to enter premises to inspect any document or data bank, except where the documents are clearly exempted from production under the Act. Cabinet documents and related policy advice would therefore be off-limits. The government is not bound to obey the commissioner's recommendation, but if the government fails to comply with it, the matter can be taken before the federal court by either the Information Commissioner or the applicant, within forty-five days of the government's decision.

Not all Canadian government information is open to access. There are five main categories of mandatory exclusions from the act, and these relate to matters of national defence, international relations, personal information, law enforcement and confidential information supplied to the government. There are in addition twelve discretionary categories relating to such matters as relations between the federal and provincial governments, police investigations, information relating to the safety of individuals, trade secrets and information which could reasonably be thought to have prejudiced the competitive position of a government corporation. The exceptions are drawn widely, and there will doubtless be pressure to narrow these exceptions when the Act is reviewed after its first three years of operation. One of the less satisfactory features of the legislation was the fact that in the course of its passage through Parliament the original exemption for Cabinet documents became extended to all Cabinet confidences. The Act can thus in theory be circumvented by marking documents 'for Cabinet eyes only'.

The Canadian Access to Information Act has made a cautious start. In its first six months of operation there were 897 requests under the Act, whereas there were 9,445 under the Privacy Act (see below). This goes some way to supporting the theory that people are rather more interested in the records kept about them by government departments than in following the details of the government decision-making process. The direct cost of administering the Act for its first nine months amounted to a modest $1,369,424.

Coupled with the Access to Information Act is the Privacy

Act 1982. The main feature of this act is the creation of a Privacy Commissioner who will investigate complaints from individuals, in this case not confined to Canadian citizens and permanent residents, who feel that their rights of privacy have been denied. The Privacy Commissioner has access to all but 19 of some 2,200 data banks, the exceptions relating principally to law enforcement, taxation and national security departments. The applicant can consult the government personal information index, which has a complete list of the banks of personal information held by each federal government institution. The relevant department must produce the information within thirty days. In the first instance, the applicant will deal with the privacy co-ordinator of the relevant department, but if there is a dispute about access or if the department refused to correct errors which the applicant says exists, a complaint can be made to the Privacy Commissioner.

The second report of the Information Commissioner showed that only limited use was being made of the Act and highlighted a number of shortcomings in the way it was administered. Foremost was the failure of the government to publicise the use that could be made of the Act. 'The Access to Information Act was supported by all parties, but it may become an unwanted offspring left to fend for itself,' Inger Hansen QC complained. 'A freedom-of-information Act cannot be improved upon, nor can it serve a country well, if its very existence is kept secret.' She further expressed herself astonished at the lack of knowledge and understanding of the Act's provisions among government departments. This contributed to inconsistency in the practice and policies of these departments.

The two principal complaints were delay – many departments failed to respond to access requests within the thirty-day statutory period – and the practice of certain departments in requiring a deposit of up to 50 per cent of the search fee before they carried out any work, with no guarantee that anything would be found. As one disappointed searcher remarked, the government was the only business which could say, 'Now you have paid the price, we will not produce the merchandise.'

The use of the Act has been surprisingly modest. From 1 July 1983 to 31 March 1985, 324 files were opened. Of the complaints investigated, 40 per cent were found to be supportable, and most of these were subsequently settled without the need for any application to court. The use of the Act to date has been mainly by journalists, lawyers and pressure groups. The largest group of requests has concerned employment and immigration matters. Some have had a uniquely Canadian flavour and have resulted in the release of the Halibut Relocation Plan Wrap-up Report and the National Broiler Hatching Egg Marketing Plan for Canada.

This legislation in Canada is a further example of how freedom of information can exist in a country with a Westminster-style government. The legislation is limited in extent; but when one looks at the attempts in Australia to limit the original freedom-of-information legislation, there is much to be said for the cautious approach of the Canadians.

Bibliography

Floyd Abrahams, 'Freedom of Information and the Law', Granada Guildhall Lecture, 1984.

Allan Adler and Morton Halperin, *The Freedom of Information Act and Privacy Act*, US Center for National Security Studies, Washington, D.C. (9th edn), 1984.

Philip Agee, *Inside the Company: CIA Diary*, Penguin, 1975.

Jonathan Aitken, *Officially Secret*, Weidenfeld & Nicolson, 1971.

Christopher Andrew, *Secret Service: The Making of the British Intelligence Community*, Heinemann, 1985.

Christopher Andrew and David Dilks (eds.), *The Missing Dimension: Governments and Intelligence Communities in the Twentieth Century*, Macmillan, 1984.

Ronald Atkey, 'Freedom of Information', *University of Western Ontario Law Review*, 1980.

Crispin Aubrey, *Who's Watching you?* Penguin, 1981.

James Bamford, *The Puzzle Palace: America's National Security Agency and its Special Relationship with Britain's GCHQ*, Sidgwick & Jackson, 1983.

Tony Benn, *The Right to Know*, Institute for Workers' Control, 1978.

Colin Bennett and Peter Hennessy, *A Consumer's Guide to Open Government: Techniques for Penetrating Whitehall*, Outer Circle Policy Unit, 1980.

Nicholas Bethell, *The Great Betrayal*, Hodder & Stoughton, 1984.

Jonathan Bloch and Patrick Fitzgerald, *British Intelligence and Covert Action*, Junction Books, 1983.

Sisslea Bok, *Secrets*, Oxford University Press, 1984.

Andrew Boyle, *The Riddle of Erskine Childers*, Hutchinson, 1977.

Andrew Boyle, *The Climate of Treason*, Hutchinson, 1979.

Fenton Bresler, *Lord Goddard*, Harrap, 1977.

John Bulloch, *MI5: The Origin and History of the British Counter-Espionage Service*, Arthur Barker, 1963.

Tony Bunyan, *The Political Police in Britain*, Julian Friedman, 1976.

Barbara Castle, *The Castle Diaries 1964–1970*, Weidenfeld & Nicolson, 1980.

David Caute, *The Espionage of the Saints*, Hamish Hamilton, 1986.

Anthony Cave Brown, *Bodyguard of Lies,* W. H. Allen, 1977.

Robert Cecil, 'The Cambridge Comintern', *Encounter*, April 1978.

Robert Cecil, 'Of Secrecy, Intelligence and the Missing Dimension', in Andrew and Dilks (eds.), op. cit., 1984.

Leslie Chapman, *Your Disobedient Servant*, Penguin, 1979.

Erskine Childers, *The Riddle of the Sands*, Collins, 1955.

Winston Churchill, *The Second World War*, Dreiburg, 1984–54.

Michael Cockerell, Peter Hennessy and David Walker, *Sources Close to the Prime Minister*, Macmillan, 1984.

A. W. Cockerill, *Sir Percy Sillitoe,* W. H. Allen, 1975.

Stanley Cohen, 'Freedom of Information and the Offical Secrets Act 1979', *McGill Law Journal*, no. 25.

Columbian Journalism Review, March 1985.

Judith Cook, *The Price of Freedom*, New English Library, 1985.

Miles Copeland, *The Real Spy World,* Weidenfeld & Nicolson, 1974.

Richard Crossman, *The Diaries of a Cabinet Minister* (3 vols.), Hamish Hamilton, 1975–7.

James Curran (ed.), *The British Press: A Manifesto,* Macmillan, 1978.

Richard Deacon, *A History of the British Secret Service*, Muller, 1969.

Rosemary Delbridge and Martin Smith, *Consuming Secrets: How Official Secrecy Affects Everyday Life in Britain,* Burnett Books, 1982.

Patrick Devlin, *Easing the Passing*, Bodley Head, 1985.

Stuart Dresner, *Open Government: Lessons from America,* Outer Circle Policy Unit, 1980.

Tom Driberg, *Guy Burgess: A Portrait with a Background,* Weidenfeld & Nicolson, 1956.

Tom Driberg, *Ruling Passions*, Cape, 1977.

John Edwards, *The Attorney-General: Politics and the Public Interest,* Sweet & Maxwell, 1985.

Harold Evans, *Good Times, Bad Times,* Weidenfeld & Nicolson, 1983.

Michael Foot, *Loyalists and Loners,* Collins, 1985.

Alexander Foote, *Handbook for Spies*, Doubleday, 1949.

Lord Francis-William, *The Right to Know*, Longman, 1969.

Ian Gilmour, *The Body Politic*, Hutchinson, 1969.

Patrick Gordon-Walker, *The Cabinet*, Heinemann, 1970.

Diana Gould, *On the Spot: The Sinking of the 'Belgrano'*, Woolf, 1984.

Peter Grigg, 'Revelations', *Granta*, 15th issue, 1984.

Richard Hall, *The Secret State*, Cassell Australia, 1978.

Morton Halperin, *The Lawless State*, Penguin, 1976.

Sir Maurice Hankey, *The Supreme Command 1914–1918*, Allen & Unwin, 1961.

Kate Harrison, *Documents, Dossiers and the Inside Dope*, Public Interest Advocacy Centre (Australia), 1986.

David Hickle, *The Prince and the Premier*, Angus & Robertson, 1985.

F. H. Hinsley, *British Intelligence in the Second World War*, HMSO, 1979–81.

Christopher Hutton, *Official Secret*, Max Parrish, 1960.

H. Montgomery Hyde, *Crime Has its Heroes: A Matter of Official Secrets*, Constable, 1976.

R. V. Jones, *Most Secret War*, Hamish Hamilton, 1978.

Justice, *The Law and the Press*, London, 1965.

Sara Keays, *A Question of Judgement*, Quintessential Press, 1985.

Ludovic Kennedy, *The Airman and the Carpenter*, Collins, 1985.

Henry Kissinger, *The White House Years*, Weidenfeld & Nicolson/ Michael Joseph, 1980.

Robert Lamphere, *The FBI–KGB War*, Random House, 1986.

Edgar Lansbury, *Lansbury, My Father*, London, 1934.

George Lansbury, *My England*, London, 1934.

Peter Laurie, *Beneath the City Streets*, Allen Lane, 1970.

David Leigh, *The Frontiers of Secrecy*, Junction Books, 1980.

Anthony Lincoln, *Freedom of Information*, Justice, 1978.

Magnus Linklater and David Leigh, *Not with Honour: The Inside Story of the Westland Scandal*, Sphere, 1986.

David Lloyd George, *War Memoirs*, Odhams, 1938.

Compton Mackenzie, *Gallipoli Memories*, Cassell, 1929.

Compton Mackenzie, *First Athenian Memories*, Cassell, 1931.

Compton Mackenzie, *Water on the Brain*, Cassell, 1933.

Compton Mackenzie, *Greek Memories*, Chatto & Windus, 1938 (2nd edn).

Compton Mackenzie, *My Life and Times: Octave 7, 1931–1938*, Chatto & Windus, 1968.

James Margach, *The Anatomy of Power*, W. H. Allen, 1979.

John Marks and Victor Marchetti, *The CIA and the Cult of Intelligence*, Coronet, 1976.

David Marquand, *Ramsay MacDonald,* Cape, 1977.

David Marr, *The Ivanov Trail,* Nelson, 1984.

David Martin, *Wilderness of Mirrors,* Harper & Row, 1980.

Charles Marvin, *The Russians at the Gates of Herat,* Samuel Tinsley, 1878.

Charles Marvin, *Our Public Offices,* Samuel Tinsley, 1879.

Sir John Masterman, *The Double Cross System in the War of 1939–45,* Yale University Press, 1972.

Sir John Masterman, *On the Chariot Wheel,* Oxford University Press, 1975.

Anthony Masters, *The Man Was M,* Blackwell, 1984.

Annabelle May and Kathryn Rowan (eds.), *Inside Information: British Government and the Media,* Constable, 1982.

John McCamus, 'Freedom of Information in Canada', *Government Publications Review,* no. 10, 1983, p. 51.

Geoffrey McDermott, *The New Diplomacy and its Apparatus,* Ward Lock, 1973.

James Michael, *The Politics of Secrecy: Confidential Government and the Public Right to Know,* Penguin, 1982.

Ewen Montagu, *The Man Who Never Was,* Evan Bros, 1955.

·David Mure, *Master of Deception,* William Kimber, 1977.

David Mure, *Practice to Deceive,* William Kimber, 1980.

John Naylor, *A Man and an Institution,* Cambridge University Press, 1984.

Richard Norton-Taylor, *The Ponting Affair,* Woolf, 1985.

Anthony Nutting, *No End of a Lesson,* Weidenfeld & Nicolson, 1976.

Outer Circle Policy Unit, *An Official Information Act,* 1977.

Bruce Page, David Leitch and Phillip Knightly (*Sunday Times* Insight team), *Philby: The Spy Who Betrayed a Generation,* Sphere, 1977.

Alasdair Palmer, 'The History of the D-Notice Committee,' in Andrew and Dilks (eds.), op. cit., 1984.

Barrie Penrose, *Stalin's Gold,* Granada, 1982.

Barrie Penrose and Roger Courtiour, *The Pencourt File*, Secker & Warburg, 1978.

Kim Philby, *My Silent War*, McGibbon & Kee, 1968.

Ben Pimlott, *Hugh Dalton,* Cape, 1985.

Chapman Pincher, *Inside Story: A Documentary of the Pursuit of Power,* Sidgwick & Jackson, 1978.

Chapman Pincher, *Their Trade Is Treachery,* Sidgwick & Jackson, 1981.

Chapman Pincher, *Too Secret Too Long,* Sidgwick & Jackson, 1984.

Clive Ponting, *The Right to Know,* Sphere, 1985.

Raymond Postgate, *The Life of George Lansbury,* Longman, 1951.

Presstime, April 1985.

Juan Pujol and Nigel West, *Garbo,* Weidenfeld & Nicolson, 1985.

T. Murray Rankin, 'The New Access to Information and Privacy Act', *Ottawa Law Review,* 1983.

Anthony Read and David Fisher, *Operation Lucy: Most Secret Spy Ring,* Hodder & Stoughton, 1980.

Anthony Read and David Fisher, *Colonel Z,* Hodder & Stoughton, 1984.

Goronwy Rees, *A Chapter of Accidents,* Chatto & Windus, 1972.

Desmond Rice and Arthur Gavshon, *The Sinking of the 'Belgrano',* Secker & Warburg, 1984.

Geoffrey Robertson, *Media Law: The Rights of Journalists and Broadcasters,* Oyez Longman, 1984.

K .G. Robertson, *Public Secrets: A Study in the Development of Government Secrecy,* Macmillan, 1982.

Stephen Roskill, *Hankey: Man of Secrets,* Collins, 1970–74.

Lord Scarman, *The Right to Know,* Granada Guildhall Lecture, 7 November 1984.

Alexander Scotland, *The London Cage,* George Mann, 1957.

Brian Sedgemore, *The Secret Constitution: An Analysis of the Political Establishment,* Hodder & Stoughton, 1980.

J. E. B. Seely, *Adventure,* Heinemann, 1930.

William Shawcross, *Sideshow: Kissinger, Nixon and the Destruction of Cambodia,* Deutsch, 1979.

Sir Percy Sillitoe, *Cloak without Dagger,* Cassell, 1955.

Tony Smythe and Donald Madgwick, *The Invasion of Privacy,* Pitman, 1973.

Frank Snepp, *Decent Interval,* Allen Lane, 1980.

Jim Spiegelman, *Secrecy and Political Censorship in Australia,* Angus & Robertson, 1972.

Neil Stammers, *Civil Liberties in Britain during the Second World War,* Croom Helm, 1983.

Michael Straight, *After Long Silence,* Collins, 1983.

Derek Tangye, *The Way to Minak,* Michael Joseph, 1968.

Hugh Thomas, *Crisis in the Civil Service,* Anthony Blond, 1968.

J. H. Thomas, *My Story,* Hutchinson, 1937.

Sir Basil Thomson, *Queer People,* Hodder & Stoughton, 1922.

Sir Basil Thomson, *The Allied Secret Service in Greece,* Hutchinson, 1932.

Sir Basil Thomson, *The Scene Changes,* Collins, 1939.

R. W. Thompson, *Churchill and Morton,* Hodder & Stoughton, 1976.

Hugh Trevor-Roper, *The Last Days of Hitler*, Macmillan, 1947.

Hugh Trevor-Roper, *The Philby Affair: Espionage, Treason and the Secret Service*, William Kimber, 1968.

Stansfield Turner, *Secrecy and Democracy: The CIA in Transition*, Sidgwick & Jackson, 1986.

Geoffrey Underwood, *Our Falklands War: The Men of the Task Force*, Maritime, 1983.

Anthony Verrier, *Through the Looking Glass: British Foreign Policy in an Age of Illusion*, Cape, 1983.

Graham Watson, *Book Society*, Deutsch, 1980.

Gordon Welchman, *The Hut Six Story*, Allen Lane, 1982.

Gordon Welchman, *From Polish Bomba to British Bomb: The Birth of Ultra*, 1985.

Nigel West, *MI5: British Security Service Operations 1909–1945*, Bodley Head, 1981.

Nigel West, *A Matter of Trust: MI5 1945–1972*, Hodder & Stoughton, 1983.

Nigel West, *MI6: British Secret Intelligence Service Operations 1909–1945*, Weidenfeld & Nicolson, 1983.

John Whitwell [Leslie Nicholson], *British Agent*, Willian Kimber, 1966.

D. G. T. Williams, *Not in the Public Interest*, Hutchinson, 1965.

Des Wilson, *The Secrets File*, Heinemann Educational, 1984.

Harold Wilson, *The Labour Government 1964–1970: A Personal Record*, Weidenfeld & Nicholson, 1971.

F. W. Winterbotham, *The Ultra Secret*, Harper & Row, 1974.

Charles Wintour, *Pressures on the Press*, Deutsch, 1972.

Horace Wyndham, *Victoria Parade*, Muller, 1934.

Greville Wynne, *The Man from Moscow*, Hutchinson, 1967.

Greville Wynne, *The Man from Odessa*, Hale, 1981.

Hugo Young, *The Crossman Affair*, Hamish Hamilton/Cape, 1976.

Official Publications

United Kingdom

Birkett Committee, *Report of the Committee on the Interception of Communications* (Cmnd 283), HMSO, 1957.

Civil Service Department, *Disclosure of Information: A Report on Overseas Practice*, HMSO, 1979.

Defence Committee: House of Commons, 4th Report, *Westland plc: the Government's Decision-Making*, HMSO, 1986.

Foreign Affairs Committee: House of Commons, 3rd Report, *Events Surrounding the Weekend of 1–2 May 1982,* HMSO, 1985.

Franks Committee, *Report and Evidence of the Committee on Section 2 of the Official Secrets Act 1911,* HMSO, 1972.

Franks Committee, *Falkland Islands Review: Report of the Committee of Privy Councillors* (Cmnd 8787), HMSO, 1983.

Fulton Committee, *The Civil Service* (Cmnd 3638), HMSO, 1968.

Green Paper, *Open Government* (Cmnd 7520), HMSO, 1979.

Home Office, *Reform of Section 2 of the Official Secrets Act 1911,* HMSO, 1978.

Lord Denning, *Report* (Cmnd 2152), HMSO, 1963.

Radcliffe Committee, *Report on D–Notice Matters* (Cmnd 3309), HMSO, 1967.

Radcliffe Committee, *Report on Ministerial Memoirs* (Cmnd 6386), HMSO, 1976.

Security Procedures in the Public Service (Cmnd 1681), 1961.

Security Commission, *Report* (Cmnd 8235), HMSO, 1981; *Report* (Cmnd 8540), HMSO, 1982; *Report* (Cmnd 9514), HMSO, 1985.

Select Committee on the Official Secrets Act, *Report,* HMSO, 1938.

White Paper, *Information and the Public Interest* (Cmnd 4089), HMSO, 1969.

White Paper, *The Falklands Campaign: The Lessons,* HMSO, 1982.

Wilson Committee, *Report* (Cmnd 8204), HMSO, 1981.

Australia

Attorney-General, *Annual Reports,* Australian Government Publishing Service. *Documents on Australian Defence and Foreign Policy 1968–75,* Angus & Robertson, 1980.

Senate Standing Committee on Constitution and Legal Affairs, *Freedom of Information,* Australian Government Publishing Service, 1979.

Canada

Annual Reports by Canadian Information Commissioner and Privacy Commissioner.

Victoria Attorney-General, *Freedom of Information Act Annual Reports.*

European Community

Council of Europe, *Report* No. 4195.

Index

DAVID HOOPER

PUBLIC SCANDAL, ODIUM AND CONTEMPT

LIBEL -- Everyone knows what it stands for, but very few can actually define it. Here is a witty, informative and entertaining account of the libel laws plus an analysis of over forty recent famous libel cases. Colourful characters emerge, gladiatorial conflicts between barrister and witness abound.

Aneurin Bevin, Jack Profumo, Sir James Goldsmith, Shirley Temple and Liberace are just a few of the famous people neatly trapped in these provocative and enthralling pages. A timely account of one of the most infamous but ignored areas of jurisdiction.

'A penetrating examination and a witty account provides admirable bedside reading'

Sunday Telegraph

'An informative and amusing introduction'

Times Literary Supplement

'A superb parody'

Punch

Post·A·Book

A Royal Mail service in association with the Book Marketing Council & The Booksellers Association.

Post·A·Book is a Post Office trademark.

JUDGE JAMES PICKLES

STRAIGHT FROM THE BENCH

Judge James Pickles is a very unusual judge. He says what he thinks and he won't shut up, even when it gets him into trouble. He thinks that there is a lot wrong with our legal system and that things won't get better unless someone makes a fuss. For instance:

* Do politics play a part when judges are appointed?
* How independent are judges anyway?
* Are the long – and often harrowing – delays in Crown Court cases really necessary?
* Plea-bargaining: shouldn't its existence be admitted   and some proper rules be worked out?
*Juries: is it time to make some changes?

Judge Pickles never minces his words. He believes that much of our judicial system has to be modernised and modernised fast. Traditionalist attitudes on the part of all too many judges have to be altered. If not, then public confidence in our judicial system may be lost.

'It is refreshing to have a judge who seeks to justify the ways of judges to men. If Judge Pickles didn't exist John Mortimer would have to invent him'

New Society

'He has made an *important* contribution to an important debate and deserves our praise for doing so.'

Ludovic Kennedy, The Independent

HODDER AND STOUGHTON PAPERBACKS

ANTHONY SUMMERS AND STEPHEN DORRIL

HONEYTRAP

The Profumo Affair: the scandal of the century.

A Conservative Minister for War and a Russian spy share the same mistress. There are daily revelations of bondage parties and of girls' cavorting at stately homes, of drugs and clubs, titled men and call girls. Some names are named. More are hinted at. Overnight, Christine Keeler and Mandy Rice-Davies are famous; the public fascinated.

The Minister, John Profumo, resigns. But the Establishment closes ranks and Dr Stephen Ward, the society doctor and artist who had made the introductions, is hounded to suicide.

Only a fraction of the truth was told at the time. Now *Honeytrap* reveals that the real story was even more sensational, that the British scandal even threatened to bring down President Kennedy in the United States.

'Bulging with new material ... This is a book which our rulers must loathe'

Tribune

'Reopens the case and once again we are left suspecting that we do indeed live in a secret society'

Woman's Journal

'Debauchery, class antagonism and espionage, a potent formula for a bestseller'

Irish Times

HODDER AND STOUGHTON PAPERBACKS

MORE TITLES AVAILABLE FROM
HODDER AND STOUGHTON PAPERBACKS

☐ 39648 2	**DAVID HOOPER** Public Scandal, Odium and Contempt	£2.95
☐ 42271 8	**JUDGE JAMES PICKLES** Straight From The Bench	£2.95
☐ 42973 9	**ANTHONY SUMMERS AND** **STEPHEN DORRIL** Honeytrap	£3.50

All these books are available at your local bookshop or newsagent, or can be ordered direct from the publisher. Just tick the titles you want and fill in the form below.

Prices and availability subject to change without notice.

HODDER AND STOUGHTON PAPERBACKS, P.O. Box 11, Falmouth, Cornwall.

Please send cheque or postal order, and allow the following for postage and packing:

U.K. – 55p for one book, plus 22p for the second book, and 14p for each additional book ordered up to a £1.75 maximum.

B.F.P.O. and EIRE – 55p for the first book, plus 22p for the second book, and 14p per copy for the next 7 books, 8p per book thereafter.

OTHER OVERSEAS CUSTOMERS – £1.00 for the first book, plus 25p per copy for each additional book.

Name ....

Address ....

....